Middle School 3-1

중간고사 완벽대비

적중100

영어 기출 문제집

중3

천재 | 정사열

Best Collection

구성과 특징

교과서의 주요 학습 내용을 중심으로 학습 영역별 특성에 맞춰 단계별로 다양한 학습 기회를 제공하여 단원별 학습능력 평가는 물론 중간 및 기말고사 시험 등에 완벽하게 대비할 수 있도록 내용을 구성

Words & Expressions

Step1 Key Words 단원별 핵심 단어 설명 및 풀이
Key Expression 단원별 핵심 숙어 및 관용어 설명
Word Power 반대 또는 비슷한 뜻 단어 배우기
English Dictionary 영어로 배우는 영어 단어

Step2 실력평가 단원별 수시평가 대비 주관식, 객관식 문제풀이

Step3 서술형 대비 학업성취도 및 수행능력평가 대비 서술형 문제풀이

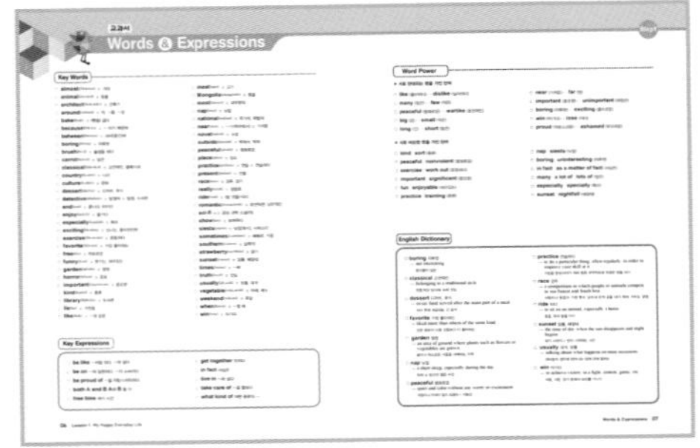

Conversation

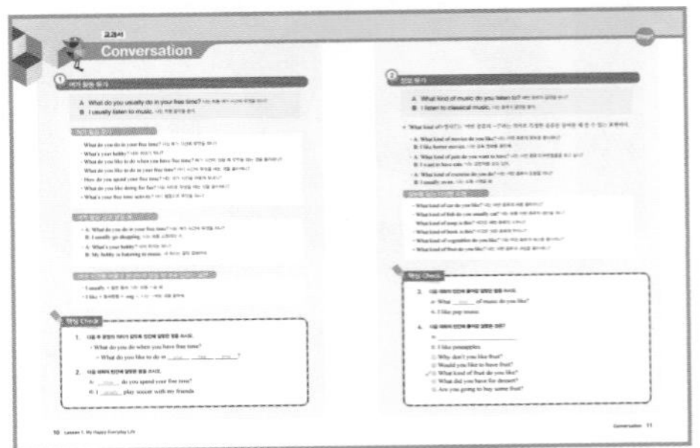

Step1 핵심 의사소통 소통에 필요한 주요 표현 방법 요약
핵심 Check 기본적인 표현 방법 및 활용능력 확인

Step2 대화문 익히기 교과서 대화문 심층 분석 및 확인

Step3 교과서 확인학습 빈칸 채우기를 통한 문장 완성 능력 확인

Step4 기본평가 시험대비 기초 학습 능력 평가

Step5 실력평가 단원별 수시평가 대비 주관식, 객관식 문제풀이

Step6 서술형 대비 학업성취도 및 수행능력평가 대비 서술형 문제풀이

Grammar

Step1 주요 문법 단원별 주요 문법 사항과 예문을 알기 쉽게 설명
핵심 Check 기본 문법사항에 대한 이해 여부 확인

Step2 기본평가 시험대비 기초 학습 능력 평가

Step3 실력평가 단원별 수시평가 대비 주관식, 객관식 문제풀이

Step4 서술형 대비 학업성취도 및 수행능력평가 대비 서술형 문제풀이

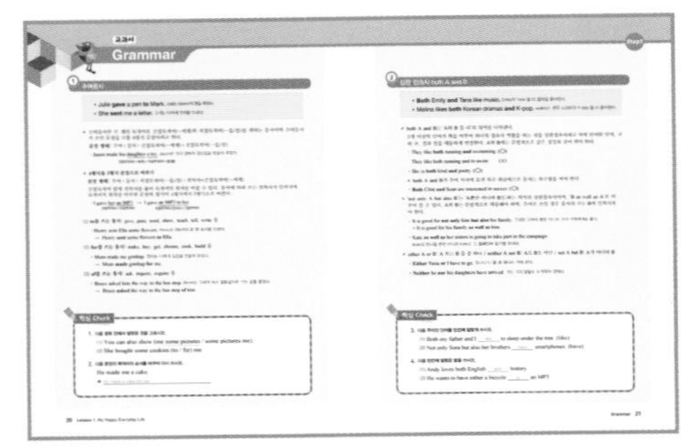

Reading

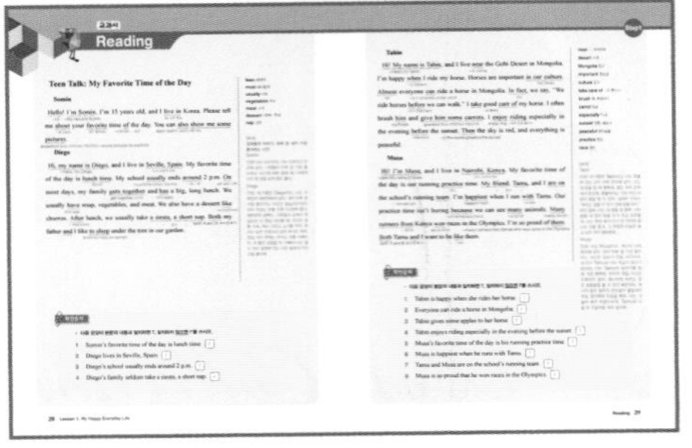

Step1 구문 분석 단원별로 제시된 문장에 대한 구문별 분석과 내용 설명
확인문제 문장에 대한 기본적인 이해와 인지능력 확인

Step2 확인학습A 빈칸 채우기를 통한 문장 완성 능력 확인

Step3 확인학습B 제시된 우리말을 영어로 완성하여 작문 능력 키우기

Step4 실력평가 단원별 수시평가 대비 주관식, 객관식 문제풀이

Step5 서술형 대비 학업성취도 및 수행능력평가 대비 서술형 문제풀이
교과서 구석구석 교과서에 나오는 기타 문장까지 완벽 학습

Composition

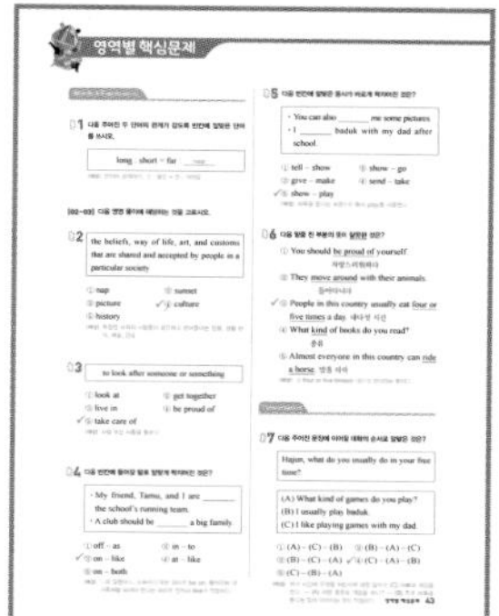

|영역별 핵심문제|

단어 및 어휘, 대화문, 문법, 독해 등 각 영역별 기출문제의 출제 유형을 분석하여 실전에 대비하고 연습할 수 있도록 문제를 배열

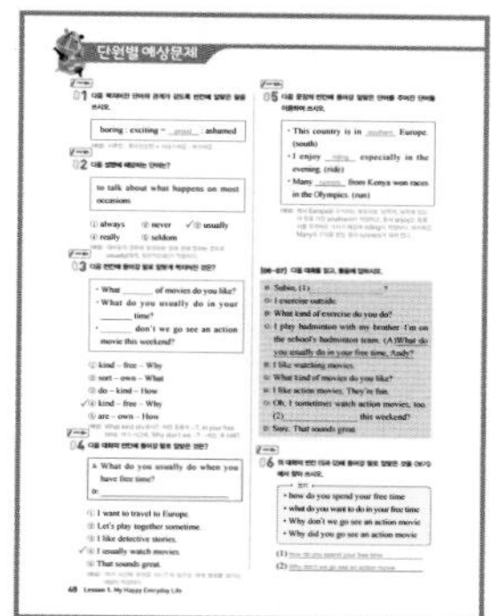

|단원별 예상문제|

기출문제를 분석한 후 새로운 시험 출제 경향을 더하여 새롭게 출제될 수 있는 문제를 포함하여 시험에 완벽하게 대비할 수 있도록 준비

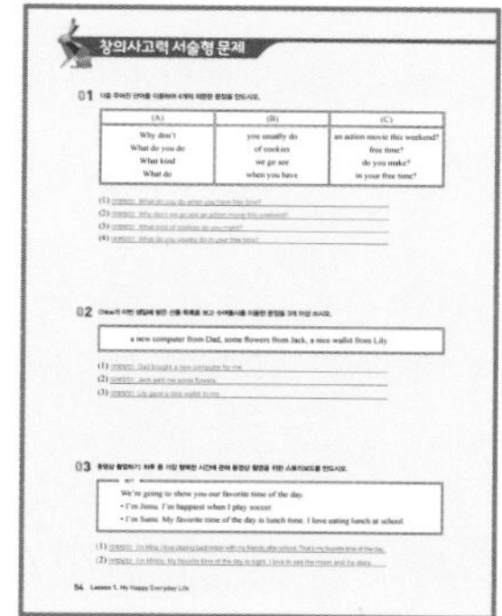

|서술형 실전 및 창의사고력 문제|

학교 시험에서 점차 늘어나는 서술형 시험에 집중 대비하고 고득점을 취득하는데 만전을 기하기 위한 학습 코너

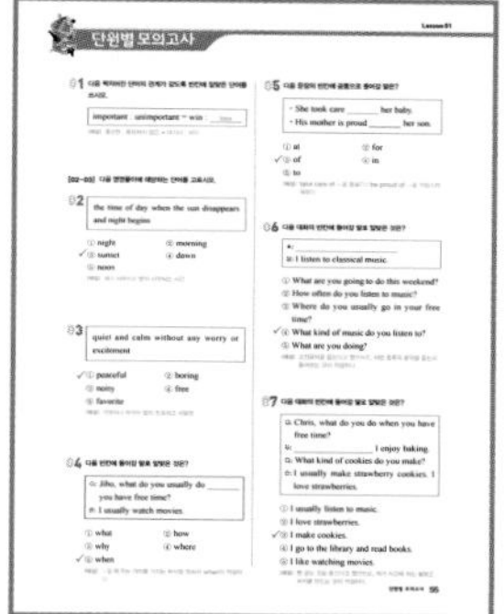

|단원별 모의고사|

영역별, 단계별 학습을 모두 마친 후 실전 연습을 위한 모의고사

교과서 파헤치기

- **단어Test1~3** 영어 단어 우리말 쓰기, 우리말을 영어 단어로 쓰기, 영영풀이에 해당하는 단어와 우리말 쓰기
- **대화문Test1~2** 대화문 빈칸 완성 및 전체 대화문 쓰기
- **본문Test1~5** 빈칸 완성, 우리말 쓰기, 문장 배열연습, 영어 작문하기 복습 등 단계별 반복 학습을 통해 교과서 지문에 대한 완벽한 습득
- **구석구석지문Test1~2** 지문 빈칸 완성 및 전문 영어로 쓰기

이책의 차례

Contents

Express Your Feelings

의사소통 기능

- 기쁨이나 슬픔에 대해 묻기
  How are you feeling?
- 기쁨 표현하기
  I'm glad to hear that.

언어 형식

- 간접의문문
  Everyone knows **what it means**.
- 관계대명사의 계속적 용법
  People also use ROFL, **which** means "Rolling On the Floor Laughing."

교과서

Words & Expressions

Key Words

- □ **actually** [ǽktʃuəli] 부 실제로
- □ **available** [əvéiləbl] 형 구할 수 있는, 이용할 수 있는
- □ **book** [buk] 동 예매하다, 예약하다
- □ **chance** [tʃæns] 명 기회, 가능성
- □ **conversation** [kὰnvərséiʃən] 명 대화
- □ **cupboard** [kʌ́bərd] 명 찬장
- □ **deliver** [dilívər] 동 전달하다
- □ **drone** [droun] 명 드론
- □ **emoji** [imóuji] 명 이모지
- □ **emoticon** [imóutikὰn] 명 이모티콘
- □ **even** [íːvən] 부 심지어, ~조차
- □ **excited** [iksáitid] 형 흥분한, 신난
- □ **expression** [ikspréʃən] 명 표현
- □ **facial** [féiʃəl] 형 얼굴의
- □ **finally** [fáinəli] 부 드디어, 마침내, 마지막으로
- □ **form** [fɔːrm] 명 형식, 방식, 형태
- □ **fried** [fraid] 형 기름에 튀긴
- □ **funny** [fʌ́ni] 형 웃긴
- □ **gentleman** [dʒéntlmən] 명 신사
- □ **grade** [greid] 명 학년, 등급, 성적
- □ **guess** [ges] 동 추측하다, 짐작하다
- □ **healthy** [hélθi] 형 건강에 좋은
- □ **human** [hjúːmən] 형 인간적인, 인간의
- □ **invite** [inváit] 동 초대하다
- □ **joke** [dʒouk] 명 농담
- □ **laughter** [lǽftər] 명 웃음
- □ **letter** [létər] 명 문자, 편지
- □ **light** [lait] 명 빛, 등
- □ **lunch break** 점심시간
- □ **lunch menu** 점심 메뉴
- □ **mark** [mɑːrk] 명 기호, 표시
- □ **mean** [miːn] 동 의미하다
- □ **meaningful** [míːniŋfəl] 형 의미 있는
- □ **miss** [mis] 동 그리워하다
- □ **move** [muːv] 동 이사하다
- □ **nervous** [nə́ːrvəs] 형 초조한
- □ **popular** [pάpjulər] 형 인기 있는
- □ **present** [préznt] 명 선물
- □ **promise** [prάmis] 동 약속하다 명 약속
- □ **quite** [kwait] 부 꽤
- □ **represent** [rèprizént] 동 나타내다, 대표하다
- □ **since** [sins] 전 ~부터, ~ 이후
- □ **stick** [stik] 명 막대기, 나뭇가지
- □ **symbol** [símbəl] 명 상징
- □ **tear** [tiər] 명 눈물
- □ **text** [tekst] 명 글, 문서, 문자 메시지
- □ **tone** [toun] 명 어조, 말투
- □ **top** [tɑp] 형 맨 위의, 최고의 명 꼭대기, 정상
- □ **travel** [trǽvəl] 동 여행하다 명 여행
- □ **try** [trai] 동 먹어 보다
- □ **type** [taip] 동 타자 치다, 입력하다
- □ **various** [vέəriəs] 형 다양한
- □ **video chat** 화상 채팅
- □ **visit** [vízit] 동 방문하다
- □ **visually** [víʒuəli] 부 시각적으로
- □ **whole** [houl] 형 완전한, 전체의, 전부의
- □ **wonder** [wʌ́ndər] 동 궁금해 하다
- □ **written** [rítn] 형 글로 쓴, 글로 표현된

Key Expressions

- □ **a group of** 한 무리의
- □ **a lot** 많이
- □ **be worried about** ~에 대해 걱정하다
- □ **break wind** 방귀를 뀌다
- □ **can't wait for** ~을 몹시 기다리다
- □ **care for** ~을 좋아하다
- □ **grow+비교급** 점점 ~해지다
- □ **happier than ever** 어느 때보다 행복한
- □ **have fun** 즐거운 시간을 보내다
- □ **keep in touch** 계속해서 연락하다
- □ **let+목적어+동사원형** ~가 …하도록 허락하다
- □ **laugh out loud** 큰 소리로 웃다
- □ **stand for** ~을 의미하다, 상징하다
- □ **such as** ~와 같은
- □ **take a look at** ~을 보다
- □ **the same ~ as** ~와 같은 …
- □ **Why don't you+동사원형 ~?** ~하는 게 어때?
- □ **with+명사+형용사** … (명사)가 ~(형용사) 한 채로

Word Power

※ 서로 반대되는 뜻을 가진 어휘

- □ **popular**(인기 있는) ↔ **unpopular**(인기 없는)
- □ **available**(구할 수 있는) ↔ **unavailable**(구할 수 없는)
- □ **healthy**(건강한) ↔ **unhealthy**(건강하지 않은)
- □ **whole**(전체의) ↔ **partial**(일부분의)
- □ **nervous**(초조한) ↔ **calm**(차분한)
- □ **top**(맨 위의) ↔ **bottom**(밑바닥의)

※ 서로 비슷한 뜻을 가진 어휘

- □ **chance** : **opportunity** (기회)
- □ **book** : **reserve** (예약하다)
- □ **various** : **diverse** (다양한)
- □ **funny** : **humorous** (재미있는)
- □ **move** : **migrate** (이사하다, 이주하다)
- □ **finally** : **eventually** (마침내, 드디어)

English Dictionary

□ **available** 구할 수 있는
→ able to be bought or used
구입되거나 사용될 수 있는

□ **book** 예약[예매]하다
→ to arrange to have a seat, room, performer, etc. at a particular time in the future
미래의 특정 시간에 좌석, 방, 공연자 등을 갖도록 준비하다

□ **conversation** 대화
→ an informal talk involving a small group of people or only two
소수의 사람들 또는 단지 두 명의 사람들이 관여한 비공식적인 이야기

□ **deliver** 전달하다
→ to bring goods, letter, etc, to the proper person
적절한 사람에게 물건이나 편지 등을 가져다 주다

□ **emoticon** 이모티콘
→ a short set of keyboard symbols that represents the facial expression used in email, etc, to show feelings
감정을 나타내기 위해 이메일 등에 사용되는 얼굴 표정을 나타내는 일련의 짧은 키보드 기호

□ **form** 형식, 방식
→ a type or variety of something
어떤 것의 유형 또는 종류

□ **gentleman** 신사
→ a man who is polite, well educated and has excellent manners
공손하고, 교육도 잘 받고, 예의가 뛰어난 남자

□ **guess** 추측하다
→ to give an answer to a particular question when you do not have all the facts and so cannot be certain if you are correct
모든 사실을 가지고 있지 않아서 당신이 옳은지 확신할 수 없을 때 특정 질문에 대답을 하다

□ **human** 인간의, 인간적인
→ being, relating to, or belonging to a person or to people as opposed to animals
동물과는 반대로 사람 또는 사람에 관계되거나 소속되어 있는

□ **represent** 나타내다, 대표하다
→ to be accepted as meaning a certain thing
어떤 것을 의미하는 것으로 받아들여지다

□ **since** ~ 이후
→ from a time in the past until a later past time or until now
과거의 어떤 시간에서부터 나중의 과거 시간까지 또는 현재까지

□ **symbol** 상징
→ a sign, shape, or object that is used to represent something else
다른 무언가를 나타내기 위해 사용되는 표시, 모양, 또는 물체

□ **tone** 어조, 말투
→ the quality of somebody's voice, especially expressing a particular emotion
특히 특정한 감정을 표현하는 누군가의 목소리의 특질

□ **type** 타자 치다, 입력하다
→ to write something using a computer or typewriter
컴퓨터나 타자기를 사용하여 무언가를 쓰다

□ **various** 다양한
→ having many different features
다양한 특징을 가지고 있는

□ **visually** 시각적으로
→ in a way that is connected with seeing or sight
보는 것 또는 시력과 연결되는 식으로

□ **written** 글로 쓴
→ involving writing rather than speaking
말하기보다는 쓰기와 관련된

서답형

01 주어진 영어 설명에 맞게 문장의 빈칸에 알맞은 말을 쓰시오.

> You can ________ tickets at a 20 percent discount.

> <영어설명> to arrange to have a seat, room, performer, etc. at a particular time in the future

➡ ____________________

02 다음 빈칸에 들어갈 말로 가장 적절한 것은?

> ________ is human. We laugh out loud when we hear a joke, see something funny or feel happy.

① Sadness ② Nature
③ Love ④ Laughter
⑤ Dialog

[03~04] 다음 설명에 해당하는 단어를 고르시오.

03

> able to be bought or used

① sale ② facial
③ advisable ④ possible
⑤ available

04

> an informal talk involving a small group of people or only two

① conversation ② proverb
③ motto ④ promise
⑤ goal

서답형

05 다음 우리말에 맞게 빈칸에 알맞은 말을 두 단어로 쓰시오.

> LOL은 '크게 소리 내어 웃기'를 상징한다.

➡ LOL ____________ "Laughing Out Loud."

06 빈칸에 공통으로 들어갈 말로 알맞은 것은?

> (A) The emoticon XD ________es our happy feelings more visually than ha-ha and LOL do.
> (B) The ________ started from London on time.

① fix ② pass ③ express
④ watch ⑤ miss

서답형

07 다음 짝지어진 단어의 관계가 같도록 알맞은 말을 주어진 철자로 시작하여 쓰시오.

> chance : opportunity
> = eventually : f________

08 다음 빈칸 (A), (B)에 들어갈 말로 알맞게 짝지어진 것은?

> These days, people use 😂 – a "face with tears of joy." This is a small picture called an "emoji." Lots of laughing emojis are __(A)__ to use online, so people can express their laughter in __(B)__.

① available – a way
② banned – various ways
③ banned – a way
④ available – various ways
⑤ banned – unique ways

01 다음 빈칸에 들어갈 말을 〈보기〉에서 찾아 쓰시오. (필요하면 변형하여 쓰시오.)

보기
mean since write work

"Ha-ha" is a form of ________ laughter. Everyone knows what it ________. Actually, it has been used ________ long ago. Even Shakespeare used "ha-ha" in his works.

중요

02 〈보기〉의 단어를 활용하여 문장의 빈칸을 완성하시오.

보기
actual fry mean face

(1) ________, I'm sad. I'll miss all of you.

(2) I'm glad to give him something ________.

(3) Laughing marks can represent our ________ expression and deliver our voice tone.

03 다음 우리말과 같은 표현이 되도록 문장의 빈칸을 채우시오.

(1) 다양한 웃음 표시를 사용함으로써, 우리는 친구들에게 우리가 얼마나 그들을 좋아하는지 보여줄 수 있다.

➡ By using ________ laughing marks, we can show our friends how much we care for them.

(2) 많은 웃음 이모지가 온라인에서 사용될 수 있다.

➡ Lots of laughing ________ are available to use online.

(3) 이 표현들은 상당히 빠르게 타자 칠 수 있어서 인기를 얻었다.

➡ These expressions have become popular because they can be ________ quite quickly.

고난이도

04 영영풀이에 해당하는 단어를 〈보기〉에서 찾아 첫 번째 빈칸에 쓰고, 두 번째 빈칸에는 우리말 뜻을 쓰시오.

보기
human guess gentleman tone

(1) ________: to give an answer to a particular question when you do not have all the facts and so cannot be certain if you are correct: ________

(2) ________: the quality of somebody's voice, especially expressing a particular emotion: ________

(3) ________: being, relating to, or belonging to a person or to people as opposed to animals: ________

05 빈칸에 공통으로 알맞은 단어를 주어진 철자로 시작하여 쓰시오.

- Read the ________ carefully and then answer the questions.
- Kids also want to express emotions in their ________s using various emoticons.

➡ t________

교과서

Conversation

1 기쁨이나 슬픔에 대해 묻기

- How are you feeling? 기분이 어떠니?

■ How are you feeling?은 '기분이 어떠니?'라는 뜻으로 상대방의 기쁨이나 슬픔 등의 감정에 대해 물을 때 사용하는 표현이다.

"I'm feeling … / I feel … / I am … "을 이용해서 응답한다.

기쁨이나 슬픔에 대해 물어보는 다른 표현

- How do you feel?
- Are you feeling happy[sad]?
- Are you happy[sad]?

- A: How are you feeling? 기분이 어떠니?
  B: I'm feeling really happy today. 오늘 정말 행복해.
- A: Are you happy? 너는 행복하니?
  B: Yes, I am. I'm happy. 응, 그래. 난 행복해.
- A: How are you feeling? 기분이 어떠니?
  B: Not so good. I'm not happy with the weather. It's raining too hard.
  그렇게 좋지 않아. 날씨가 마음에 들지 않아. 비가 너무 많이 내리고 있어.

핵심 Check

1. 다음 대화의 빈칸에 들어갈 알맞은 것은?

B: Yena, ______________________________

G: I'm feeling very sad, Seho. My best friend Juhin is moving away.

① How do you do?
② What do you think about my friend?
③ Why don't you get some sleep?
④ How are you feeling?
⑤ Can you tell me about your friend, Seho?

2 기쁨 표현하기

• I'm glad to hear that. 그 말을 들으니 기쁘구나.

■ 'I'm (very) glad to ~'는 '~해서 (매우) 기쁘다'라는 뜻으로 'to' 뒤에는 동사원형이 온다. 이어지는 내용을 절로 쓸 때는 "I'm glad (that) ~"으로 말한다.

• A: I'm very glad to be a 3rd grader. How about you? 3학년이 되어서 매우 기뻐. 너는 어때?
B: I'm glad, too. 나도 기뻐.

■ 기쁨을 표현할 때 다음과 같이 말할 수 있다.

• I'm glad to+동사원형 ~.

e.g. I'm glad to be here. 여기 와서 기뻐.

• I'm glad (that)+주어+동사 ~.

e.g. I'm glad that we won the game. 우리가 경기에서 이겨서 기뻐.

• I'm delighted to+동사원형 ~.

e.g. I'm delighted to get a present from him. 그로부터 선물을 받아서 기뻐.

■ 다음과 같은 표현들은 강한 기쁨을 표현한다.

• I feel like a million dollars. 기분이 아주 좋아.
• I'm walking on air right now. 지금 하늘을 나는 기분이야. (기분이 매우 좋아.)
• I couldn't be happier. 난 이보다 더 행복할 수가 없을 거야.
• I've never been better. 이보다 더 좋을 순 없어.

핵심 Check

2. 다음 우리말에 맞도록 빈칸에 들어갈 알맞은 말을 쓰시오.

새로운 나라로 여행할 기회를 얻게 되어 기뻐.

= I'm ____________ have a chance to travel to a new country.

① glad that ② happy for
③ glad to ④ nice of
⑤ feeling like

Step Up – Real-life Scene

I Like Their Emojis

Nari: Hi, Jiho. ❶How are you feeling?

Jiho: ❷I'm happier than ever, Nari.

Nari: I know why. ❸You did it, didn't you?

Jiho: Yes. I finally booked four tickets for the VTS concert!

Nari: Good job. Did you tell Minsu and Yujin about ❹that?

Jiho: Sure. Oh, I just got messages from them. They said they are really happy. Look.

Nari: ❺How cute! I like their emojis. They will bring light sticks and a nice camera.

Jiho: ❻I'm glad to hear that. We're going to have lots of fun!

나는 그들의 이모지가 마음에 들어

나리: 안녕, 지호. 기분이 어떠니?

지호: 어떤 때보다 행복해, 나리야.

나리: 왜 그런지 알겠다. 너 해냈구나, 그렇지?

지호: 그래. 내가 마침내 VTS 콘서트 표를 4장 예매했어!

나리: 잘했어. 민수와 유진이에게도 그것에 대해 말했니?

지호: 물론이지. 오, 그들에게서 방금 메시지를 받았어. 그 애들도 정말 기쁘다고 말했어. 봐.

나리: 정말 귀엽구나! 나는 그들의 이모지가 마음에 들어. 그 애들은 광선 막대기와 멋진 카메라를 가져올 거야.

지호: 그 말을 들으니 기쁘다. 우리는 정말 재미있을 거야!

❶ '기분이 어떠니?'라는 뜻으로 상대방의 기쁨이나 슬픔 등의 감정에 대해 물을 때 사용하는 표현이다.
❷ '비교급 than ~' 구문으로 기쁨을 표현하는 것이다. 'ever'는 비교급과 함께 '지금까지', '이제까지'의 의미로 사용된다.
❸ 'didn't you?'는 부가의문문 형태로 앞 문장의 평서문이 일반동사 긍정문일 때 부가의문문은 부정문 형태로 사용한다.
❹ that은 지시대명사로 'VTS 콘서트 표를 4장 예매한 것(booking four tickets for the VTS concert)'을 가리킨다.
❺ 감탄문으로 'How+형용사(+주어+동사)!' 형태를 사용한다. 'they are'가 생략되어 있다.
❻ 기쁨을 표현하는 말이다.

Check(√) True or False

(1) Jiho told Yujin and Minsu about booking the tickets. T ☐ F ☐

(2) Nari likes emojis which Jiho sent Minsu and Yujin. T ☐ F ☐

Start Off – Listen & Talk A 1

G: Jihun, you're moving to another country next week. How are you feeling?

B: ❶I'm excited to go to a whole new world, Yunju.

G: I'm glad to hear that. ❷I was worried about you.

B: Actually, I'm sad, too. I'll miss all of you a lot.

G: ❸Let's keep in touch online.

B: Okay. Let's have video chats often.

G: 지훈아, 너 다음 주에 다른 나라로 이사 가지. 기분이 어때?

B: 완전히 새로운 나라에 가게 되어 흥분돼, 윤주야.

G: 그 말을 들으니 기쁘구나. 나는 너를 걱정했어.

B: 사실, 슬프기도 해. 너희 모두를 많이 그리워할 거야.

G: 온라인으로 계속 연락하자.

B: 좋아. 자주 화상 채팅하자.

❶ 'I'm excited to V'는 '…해서 흥분돼'라는 의미로 기쁨의 감정을 나타내는 표현이다.
❷ 'be worried about'은 '~에 관해 걱정하다'라는 의미이다.
❸ 'keep in touch'는 '계속 연락하다'라는 의미이다.

Check(√) True or False

(3) Jihun is going to move to a new country next week. T ☐ F ☐

(4) Jihun and his friends will have video chats. T ☐ F ☐

Start Off B – Listen & Talk B

B: Yena, ❶how are you feeling?

G: ❷I'm feeling very sad, Seho. My best friend Jihun is moving away.

B: Really? I'm sorry. But don't be so sad. You two can have video chats online.

G: You're right.

B: ❸Why don't we make him a photo book as a goodbye gift?

G: Great idea. ❹I'm glad to give him something meaningful.

B: 예나야, 기분이 어떠니?
G: 아주 슬퍼, 세호야. 내 가장 친한 친구인 지훈이가 이사 간대.
B: 정말? 유감이구나. 하지만 너무 슬퍼하지 마. 너희 둘은 온라인으로 화상 채팅을 할 수 있잖아.
G: 네 말이 맞아.
B: 우리 이별 선물로 그에게 사진책을 만들어 주는 게 어때?
G: 좋은 생각이야. 그에게 뭔가 의미 있는 것을 준다니 기뻐.

❶ '기분이 어떠니?'라는 뜻으로 상대방의 기쁨이나 슬픔을 물어볼 때 사용하는 표현이다.
❷ 'I'm feeling ~.'은 'How are you feeling?'에 대한 대답으로 감정 상태를 표현할 때 사용한다.
❸ 'Why don't we+동사원형 ~?'은 제안을 할 때 사용하는 표현으로 '우리 ~하는 게 어때?'라는 의미이다.
❹ '-thing'으로 끝나는 대명사는 형용사가 뒤에서 수식한다.

Check(√) True or False

(5) Yena is feeling sad because her best friend Jihun is moving away. T ☐ F ☐

(6) Yena will give Jihun a yearbook as a goodbye gift. T ☐ F ☐

Check Yourself – Listen & Speak 1

G: Minsu, how are you feeling?

B: I'm really excited, Miso. We have a new student in our class. His name is Kim Kihun.

G: So why are you excited?

B: He was a soccer player on his school team. ❶As you know, my team needs a player.

G: I'm glad to hear that. ❷I hope he joins your team.

B: Thanks a lot.

G: 민수야, 기분이 어떠니?
B: 나 정말 신나, 미소야. 우리 반에 새 학생이 한 명 왔어. 이름은 김기훈이야.
G: 그래서 네가 왜 신나는데?
B: 그는 학교 팀 축구 선수였대. 너도 알다시피, 우리 팀은 선수가 한 명 필요하잖아.
G: 그 말을 들으니 기뻐. 그가 너희 팀에 합류하길 바랄게.
B: 고마워.

❶ As you know: 너도 알다시피, 이때의 as는 접속사로 '~이듯이'의 뜻이다.
❷ I hope (that) ~.: 나는 ~하기를 바란다.

Check(√) True or False

(7) There is a new student in the boy's class. T ☐ F ☐

(8) The new student joined the boy's team. T ☐ F ☐

Get Ready 2

(1) B: You don't look happy. Are you all right?
G: No, I'm really sad. My dog is sick. He won't eat at all.
B: ❶That's too bad.

(2) B: It'll be a good day today! Take a look at today's lunch menu.
G: Wow! ❷I'm glad to eat fried chicken! ❸I can't wait for lunch break.

(3) W: Good morning, Mr. Lee. How are you feeling?
M: I'm feeling very happy this morning. ❹ Some students are helping me clean the school.
W: I'm glad to hear that.

(4) G: You look upset. Are you all right?
B: My mom won't ❺let me play soccer after school.
G: Why don't you ask her one more time?

❶ 유감을 나타낼 때 사용하는 표현이다.
❷ '~해서 기쁘다'라는 의미로 기쁨을 나타낼 때 사용하는 표현이다.
❸ 'I can't wait for ~'는 '~가 무척 기다려진다'는 뜻이다.
❹ help+목적어+목적보어(동사원형/to부정사): ~가 …하는 것을 돕다
❺ '사역동사(let)+목적어+목적보어(동사원형)' 형태로 '…가 ~하도록 허락하다'는 의미이다.

Start Off – Listen & Talk A 2

G: Minsu, ❶Jihun is moving to Abu Dhabi in the UAE next week. How are you feeling?
B: I'm sad. ❷I'm going to miss him a lot.
G: I'm sad, too, but I'm also happy. We can visit Abu Dhabi. He is going to invite us. He promised.
B: That's great! I'm glad to have a chance to travel to a new country.

❶ 현재진행형이 미래의 부사구(next week)와 사용될 때는 '~할 예정이다'로 해석한다.
❷ 'be going to+동사원형'은 '~할 예정이다'라는 의미이고, 여기서 miss는 '그리워하다'라는 뜻이다.

Fun Time

A: How are you feeling?
B: I'm nervous. ❶I forgot to bring my math homework. How are you feeling?
A: I'm nervous, too. I have a math test tomorrow. ❷I'm glad to find someone who feels the same.
B: Me, too.

❶ 'forget to+동사원형'은 '~할 것을 잊다'라는 의미이다. 'forget+V-ing(동명사)'는 '~한 것을 잊다'라는 의미이다.
❷ 'I'm glad to+동사원형'은 '~해서 기뻐'라는 의미이고, who는 관계대명사로 선행사 someone을 수식하는 형용사절을 이끈다.

Express Yourself A 1

G: How are you feeling today?
B: ❶I'm really glad to get a present for my birthday.
G: What is the present?
B: It's this drone, ❷which our grandpa sent for my birthday.
G: Wow! I wonder how high it can fly.
B: Let me show you.
G: Thanks.

❶ 'I'm glad to+동사원형'에서 to부정사는 '~해서'라는 감정의 원인을 나타낸다.
❷ 콤마(comma) 뒤의 관계대명사 which는 계속적 용법으로 '접속사+대명사(and our grandpa sent it for my birthday)'로 바꾸어 사용할 수 있다.

Express Yourself A 2

G: How are you feeling?
M: I'm really glad to cook my favorite food.
G: I want to know ❶what it is.
M: It's *japchae*, which is delicious and healthy.
G: I want to ❷try some.
M: Okay. Wait for 30 minutes!

❶ what it is는 간접의문문으로 know의 목적어이다.
❷ try some = try some *japchae*

• 다음 우리말과 일치하도록 빈칸에 알맞은 말을 쓰시오.

Get Ready 2

(1) B: You don't ________ ________. Are you all ________?
G: No, I'm ________ sad. My dog is ________. He won't eat ________ ________.
B: ________ ________ ________.

(2) B: It'll be a good day today! ________ ________ ________ at today's lunch menu.
G: Wow! I'm ________ ________ ________ fried chicken! I ________ ________ ________ lunch break.

(3) W: Good morning, Mr. Lee. ________ are you ________?
M: I'm feeling very happy this morning. Some students are ________ me ________ the school.
W: I'm________ ________ ________ ________.

(4) G: You look ________. Are you ________ ________?
B: My mom won't ________ me ________ soccer after school.
G: ________ ________ ________ ask her one more time?

(1) B: 기분이 좋아 보이지 않는구나. 너 괜찮니?
G: 아니, 나 정말 슬퍼. 내 개가 아파. 그는 아무것도 안 먹으려고 해.
B: 정말 안됐구나.
(2) B: 오늘은 좋은 날이 될 거야! 오늘 점심 메뉴 좀 봐.
G: 와! 닭튀김을 먹게 되어 기뻐! 점심시간이 무척 기다려져.
(3) W: 안녕하세요, 이 선생님. 기분이 어떠세요?
M: 오늘 아침에는 기분이 아주 좋습니다. 몇몇 학생들이 학교 청소하는 것을 돕고 있어요.
W: 그 말을 들으니 기쁘군요.
(4) G: 기분이 언짢아 보인다. 너 괜찮니?
B: 엄마가 방과 후에 축구하는 것을 허락하지 않으셔.
G: 한 번 더 말씀드려 보지 그러니?

Start Off – Listen & Talk A

1. G: Jihun, you're ________ to another country next week. ________ are you feeling?
B: I'm ________ to go to a ________ new world, Yunju.
G: I'm glad ________ ________ that. I ________ ________ ________ you.
B: ________, I'm sad, too. I'll ________ all of you a lot.
G: Let's ________ ________ ________ online.
B: Okay. Let's ________ video chats often.

2. G: Minsu, Jihun ________ ________ to Abu Dhabi in the UAE next week. How are you feeling?
B: I'm sad. I'm going to ________ him a lot.
G: I'm sad, too, but I'm also happy. We can visit Abu Dhabi. He ________ ________ to ________ us. He ________.
B: That's great! I'm ________ ________ ________ a ________ to travel to a new country.

1. G: 지훈아, 너 다음 주에 다른 나라로 이사가지. 기분이 어때?
B: 완전히 새로운 나라에 가게 되어 흥분돼, 윤주야.
G: 그 말을 들으니 기쁘구나. 나는 너를 걱정했어.
B: 사실, 슬프기도 해. 너희 모두를 많이 그리워할 거야.
G: 온라인으로 계속 연락하자.
B: 좋아. 자주 화상 채팅하자.

2. G: 민수야, 지훈이가 다음 주에 아랍에미리트의 아부다비로 이사 간대. 기분이 어떠니?
B: 슬퍼. 그 애가 많이 보고 싶을 거야.
G: 나도 슬퍼, 하지만 기쁘기도 해. 우리는 아부다비를 방문할 수 있잖아. 그가 우리를 초대할 거야. 약속했어.
B: 그거 굉장하다! 새로운 나라로 여행할 기회를 얻게 되어 기뻐.

Start Off – Listen & Talk B

B: Yena, ________ ________ ________ ________?

G: I'm feeling very sad, Seho. My best friend Jihun is ________ ________.

B: Really? I'm ________. But ________ ________ so sad. You two can have video chats online.

G: You're right.

B: ________ ________ ________ make him a photo book ________ a goodbye gift?

G: Great idea. I'm glad to give him ________ ________.

해석

B: 예나야, 기분이 어떠니?
G: 아주 슬퍼, 세호야. 내 가장 친한 친구인 지훈이가 이사 간대.
B: 정말? 유감이구나. 하지만 너무 슬퍼하지 마. 너희 둘은 온라인으로 화상 채팅을 할 수 있잖아.
G: 네 말이 맞아.
B: 우리 이별 선물로 그에게 사진책을 만들어 주는 게 어때?
G: 좋은 생각이야. 그에게 뭔가 의미 있는 것을 준다니 기뻐.

Start Off – Speak Up – Mission

A: ________ ________ ________ feeling today?

B: I'm ________ happy. Today's lunch is great.

A: I'm ________ ________ ________ ________.

A: 오늘 기분이 어떠니?
B: 기분이 좋아. 오늘 점심이 훌륭해.
A: 그 말을 들으니 기쁘구나.

Step Up – Real-life Scene

I Like Their Emojis

Nari: Hi, Jiho. ________ are you feeling?

Jiho: I'm ________ than ________, Nari.

Nari: I know ________. You did it, ________ you?

Jiho: Yes. I finally ________ four tickets for the VTS concert!

Nari: Good job. Did you tell Minsu and Yujin ________ that?

Jiho: Sure. Oh, I just ________ ________ from them. They said they are really happy. Look.

Nari: ________ ________! I like their ________. They will ________ light ________ and a nice camera.

Jiho: ________ ________ ________ ________ ________. We're going to have lots of ________!

나는 그들의 이모지가 마음에 들어

나리: 안녕, 지호. 기분이 어떠니?
지호: 어떤 때보다 행복해, 나리야.
나리: 왜 그런지 알겠다. 너 해냈구나, 그렇지?
지호: 그래. 내가 마침내 VTS 콘서트 표를 4장 예매했어!
나리: 잘했어. 민수와 유진이에게도 그것에 대해 말했니?
지호: 물론이지. 오, 그들에게서 방금 메시지를 받았어. 그 애들도 정말 기쁘다고 말했어. 봐.
나리: 정말 귀엽구나! 나는 그들의 이모지가 마음에 들어. 그 애들은 광선 막대기와 멋진 카메라를 가져올 거야.
지호: 그 말을 들으니 기쁘다. 우리는 정말 재미있을 거야!

Fun Time

A: How are you ________?

B: I'm ________. I ________ ________ ________ my math homework. ________ ________ you feeling?

A: I'm ________, too. I have a math test tomorrow. I'm glad to find someone ________ ________ the same.

B: Me, too.

A: 기분이 어떠니?
B: 나는 초조해. 수학 숙제 가져오는 걸 잊어버렸어. 너는 기분이 어떠니?
A: 나도 초조해. 내일 수학 시험이 있어. 같은 감정을 가진 사람을 찾아서 기뻐.
B: 나도 그래.

A: ________ are you feeling?

B: I'm ________. I ________ a good grade. How are you feeling?

A: I'm ________. Someone ________ my glasses.

A: 기분이 어떠니?
B: 나는 기분이 좋아. 좋은 점수를 받았어. 너는 기분이 어떠니?
A: 나는 화가 나. 누군가가 내 안경을 망가뜨렸어.

Express Yourself A 1

G: ________ ________ you feeling today?

B: I'm really glad to ________ ________ ________ for my birthday.

G: What is the ________?

B: It's this drone, ________ our grandpa sent for my birthday.

G: Wow! I ________ ________ ________ it can fly.

B: ________ ________ ________ you.

G: Thanks.

해석

G: 넌 오늘 기분이 어때?
B: 생일 선물을 받아서 정말 기뻐.
G: 선물이 뭔데?
B: 이 드론인데, 우리 할아버지가 내 생일에 보내 주셨어.
G: 와! 그게 얼마나 높이 날 수 있는지 궁금하다.
B: 내가 보여 줄게.
G: 고마워.

Express Yourself A 2

G: ________ are you ________?

M: I'm really glad ________ ________ my ________ food.

G: I want to know ________ ________ ________.

M: It's *japchae*, ________ is ________ and ________.

G: I want ________ ________ some.

M: Okay. ________ ________ 30 minutes!

G: 기분이 어떠세요?
M: 내가 가장 좋아하는 음식을 요리해서 정말 기뻐.
G: 그게 뭔지 알고 싶은데요.
M: 그건 잡채인데, 맛있고 건강에도 좋아.
G: 저도 좀 먹어 보고 싶어요.
M: 좋아. 30분만 기다려!

Check Yourself – Listen & Speak 1

G: Minsu, ________ ________ ________ ________?

B: I'm really ________, Miso. We ________ a new student ________ our class. His name is Kim Kihun.

G: So ________ are you ________?

B: He was a soccer player ________ his school ________. ________ ________ ________, my team ________ a player.

G: ________ ________ ________ ________ that. I ________ he ________ your team.

B: Thanks a lot.

G: 민수야, 기분이 어떠니?
B: 나 정말 신나, 미소야. 우리 반에 새 학생이 한 명 왔어. 이름은 김기훈이야.
G: 그래서 네가 왜 신나는데?
B: 그는 학교 팀 축구 선수였대. 너도 알다시피, 우리 팀은 선수가 한 명 필요하잖아.
G: 그 말을 들으니 기뻐. 그가 너희 팀에 합류하길 바랄게.
B: 고마워.

01 우리말에 맞도록 주어진 단어를 이용하여 5 단어로 쓰시오.

넌 오늘 기분이 어때? (how, feeling)

➡ ______________________________

02 다음 대화의 빈칸에 들어갈 말로 알맞은 것은?

W: Good morning, Mr. Lee. How are you feeling?
M: I'm feeling very happy this morning. Some students are helping me clean the school.
W: ______________________

① That's too bad.
② I'm sorry to hear that.
③ I don'k know how to help you.
④ You did a good job.
⑤ I'm glad to hear that.

03 다음 대화의 빈칸에 들어갈 말로 적절하지 <u>않은</u> 것은?

B: You don't look happy. Are you all right?
G: No, I'm really sad. ______________________
B: That's too bad.

① I don't know whether Kirk likes me.
② I am having trouble with playing the guitar.
③ My dog is sick. He won't eat at all.
④ I'm glad to eat fried chicken!
⑤ My best friend Jihun is moving away.

04 다음 대화의 밑줄 친 우리말에 맞게 주어진 단어를 이용하여 문장의 빈칸을 채우시오.

B: I'm excited to go to a whole new world, Yunju.
G: I'm glad to hear that. <u>나는 너를 걱정했어.</u> (worry)

➡ I ____________________ you.

[01~02] 다음 대화를 읽고 물음에 답하시오.

G: Jihun, you're moving to another country next week. How are you ⓐfeeling?
B: I'm ⓑsad to go to a whole new world, Yunju.
G: I'm ⓒglad to hear that. I was ⓓworried about you.
B: Actually, I'm ⓔsad, too. I'll miss all of you a lot.
G: ______(A)______
B: Okay. Let's have video chats often.

중요
01 위 대화의 흐름상 밑줄 친 ⓐ~ⓔ 중 어휘의 쓰임이 어색한 것은?

① ⓐ ② ⓑ ③ ⓒ ④ ⓓ ⑤ ⓔ

02 위 대화의 빈칸 (A)에 들어갈 말로 알맞은 것은?

① I can visit you.
② We can write letters to each other.
③ My best friend is moving away, too.
④ Let's keep in touch online.
⑤ Why don't you buy a gift for me?

서답형
03 다음 대화의 밑줄 친 우리말에 맞게 주어진 단어를 이용하여 영어로 쓰시오.

A: How are you feeling today?
B: I'm feeling sad. My friend is sick.
A: 그 말을 들으니 안됐구나.

sorry / hear / that

➡ ________________

[04~05] 다음 대화를 읽고 물음에 답하시오.

G: ______(A)______
B: I'm really glad to get a present for my birthday.
G: What is the present?
B: It's this drone, which our grandpa sent for my birthday.
G: Wow! (B)그게 얼마나 높이 날 수 있는지 궁금하다.
B: Let me show you.
G: Thanks.

04 위 대화의 빈칸 (A)에 들어갈 말로 알맞은 것은?

① How are you feeling today?
② What's your favorite present for your birthday?
③ What do you think of this drone?
④ Do you like the present?
⑤ What do you want to get?

서답형
05 위 대화의 밑줄 친 (B)의 우리말에 맞게 주어진 단어를 이용하여 쓰시오.

wonder / high / it / can

➡ ________________

06 다음 대화의 밑줄 친 부분의 의도로 알맞은 것은?

A: I have bad news.
B: What is it?
A: John fell down and broke his leg.
B: I'm sorry to hear that.

① 실망 표현하기 ② 상기시켜 주기
③ 격려에 답하기 ④ 기대 표현하기
⑤ 유감 표현하기

[07~08] 다음 대화를 읽고 물음에 답하시오.

Nari: Hi, Jiho. How are you feeling?
Jiho: I'm ⓐhappy than ever, Nari.
Nari: I know why. You did it, ⓑdidn't you?
Jiho: Yes. I finally ⓒbooked four tickets for the VTS concert!
Nari: Good job. Did you tell Minsu and Yujin about that?
Jiho: Sure. Oh, I just got messages from them. They said they are really happy. Look.
Nari: ⓓHow cute! I like their emojis. They will bring light sticks and a nice camera.
Jiho: I'm glad to hear that. We're going to have ⓔlots of fun!

07 위 대화의 밑줄 친 ⓐ~ⓔ 중 어법상 어색한 것은?

① ⓐ ② ⓑ ③ ⓒ ④ ⓓ ⑤ ⓔ

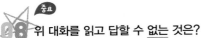

08 위 대화를 읽고 답할 수 없는 것은?

① How is Jiho feeling now?
② Why is Jiho so happy?
③ What did Minsu and Yujin send to Jiho?
④ How did Jiho book the tickets for the VTS concert?
⑤ What does Nari like?

서답형

09 다음 대화의 빈칸에 공통으로 들어갈 말에 대한 영어 풀이를 보고 주어진 철자로 시작하여 쓰시오.

A: How are you feeling?
B: I'm ________. I forgot to bring my math homework. How are you feeling?
A: I'm ________, too. I have a math test tomorrow.

worried or frightened about something, and unable to relax

➡ n________________

10 주어진 문장에 이어질 대화의 순서로 알맞은 것은?

G: How are you feeling?

(A) I want to try some.
(B) It's *japchae*, which is delicious and healthy.
(C) I'm really glad to cook my favorite food.
(D) I want to know what it is.

M: Okay. Wait for 30 minutes!

① (B) – (A) – (C) – (D)
② (B) – (C) – (A) – (D)
③ (C) – (B) – (D) – (A)
④ (C) – (D) – (B) – (A)
⑤ (D) – (B) – (C) – (A)

중요

11 다음 두 사람의 대화가 어색한 것은?

① A: You don't look happy. Are you all right?
B: No, I'm really sad.
② A: How are you feeling?
B: I'm happier than ever.
③ A: My best friend is moving to another country next week.
B: I'm glad to hear that.
④ A: Some students are helping me clean the school.
B: I'm glad to hear that.
⑤ A: I'm feeling sad. My friend is sick.
B: I'm sorry to hear that.

[01~02] 다음 대화를 읽고 물음에 답하시오.

Nari: Hi, Jiho. How are you feeling?
Jiho: (A)나는 어느 때보다 더 행복해, Nari.
Nari: I know why. You did it, didn't you?
Jiho: Yes. I finally booked four tickets for the VTS concert!
Nari: Good job. Did you tell Minsu and Yujin about that?
Jiho: Sure. Oh, I just got messages from them. They said they are really happy. Look.
Nari: How cute! I like their emojis. They will bring light sticks and a nice camera.
Jiho: I'm glad to hear that. We're going to have lots of fun!

01 위 대화를 읽고 다음 물음에 영어로 답하시오. (5 단어로 쓸 것)

Q: What does Nari think of the emojis?

➡ ______________________

02 위 대화의 밑줄 친 (A)의 우리말에 맞게 'happy'와 'ever'를 활용하여 영작하시오.

➡ ______________________

중요

03 다음 대화의 빈칸에 들어갈 말로 자연스러운 것을 〈보기〉에서 찾아 쓰시오.

B: Yena, ________(A)________
G: I'm feeling very sad, Seho. My best friend Jihun is moving away.
B: ______(B)______ But don't be so sad. You two can have video chats online.
G: You're right.
B: ________(C)________
G: Great idea. I'm glad to give him something meaningful.

보기
- Why don't we make him a photo book as a goodbye gift?
- how are you feeling?
- Really? I'm sorry.

➡ (A) ______________________
(B) ______________________
(C) ______________________

고난이도

04 다음 대화의 밑줄 친 질문에 대한 답을 주어진 단어를 활용하여 〈조건〉에 맞게 영작하여 빈칸 (A)를 채우시오.

조건
- 관계대명사의 계속적 용법을 사용할 것.
- this drone, our grandpa, send, for my birthday

G: How are you feeling today?
B: I'm really glad to get a present for my birthday.
G: What is the present?
B: ________(A)________
G: Wow! I wonder how high it can fly.
B: Let me show you.
G: Thanks.

➡ It's ______________________
______________________.

05 다음 대화의 빈칸에 들어갈 말을 주어진 단어를 알맞게 배열하여 쓰시오.

B: It'll be a good day today! Take a look at today's lunch menu.
G: Wow! I'm glad to eat fried chicken!
____
(for / break / I / can't / lunch / wait)

교과서

Grammar

1 간접의문문

• Everyone knows **what it means.** 모두가 그것이 무엇을 의미하는지 안다.

■ 형태: 의문사+주어+동사
의미: ~인지/일지

■ 다른 문장 뒤에 이어져서 간접의문문이 되며 '의문사+주어+동사'의 어순이 된다.

• Do you know? + What time is it? (의문사+동사+주어)
= Do you know **what time it is**? (의문사+주어+동사) 너는 몇 시인지 아니?

■ 의문사가 주어인 경우에는 의문사 뒤에 바로 동사가 이어진다.

• Can you tell me? + Who visited our school today? (의문사(=주어)+동사)
= Can you tell me **who visited our school today**? (의문사(=주어)+동사)
오늘 누가 우리 학교를 방문했는지 내게 말해 줄 수 있니?

■ 'how often, how much, how many people, what kind of food'처럼 하나의 의미 단위로 쓰이는 의문사구는 하나의 의문사로 취급한다.

• Tell me. + What kind of food does she enjoy? (의문사구+조동사+주어+동사원형)
= Tell me **what kind of food she enjoys**. (○) 그녀가 어떤 종류의 음식을 좋아하는지 내게 말해 줘.
Tell me what she enjoys kind of food. (X)

■ 주절이 Do you think(believe, guess, suppose 등)일 때 간접의문문의 의문사는 맨 앞으로 보내진다.

• Do you think? + When did Tom leave?
= **When** do you think **Tom left**? 넌 Tom이 언제 떠났다고 생각하니?

■ 의문사가 없는 의문문은 의문사 대신 두 절을 연결하는 접속사로 whether 또는 if를 쓰고 '접속사+주어+동사'의 어순이 된다.

• I wonder. + Is he satisfied with his job? (동사+주어)
= I wonder **whether[if] he is satisfied with his job**. (접속사+주어+동사)
그가 자기 직업에 만족하는지 궁금해.

핵심 Check

1. 다음 괄호 안에서 알맞은 것을 고르시오.
(1) Do you know (who is he / who he is)?
(2) Do you know (where does he come from / where he comes from)?
(3) Tell me (how old he is / how he is old).

2 관계대명사의 계속적 용법

• People also use ROFL, **which** means "Rolling On the Floor Laughing."
사람들은 또한 ROFL를 사용하는데, 그것은 '바닥을 구르면서 웃기'를 의미한다.

■ 형태: 쉼표(,) + 관계대명사
쓰임: 관계대명사절이 선행사에 대해 부연 설명할 때 사용함

■ 선행사가 사람이면 'who[whom]', 사람이 아니면 'which'를 사용한다. 그러나 'that'은 사용하지 않는다.

• Last Friday, I met my friend, Jack, **who** is a police officer.
지난 금요일, 나는 내 친구 Jack을 만났는데, 그는 경찰관이다.

• This is my new laptop, **which** my mom bought for me.
이것은 나의 새 노트북인데, 엄마가 나에게 사 주셨다.

• We visited the building, **which** was built by my company.
우리는 그 건물을 방문했는데, 그것은 우리 회사에 의해서 지어졌다.

■ 관계대명사의 제한적 용법은 선행사를 꾸밀 때 사용하고 관계사절을 먼저 해석하지만, 관계대명사의 계속적 용법은 선행사를 부연 설명할 때 사용하므로 관계사절을 나중에 사용한다.

• Mrs. Irene has a daughter **who** is a lawyer. (Mrs. Irene은 변호사인 딸이 하나 있다. → 다른 직업을 가진 다른 딸이 있을 수 있음)

• Mrs. Irene has a daughter, **who** is a lawyer. (Mrs. Irene은 딸이 하나 있는데, 그녀는 변호사이다. → 딸이 한 명 밖에 없고, 그 딸이 변호사임)

■ 선행사가 앞선 절의 일부이거나 전체인 경우, 'which'를 사용한 관계대명사의 계속적 용법으로 문장을 쓴다.

• He lost his new backpack, **which** made his mother angry. 〈선행사가 앞 문장 전체〉
그는 그의 새 책가방을 잃어버렸는데, 그것이 그의 어머니를 화나게 만들었다.

핵심 Check

2. 다음 괄호 안에서 알맞은 것을 고르시오.
(1) This is Hannah, (who / that) is kind and smart.
(2) We wrote a letter to Jimin, (who / which) made him happy.
(3) My aunt, (who / that) is a teacher, lives in Incheon.

01 다음 우리말에 맞게 괄호 안에 주어진 어구를 바르게 배열하시오.

(1) 당신 학교의 이름이 무엇인지 제게 말해 주세요. (the name, tell, is, what, me, of your school)

➡ ______________________

(2) 저는 당신의 영어 선생님이 어디 출신인지 알고 싶습니다. (where, to know, like, your English teacher, I'd, comes from)

➡ ______________________

(3) 이 가방이 얼마인지 제게 말해 줄 수 있나요? (how much, tell, can, you, me, is, this bag)

➡ ______________________

(4) 저는 왜 당신이 슬픈지 알고 싶습니다. (why, to know, feeling, I'd like, sad, you, are)

➡ ______________________

02 다음 문장에서 어법상 어색한 부분을 바르게 고쳐 쓰시오.

(1) She has an office, where is located on Worchester Street.

__________ ➡ __________

(2) I have been to Wellington, that is the capital of New Zealand.

__________ ➡ __________

(3) Can you tell me where did Ann spend her vacation?

__________ ➡ __________

(4) I don't know why was he absent from school.

__________ ➡ __________

03 다음 우리말에 맞게 주어진 어휘를 바르게 배열하시오.

> 보기
>
> I asked Jane. + What did she eat for lunch yesterday?
>
> → I asked Jane what she ate for lunch yesterday.

(1) Tell me. + When is your birthday?

➡ ______________________

(2) I didn't know. + What did she major in?

➡ ______________________

(3) Do you know? + What is the most famous online game these days?

➡ ______________________

Grammar 시험대비 실력평가 Step3

01 다음 중 어법상 어색한 문장을 고르시오.

① Do you know who visited the museum?
② Can you tell me what it is time?
③ I wonder if we will have an exam.
④ What do you think he likes to eat for dinner?
⑤ I'm not sure how many people will come to my birthday party.

02 다음 두 문장을 한 문장으로 바르게 쓴 것을 고르시오.

• Can you tell me?
• How many hours do you sleep a day?

① Can you tell me how many hours do you sleep a day?
② Can you tell me how you sleep many hours a day?
③ How can you tell me many hours you sleep a day?
④ Can you tell me how many hours you sleep a day?
⑤ How many hours can you tell me sleep a day?

03 다음 빈칸에 들어갈 말로 적절한 것은?

This is my friend, Minseung, ________ has a cute younger sister.

① that ② who
③ whom ④ whose
⑤ which

중요

04 다음 빈칸에 들어갈 수 있는 말이 다른 하나는?

① She has a son, ________ is studying in Vancouver.
② My homeroom teacher, ________ teaches English, lives in Seoul.
③ Ted seems to like Jenny, ________ is very shocking to us.
④ I'm glad to meet Tom again, ________ I haven't heard from for a long time.
⑤ Look at that girl, ________ is smiling brightly.

05 빈칸에 들어갈 말을 순서대로 바르게 연결한 것은?

• I wonder ________ he put his pencil case.
• Can you guess ________ my brother got for his birthday?

① what – when
② where – how
③ how – who
④ how – when
⑤ where – what

중요

06 다음 밑줄 친 who의 성격이 나머지 넷과 다른 것은?

① Can you guess who will be the next leader of our team?
② I haven't decided who to meet next Monday.
③ Who do you think is your best friend?
④ Please tell her who should be invited.
⑤ Meet my friend, Mingyu, who is the most popular boy.

서답형

07 다음 괄호 안에 주어진 단어들을 바르게 배열하여 문장을 완성하시오.

The soccer ball is from Messi, (a big soccer game, whom, Amy, after, met).

➡ ______________________

08 다음 두 문장을 한 문장으로 바르게 옮긴 것은?

• Do you know? • Does he have brothers or sisters?

① Do you know that he has brothers or sisters?
② Do you know whether does he have brothers or sisters?
③ Do you know whether he have brothers or sisters?
④ Do you know whether he has brothers or sisters?
⑤ Do you know he has brothers or sisters?

서답형

09 다음 문장에서 어법상 어색한 것을 바르게 고쳐 다시 쓰시오.

(1) I wonder how you need many books.
➡ ______________________

(2) Tell me why did he invent the machine.
➡ ______________________

서답형

10 다음 두 문장을 관계대명사의 계속적 용법을 사용하여 한 문장으로 바르게 바꿔 쓰시오.

• I'm going to show you the photo. • My friend, Amy, sent it to me.

➡ ______________________

11 다음 중 어법상 어색한 문장을 고르시오.

① She lives in Seoul, which is the biggest city in Korea.
② This is the microwave oven, which was invented by Dr. Spencer.
③ What do you think he will bring tomorrow?
④ I wonder that my teacher will ask me a question or not.
⑤ They welcomed me with a warm heart, which moved me.

서답형

12 다음 괄호 안에서 알맞은 말을 고르시오.

(1) I have grandparents, and (who / they) live in Busan.
(2) We sang a song, (who / which) sounded beautiful.
(3) She works at the bank, (which / where) is located on Downing Street.
(4) Mason won the gold medal, (which / who) made his family happy.
(5) I have a cat, (that / which) can jump high.

서답형

13 다음 괄호 안에 주어진 어구들을 바르게 배열하여 문장을 완성하시오.

Can you tell me (for, many, we, class, to, pencils, how, need, bring, the next)?

➡ ______________________

서답형

[14~15] 주어진 어휘를 이용하여 다음 우리말을 영어로 쓰시오.

14

너는 왜 과학자가 되고 싶은지 나에게 말해 줄 수 있니? (can, tell, why, become, scientist)

➡ ______________________________
____

15

나는 언니가 한 명 있는데, 그녀는 New York에서 음악을 공부하는 중이야. (older, music, studying)

➡ ______________________________
____

16 다음 중 밑줄 친 부분의 쓰임이 어색한 것을 고르시오.

① This is Ms. Kim, who is my art teacher.
② My uncle has a son, who will go to high school next year.
③ I had dinner with Mike, who is one of my friends.
④ I bought a camera for June, who was very expensive.
⑤ I met an old friend, who didn't recognize me at first.

중요

17 빈칸에 들어갈 말을 순서대로 바르게 연결한 것은?

• This is Nancy, ________ took this photo. • Do you know ________ your parents' favorite food are.

① who – why
② who – what
③ which – who
④ which – what
⑤ what – why

18 다음 문장에서 'who'가 들어갈 위치로 알맞은 것을 고르시오.

① Nancy, ② will throw ③ a birthday party tomorrow, ④ is ⑤ my classmate.

① ② ③ ④ ⑤

중요

19 다음 중 어법상 어색한 문장을 고르시오.

① I like Junho, who is gentle and kind.
② I met my friend at night, who was a secret.
③ I bought new pants, which were too tight.
④ I made friends with Chris, who speaks Korean fluently.
⑤ The books, which you gave me, were very helpful.

서답형

20 다음 문장을 두 문장으로 나누어 쓰시오.

(1) Do you know what the color red means?
➡ ______________________________

(2) My best friends are Ken and Mary, who are nice and smart.
➡ ______________________________
____

(3) I wonder how often Mary meets Ken.
➡ ______________________________

21 다음 빈칸에 들어갈 말이 순서대로 짝지어진 것은?

• I wonder ________ high the drone can fly. • The present is this drone, ________ our grandpa sent to me for my birthday.

① why – what
② how – who
③ how – which
④ when – which
⑤ why – which

Grammar 서술형 시험대비

고난이도

01 다음 두 문장을 간접의문문을 이용하여 한 문장으로 연결하여 쓰시오.

(1) • Do you know?
• Why is Mira smiling?
➡ ______________________

(2) • Do you think?
• What is my dad cooking?
➡ ______________________

(3) • Do you guess?
• How did she find out the answer?
➡ ______________________

(4) • I want to know.
• What made him happy?
➡ ______________________

(5) • I wonder.
• How much time do they spend studying?
➡ ______________________

02 다음 우리말을 주어진 어휘를 이용하여 영어로 옮기시오.

(1) 나는 네가 그 인형을 어떻게 만들었는지 궁금해. (wonder, how, doll)
➡ ______________________

(2) 너는 그 영화가 언제 시작하는지 아니? (know, movie, start)
➡ ______________________

(3) 그녀에게 네가 뭐라고 말했는지 말해 줄 수 있니? (tell, what, said)
➡ ______________________

03 주어진 문장을 계속적 용법의 관계대명사를 사용하여 다시 쓰시오.

(1) Minsu got a drone from his grandpa, and he lives in Busan.
➡ ______________________

(2) He is cooking *japchae*, and he likes it the most.
➡ ______________________

중요

04 잘못된 부분을 바르게 고쳐 문장을 다시 쓰시오.

(1) Do you know how he is old?
➡ ______________________

(2) The girl is Amy, that enjoys cooking.
➡ ______________________

(3) Look at this guitar, which I gave it to Amy for her birthday.
➡ ______________________

(4) The cute dog is Lucky, which like catching balls.
➡ ______________________

(5) Do you know when did he came to Korea?
➡ ______________________

05 다음 주어진 빈칸에 괄호 안의 문장을 알맞은 형태로 바꾸어 쓰시오.

I want to learn ________________.
(What does he do in his free time?)

➡ ________________

중요

06 다음 괄호 안의 단어를 바르게 배열하여 대화를 완성하시오.

(1)

A: Can you ________________?
(live, tell, where, me, you)
B: Sure, I live in Mokpo.

➡ ________________

(2)

A: Can you tell me ________________?
(the, will, bus, when, come, next)
B: Sure, it will come in 10 minutes.

➡ ________________

07 다음 중 어법상 어색한 문장을 바르게 고치시오. (3개)

a. Koreans use Hangeul, which was invented by King Sejong.
b. Emma, who is very young, is good at chess.
c. She wants to visit the Eiffel Tower, it is located in Paris.
d. I climbed Mt. Halla with Mary, who is famous for its beauty.
e. I hate those guys, who tells lies to me.

➡ ________ ➡ ________
________ ➡ ________
________ ➡ ________

고난이도

08 다음 문장을 어법에 맞게 고쳐 쓰시오.

(1) She met my sister, who live in Hawaii.
➡ ________________

(2) He is dancing with Nancy, she is 20 years old.
➡ ________________

(3) He is happy to get a cat, Milky, that is white like milk.
➡ ________________

(4) Do you know why is the boy happy?
➡ ________________

(5) Do you guess what Mr. Lee is doing?
➡ ________________

09 두 문장을 간접의문문을 사용하여 한 문장으로 썼을 때, 빈칸에 해당하는 문장을 쓰시오.

(1) Do you know?
+ ________________
→ Do you know when the game starts?

(2) I want to know.
+ Where did she go last night?
→ ________________

(3) I wonder.
+ Who broke the glasses?
→ ________________

(4) Can you tell me?
+ What color do you like?
→ ________________

교과서

Reading

How Do You "Ha-Ha" in Your Texts?

Laughter is human. We laugh out loud when we hear a joke, see something funny, or feel happy. We laugh even in our writings, such as emails or texts, as we do in our conversations. How do we do that?

때를 나타내는 부사절 / something과 같이 -thing으로 끝나는 부정대명사는 꾸며 주는 형용사가 뒤에 온다. / 쉼표를 앞뒤에 넣은 삽입구 / ~하는 것처럼, ~하듯이(접속사)

"Ha-ha" is a form of written laughter. Everyone knows what it means. Actually, it has been used since long ago. Even Shakespeare used "ha-ha" in his works.

과거분사형 형용사로 쓰여 뒤에 나오는 명사 laughter를 수식. / 간접의문문(의문사+주어+동사) / 현재완료 수동태 / ~조차

DOGBERRY: Ha, ha, ha! Well, gentlemen, good night. And if anything important happens, find me and let me know.

(Shakespeare, *Much Ado About Nothing* Act 3, Scene 3, Page 4)

Another form of written laughter is LOL. It stands for "Laughing Out Loud." People also use ROFL quite often, which means "Rolling On the Floor Laughing." These expressions have become popular because they can be typed quite quickly.

= and it 계속적 용법의 관계대명사 / 현재완료시제 / 조동사가 쓰인 수동태로, 조동사 can 뒤에 be동사가 원형으로 쓰임

A: Have a safe trip 2mrw. Make sure u don't miss me too much. LOL

B: OK. I'll try to make sure I don't miss u. LOL. Thanks for wishing me a safe trip.

= make sure (that) / 동명사(전치사의 목적어)

XD also represents laughter in text. It shows a laughing face with a mouth open and eyes closed tightly. XD is not a word. It's an emoticon, which is a group of letters or symbols used to represent a facial expression. The emoticon XD expresses our happy feelings more visually than ha-ha and LOL do.

with+명사+형용사: '…(명사)가 ~(형용사) 한채로'의 뜻으로 부대상황을 의미함 / 계속적 용법의 관계대명사 / used는 과거분사로, 뒤에서 명사를 수식하는 형용사 역할 / to부정사의 부사적 용법(목적)

I can't wait to go to Disneyland. XD

can't wait to 동사원형: …하기를 몹시 바라다, 어서 빨리 …하고 싶어 하다

- text 글, 문서, 문자 메시지
- conversation 대화
- human 인간의, 인간적인
- laugh out loud 큰 소리로 웃다
- such as …와 같은
- form 형식, 방식, 형태
- written 글로 쓴, 글로 표현된
- since …부터, … 이후
- gentleman 신사
- stand for …을 의미하다, …을 상징하다
- type 치다, 입력하다
- represent 나타내다, 대표하다
- emoticon 이모티콘 (emotion+icon)
- a group of 한 무리의
- symbol 상징
- facial 얼굴의
- visually 시각적으로

확인문제

- 다음 문장이 본문의 내용과 일치하면 T, 일치하지 않으면 F를 쓰시오.

1. We laugh even in our writings. ☐
2. "Ha-ha" is a form of spoken laughter. ☐
3. Shakespeare didn't use "ha-ha" in his works. ☐
4. LOL stands for "Laughing Out Loud." ☐
5. XD is a word. ☐

These days, people use 😂 — a "face with tears of joy." This is a small picture called an "emoji." Lots of laughing emojis are available to use online, so people can express their laughter in various ways.

앞에 나온 picture를 꾸며 주는 과거분사. 앞에 'which is'가 생략 / 그래서

A: I hit my head on the cupboard.

B: Oh, my! Are you okay?

아, 저런!

A: I hit my head on the cupboard. 😂

B: Uh-oh! Is the cupboard okay? 😂

Some emojis have grown bigger, and some even move or make laughing sounds.

현재완료 / 웃음소리

A: So yesterday, I was in a restaurant, and I really needed to break wind.

need to: ~할 필요가 있다

B: And ...

A: Well, the music was really loud, so I just did it.

B: And ...

A: And then I realized I was listening to music with my earphones.

I was 앞에 접속사 that이 생략

B:

Laughing marks can represent our facial expressions and deliver our voice tones. By using various laughing marks, we can show our friends how much we care for them or how happy we are with them. Laugh, even in written forms, and your friends will laugh with you.

represent와 병렬 관계 / by -ing: …함으로써 / 'show+간접목적어+직접목적어' (4형식 구문). 직접목적어에 간접의문문 두 개가 쓰였음. / 명령문,+and …: ~해라, 그러면 …

A: Me when it's cold out

B: This was me yesterday

tear 눈물
joy 기쁨
emoji 이모지
available 구할 수 있는, 이용할 수 있는
various 다양한
cupboard 찬장
break wind 방귀를 뀌다
mark 기호, 표시
deliver 배달하다, 전달하다
tone 어조, 말투

확인문제

● 다음 문장이 본문의 내용과 일치하면 T, 일치하지 않으면 F를 쓰시오.

1 😂 is known as a "face with tears of joy." ☐

2 Lots of laughing emojis are often used offline. ☐

3 Some emojis have grown bigger. ☐

4 Emojis can't move or make laughing sounds. ☐

5 Laughing marks can represent our facial expressions. ☐

6 Laughing marks can't deliver our voice tones. ☐

Reading 교과서 확인학습 A

- 우리말을 참고하여 빈칸에 알맞은 말을 쓰시오.

1 _______ Do You "Ha-Ha" in Your _______?

2 Laughter is _______.

3 We _______ _______ _______ when we hear a joke, see something funny, or feel happy.

4 We _______ _______ _______ _______ _______, such as emails or texts, as we do in our conversations.

5 _______ do we do that?

6 "Ha-ha" is a form of _______ _______.

7 Everyone knows _______ _______ _______.

8 Actually, it _______ _______ _______ since long ago.

9 Even Shakespeare used "ha-ha" _______ _______ _______.

10 **DOGBERRY**: Ha, ha, ha! Well, _______, _______ night.

11 And if _______ _______ happens, find me and let me know.

12 (Shakespeare, *Much Ado About Nothing* _______ 3, _______ 3, Page 4)

13 Another form of _______ _______ is LOL.

14 It _______ _______ "Laughing Out Loud."

15 People also use ROFL quite often, which means "_______ _______ _______ _______ _______."

16 These expressions have become popular because they _______ _______ _______ quite quickly.

17 A: _______ _______ _______ _______ 2mrw.

18 _______ _______ u don't miss me too much. LOL

19 B: OK. I'll try to make sure I don't _______ _______. LOL

20 Thanks for _______ _______ _______ _______ _______.

21 XD also _______ laughter in text.

22 It shows a laughing face _______ a mouth _______ and eyes _______ _______.

1 글에서는 어떻게 "하하"라고 웃나요?
2 웃음은 인간 고유의 것이다.
3 우리는 농담을 듣거나 우스운 것을 보거나 행복감을 느끼면 소리 내어 웃는다.
4 우리는 이메일이나 문자 메시지 같은 글 속에서조차 대화에서 하듯이 웃는다.
5 어떻게 그렇게 하는가?
6 "하하"는 문자로 된 웃음의 한 형태이다.
7 모두가 그것이 무엇을 의미하는지 안다.
8 실제로 그것은 오래전부터 사용되어 왔다.
9 셰익스피어조차도 "하하"를 자신의 작품에 사용하였다.
10 DOGBERRY: 하하하! 자, 신사분들, 좋은 밤 보내시오.
11 그리고 만일 뭔가 중요한 일이 일어난다면 나를 찾아서 알려 주시오.
12 (셰익스피어, 헛소동, 3막 3장 4쪽)
13 또 다른 형태의 문자로 된 웃음은 LOL이다.
14 그것은 '크게 소리 내어 웃기'를 상징한다.
15 사람들은 또한 ROFL도 꽤 자주 사용하는데, 그것은 '바닥을 구르면서 웃기'를 의미한다.
16 이 표현들은 상당히 빠르게 타자를 칠 수 있어서 인기를 얻었다.
17 A: 내일 안전한 여행을 해.
18 나를 너무 많이 그리워하지 않도록 해. LOL
19 B: 좋아. 너를 그리워하지 않도록 할게. LOL
20 안전한 여행을 기원해 줘서 고마워.
21 XD 또한 문자 메시지에서 웃음을 나타낸다.
22 그것은 입을 벌리고 눈을 질끈 감은 채 웃는 얼굴을 보여 준다.

23 XD is not ________ ________.

24 It's an emoticon, which is a group of letters or symbols ________ ________ ________ ________ ________ ________.

25 The emoticon XD expresses our happy feelings ________ ________ than ha-ha and LOL do.

26 I ________ ________ ________ go to Disneyland. XD

27 These days, people use — a "________ ________ ________ ________ ________."

28 This is a small picture ________ an "emoji."

29 Lots of laughing emojis are ________ ________ ________ online, so people can express their laughter in ________ ________.

30 A: I ________ ________ ________ on the cupboard.

31 B: Oh, my! Are you ________?

32 A: I hit my head ________ ________ ________.

33 B: Uh-oh! Is the cupboard ________?

34 Some emojis ________ ________ bigger, and some even move or make ________ ________.

35 A: So yesterday, I was in a restaurant, and I really needed to ________ ________.

36 B: And ...

37 A: Well, the music was really loud, so I ________ ________ ________.

38 B: And ...

39 A: And then I realized I was listening to music ________ ________ ________.

40 Laughing marks can represent our ________ ________ and deliver our ________ ________.

41 By using various laughing marks, we can show our friends how much we ________ ________ them or how happy we are ________ ________.

42 ________, even in written forms, ________ your friends will laugh with you.

43 Me when it's ________ ________

44 ________ ________ me yesterday

23 XD는 단어가 아니다.

24 그것은 이모티콘이고, 얼굴 표정을 나타내기 위해 사용되는 한 무리의 문자나 상징이다.

25 이모티콘 XD는 우리의 행복한 감정을 하하와 LOL보다 더 시각적으로 표현한다.

26 나는 디즈니랜드에 가는 게 몹시 기다려져. XD

27 요즘 사람들은 '기쁨의 눈물을 흘리는 얼굴'인 를 사용한다.

28 이것은 '이모지'라고 불리는 작은 그림이다.

29 많은 웃는 이모지가 온라인에서 사용될 수 있고, 그래서 사람들은 다양한 방식으로 자신들의 웃음을 표현할 수 있다.

30 A: 찬장에 머리를 부딪쳤어.

31 B: 오, 이런! 너 괜찮니?

32 A: 찬장에 머리를 부딪쳤어.

33 B: 어 어! 찬장 괜찮니?

34 어떤 이모지들은 크기가 커졌고, 또 어떤 것들은 심지어 움직이거나 웃음소리를 내기까지 한다.

35 A: 그래서 어제 나는 식당에 있었는데 정말 방귀를 뀌어야 했어.

36 B: 그리고 …

37 A: 음, 음악이 정말 시끄럽길래 나는 그냥 뀌어 버렸어.

38 B: 그리고 …

39 A: 그리고 그때 나는 내가 이어폰을 끼고 음악을 듣고 있다는 걸 깨달았지.

40 웃음 표시는 우리의 얼굴 표정을 나타내고 우리의 목소리 어조를 전달할 수 있다.

41 다양한 웃음 표시를 사용함으로써, 우리는 친구들을 얼마나 좋아하는지 또는 그들과 함께 있어서 얼마나 행복한지를 그들에게 보여 줄 수 있다.

42 웃어라, 문자로 된 형태로라도. 그러면 친구들도 여러분과 함께 웃을 것이다.

43 추울 때 내 모습이네.

44 이건 어제의 나야.

Reading 교과서 확인학습 B

• 우리말을 참고하여 본문을 영작하시오.

1 글에서는 어떻게 "하하"라고 웃나요?
➡ ________________

2 웃음은 인간 고유의 것이다.
➡ ________________

3 우리는 농담을 듣거나 우스운 것을 보거나 행복감을 느끼면 소리 내어 웃는다.
➡ ________________

4 우리는 이메일이나 문자 메시지 같은 글 속에서조차 대화에서 하듯이 웃는다.
➡ ________________

5 어떻게 그렇게 하는가?
➡ ________________

6 "하하"는 문자로 된 웃음의 한 형태이다.
➡ ________________

7 모두가 그것이 무엇을 의미하는지 안다.
➡ ________________

8 실제로 그것은 오래전부터 사용되어 왔다.
➡ ________________

9 셰익스피어조차도 "하하"를 자신의 작품에 사용하였다.
➡ ________________

10 DOGBERRY: 하하하! 자, 신사분들, 좋은 밤 보내시오.
➡ ________________

11 그리고 만일 뭔가 중요한 일이 일어난다면 나를 찾아서 알려 주시오.
➡ ________________

12 (셰익스피어. 헛소동. 3막 3장 4쪽)
➡ ________________

13 또 다른 형태의 문자로 된 웃음은 LOL이다.
➡ ________________

14 그것은 '크게 소리 내어 웃기'를 상징한다.
➡ ________________

15 사람들은 또한 ROFL도 꽤 자주 사용하는데. 그것은 '바닥을 구르면서 웃기'를 의미한다.
➡ ________________

16 이 표현들은 상당히 빠르게 타자를 칠 수 있어서 인기를 얻었다.
➡ ________________

17 A: 내일 안전한 여행을 해.
➡ ________________

18 나를 너무 많이 그리워하지 않도록 해. LOL
➡ ________________

19 B: 좋아. 너를 그리워하지 않도록 할게. LOL.
➡ ________________

20 안전한 여행을 기원해 줘서 고마워.
➡ ________________

21 XD 또한 문자 메시지에서 웃음을 나타낸다.
➡ ________________

22 그것은 입을 벌리고 눈을 질끈 감은 채 웃는 얼굴을 보여 준다.
➡ ________________

23 XD는 단어가 아니다.

➡ ______

24 그것은 이모티콘이고, 얼굴 표정을 나타내기 위해 사용되는 한 무리의 문자나 상징이다.

➡ ______

25 이모티콘 XD는 우리의 행복한 감정을 하하와 LOL보다 더 시각적으로 표현한다.

➡ ______

26 나는 디즈니랜드에 가는 게 몹시 기다려져. XD

➡ ______

27 요즘 사람들은 '기쁨의 눈물을 흘리는 얼굴'인 😂를 사용한다.

➡ ______

28 이것은 '이모지'라고 불리는 작은 그림이다.

➡ ______

29 많은 웃는 이모지가 온라인에서 사용될 수 있고, 그래서 사람들은 다양한 방식으로 자신들의 웃음을 표현할 수 있다.

➡ ______

30 A: 찬장에 머리를 부딪쳤어.

➡ ______

31 B: 오. 이런! 너 괜찮니?

➡ ______

32 A: 찬장에 머리를 부딪쳤어. 😂

➡ ______

33 B: 어 어! 찬장 괜찮니? 😂

➡ ______

34 어떤 이모지들은 크기가 커졌고, 또 어떤 것들은 심지어 움직이거나 웃음소리를 내기까지 한다.

➡ ______

35 A: 그래서 어제 나는 식당에 있었는데 정말 방귀를 뀌어야 했어.

➡ ______

36 B: 그리고 …

➡ ______

37 A: 음, 음악이 정말 시끄럽길래 나는 그냥 뀌어 버렸어.

➡ ______

38 B: 그리고 …

➡ ______

39 A: 그리고 그때 나는 내가 이어폰을 끼고 음악을 듣고 있다는 걸 깨달았지.

➡ ______

40 웃음 표시는 우리의 얼굴 표정을 나타내고 우리의 목소리 어조를 전달할 수 있다.

➡ ______

41 다양한 웃음 표시를 사용함으로써, 우리는 친구들을 얼마나 좋아하는지 또는 그들과 함께 있어서 얼마나 행복한지를 그들에게 보여 줄 수 있다.

➡ ______

42 웃어라, 문자로 된 형태로라도. 그러면 친구들도 여러분과 함께 웃을 것이다.

➡ ______

43 추울 때 내 모습이네.

➡ ______

44 이건 어제의 나야.

➡ ______

[01~03] 다음 글을 읽고 물음에 답하시오.

XD also represents laughter in text. ⓐIt shows a laughing face with a mouth open and eyes closing tightly. XD is not a word. It's an emoticon, which is a group of letters or symbols used ⓑto represent a facial expression. The emoticon XD expresses our happy feelings more visually than ha-ha and LOL do.

서답형

01 위 글의 밑줄 친 ⓐ에서 어법상 틀린 부분을 찾아 고치시오.

______ ➡ ______

02 아래 <보기>에서 위 글의 밑줄 친 ⓑto represent와 to부정사의 용법이 다른 것의 개수를 고르시오.

보기

① It is interesting to watch the show.
② You are nice to help the poor.
③ He has no house to live in.
④ My hobby is to play the piano.
⑤ He is a fool to say so.

① 1개 ② 2개 ③ 3개 ④ 4개 ⑤ 5개

03 위 글을 읽고 대답할 수 없는 질문은?

① What does XD represent in text?
② What does XD show?
③ What is an emoticon?
④ What emoticon expresses our happy feelings most effectively?
⑤ Which expresses our happy feelings more visually, ha-ha or XD?

[04~06] 다음 글을 읽고 물음에 답하시오.

Laughter is human. We laugh out loud when we hear a joke, see something funny, or feel happy. We laugh even in our writings, such as emails or texts, ⓐas we do in our conversations. How do we do that?

"Ha-ha" is a form of written laughter. Everyone knows what it means. ___ⓑ___, it has been used since long ago. Even Shakespeare used "ha-ha" in his works.

04 위 글의 밑줄 친 ⓐas와 같은 의미로 쓰인 것을 고르시오.

① As you were out, I left a message.
② He doesn't earn as much as me.
③ He sat watching her as she got ready.
④ He is famous as a statesman.
⑤ As you know, Mary is leaving soon.

05 위 글의 빈칸 ⓑ에 들어갈 알맞은 말을 고르시오.

① Therefore ② However
③ Instead ④ Actually
⑤ In other words

06 According to the passage, which is NOT true?

① Laughter is unique to humans.
② We laugh loudly when we hear a joke, see something funny, or feel happy.
③ It's impossible for us to laugh in our writings.
④ Everyone knows what "ha-ha" means.
⑤ "Ha-ha" was used even in Shakespeare's works.

[07~10] 다음 글을 읽고 물음에 답하시오.

These days, people use 😂 — a "face with tears of joy." ⓐThis is a small picture calling an "emoji." Lots of laughing emojis are available to use online, so people can express their laughter in various ways.

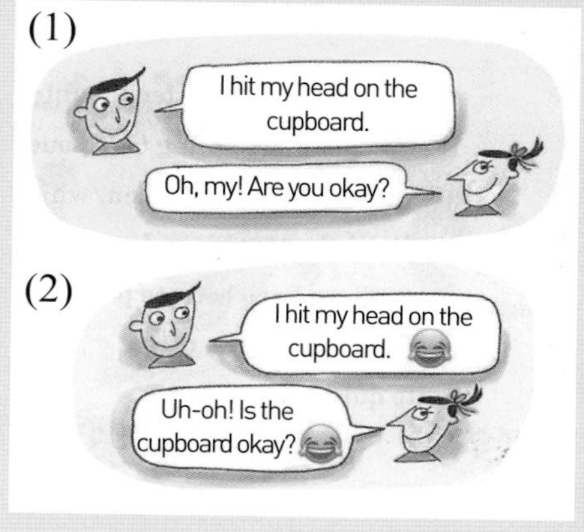

(1)
I hit my head on the cupboard.
Oh, my! Are you okay?
(2)
I hit my head on the cupboard.
Uh-oh! Is the cupboard okay?

서답형

07 다음 빈칸에 알맞은 단어를 넣어 😂에 대한 소개를 완성하시오.

It is a ________ ________ and is known as a "face with tears of joy."

08 다음 중 "emoji"에 해당하는 것을 고르시오.

① XD ② ha-ha ③ LOL
④ 👍 ⑤ ROFL

서답형

09 위 글의 밑줄 친 ⓐ에서 어법상 틀린 부분을 찾아 고치시오.

________ ➡ ________

서답형

10 다음 빈칸 (A)와 (B)에 알맞은 단어를 넣어 위의 그림 (1)과 (2)의 차이점을 완성하시오.

The dialogue (2) which uses (A)________ ________ can communicate laughter more visually than the dialogue (1) which doesn't use an emoji. Besides, the woman in the second dialogue expresses the humorous mood more interestingly by replacing "Are you okay?" with "(B)________ ________ ________ ________?"

[11~13] 다음 글을 읽고 물음에 답하시오.

Another form of written laughter is LOL. It stands for "Laughing Out Loud." People also use ROFL quite often, which means "Rolling On the Floor Laughing." These expressions have become popular because they can ___ⓐ___ quite quickly.

서답형

11 위 글의 빈칸 ⓐ에 type를 알맞은 형태로 쓰시오.

➡ ________________

중요

12 위 글의 앞에 올 내용으로 가장 알맞은 것을 고르시오.

① 대화에서 웃음을 터뜨리는 상황들 소개
② 문자로 된 웃음의 형태에 대한 소개
③ LOL이 생기게 된 배경 설명
④ ROFL을 주로 사용하는 상황들 소개
⑤ 이모티콘의 탄생 비화

서답형

13 Why have LOL and ROFL become popular? Fill in the blanks with suitable words.

Because people can type them ________ ________.

[14~16] 다음 글을 읽고 물음에 답하시오.

Laughter is human. We laugh out loud when we hear a joke, see something funny, or feel happy. We laugh even in our writings, such as emails or texts, as we do in our conversations. How do we do that?

"Ha-ha" is a form of written laughter. ⓐ 모두가 그것이 무엇을 의미하는지 안다. Actually, ⓑit has been used since long ago. Even Shakespeare used "ha-ha" in his works.

서답형

14 위 글의 밑줄 친 ⓐ의 우리말에 맞게 주어진 어휘를 알맞게 배열하시오.

what / means / everyone / knows / it

➡ ______________________

서답형

15 위 글의 밑줄 친 ⓑit이 가리키는 것을 본문에서 찾아 쓰시오.

➡ ______________

서답형

16 How can we laugh in our writings? Fill in the blanks below with suitable words. (two words)

We can use a form of ________ ________ like "ha-ha" in our writings.

[17~19] 다음 글을 읽고 물음에 답하시오.

Some emojis have grown bigger, and some even move or make laughing sounds.

A: So yesterday, I was in a restaurant, and I really needed to break wind.

B: And ...

A: Well, the music was really loud, so I just did it.

B: And ...

A: ⓐAnd then I realized I was listening to music with my earphones.

서답형

17 주어진 영영풀이에 해당하는 어구를 본문에서 찾아 쓰시오.

let gas out from the intestine

➡ ______________

중요

18 위 글의 밑줄 친 ⓐ에서 알 수 있는 'A'의 심경으로 가장 알맞은 것을 고르시오.

① disappointed ② comfortable
③ refreshed ④ pleased
⑤ embarrassed

서답형

19 Yesterday, could 'A' break wind undetected in a restaurant? Choose the right answer between (1) and (2) below. If you choose (2), write the reason by filling in the blanks ⓐ and ⓑ with suitable words. 〈*undetected: 아무에게도 들키지 않는〉

(1): Yes, he could. (2): No, he couldn't. When he broke wind thinking the music was really ⓐ________ in a restaurant, actually he was listening to music with ⓑ________ ________.

➡ ________번,
ⓐ ________ ⓑ ________ ________

[20~23] 다음 글을 읽고 물음에 답하시오.

XD also represents laughter in text. It shows a laughing face (A)with a mouth open and eyes closed tightly. XD is not a word. It's an emoticon, which is a group of letters or symbols used to represent a facial expression. The emoticon XD expresses our happy feelings more ___ⓐ___ than ha-ha and LOL (B)do.

20 위 글의 빈칸 ⓐ에 들어갈 알맞은 말을 고르시오.

① musically ② interestingly
③ indirectly ④ visually
⑤ fantastically

중요
21 위 글의 밑줄 친 (A)with와 문법적 쓰임이 같은 것을 모두 고르시오.

① She lives with her parents.
② Don't speak with your mouth full.
③ Look at the girl with red hair.
④ Cut it with a knife.
⑤ He stood there with his hands in his pockets.

서답형
22 위 글의 밑줄 친 (B)do가 가리키는 내용을 영어로 쓰시오.

➡ ______________________

23 본문의 그림 속에 밑줄 친 can't wait to go와 바꿔 쓸 수 없는 말을 고르시오.

① am looking forward to going
② am eager to go
③ am unwilling to go
④ am anxious to go
⑤ am dying to go

[24~26] 다음 글을 읽고 물음에 답하시오.

Laughter is human. We laugh out loud when we hear a joke, see something funny, or feel happy. We laugh even in our writings, ⓐsuch as emails or texts, as we do in our conversations. How do we do that?

"Ha-ha" is a form of written laughter. Everyone knows what it means. Actually, it has been used since long ago. Even Shakespeare used "ha-ha" in his works.

24 위 글의 밑줄 친 ⓐ를 한 단어로 바꿔 쓰시오.

➡ ______________________

중요
25 위 글의 제목으로 알맞은 것을 고르시오.

① Various Kinds of Laughing Marks
② Can You "Ha-Ha" in Your Texts?
③ What Makes You Laugh?
④ How Can We Make Our Writings Fun?
⑤ Why Did Shakespeare Use "Ha-ha" in His Works?

서답형
26 본문의 내용과 일치하도록 다음 빈칸에 알맞은 단어를 쓰시오. (세 단어)

Jokes, funny sights, or happy feelings can make us ________ ________ ________.

[01~03] 다음 글을 읽고 물음에 답하시오.

Laughter is human. We laugh out loud when we hear a joke, see something funny, or feel (A)[happy / happily]. We laugh even in our writings, such as emails or texts, as we (B) [are / do] in our conversations. How do we ⓐdo that?

"Ha-ha" is a form of written laughter. Everyone knows what it means. Actually, it has been used (C)[for / since] long ago. Even Shakespeare used "ha-ha" in his works.

중요

01 위 글의 괄호 (A)~(C)에서 문맥이나 어법상 알맞은 낱말을 골라 쓰시오.

➡ (A) ________ (B) ________ (C) ________

고난이도

02 다음 빈칸에 알맞은 단어를 넣어 위 글의 밑줄 친 ⓐdo that이 가리키는 것을 완성하시오. (5 단어)

________ ________ ________ ________
________ as we do in our conversations

03 위 글의 내용을 다음과 같이 정리하고자 한다. 빈칸 (A)와 (B)에 공통으로 들어갈 알맞은 단어를 본문에서 찾아 쓰시오.

Not only do we burst into (A)________ when we experience something funny or happiness, but we can express laughing sound in our writings by using a form of written (B)________, "ha-ha," as well.

*burst into: ~을 터뜨리다

➡ ________________

[04~06] 다음 글을 읽고 물음에 답하시오.

Another form of written laughter is LOL. It stands for "Laughing Out Loud." People also use ROFL quite often, which means "Rolling On the Floor Laughing." These expressions have become popular because they can be typed quite quickly.

XD also represents laughter in text. ⓐ그것은 입을 벌리고 눈을 질끈 감은 채 웃는 얼굴을 보여 준다. XD is not a word. It's an emoticon, which is a group of letters or symbols used to represent a facial expression. The emoticon XD expresses our happy feelings more visually than ha-ha and LOL do.

중요

04 What does ROFL stand for? Answer in English in a full sentence.

➡ ________________

05 위 글의 밑줄 친 ⓐ의 우리말에 맞게 한 단어를 보충하여, 주어진 어휘를 알맞게 배열하시오.

a mouth / and / shows / closed tightly / it / open / a laughing face / eyes

➡ ________________
____

고난이도

06 다음 문장에서 위 글의 내용과 다른 부분을 찾아서 고치시오.

LOL and ROFL are a group of letters or symbols used to represent a facial expression.

➡ ________ → ________ 또는
____
________ → ________

[07~11] 다음 글을 읽고 물음에 답하시오.

Laughing marks can represent our facial expressions and deliver our voice tones. By using various laughing marks, we can show our friends how much we ⓐcare for them or how happy we are with ⓑthem. ⓒLaugh, even in written forms, and your friends will laugh with you.

07 위 글의 밑줄 친 ⓐcare for와 바꿔 쓸 수 있는 말을 한 단어로 쓰시오.

➡ ______________________

08 위 글의 밑줄 친 ⓑthem이 가리키는 것을 본문에서 찾아 쓰시오.

➡ ______________________

중요

09 위 글의 밑줄 친 ⓒ를 If를 사용하여 고치시오.

➡ ______________________

____

10 다음 빈칸 (A)와 (B)에 알맞은 단어를 넣어 laughing marks에 대한 설명을 완성하시오.

Using various laughing marks enables us to show our friends (A)________ ________ we care for them or (B)________ ________ we are with them.

중요

11 What can laughing marks represent and deliver? Answer in English in a full sentence.

➡ ______________________

____

[12~14] 다음 글을 읽고 물음에 답하시오.

Another form of written laughter is LOL. It ⓐstands for "Laughing Out Loud." People also use ROFL quite often, which means "Rolling On the Floor Laughing." These expressions have become popular because they can be typed quite quickly.

A: ⓑHave a safe trip 2mrw. Make sure u don't miss me too much. LOL

B: OK. I'll try to make sure I don't miss u. LOL. Thanks for wishing me a safe trip.

XD also represents laughter in text. It shows a laughing face with a mouth open and eyes closed tightly. XD is not a word. It's an emoticon, which is a group of letters or symbols used to represent a facial expression. The emoticon XD expresses our happy feelings more visually than ha-ha and LOL do.

12 위 글의 밑줄 친 ⓐstands for와 바꿔 쓸 수 있는 말을 본문에서 찾아 쓰시오.

➡ ______________________

13 위 글의 밑줄 친 ⓑ를 축약된 단어들의 본래 형태를 사용하여 문장을 다시 쓰시오.

➡ ______________________

____

고난이도

14 본문의 내용과 일치하도록 다음 빈칸 (A)와 (B)에 알맞은 단어를 쓰시오. (한 칸에 여러 단어를 쓸 수 있음.)

If you want to express your happy feelings more visually, it would be better for you to use (A)________________ than to use (B)________________.

교과서

구석구석

Self-study Guide

A: Can you tell me where you live?
tell의 직접목적어 자리에 사용된 간접의문문이다.

B: Sure. I live in Mokpo.
~에 살다

A: Could you tell me when the next bus will come?
정중한 부탁의 표현 / tell의 직접목적어 자리에 사용된 간접의문문이다.

B: Sure. It will come in ten minutes.
in+시간: ~ 후에

해석

A: 당신이 어디에 사는지 제게 말해 줄 수 있나요?

B: 물론이죠. 저는 목포에 살아요.

A: 다음 버스가 언제 올지 제게 말씀해 주실 수 있으신가요?

B: 물론이죠. 그건 10분 후에 올겁니다.

Link to the World

Do you know what the color red means.
간접의문문: 의문사+주어+동사

- This is the uniform of the Reds, who cheer for the Korean soccer team. Red means "power" on this uniform.
  관계대명사의 계속적 용법
- Red on a traffic light means "stop."
- Of all the meanings of red, "love" is my favorite. "Love never fails."
  'all the+복수명사'의 어순

구문해설 • cheer for: ~을 응원하다 • of ~: ~ 중에서 • meaning: 의미

빨간색이 무엇을 의미하는지 알고 있니?

- 이것은 붉은 악마들의 유니폼인데, 그들은 한국 축구팀을 응원한다. 이 유니폼에서 빨간색은 "힘"을 의미한다.
- 교통 신호등의 빨간색은 "멈추시오"라는 뜻이다.
- 빨간색의 모든 의미 중에서, '사랑'이 나는 가장 좋다. "사랑은 절대 실패하지 않는다."

Express Yourself C

Yeji: Can you guess what my brother got for his birthday? He got a drone from our grandpa, who lives in Busan.
Can you guess?와 What did my brother get for his birthday?를 합친 간접의문문
= and he

구문해설 • guess: 추측하다 • drone: 드론 • grandpa: 할아버지(= grandfather)

예지: 내 남동생이 그의 생일 선물로 무엇을 받았는지 추측할 수 있니? 그는 우리 할아버지로부터 드론을 받았는데, 할아버지는 부산에 사셔.

영역별 핵심문제

Words & Expressions

01 다음 주어진 두 단어의 관계가 같도록 빈칸에 알맞은 단어를 쓰시오.

popular – unpopular : ________ – partial

02 다음 글의 빈칸 (a)와 (b)에 들어갈 단어가 바르게 짝지어진 것은?

> • Laughing marks can represent our facial expression and __(a)__ our voice tones.
> • Lots of laughing emojis are available to use online, so people can __(b)__ their laughter in various ways.

① destroy – deliver ② make – buy
③ create – make ④ deliver – express
⑤ deliver – form

[03~04] 다음 영영 풀이에 해당하는 것을 고르시오.

03

involving writing rather than speaking

① typed ② delivered
③ text ④ represented
⑤ written

04

> a short set of keyboard symbols that represents the facial expression used in email, etc, to show feelings

① emoticon ② sign
③ photograph ④ symbol
⑤ signal

05 (A)와 (B)의 빈칸에 공통으로 들어갈 말을 쓰시오.

> (A) If you have been good, Santa will give you a nice ________ tomorrow!
> (B) Students in groups will ________ how they have reached their conclusions to certain questions.

➡ ________________

06 다음 밑줄 친 부분의 뜻이 잘못된 것은?

① I'm glad to get a book from Junho. (예약하다)
② Can you guess who my mom met? (추측하다)
③ Shakespeare used "ha-ha" in his works. (작품)
④ Another form of written laughter is LOL. (형태)
⑤ XD represents laughter in text. (나타내다)

Conversation

07 다음 대화의 빈칸에 들어갈 말로 적절한 것은?

> G: ________________ Are you all right?
> B: My mom won't let me play soccer after school.
> G: Why don't you ask her one more time?

① You look bored.
② You look upset.
③ You look tired.
④ You look refreshed.
⑤ You look pleased.

08 주어진 문장에 이어질 대화를 순서에 맞게 바르게 배열한 것은?

Minsu, how are you feeling?

(A) I'm glad to hear that. I hope he joins your team.
(B) He was a soccer player on his school team. As you know, my team needs a player.
(C) I'm really excited, Miso. We have a new student in our class. His name is Kim Kihun.
(D) So why are you excited?

① (A) – (D) – (B) – (C)
② (B) – (A) – (C) – (D)
③ (B) – (D) – (C) – (A)
④ (C) – (A) – (D) – (B)
⑤ (C) – (D) – (B) – (A)

[09~10] 다음 대화를 읽고 물음에 답하시오.

A: How are you feeling?
B: I'm nervous. ______(A)______ How are you feeling?
A: I'm nervous, too. I have a math test tomorrow. ______(B)______
B: Me, too.

09 대화의 빈칸 (A)에 들어갈 말로 알맞은 것은?

① I got a good grade.
② I got a present for my birthday.
③ I forgot to bring my math homework.
④ I had a chance to travel to a new country.
⑤ It'll be a good day today!

10 대화의 빈칸 (B)에 들어갈 말을 주어진 단어를 알맞게 배열하여 쓰시오.

(to / the / someone / I'm / feels / glad / find / who / same)

➡ ________________________________
____

[11~12] 다음 대화를 읽고 물음에 답하시오.

Nari: Hi, Jiho. How are you feeling?
Jiho: I'm happier than ever, Nari. (①)
Nari: I know why. You did it, didn't you?
Jiho: Yes. I finally booked four tickets for the VTS concert! (②)
Nari: Good job. Did you tell Minsu and Yujin about that? (③)
Jiho: Sure. Oh, I just got messages from them. They said they are really happy. Look. (④)
Nari: How cute! I like their emojis. (⑤)
Jiho: I'm glad to hear that. We're going to have lots of fun!

11 주어진 문장이 들어갈 위치로 알맞은 것은?

They will bring light sticks and a nice camera.

① ② ③ ④ ⑤

12 위 대화의 내용과 일치하지 않는 것은?

① Jiho is happier than ever.
② Jiho booked four tickets for the VTS concert.
③ Minsu and Yujin sent messages with cute emojis.
④ Minsu and Yujin will not bring a camera.
⑤ Jiho told Minsu and Yujin about booking the tickets.

Grammar

13 다음 중 어법상 어색한 문장을 고르시오.

① Do you think who he liked?
② Can you tell me where she wants to go?
③ Who do you guess that man is?
④ What do you think is wrong with your computer?
⑤ I don't know if Jihoon likes inline skating.

14 다음 글에서 어법상 어색한 부분을 찾아 바르게 고치시오.

> This is the uniform of the Reds, which cheer for the Korean soccer team. Red means "power" on this uniform.

________ ➡ ________

15 주어진 〈조건〉에 맞추어, 괄호 안의 단어를 이용하여 영어로 쓰시오.

조건
a. 우리말의 의미에 유의한다.
b. 필요하면 쉼표(,)를 적절히 사용한다.
c. 괄호 안에 주어진 영어 단어를 문법상 올바르게 변형한다.

(1) 그는 검은색인 고양이가 두 마리가 있다. (have, two cats, which)
➡ ________
(2) 그는 고양이가 두 마리 있는데, 그것들은 검은색이다. (have, two cats, which)
➡ ________
(3) 나는 노란 모자를 쓰고 있는 한 어린이를 보았다. (see, a child, who, wearing, a yellow cap)
➡ ________
(4) 나는 한 어린이를 보았는데, 그는 노란 모자를 쓰고 있었다. (see, a child, who, wearing, a yellow cap)
➡ ________

16 다음 두 문장을 한 문장으로 바르게 옮긴 것은?

> Do you know? What does the color red mean?

① Do you know what the color red mean?
② Do you know what the color red means?
③ What do you know the color red means?
④ Do you know what the color red mean does?
⑤ Do you know what does the color red mean?

17 다음 중 어법상 어색한 문장의 개수로 알맞은 것은?

> a. Do you think where they will go?
> b. Do you know who invented the machine?
> c. Did you ask me where did he go?
> d. I met Jinhee, who was one of my classmates.
> e. I borrowed a watch from Minji, who was broken.
> f. I can't buy a car, which is very expensive.

① 1개 ② 2개 ③ 3개 ④ 4개 ⑤ 5개

18 다음 빈칸에 공통으로 알맞은 말을 쓰시오.

> • I wonder ________ will win the contest.
> • I read a book about a man, ________ sacrificed himself for others.

➡ ________

19 다음 우리말을 주어진 어휘를 이용하여 영어로 옮기시오.

(1) 너는 왜 선생님이 되고 싶은지 나에게 말해 줄 수 있니? (tell, me, want, be)

➡ ______________________

____

(2) 너의 새로운 과학 선생님이 어떠신지 말해 줘. (Please, tell, what, science, like)

➡ ______________________

____

Reading

[20~22] 다음 글을 읽고 물음에 답하시오.

Laughter is human. We laugh out loud when we hear a joke, see something funny, or feel happy. We laugh even in our ___ⓐ___, such as emails or texts, as we do in our conversations. How do we do that?

"Ha-ha" is a form of written laughter. Everyone knows what it means. Actually, it ⓑhas been used since long ago. Even Shakespeare used "ha-ha" in his works.

20 위 글의 빈칸 ⓐ에 들어갈 알맞은 말을 고르시오.

① drawings ② writings ③ songs
④ pictures ⑤ poems

21 위 글의 밑줄 친 ⓑhas been used와 현재완료 용법이 같은 것을 모두 고르시오.

① How long has it been used in our writings?
② How many times has it been used in our writings?
③ It has already been used in our writings.
④ It has never been used in our writings.
⑤ It has been used for ten years in our writings.

22 위 글의 주제로 가장 알맞은 것을 고르시오.

① Laughter is human.
② We laugh out loud when we hear a joke.
③ We can laugh even in our writings.
④ "Ha-ha" is the most widely used written laughter.
⑤ We can find "ha-ha" even in Shakespeare's works.

[23~25] 다음 글을 읽고 물음에 답하시오.

Another form of written laughter is LOL. It stands for "Laughing Out Loud." People also use ROFL quite often, which means "Rolling On the Floor Laughing." These expressions have become popular ⓐ상당히 빠르게 타자를 칠 수 있어서.

XD also represents laughter in text. It shows a laughing face with a mouth open and eyes closed tightly. XD is not a word. ⓑIt's an emoticon, that is a group of letters or symbols used to represent a facial expression. The emoticon XD expresses our happy feelings more visually than ha-ha and LOL do.

23 위 글의 밑줄 친 ⓐ의 우리말에 맞게 주어진 어휘를 이용하여 7 단어로 영작하시오.

they, quite, typed

➡ ______________________

24 위 글의 밑줄 친 ⓑ에서 어법상 틀린 부분을 찾아 고치시오.

______ ➡ ______

25 According to the passage, which is NOT true?

① LOL is a form of written laughter.
② ROFL is also used quite often.
③ XD represents alphabet X and D.
④ An emoticon is a group of letters or symbols used to represent a facial expression.
⑤ Ha-ha and LOL are less effective than XD in expressing our happy feelings visually.

[26~27] 다음 글을 읽고 물음에 답하시오.

Laughing marks can represent our facial expressions and deliver our voice tones. By using various laughing marks, we can show our friends how much we care for them or how happy we are with them. Laugh, even in written forms, and your friends will laugh with you.

26 위 글의 주제로 알맞은 것을 고르시오.

① pros and cons about laughing marks
② the role of laughing marks
③ the strong and weak points of laughing marks
④ the effective way of expressing laughter
⑤ various kinds of laughing marks

27 다음 중 위 글에 대한 이해가 올바르지 못한 사람을 고르시오.

① 수진: 웃음 표시는 우리의 얼굴 표정을 나타낼 수 있어.
② 미경: 웃음 표시로 우리의 목소리 어조를 전달하는 것은 힘들어.
③ 영미: 다양한 웃음 표시를 사용함으로써, 우리가 친구들을 얼마나 좋아하는지를 그들에게 보여 줄 수 있어.
④ 진규: 다양한 웃음 표시를 사용함으로써, 우리는 또한 친구들과 함께 있어서 얼마나 행복한지도 그들에게 보여 줄 수 있어.
⑤ 희성: 문자로 된 형태로라도 웃으면, 친구들도 우리와 함께 웃을 거야.

[28~29] 다음 글을 읽고 물음에 답하시오.

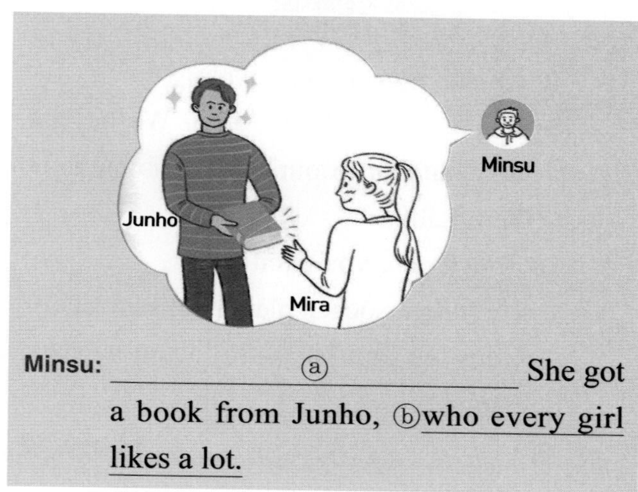

Minsu: ______ⓐ______ She got a book from Junho, ⓑwho every girl likes a lot.

28 위 글의 빈칸 ⓐ에 Can you guess?와 Why is Mira smiling?을 한 문장으로 합쳐 쓰시오.

➡ ______________________

29 위 글의 밑줄 친 ⓑ를 다음과 같이 바꿔 쓸 때 빈칸에 들어갈 알맞은 말을 두 단어로 쓰시오.

➡ ______ every girl likes ______ a lot

단원별 예상문제

출제율 90%

01 다음 짝지어진 단어의 관계가 같도록 빈칸에 알맞은 말을 쓰시오.

chance : opportunity = diverse : ________

출제율 95%

02 다음 영영 풀이에 해당하는 단어는?

a sign, shape, or object that is used to represent something else

① emoticon ② symbol
③ space ④ forest
⑤ emoji

출제율 90%

03 다음 대화를 읽고 Minsu의 상황에 맞는 Miso의 말을 빈칸 (A)에 영어 문장으로 완성하시오.

G: Minsu, how are you feeling?
B: I'm really excited, Miso. We have a new student in our class. His name is Kim Kihun.
G: So why are you excited?
B: He was a soccer player on his school team. As you know, my team needs a player.
G: ________(A)________ I hope he joins your team.
B: Thanks a lot.

➡ ____________________

[04~05] 다음 대화를 읽고 물음에 답하시오.

B: Yena, how are you feeling?
G: I'm feeling very sad, Seho. My best friend Jihun is moving away.
B: Really? I'm sorry. But don't be so sad. You two can have video chats online.
G: You're right.
B: Why don't we make him a photo book as a goodbye gift?
G: Great idea. <u>그에게 뭔가 의미 있는 것을 준다니 기뻐.</u> (give / I'm / meaningful / to / something / him / glad)

출제율 100%

04 위 대화를 읽고 다음 빈칸에 알맞은 내용을 영어로 쓰시오. (to부정사로 시작하여 쓸 것.)

(1) Yena와 Jihun이 할 일: ____________________
____

(2) Yena와 Seho가 할 일: ____________________
____

출제율 90%

05 위 대화의 밑줄 친 우리말에 맞게 주어진 단어를 알맞게 배열하시오.

➡ ____________________

출제율 95%

06 다음 대화의 빈칸에 들어갈 말로 알맞은 것은?

W: Good morning, Mr. Lee. How are you feeling?
M: ____________________ Some students are helping me clean the school.
W: I'm glad to hear that.

① I'm feeling very sad this morning.
② I'm nervous this morning.
③ I'm glad to hear that.
④ I'm feeling very happy this morning.
⑤ I'm very upset this morning.

[07~08] 다음 대화를 읽고 물음에 답하시오.

G: Jihun, you ⓐare moving to another country next week. How are you feeling?
B: I'm ⓑexcited to go to a whole new world, Yunju.
G: I'm glad to hear that. I was ⓒworrying about you.
B: Actually, I'm sad, too. I'll miss all of you ⓓ a lot.
G: Let's ⓔkeep in touch online.
B: Okay. Let's have video chats often.

출제율 95%

07 위 글의 밑줄 친 ⓐ~ⓔ 중 어법상 어색한 것은?

① ⓐ ② ⓑ ③ ⓒ ④ ⓓ ⑤ ⓔ

출제율 100%

08 위 대화의 내용과 일치하지 않는 것은?

① Jihun is going to move to another country next week.
② Yunju was concerned about Jihun.
③ Jihun was excited to move to a new country.
④ Jihun is sad as he will miss his friends.
⑤ Yunju is glad to hear that Jihun is moving to another country next week.

출제율 90%

09 다음 대화의 빈칸 (A)와 (B)에 들어갈 표현으로 알맞은 것은?

(1) B: You don't look happy. Are you all right?
G: No, I'm really sad. My dog is sick. He won't eat at all.
B: ______(A)______

(2) B: It'll be a good day today! Take a look at today's lunch menu.
G: Wow! I'm glad to eat fried chicken! ______(B)______

① (A) That's too bad.
(B) I'm not happy with today's lunch menu.
② (A) That's too bad.
(B) I can't wait for lunch break.
③ (A) I'm glad to hear that.
(B) I can't wait for lunch break.
④ (A) I'm happy to hear that.
(B) I can wait for lunch break.
⑤ (A) I'm feeling very happy.
(B) I'm happy with today's lunch menu.

출제율 90%

10 다음 빈칸에 들어갈 말로 적절한 것을 모두 고르시오.

That fire fighter is Fred, ________ saved a boy from the fire.

① which ② he ③ who
④ what ⑤ and he

출제율 100%

11 잘못된 부분을 바르게 고쳐 문장을 다시 쓰시오.

(1) Do you know where did Tom work last year?
➡ ________________________

(2) She made chocolate cookies for me, which was very delicious.
➡ ________________________
____

(3) I met Sue, who gives me a free ticket.
➡ ________________________

출제율 90%

12 다음 밑줄 친 우리말을 괄호 안의 어구를 사용하여 영어로 옮기시오.

(1) 빨간색이 무엇을 의미하는지 알고 있니? (color, mean) (8 words)
(2) 이것은 붉은 악마들의 유니폼인데, 그들은 한국 축구팀을 응원한다. (uniform of the Reds, cheer) (14 words)

➡ (1) ______________________
(2) ______________________
____

[13~15] 다음 글을 읽고 물음에 답하시오.

Laughter is human. We laugh out loud when we hear a joke, see something funny, or feel happy. We laugh even in our writings, such as emails or texts, as we do in our conversations. How do we do that?

"Ha-ha" is a form of ___ⓐ___ laughter. Everyone knows what it means. Actually, it has been used since long ago. Even Shakespeare used "ha-ha" in his ⓑworks.

출제율 90%

13 위 글의 빈칸 ⓐ에 write를 알맞은 형태로 쓰시오.

➡ ______________________

출제율 100%

14 위 글의 밑줄 친 ⓑworks와 같은 의미로 쓰인 것을 고르시오.

① She works for a bank.
② I have the complete works of J. K. Rowling.
③ He is the owner of the engineering works.
④ This machine works by electricity.
⑤ I'm interested in the works of a clock.

출제율 100%

15 다음 중 위 글의 내용을 올바르게 이해하지 못한 사람을 고르시오.

① 수호: 웃음은 인간 고유의 것이야.
② 태경: 이메일을 보낼 때도 우리는 웃음을 표현할 수 있어.
③ 영미: 우리 모두 "하하"의 의미를 알지.
④ 철수: "하하"는 오래전부터 글 속에서 사용되어 왔어.
⑤ 희진: 셰익스피어가 글에서 "하하"를 사용한 첫 번째 작가야.

[16~18] 다음 글을 읽고 물음에 답하시오.

Another form of written laughter is LOL. It stands for "Laughing Out Loud." People also use ROFL quite often, (A)which means "Rolling On the Floor Laughing." These expressions have become popular because they can be typed quite quickly.

XD also represents laughter in text. It shows a laughing face with a mouth open and eyes closed tightly. XD is not a word. It's an emoticon, which is a group of letters or symbols used to represent a ___ⓐ___ expression. The emoticon XD expresses our happy feelings more visually than ha-ha and LOL do.

출제율 90%

16 위 글의 한 단어를 변형하여 빈칸 ⓐ에 들어갈 알맞은 단어를 쓰시오.

➡ ______________________

출제율 95%

17 위 글의 밑줄 친 (A)를 두 단어로 바꿔 쓰시오.

➡ ______________________

출제율 100%

18 위 글의 제목으로 알맞은 것을 고르시오.

① Which Do You Prefer, LOL or ROFL?
② What Does XD Show?
③ How to Represent Laughter in Writings
④ What Is an Emoticon?
⑤ More Suitable Form for Expressing Happy Feelings Visually

[19~22] 다음 글을 읽고 물음에 답하시오.

These days, people use 😂 — a "face with tears of joy." This is a small picture called an "emoji." Lots of laughing emojis are available (A)to use online, so people can express their laughter in various ways.

A: I hit my head on the cupboard.
B: Oh, my! Are you okay?

A: I hit my head on the cupboard. 😂
B: Uh-oh! Is ___ⓐ___ okay? 😂

Some emojis have grown bigger, and some even move or make laughing sounds.

출제율 90%

19 위 글의 대화가 더 유머러스한 분위기를 표현할 수 있도록, 본문의 단어를 사용하여 빈칸 ⓐ에 들어갈 알맞은 말을 쓰시오. (2 words)

➡ ____________________

출제율 100%

20 위 글의 밑줄 친 (A)to use와 to부정사의 용법이 같은 것을 모두 고르시오.

① Can you tell me how to use it?
② I want a chance to use this coupon.
③ This tool is easy to use.
④ I would be happy to use this money.
⑤ He told me to use the locker.

출제율 100%

21 According to the passage, which is NOT true?

① 😂 is known as a "face with tears of joy."
② We can find and use lots of laughing emojis online.
③ People can express their laughter in a few ways.
④ Some emojis even move.
⑤ Some emojis make laughing sounds.

출제율 90%

22 What is an emoji? Answer in English in a full sentence.

➡ ____________________
____

[23~24] 다음 글을 읽고 물음에 답하시오.

Laughing marks can represent our facial expressions and deliver our voice tones. By using various laughing marks, we can show our friends ⓐ친구들을 얼마나 좋아하는지 또는 그들과 함께 있어서 얼마나 행복한지를. Laugh, even in written forms, and your friends will laugh with you.

출제율 90%

23 위 글의 밑줄 친 ⓐ의 우리말에 맞게 한 단어를 보충하여, 주어진 어휘를 알맞게 배열하시오.

them / we / how happy / care for / we are / or / them / how much

➡ ____________________
____

출제율 100%

24 위 글을 읽고 대답할 수 없는 것을 고르시오.

① What can laughing marks represent?
② What can laughing marks deliver?
③ What can you show by using various laughing marks?
④ What kind of laughing marks do people like most?
⑤ Can you make your friends laugh with you?

서술형 실전문제

01 다음 대화의 우리말과 <조건>에 맞게 주어진 단어를 이용하여 영어로 쓰시오.

(1) W: Good morning, Mr. Lee. How are you feeling?
M: I'm feeling very happy this morning. (A)몇몇 학생들이 학교 청소하는 것을 돕고 있어요.
W: I'm glad to hear that.

(2) G: You look upset. Are you all right?
B: (B)엄마가 방과 후에 축구하는 것을 허락하지 않으셔.
G: Why don't you ask her one more time?

조건
(A) • 진행형을 사용할 것. / 목적보어 자리에 동사원형을 사용할 것.
• some / me / clean
(B) • 미래 부정문의 축약형을 사용할 것.
• let / me / soccer / after school

➡ (A) ______________________
(B) ______________________

02 다음 대화의 흐름상 주어진 단어를 이용하여 빈칸 (A)에 들어갈 Miso의 질문을 완성하시오.

G: Minsu, how are you feeling?
B: I'm really excited, Miso. We have a new student in our class. His name is Kim Kihun.
G: So ______(A)______ (excited)
B: He was a soccer player on his school team. As you know, my team needs a player.
G: I'm glad to hear that. I hope he joins your team.

➡ ______________________

03 대화를 읽고 물음에 영어로 답하시오.

Nari: Hi, Jiho. How are you feeling?
Jiho: I'm happier than ever, Nari.
Nari: I know why. You did it, didn't you?
Jiho: Yes. I finally booked four tickets for the VTS concert!
Nari: Good job. Did you tell Minsu and Yujin about that?
Jiho: Sure. Oh, I just got messages from them. They said they are really happy. Look.
Nari: How cute! I like their emojis. They will bring light sticks and a nice camera.
Jiho: I'm glad to hear that. We're going to have lots of fun!

(1) Why is Jiho so happy?
➡ ______________________

(2) What did Minsu and Yujin send to Jiho?
➡ ______________________

04 <보기>에서 알맞은 문장을 골라 관계대명사의 계속적 용법으로 문장을 완성하시오.

보기
• The letter cheered him up.
• She wrote a poem about love.

(1) My favorite poet is Alice. + ______________________
→ My favorite poet is Alice, ______________________.

(2) Dennis got a letter. + ______________________
→ Dennis got a letter, ______________________.

05 다음 문장의 밑줄 친 부분을 '접속사+대명사'의 형태로 고치시오.

(1) The artist is Leonardo da Vinci, <u>who</u> painted the masterpiece, *The Last Supper*.
→ The artist is Leonardo da Vinci, ________ ________ painted the masterpiece, *The Last Supper*.

(2) I like my school bag, <u>which</u> was given to me by my mom for my birthday.
→ I like my school bag, ________ ________ was given to me by my mom for my birthday.

[06~08] 다음 글을 읽고 물음에 답하시오.

Laughter is human. We laugh out loud when we hear a joke, see something funny, or feel happy. We laugh even in our writings, such as emails or texts, as we (A)<u>do</u> in our conversations. How do we do that?

"Ha-ha" is a form of written laughter. Everyone knows what it means. Actually, it ⓐ________ ________ ________ since long ago. Even Shakespeare used "ha-ha" in his works.

06 다음과 같은 뜻이 되도록 위 글의 빈칸 ⓐ에 들어갈 알맞은 말을 쓰시오. (세 단어)

Actually, it started to be used long ago and is still used now.

➡ ____________________

07 위 글의 밑줄 친 (A)<u>do</u>가 가리키는 것을 본문에서 찾아 쓰시오.

➡ ____________________

08 다음 빈칸 (A)와 (B)에 알맞은 단어를 넣어 "ha-ha"에 대한 소개를 완성하시오.

It is a form of written laughter which we use to laugh even in our (A)________ as we do in our (B)__________.

[09~10] 다음 글을 읽고 물음에 답하시오.

Another form of written laughter is LOL. It stands for "Laughing Out Loud." People also use ROFL quite often, which means "Rolling On the Floor Laughing." These expressions have become popular because they can (A)[type / be typed] quite quickly.

XD also represents laughter in text. It shows a laughing face with a mouth (B)[open / opening] and eyes closed tightly. XD is not a word. It's an emoticon, which is a group of letters or symbols (C)[using / used] to represent a facial expression. The emoticon XD expresses our happy feelings more visually than ha-ha and LOL do.

09 위 글의 괄호 (A)~(C)에서 문맥이나 어법상 알맞은 낱말을 골라 쓰시오.

➡ (A) ________ (B) ________ (C) ________

10 본문의 내용과 일치하도록 다음 빈칸에 들어갈 알맞은 단어를 본문에서 찾아 쓰시오.

People can express laughter in their writings ________ ________ by using LOL instead of spelling the whole words "Laugh Out Loud."

창의사고력 서술형 문제

01 아래 표의 (A)는 감정 상태를, (B)는 그 이유를 나타낸다. 제시된 〈보기〉처럼 감정을 묻는 표현과 감정의 이유를 쓰시오.

(A)	(B)
• happy	• I got a good grade.
• nervous	• I forgot to bring my math homework.
• angry	• Someone broke my glasses.
• sad	• My brother is sick in bed.

보기

A: How are you feeling?

B: I'm nervous. I forgot to bring my math homework.

02 다음 〈보기〉와 같이, 관계대명사의 계속적 용법으로 부가 정보를 제공하는 문장을 쓰시오.

보기

I ate *Ceviche* in Peru, which is a traditional fish dish.

(1) My sister studied in Paris, ________________________.

(2) We learned Hula, ________________________.

(3) ________________________________

(4) ________________________________

03 다음 사진을 바탕으로 사진을 설명하는 글을 쓰시오.

A boy is holding a box with a white cat in it. The cat's name is Milky.

Yuna

Yuna: Can you guess (A)________ the boy is happy? He is happy to get (B)________, Milky, which is (C)________ like milk.

단원별 모의고사

01 다음 단어에 대한 영어 설명이 어색한 것은?

① form: a type or variety of something
② since: from a time in the past until a later past time or until now
③ gentleman: a man who is polite, well educated and has excellent manners
④ deliver: to be accepted as meaning a certain thing
⑤ type: to write something using a computer or typewriter

02 다음 짝지어진 단어의 관계가 같도록 빈칸에 알맞은 말을 쓰시오.

partial : whole = top : ________

03 다음 영영풀이에 해당하는 단어를 고르시오.

in a way that is connected with seeing or sight

① variously ② visually
③ available ④ nervously
⑤ written

04 다음 대화의 빈칸에 알맞은 것은?

G: You look upset. Are you all right?
B: ______________________________
G: Why don't you ask her one more time?

① Someone broke my cell phone.
② My dad cooked my favorite pie.
③ My sister is sick in bed.
④ My mom won't let me play soccer after school.
⑤ My sister got a bad grade.

05 다음 대화의 빈칸에 들어갈 말로 알맞은 것을 고르시오.

G: Jihun, you're moving to another country next week. How are you feeling?
B: ______________________, Yunju.
G: I'm glad to hear that. I was worried about you.
B: Actually, I'm sad, too. I'll miss all of you a lot.
G: Let's keep in touch online.
B: Okay. Let's have video chats often.

① I'm really sad
② I'm so nervous to move to another country
③ I hope things will get better
④ That sounds like fun
⑤ I'm excited to go to a whole new world

06 다음 중 짝지어진 대화가 어색한 것은?

① A: How are you feeling?
B: I'm happy. I got a good grade.
② A: How are you feeling today?
B: I'm really glad to get a present for my birthday.
③ A: How are you feeling?
B: I'm really bored to cook my favorite food.
④ A: How are you feeling?
B: I'm really excited.
⑤ A: How are you feeling today?
B: I'm feeling sad. My friend is sick.

[07~09] 다음 대화를 읽고 물음에 답하시오.

(Nari and Jiho are at the bus stop.)
Nari: Hi, Jiho. How are you feeling?
Jiho: I'm happier than ever, Nari.
Nari: I know why. (①) You did it, didn't you?
Jiho: Yes. I finally booked four tickets for the VTS concert! (②)
Nari: Good job. Did you tell Minsu and Yujin about that? (③)
Jiho: Sure. Oh, I just got messages from them. (④) Look.
Nari: How cute! I like their emojis. (⑤) They will bring light sticks and a nice camera.
Jiho: I'm glad to hear that. We're going to have lots of fun!

07 위 대화의 ①~⑤ 중 주어진 문장이 들어갈 위치로 알맞은 것은?

They said they are really happy.

① ② ③ ④ ⑤

08 What will Minsu and Yujin bring to the VTS concert? (9 단어로 답할 것)

➡ ______________________

09 다음은 위 대화를 요약한 문장이다. 빈칸에 알맞은 말을 찾아 쓰시오.

Jiho is talking with Nari at the bus stop. He is ________ than ever because he ________ four tickets for the VTS concert. He told Minsu and Yujin about it, and they sent ____________. Nari tells him that they will ________________. Jiho is very glad to hear that.

10 다음 대화의 빈칸에 'how'를 이용하여 상대방의 감정에 대해 묻는 말을 완성하시오.

A: ____________________ today?
B: I'm feeling sad. My friend is sick.
A: I'm sorry to hear that.

➡ ______________________

11 다음 주어진 문장에 이어질 대화의 순서로 알맞은 것은?

G: Minsu, Jihun is moving to Abu Dhabi in the UAE next week. How are you feeling?

(A) That's great! I'm glad to have a chance to travel to a new country.
(B) I'm sad. I'm going to miss him a lot.
(C) I'm sad, too, but I'm also happy. We can visit Abu Dhabi. He is going to invite us. He promised.

① (A) – (B) – (C)
② (B) – (A) – (C)
③ (B) – (C) – (A)
④ (C) – (A) – (B)
⑤ (C) – (B) – (A)

12 다음 대화의 빈칸에 들어갈 말로 알맞은 것은?

B: Yena, how are you feeling?
G: I'm feeling very sad, Seho. My best friend Jihun is moving away.
B: Really? I'm sorry. But don't be so sad. You two can have video chats online.
G: You're right.
B: Why don't we make him a photo book as a goodbye gift?
G: Great idea. ________________

① We're going to have lots of fun!
② I'm sorry to hear that. But it was just a photo book.
③ I'm sorry to give him something simple.
④ I'm glad to give him something meaningful.
⑤ I'm glad to find someone who feels the same.

13 다음 중 어법상 올바른 문장을 고르시오.

① What do you think I should do?
② I wonder if what went wrong.
③ Do you know what do I mean?
④ I don't know whether can he do it.
⑤ Tell me who the window broke.

14 다음 우리말을 영어로 바르게 옮긴 것은?

너는 누가 다음 우승자가 될 것이라고 생각하니?

① Do you think who will become the next winner?
② Do you think who the next winner will become?
③ Do you think who will the next winner become?
④ Who do you think the next winner will become?
⑤ Who do you think will become the next winner?

15 주어진 문장을 활용하여 대화를 완성하시오.

> A: The painting looks so special.
> B: Right. It was painted by Basquiat, ________________________________ ________________. (Basquiat is one of the most famous artists of our time.)

16 다음 중 어법상 <u>어색한</u> 문장을 고르시오.

① Tell me why you didn't invite me.
② I want to know how the mountain is high.
③ I asked him how much money he earned a month.
④ I'm not sure who will be our new leader.
⑤ Do you know whom Daniel went out with?

17 우리말과 일치하도록 할 때, 빈칸에 알맞은 것은?

> 한 낯선 사람이 내게 내 휴대전화를 사용해도 되는지 물었다.
> → A stranger asked me ________ he could use my cell phone.

① whether ② who ③ that
④ how ⑤ which

[18~19] 다음 글을 읽고 물음에 답하시오.

> Laughter is human. (①) We laugh out loud when we hear a joke, see something funny, or feel happy. (②) We laugh even in our writings, such as emails or texts, as we do in our conversations. (③) How do we do that? (④) "Ha-ha" is a form of written laughter. (⑤) ⓐ<u>Actually</u>, it has been used since long ago. Even Shakespeare used "ha-ha" in his works.

18 위 글의 흐름으로 보아, 주어진 문장이 들어가기에 가장 적절한 곳은?

Everyone knows what it means.

① ② ③ ④ ⑤

19 위 글의 밑줄 친 ⓐActually와 바꿔 쓸 수 있는 말을 모두 고르시오.

① Probably ② In fact
③ Exactly ④ Especially
⑤ As a matter of fact

[20~22] 다음 글을 읽고 물음에 답하시오.

Another form of written laughter is LOL. It stands for "Laughing Out Loud." People also use ROFL quite often, which means "Rolling On the Floor Laughing." These expressions have become popular because ⓐthey can be typed quite quickly.

XD also represents laughter in text. It shows a laughing face with a mouth open and eyes closed tightly. XD is not a word. It's an emoticon, which is a group of letters or symbols ⓑused to represent a facial expression. The emoticon XD expresses our happy feelings more visually than ha-ha and LOL do.

20 위 글의 밑줄 친 ⓐthey가 가리키는 것을 본문에서 찾아 쓰시오.

➡ ____________________

21 위 글의 밑줄 친 ⓑ 앞에 생략된 말을 쓰시오.

➡ ____________________

22 위 글의 주제로 알맞은 것을 고르시오.

① What is the reason why we use LOL instead of "Laugh Out Loud"?
② Why have LOL and ROFL become popular?
③ We can represent laughter even in writings by using LOL, ROFL and XD.
④ There are many kinds of emoticons used to represent a facial expression.
⑤ Why is XD more effective than ha-ha to express our happy feelings visually?

[23~25] 다음 글을 읽고 물음에 답하시오.

Some emojis have ⓐgrown bigger, and some even move or make laughing sounds.

A: So yesterday, I was in a restaurant, and I really needed to break wind.
B: And ...
A: Well, the music was really loud, so I just ⓑ did it.
B: And ...
A: And then I realized I was listening to music with my earphones.
B:

23 위 글의 밑줄 친 ⓐgrown과 바꿔 쓸 수 있는 말을 모두 고르시오.

① done ② become
③ fallen ④ gotten
⑤ given

24 요즈음 사용할 수 있는 이모지의 특성으로 언급되지 않은 것은? (2개)

① 크기가 커졌다.
② 움직이기도 한다.
③ 온라인에서만 사용할 수 있다.
④ 웃음소리를 내기까지 한다.
⑤ 색깔이 다양하다.

25 위 글의 밑줄 친 ⓑ가 가리키는 것을 영어로 쓰시오. (시제를 일치시킬 것.)

➡ ____________________

Let's Make Our Town Better

의사소통 기능

- 주제 소개하기
  Let's talk about the class party.
- 감사하기
  Thank you for helping me.

언어 형식

- 과거완료
  I was glad my dad **had made** me wear gloves.
- 비교급 강조
  I had to admit the lot looked **much** better.

교과서

Words & Expressions

Key Words

- □ **activity** [æktívəti] 명 활동
- □ **admit** [ædmít] 동 인정하다, 시인하다
- □ **agree** [əgríː] 동 동의하다
- □ **among** [əmʌ́ŋ] 전 ~ 중에, ~ 사이에
- □ **assign** [əsáin] 동 배정하다, 배치하다, 맡기다
- □ **awful** [ɔ́ːfəl] 형 끔찍한, 지독한
- □ **bake** [beik] 동 굽다
- □ **bean** [biːn] 명 콩
- □ **board** [bɔːrd] 명 게시판
- □ **bring** [briŋ] 동 가져오다
- □ **bus stop** 버스 정류장
- □ **class leader** 반장
- □ **clean** [kliːn] 동 청소하다
- □ **complain** [kəmpléin] 동 불평하다, 투덜거리다
- □ **corner** [kɔ́ːrnər] 명 구석, 모서리
- □ **dirty** [də́ːrti] 형 더러운
- □ **double** [dʌ́bl] 동 두 배가 되다
- □ **dust** [dʌst] 명 먼지
- □ **else** [els] 형 다른, 그 밖의
- □ **empty** [émpti] 형 텅 빈, 비어 있는
- □ **event** [ivént] 명 행사
- □ **far** [fɑːr] 부 (비교급 강조) 훨씬
- □ **fill** [fil] 동 채우다
- □ **fix** [fiks] 동 수리하다
- □ **guide** [gaid] 동 안내하다
- □ **hang** [hæŋ] 동 걸다, 매달다
- □ **heavy** [hévi] 형 무거운
- □ **helpful** [hélpfəl] 형 도움이 되는, 유용한
- □ **hit** [hit] 동 (생각이) ~에게 떠오르다
- □ **imagine** [imǽdʒin] 동 상상하다
- □ **kitchen** [kítʃən] 명 부엌
- □ **learn** [ləːrn] 동 알게 되다
- □ **lettuce** [létis] 명 상추
- □ **lot** [lɑt] 명 부지, 구획
- □ **mess** [mes] 명 쓰레기 더미, 지저분함, 엉망진창
- □ **neighborhood** [néibərhùd] 명 이웃, 인근 주민
- □ **newspaper** [nuzpeipər] 명 신문(지)
- □ **noodle** [núːdl] 명 국수
- □ **nursing home** 양로원
- □ **plant** [plænt] 동 심다
- □ **pleasure** [pléʒər] 명 기쁨
- □ **popular** [pɑ́pjulər] 형 인기 있는
- □ **pot** [pɑt] 명 분, 항아리, 단지
- □ **put** [put] 동 두다
- □ **remember** [rimémbər] 동 기억하다
- □ **row** [rou] 명 열, 줄
- □ **sight** [sait] 명 광경
- □ **snake** [sneik] 명 뱀
- □ **sneeze** [sniːz] 동 재채기하다
- □ **string** [striŋ] 명 끈, 줄
- □ **suggest** [sədʒést] 동 제안하다
- □ **sweaty** [swéti] 형 땀투성이의, 땀에 젖은
- □ **the elderly** 노인들
- □ **tight** [tait] 부 단단히, 꽉
- □ **together** [təgéðər] 부 함께, 같이
- □ **tough** [tʌf] 형 힘든
- □ **trash** [træʃ] 명 쓰레기
- □ **trash bag** 쓰레기 봉투
- □ **ugly** [ʌ́gli] 형 추한, 보기 싫은
- □ **volunteer** [vɑ̀ləntíər] 동 지원[자원]하다
- □ **volunteer work** 자원 봉사
- □ **water** [wɔ́ːtər] 동 물을 주다
- □ **wild plant** 야생식물
- □ **wonder** [wʌ́ndər] 동 궁금해 하다, ~할까 생각하다
- □ **wrap** [ræp] 명 포장지

Key Expressions

- □ **across from** ~ 맞은편에
- □ **be full of** ~로 가득 차다
- □ **be ready to-V** ~할 준비가 되다
- □ **divide A into B** A를 B로 나누다
- □ **fill A with B** A를 B로 채우다
- □ **How about+V-ing?** ~하는 게 어때?
- □ **I bet** 틀림없이 ~이다
- □ **in charge of** ~을 맡아, ~을 담당하여
- □ **let+목적어+동사원형** ~가 …하도록 허락하다
- □ **one of+복수명사** ~ 중 하나
- □ **pop up** 갑자기 나오다, 불쑥 나타나다
- □ **set up** 설치하다, 마련하다
- □ **Shall we+동사원형?** ~하는 게 어때?
- □ **take care of** ~을 돌보다
- □ **turn A into B** A를 B로 바꾸다
- □ **What do you think of ~?** ~을 어떻게 생각해?
- □ **Why don't you+동사원형?** ~하는 게 어때?
- □ **work on** ~에 공들이다[애쓰다]

Word Power

※ 서로 반대되는 뜻을 가진 어휘

- □ **popular**(인기 있는) ↔ **unpopular**(인기 없는)
- □ **fill** (채우다) ↔ **empty** (비우다)
- □ **remember** (기억하다) ↔ **forget** (잊다)
- □ **whole** (전체의) ↔ **partial** (일부분의)
- □ **awful** (끔찍한) ↔ **wonderful** (멋진)
- □ **empty** (비어 있는) ↔ **full** (가득 찬)

※ 서로 비슷한 뜻을 가진 어휘

- □ **awful** : **disgusting** (끔찍한, 역겨운)
- □ **empty** : **vacant** (비어 있는)
- □ **assign** : **allocate** (배치하다)
- □ **complain** : **moan** (불평하다)
- □ **plant** : **implant** (심다)
- □ **hang** : **suspend** (매달다)
- □ **fix** : **mend** (수리하다, 고치다)
- □ **string** : **cord** (끈)

English Dictionary

□ **admit** 인정[시인]하다
→ to agree that something is true, especially unwillingly
특히 내키지 않게 무언가가 사실이라는 것에 동의하다

□ **assign** 배치하다, 맡기다
→ to give a particular job or piece of work to someone
누군가에게 특정한 직업이나 일을 주다

□ **awful** 끔찍한
→ extremely bad or unpleasant
매우 나쁘거나 불쾌한

□ **complain** 불평하다
→ to say that something is wrong or not satisfactory
무언가 잘못되었거나 만족스럽지 않다고 말하다

□ **double** 두 배가 되다
→ to make something twice as much or many
어떤 것을 양이나 수가 두 배가 되게 하다

□ **dust** 먼지
→ dry dirt in the form of powder that covers surfaces inside a building, or very small dry pieces of soil, sand, or other substances
건물 내부의 표면을 덮는 분말 형태의 건조한 오물 또는 매우 작은 건조한 토양, 모래 또는 기타 물질 조각

□ **empty** 텅 빈, 비어 있는
→ not containing any things or people
어떤 물건이나 사람을 담고 있지 않은

□ **fill** 채우다
→ to make or become full
가득 채우거나 가득해지다

□ **fix** 고치다
→ to repair something
무언가를 수리하다

□ **hang** 매달다
→ to put something in a position so that the top part is fixed or supported, and the bottom part is free to move and does not touch the ground
상부가 고정 또는 지지되도록 어떤 위치에 놓이도록 하고, 바닥 부분은 자유롭게 이동할 수 있고, 지면에 닿지 않도록 하다

□ **kitchen** 부엌
→ a room where food is kept, prepared, and cooked and where the dishes are washed
음식이 보관, 준비, 조리되고, 설거지를 하는 방

□ **lot** 부지, 구획
→ an area of land 땅의 한 구역

□ **nursing home** 양로원
→ a place where very old people who are ill live and receive medical treatment and care
병든 매우 나이 든 사람들이 살고 의학 치료와 돌봄을 받는 곳

□ **row** 열, 줄
→ a line of things or people next to each other
서로 옆에 있는 사물이나 사람의 줄

□ **suggest** 제안하다
→ to tell someone your ideas about what they should do, where they should go, etc.
자신이 무엇을 해야 하는지, 어디로 가야 하는지 등에 대한 당신의 생각을 누군가에게 말하다

□ **sweaty** 땀에 젖은
→ covered in sweat or smelling of sweat
땀 또는 땀 냄새로 뒤덮인

□ **tough** 힘든
→ difficult to do or to deal with
하거나 다루기에 어려운

□ **volunteer** 자원하다
→ to offer to do something that you do not have to do
할 필요가 없는 일을 하겠다고 제안하다

서답형

01 다음은 어떤 단어에 관한 영어 설명이다. 빈칸에 들어갈 알맞은 단어를 쓰시오.

> When you ________, air and often small drops of liquid suddenly come out of your nose and mouth in a way you cannot control.

중요

02 다음 빈칸에 들어갈 말로 가장 적절한 것은?

> The hotel was ________! To begin with, our room was too small.

① wonderful ② terrific
③ popular ④ awful
⑤ ugly

[03~04] 다음 영어 설명에 해당하는 단어를 고르시오.

03

> to say that something is wrong or not satisfactory

① blame ② appreciate
③ complain ④ praise
⑤ enable

04

> a place where very old people who are ill live and receive medical treatment and care

① daycare center ② kindergarten
③ nursery ④ kitchen
⑤ nursing home

서답형

05 다음 우리말에 맞게 빈칸에 알맞은 단어를 쓰시오.

> 선생님은 학생들을 두 팀으로 나누었다.

➡ The teacher ________ the students ________ two teams.

06 빈칸에 공통으로 들어갈 말로 알맞은 것은? (대 · 소문자 무시)

> (A) ________ foods are fruits and vegetables that do not have a nice, visual appearance.
> (B) A goodwill basketball game between China and the United States turned ________.

① tough ② ugly
③ tasty ④ awesome
⑤ empty

07 다음 짝지어진 단어의 관계가 같도록 알맞은 말을 쓰시오.

> string – cord : mend – ________

중요

08 다음 빈칸에 들어갈 말이 바르게 짝지어진 것은?

> • Recently, Hawking surprised the world by ________ a shocking idea.
> • Interestingly, a small colorful rainbow is ________ in the sky!

① suggesting – hanging
② suggesting – imagining
③ banning – hanging
④ banning – sneezing
⑤ suggesting – guiding

01 <보기>에서 알맞은 단어를 선택하여 문장의 빈칸을 완성하시오. (필요하면 변형하여 쓰시오.)

보기
hang heavy pot corner bring

(1) The woman placed the flower ________ next to the window.

(2) The ________ box doesn't move an inch.

(3) Jason is ________ a painting on the wall.

(4) Let's put this box in the ________.

02 다음 대화의 빈칸에 <영영풀이>에 해당하는 단어를 쓰시오.

A: It smells good. What did you make?
B: I made a pizza. Let's eat it together.
A: Great. Then, let's ________ it into several pieces.

➡ ________________

<영영풀이> to separate into parts or groups

중요

03 다음 우리말에 맞게 주어진 문장의 빈칸에 알맞은 단어를 쓰시오.

• 학급 반장들이 이 판에 몇 개의 포스터를 붙였습니다. 그 전에, 그들은 학교 정문 앞에 판을 세웠었습니다. 학급 반장들 덕분에, 이 장소는 이전보다 훨씬 더 인기 있습니다.

➡ The class ________ put up some posters on this board. Before that, they had ________ ________ the ________ in front of the school gate. Thanks to the class ________, this place is much more ________ than before.

고난이도

04 영영풀이에 해당하는 단어를 <보기>에서 찾아 첫 번째 빈칸에 쓰고, 두 번째 빈칸에는 우리말 뜻을 쓰시오.

보기
dust suggest admit kitchen

(1) ________: a room where food is kept, prepared, and cooked and where the dishes are washed: ________

(2) ________: dry dirt in the form of powder that covers surfaces inside a building, or very small dry pieces of soil, sand, or other substances: ________

(3) ________: to agree that something is true, especially unwillingly: ________

(4) ________: to tell someone your ideas about what they should do, where they should go, etc.: ________

05 다음 글의 빈칸에 주어진 철자로 시작하는 알맞은 단어를 쓰시오.

(1) My bedroom was a m________, so my mom told me to clean it up.

(2) She hates summer because it is too hot and very s________.

(3) Why didn't you cover your mouth when you s________?

(4) My dad reads the n________ every morning.

교과서

Conversation

1 주제 소개하기

• Let's talk about the class party. 학급 파티에 대해 이야기해 보자.

■ "Let's talk about ~."는 '~에 대해서 말해 보자.'라는 뜻으로 함께 대화하고자 하는 주제를 소개할 때 쓰는 표현이다. 또는 대화나 발표 도입부에서 특정 주제를 언급하고자 할 때 'I'd like to talk about ~.'을 쓸 수 있다. 상황에 따라 'talk about' 대신 'introduce', 'discuss', 'mention' 등도 사용할 수 있다. 또한 상대방과 친밀도가 높은 대화 상황에서는 'would like to' 대신 'want to'를 사용하는 것이 가능하다.

■ 이에 대한 응답으로 해당 주제에 관한 자신의 의견을 말할 수 있다.

주제를 소개하는 다른 표현들

• I'd like to say something about ~.
• I'd like to introduce ~.
• Let me tell you about ~.
• Why don't we talk about ~?
• I'd like to discuss ~.

자신의 의견을 말할 때

• I think ~. / How about ~? / In my opinion, ~.

• A: Let's talk about our trip. 우리의 여행에 대해 이야기해 보자.
B: How about going to the national park? 국립공원으로 가는 게 어때?

• A: I'd like to talk about the movie we watched yesterday. 나는 어제 우리가 본 영화에 대해 얘기하고 싶어.
B: Yes, what would you like to talk first? 그래, 어떤 부분을 먼저 말할래?

핵심 Check

1. 다음 대화의 빈칸에 들어갈 말로 알맞지 <u>않은</u> 것은?

A: ______________________ a book I read recently.
B: Please share your thoughts with us.

① Let's talk about
② It is likely that
③ Let me say something about
④ I'd like to say something about
⑤ Allow me to say something about

2 감사하기

• Thank you for helping me. 도와줘서 고마워.

■ "Thank you for ~."는 '~에 대해서 고마워.'라는 뜻으로 감사를 나타낼 때 쓰는 표현이다. 이에 대한 응답으로 "You're welcome.", "(It's) My pleasure."와 같이 표현할 수 있다.

■ **감사하기 표현**

고마움과 감사의 표현으로 'Thank you'보다 더욱 공손하게 표현하고자 할 때는 'I appreciate ~.'를 사용할 수 있고 appreciate 뒤에는 목적어를 사용해야 한다.

• A: I really appreciate your advice. 당신의 충고에 정말 감사드립니다.
  B: Not at all. I'm glad that I could help you. 천만에요. 당신을 도울 수 있어서 기쁩니다.

■ **감사하기 표현에 대한 응답 표현**

'Thank you.'나 'I appreciate ~.'에 대한 대답은 'You're welcome.', 'No problem.', 'Not at all.', 'Don't mention it.' 등을 사용한다.

• A: Jihun, I heard you passed the math exam. 지훈아, 네가 수학 시험에 합격했다고 들었어.
  B: You helped me a lot. I really appreciate your help. 네가 많이 도와주었잖아. 너의 도움 정말 고마워.

• A: I really appreciate your help. 도와줘서 정말 고마워.
  B: You're welcome. 천만에.

핵심 Check

2. 다음 우리말에 맞도록 빈칸에 들어갈 알맞은 말을 고르시오.

• 그렇게 말해 주니 고마워.

Thank you ______________ that.

① of say ② to say ③ for saying
④ for to say ⑤ with saying

Conversation 교과서 대화문 익히기

Step Up – Real-life Scene

G1: ❶Let's talk about how we can make our town better.
B: ❷Let me tell you first. There's too much trash at the bus stop.
G2: I agree. ❸Why don't we clean the place together?
B: Good. We can put a bench there, too.
G1: Great idea. It'll be helpful for ❹the elderly.
G2: ❺How about putting some flower pots around the bench? They'll make the bus stop more beautiful.
G1: ❻Thank you for suggesting great ideas, everyone. Then, shall we start tomorrow?
G2, B: ❼No problem.

G1: 우리 마을을 어떻게 하면 더 좋게 만들 수 있을지를 이야기해 보자.
B: 내가 먼저 말할게. 버스 정류장에 쓰레기가 너무 많아.
G2: 동의해. 그 장소를 함께 치우는 게 어때?
B: 좋아. 우리가 거기에 벤치를 놓을 수도 있을 것 같아.
G1: 좋은 생각이야. 그것은 어르신들에게 도움이 될 거야.
G2: 벤치 주변에 화분도 좀 놓는 게 어때? 그것들은 버스 정류장을 더 아름답게 할 거야.
G1: 모두 좋은 의견을 내줘서 고마워. 그러면, 내일 시작하는 게 어때?
G2, B: 좋아.

❶ 'Let's talk about ~.'는 '~에 대해서 말해 보자'라는 뜻으로 함께 대화하고자 하는 주제를 소개할 때 쓰는 표현이다.
❷ 'Let+목적어+동사원형'은 '…가 ~하게 해주다'라는 의미이다.
❸ 'Why don't we+동사원형?'은 '~하는 게 어때?'라는 의미로 'Let's+동사원형'과 같이 주제를 소개할 때 쓰는 표현이다.
❹ 'the+형용사'는 복수명사로 '~한 사람들'의 의미로 '노인들'의 의미이다.
❺ 'How about+동명사?'는 '~는 어때?'라는 의미로 제안하는 표현이다.
❻ 'Thank you for+동명사'는 감사하는 표현으로 '~해 줘서 고마워'라는 의미이다.
❼ 감사하기 표현에 대한 응답 표현이다. 같은 표현으로 'You're welcome.' 'Not at all.' 'Don't mention it.' 등을 사용한다.

Check(√) True or False

(1) They are going to put a bench at the bus stop. T ☐ F ☐
(2) Some flower pots will make the bench more beautiful. T ☐ F ☐

Start Off – Listen & Talk B

G: Seho, we need something on the wall, too. Don't you think so?
B1: You're right. Let's talk about it together.
G: I think we need to put the club member list there. ❶It'll be helpful for us to learn the new members' names.
B2: That's a good idea. We also need our plan for this school year on the wall.
G: Right! That'll really ❷help us remember important school events.
B1: ❸Thank you for suggesting great ideas, everyone. We are a good team.

G: 세호야, 우리는 벽에도 뭔가 필요해. 그렇게 생각하지 않니?
B1: 네 말이 맞아. 그것에 대해서 함께 이야기해 보자.
G: 내 생각에는 거기에 동아리 회원 목록을 붙일 필요가 있는 것 같아. 그것은 우리가 신입 회원들의 이름을 알게 되는 데 도움이 될 거야.
B2: 좋은 생각이야. 이번 학년도의 우리 계획도 벽에 필요해.
G: 맞아! 그러면 우리가 중요한 학교 행사를 기억하는 데 정말 도움이 될 거야.
B1: 모두 좋은 의견을 내줘서 고마워. 우린 좋은 팀이야.

❶ It은 'to put the club member list there'를 가리키는 대명사이고, for us는 to부정사의 의미상 주어이다.
❷ 'help+목적어+목적보어(동사원형)' 형태로 '…가 ~하는 데 도움이 되다'라는 의미이다.
❸ 'Thank A for B' 구문은 'B 때문에 A에게 고마워하다'라는 의미로 전치사 for 뒤에는 동명사나 명사가 온다.

Check(√) True or False

(3) Seho doesn't think that they need something on the wall. T ☐ F ☐
(4) Seho thanks G and B2 for suggesting great ideas. T ☐ F ☐

Get Ready 2

(1) B: The flower pot ❶looks heavy. ❷Can I help you, Ms. Min?

W: You're so kind. Thank you very much.

(2) G: ❸Let me help you fix the bench.

M: Please hold this tight. ❹Thank you for helping me.

(3) B: Let's talk about ❺what we can do for our town.

G: ❻How about drawing pictures on the dirty walls?

B: Sounds good. ❼Anything else?

❶ 'look+형용사'는 '~하게 보이다'라는 의미이다.
❷ '도와 드릴까요?'라는 의미로 'May I help you?'를 대신 사용할 수 있다.
❸ 'let+목적어+동사원형'은 '…가 ~하게 하다'라는 의미이다.
❹ 감사를 표현하는 말로 전치사 for 뒤에는 동명사 helping이 온다.
❺ 전치사 about의 목적어 자리에 사용된 간접의문문으로 '의문사+주어+동사' 어순을 취한다.
❻ 'How about -ing?'는 '~하는 게 어때?'라는 의미로 'What about -ing?'를 사용할 수 있다.
❼ '-thing'으로 끝나는 부정대명사는 형용사가 뒤에서 수식한다.

Start Off – Listen & Talk A

1. B: What do we need in our club room? ❶Let's talk about it.

G: Sure. Well, how about putting some flower pots by the windows? They'll ❷make our room prettier.

B: That's a good idea. Thank you, Jiu.

2. B: ❸How about hanging some pictures?

G: Good. ❹Why don't you bring one of your pictures? You're good at painting, Seho.

B: Thank you for saying that. I'll bring one of ❺mine.

3. B: Let's talk about the corner this time. Any ideas?

G: How about making a small library in the corner of the club room? I will bring some books tomorrow.

B: Great idea! Thank you for suggesting it, Minju.

❶ 'Let's talk about ~.'는 '~에 대해서 말해 보자'라는 뜻이다.
❷ 'make+목적어+목적보어(형용사)' 구문으로 '…을 ~하게 만들다'라는 뜻이다.
❸ 전치사 about 뒤에 동명사 hanging을 사용한다.
❹ 'Why don't you+동사원형?' 형태로 '(네가) ~하는 게 어때?'라는 제안의 표현이다.
❺ mine은 'my pictures'를 대신하는 소유대명사이다.

Fun Time

A: Let's talk about the town party.

B: Okay. Why don't we cook *bibimbap*?

A: Wonderful. ❶Thank you for your idea.

❶ 감사의 표현으로 전치사 for 뒤에 명사가 온다.

Express Yourself A

1. M1: Thank you for coming, everyone. Let's talk about the Clean School Project.

W: I like the corner under the tree most. ❶ The Science Club cleaned around the corner and planted the tree.

M2: I like it, too. It is a very popular place among the students.

2. M1: Let's talk about the school gate this time. ❷What do you think of it?

W: The class leaders ❸set up the board and put up some posters. We can know ❹a lot more about school events.

M2: Right! They did a good job. Let's thank the class leaders.

❶ The Science Club cleaned ~ and planted ~ 형태로 동사 cleaned와 planted가 병렬 구조이다.
❷ 'What do you think of ~?'는 '~에 대해 어떻게 생각하니?'라는 뜻으로 의문사 'how'를 사용하지 않도록 주의한다.
❸ 동사 'set'과 'put'은 현재형과 과거형이 같은 형태의 동사로 여기서는 과거형으로 사용되었다.
❹ 'a lot'은 비교급 강조로 '훨씬'의 의미를 가진다. 'much, even, still, far' 등으로 바꾸어 사용할 수 있다.

● 다음 우리말과 일치하도록 빈칸에 알맞은 말을 쓰시오.

Get Ready 2

(1) B: The flower ________ looks ________. ________ ________ help you, Ms. Min?
W: You're so kind. ________ ________ very much.

(2) G: ________ me ________ you ________ the bench.
M: Please ________ this ________. Thank you ________ ________ me.

(3) B: ________ ________ ________ what we can do ________ our town.
G: ________ ________ ________ pictures on the ________ walls?
B: ________ good. ________ ________?

Start Off – Listen & Talk A

1. B: What do we ________ in our club room? ________ talk about it.
G: Sure. Well, ________ ________ ________ some ________ ________ ________ the windows? They'll ________ our room ________.
B: That's a ________ ________. Thank you, Jiu.

2. B: How about ________ some pictures?
G: Good. ________ ________ ________ ________ one of your pictures? You're good at ________, Seho.
B: ________ you ________ ________ that. I'll ________ one of ________.

3. B: Let's talk ________ the ________ this time. ________ ideas?
G: ________ ________ ________ a small library in the ________ of the club room? I will ________ some books tomorrow.
B: Great idea! Thank you for ________ it, Minju.

Start Off – Listen & Talk B

G: Seho, we need something on the wall, too. ________ you think so?
B1: You're right. ________ ________ about it ________.
G: I think we need to ________ the club ________ list there. It'll be ________ ________ ________ ________ ________ the new ________ names.
B2: That's a good idea. We also need our ________ for this ________ ________ on the wall.
G: Right! That'll really ________ us ________ important school events.
B1: Thank you for ________ great ideas, everyone. We are a good team.

해석

(1) B: 화분이 무거워 보여요. 민 선생님, 도와드릴까요?
W: 아주 친절하구나. 정말 고마워.

(2) G: 제가 의자 고치시는 걸 도와 드릴게요.
M: 이걸 좀 꽉 잡아 다오. 도와줘서 고맙구나.

(3) B: 우리가 마을을 위해 무엇을 할 수 있는지 이야기해 보자.
G: 지저분한 벽에 그림을 그리는 게 어떠니?
B: 좋아. 또 다른 건?

1. B: 우리 동아리실에 무엇이 필요할까? 그것에 대해 이야기해 보자.
G: 좋아. 음, 창가에 몇 개의 화분을 두는 게 어때? 그것들은 우리 동아리실을 더 예쁘게 할 거야.
B: 좋은 생각이야. 지우야, 고마워.

2. B: 그림을 좀 거는 게 어때?
G: 좋아. 네 그림 중의 하나를 가져오는 게 어때? 세호야, 넌 그림을 잘 그리잖아.
B: 그렇게 말해 주니 고마워. 내가 내 그림 중에서 하나를 가져올게.

3. B: 이번에는 모퉁이에 대해 이야기해 보자. 의견 있니?
G: 동아리실 모퉁이에 작은 도서관을 만드는 게 어때? 내가 내일 책 몇 권을 가져올게.
B: 좋은 생각이야! 민주야, 제안해 줘서 고마워.

G: 세호야, 우리는 벽에도 뭔가 필요해. 그렇게 생각하지 않니?
B1: 네 말이 맞아. 그것에 대해서 함께 이야기해 보자.
G: 내 생각에는 거기에 동아리 회원 목록을 붙일 필요가 있는 것 같아. 그것은 우리가 신입 회원들의 이름을 알게 되는 데 도움이 될 거야.
B2: 좋은 생각이야. 이번 학년도의 우리 계획도 벽에 필요해.
G: 맞아! 그러면 우리가 중요한 학교 행사를 기억하는 데 정말 도움이 될 거야.
B1: 모두 좋은 의견을 내줘서 고마워. 우린 좋은 팀이야.

[01~02] 다음 대화를 읽고 물음에 답하시오.

B: ___(a)___ the corner this time. Any ideas?
G: How about ___(A)___ (make) a small library in the corner of the club room? I will bring some books tomorrow.
B: Great idea! Thank you for ___(B)___ (suggest) it, Minju.

01 위 대화의 빈칸 (a)에 들어갈 말로 알맞은 것은?

① Let us talk to
② Let's talk with
③ Let's talk to
④ Let's talk about
⑤ Let us to talk about

서답형

02 위 대화의 빈칸 (A)와 (B)에 주어진 단어를 알맞은 형태로 고치시오.

➡ (A) ____________ (B) ____________

서답형

03 다음 대화의 밑줄 친 우리말에 맞게 주어진 단어를 알맞은 순서로 배열하여 쓰시오.

G: 제가 의자 고치시는 걸 도와 드릴게요. (fix / let / you / me / the bench / help)
M: Please hold this tight. Thank you for helping me.

➡ ______________________________

[04~05] 다음 대화를 읽고 물음에 답하시오.

G: Seho, we need something on the wall, too. Don't you think so?
B1: You're right. Let's talk about it together.
G: I think we need to put the club member list there. It'll be ___(A)___ for us to learn the new members' names.
B2: That's a good idea. We also need our plan for this school year on the wall.
G: Right! That'll really help us remember important school events.
B1: ___________(B)___________, everyone. We are a good team.

서답형

04 위 대화의 빈칸 (A)에 들어갈 말에 대한 영어 풀이를 보고 주어진 철자로 시작하여 쓰시오.

providing useful help in making a situation better or easier

➡ h____________

05 위 대화의 빈칸 (B)에 들어갈 말로 알맞은 것은?

① Thank you for informing me of the new members' names
② Thank you for teaching me how to make the wall
③ Thank you for suggesting great ideas
④ Thank you for volunteering
⑤ Thank you for helping me with remembering important school events

중요

06 다음 글의 밑줄 친 부분의 의도로 알맞은 것은?

Let's talk about the school gate this time. What do you think of it?

① 실망 표현하기
② 상기시켜 주기
③ 격려하기
④ 기대 표현하기
⑤ 주제 소개하기

[07~08] 다음 대화를 읽고 물음에 답하시오.

G1: Let's talk about ________(A)________.
B: Let me tell you first. There's too much trash at the bus stop.
G2: I agree. Why don't we clean the place together?
B: Good. We can put a bench there, too.
G1: Great idea. It'll be helpful for the elderly.
G2: How about putting some flower pots around the bench? They'll make the bus stop more beautiful.
G1: Thank you for suggesting great ideas, everyone. Then, shall we start tomorrow?
G2, B: No problem.

07 위 대화의 빈칸 (A)에 들어갈 말로 알맞은 것은?

① the class field trip
② how we can make our town better
③ how to make the town sports day more interesting
④ what we'll do to help the elderly
⑤ how we can make the trash can more beautiful

08 위 대화를 읽고 답할 수 없는 질문은?

① What is the problem in the town?
② What are they going to do after cleaning the bus stop?
③ Who is going to clean the bus stop?
④ What will they put on the bench?
⑤ When are they going to start working?

[09~10] 다음 대화를 읽고 물음에 답하시오.

M1: Let's talk about the school gate this time. (A)그것에 대해 어떻게 생각하나요? (think of it)
W: The class leaders set up the board and put up some posters. We can know a lot more about school events.
M2: Right! They did a good job. Let's thank the class leaders.

서답형

09 위 대화의 밑줄 친 우리말 (A)에 맞게 주어진 단어를 이용하여 영어로 쓰시오.

➡ ____________________

서답형

10 위 대화를 읽고 다음 질문에 영어로 답하시오.

Q: What did the class leaders do before they put up some posters on the board?
➡ They ____________.

[11~13] 다음 대화를 읽고 물음에 답하시오.

B: How about hanging some pictures?
G: Good. ____(A)____ take one of your pictures? You're good at painting, Seho.
B: Thank you for saying that. I'll bring one of (B)mine.

서답형

11 위 대화의 빈칸 (A)에 제안하는 표현을 세 단어로 쓰시오. (you를 이용할 것)

➡ ____________

서답형

12 위 대화의 밑줄 친 (B)가 가리키는 것을 찾아 쓰시오.

➡ ____________

서답형

13 위 대화에서 어색하게 쓰인 어휘를 하나 찾아서 바르게 고쳐 쓰시오.

________ ➡ ________

[01~02] 다음 대화를 읽고 물음에 답하시오.

G1: Let's talk about how we can make our town better.
B: Let me tell you first. There's too much trash at the bus stop.
G2: I agree. (A)그 장소를 함께 치우는 게 어때?
B: Good. We can put a bench there, too.
G1: Great idea. It'll be helpful for the elderly.
G2: How about putting some flower pots around the bench? They'll make the bus stop more beautiful.
G1: Thank you for suggesting great ideas, everyone. Then, shall we start tomorrow?
G2, B: No problem.

01 위 대화를 읽고 다음 물음에 영어로 답하시오. (9 단어로 쓸 것)

Q: What are they going to do to make the bus stop more beautiful?

➡ ______________________________

중요

02 위 대화의 밑줄 친 (A)의 우리말에 맞게 'why'와 'we'를 활용하여 영작하시오.

➡ ______________________________

03 다음 대화의 빈칸에 들어갈 말로 자연스러운 것을 <보기>에서 찾아 쓰시오.

G: Seho, we need something on the wall, too. Don't you think so?
B1: You're right. ______(A)______
G: I think we need to put the club member list there. It'll be helpful for us to learn the new members' names.
B2: That's a good idea. ______(B)______
G: Right! That'll really help us remember important school events.
B1: ______(C)______ We are a good team.

보기

- Thank you for suggesting great ideas, everyone.
- Let's talk about it together.
- Really? I'm sorry.
- We also need our plan for this school year on the wall.

➡ (A) ______________________________
(B) ______________________________
(C) ______________________________

고난이도

04 다음 대화의 밑줄 친 우리말을 주어진 <조건>에 맞게 영작하시오.

B: Let's talk about the corner this time. Any ideas?
G: 동아리실 모퉁이에 작은 도서관을 만드는 게 어때? I will bring some books tomorrow.
B: Great idea! Thank you for suggesting it, Minju.

조건

- 'How'를 사용할 것.
- make, small, in the corner, the club room 등의 단어를 이용할 것.

➡ ______________________________
____

교과서

Grammar

1 과거완료

• I was glad my dad **had made** me wear gloves.
나는 아버지가 나를 장갑을 착용하게 하셔서 기뻤다.

■ 형태: had+과거분사(p.p.)
의미: '~했었다'

■ 과거의 특정 시점보다 더 이전에 일어난 일이나 그때까지 지속된 상태

• I looked at the photo that I **had taken** a week earlier.
나는 일주일 전에 찍은 사진을 보았다. (사진을 본 것보다 사진을 찍은 것이 더 이전의 일)

• When I arrived there, he **had been waiting** for me for 2 hours.
내가 거기에 도착했을 때 그는 나를 2시간 동안 기다리고 있었다. (내가 거기에 도착한 과거의 특정 시점까지 그가 기다리는 행동이 그 이전부터 지속됨) (과거완료진행형)

■ 과거완료의 수동은 'had been+과거분사'로 쓰고, 과거완료의 진행은 'had been+현재분사'의 형태로 쓴다.

• My son spent all the money that **had been given** to him.
나의 아들은 그에게 주어진 모든 돈을 다 써버렸다. (과거완료수동태)

• When she visited my house, I **had been cleaning** the bathroom. (과거완료진행형)
그녀가 나의 집을 방문했을 때 나는 욕실을 청소하고 있었다.

■ 역사적 사실은 과거완료를 쓰지 않고 항상 과거로 쓴다.

• I knew that the North Korean army **had invaded** South Korea. (×)
→ I knew that the North Korean army **invaded** South Korea. (○)
나는 북한군이 남한을 침략했다는 사실을 알고 있었다.

핵심 Check

1. 다음 괄호 안에서 알맞은 것을 고르시오.
(1) I read the book that he (has / had) bought for me.
(2) The old lady found out that she (left / had left) her key in the car.
(3) When I (turned / had turned) on the radio, my favorite song had already been played.

2 비교급 강조

- I had to admit the lot looked **much** better.
  나는 그 지역이 훨씬 더 좋아 보이는 것을 인정해야만 했다.

■ 형태: much/far/even/still/a lot + 비교급
의미: 훨씬 더 ~한

■ 'much/far/even/still/a lot'은 비교급 앞에서 '훨씬'의 뜻으로 비교급을 강조한다.

- Your dog is **much** bigger than my dog. 너의 개가 나의 개보다 훨씬 더 크다.
- The novel is **far** more interesting than the movie. 그 소설이 영화보다 훨씬 더 흥미롭다.

■ 'very'는 원급을 강조할 때 쓰고, 비교급 강조에는 사용할 수 없다.

- This computer is **very** cheap. (○)
  This computer is very cheaper than that phone. (×)
  → This computer is **much** cheaper than that phone. (○)
  이 컴퓨터는 저 전화기보다 훨씬 더 싸다.
- My dad is **very** fat. (○)
  My dad is very fatter than my uncle. (×)
  → My dad is **even** fatter than my uncle. (○)
  나의 아빠는 삼촌보다 훨씬 더 뚱뚱하시다.

핵심 Check

2. 다음 괄호 안에서 알맞은 것을 고르시오.

(1) The red shirt looks (many / much) more cheaper than the blue one.
(2) I like summer (a lot / a lot of) more than winter.
(3) We are (far / very) tired today.

01 다음 우리말에 맞게 괄호 안에 주어진 단어를 이용하여 문장을 완성하시오.

(1) 수학 시험은 내가 예상한 것보다 훨씬 더 어려웠다. (much, difficult, expected)
➡ The math test ________________________.

(2) 그는 고양이보다 개를 훨씬 더 좋아한다. (much, cats)
➡ He likes ________________________.

(3) 너는 상자를 어디에 두었는지 기억했니? (where, put)
➡ Did you remember ________________________?

(4) 너는 그 집이 새로 칠해졌다는 것을 알아챘니? (newly, painted)
➡ Did you notice that ________________________?

02 다음 문장에서 어법상 어색한 부분을 바르게 고쳐 쓰시오.

(1) My teacher was looking at the pictures that her students had been drawn.
➡ ________________________

(2) When I arrived at the station, the train has just left.
➡ ________________________

(3) I jumped many higher than he did.
➡ ________________________

(4) He grew far tall than his father.
➡ ________________________

03 다음 〈보기〉의 문장을 참고하여 주어진 두 문장을 한 문장으로 바꾸어 쓰시오.

보기
At 2, my mom left the house. + At 3, I arrived at the house. → When I arrived at the house, my mom had left the house.

(1) At 7, my friends prepared for my birthday party. + At 8, I entered the classroom.
➡ ________________________

(2) At 6 :30, my husband ate all the sandwiches. + At 7, I got up.
➡ ________________________

01 다음 빈칸에 들어갈 말로 적절하지 않은 것은?

> You helped me _______ more than anyone else.

① much　② still
③ far　④ really
⑤ even

02 중요 다음 중 어법상 어색한 문장을 고르시오.

① She was tired because she had run for hours.
② We hadn't met each other before we worked together.
③ The letter had already arrived at my office when I came in.
④ He said that he had heard about the rules before the contest.
⑤ The teacher said that the Civil War had been between the north and south part of America.

03 다음 빈칸에 들어갈 수 있는 말이 다른 하나는?

① You helped me _______. Thanks to you, I passed the test.
② She works out regularly these days. She looks _______ healthier than before.
③ As I'm working as a salesperson, I need to meet _______ people every day.
④ Learning Spanish is _______ more interesting than learning Japanese.
⑤ We hope you enjoy this show _______.

04 다음 두 문장을 '과거완료시제'를 사용하여 한 문장으로 바르게 바꾸면?

> • She was sick.
> • I found it later.

① I found that she was sick.
② I found that she had been sick.
③ I had found that she was sick.
④ She had been sick and I had found it.
⑤ She was sick and I had found it.

05 중요 다음 밑줄 친 much의 용법이 나머지 넷과 다른 것은?

① We can't spend much time on this problem.
② The student has much interest in science.
③ The child wanted to have much more love.
④ Mike has never earned much money.
⑤ Much oil spilled out of the bottle.

06 중요 빈칸에 들어갈 말을 순서대로 바르게 연결한 것은?

> Your brothers _______ the snowman that _______ by me.

① destroyed – made
② destroyed – had made
③ destroyed – had been made
④ had destroyed – had made
⑤ had destroyed – had been made

서답형

07 다음 괄호 안에 주어진 단어들을 바르게 배열하여 문장을 완성하시오.

> When I visited him, (fixed, he, already, bike, had, my).

➡ ______________________

08 다음 중 어법상 어색한 문장을 고르시오.

① He said he had paid the phone bill.
② I remembered that I had once lived in Seoul.
③ Because she broke my earphones, I had yelled at my sister.
④ She was not the one who had broken the copy machine.
⑤ He had already packed his suitcase when I entered his room.

서답형

09 다음 문장에서 어법상 어색한 것을 바르게 고쳐 다시 쓰시오.

(1) When Jiyeon came back home, she found that her mother already set the table for her.
➡ ______________________
____

(2) He is much more cool than you think. I'm sure you will like him.
➡ ______________________
____

10 다음 빈칸에 들어갈 말로 어색한 것은?

> Ms. Miller was eating the chicken that her husband had ________.

① left ② baked
③ cooked ④ bought
⑤ took

11 다음 두 문장을 한 문장으로 바르게 옮긴 것은?

> • He moved to New York.
> • Before that, he lived in LA for 2 years.

① He lived in LA for 2 years before he had moved to New York.
② He had lived in LA for 2 years after he moved to New York.
③ He has lived in LA for 2 years before he moved to New York.
④ He had lived in LA for 2 years before he moved to New York.
⑤ After he lived in LA for 2 years, he had moved to New York.

서답형

12 다음 괄호 안에서 알맞은 말을 고르시오.

(1) I missed the bus because I (was / had) gotten up late.
(2) When they arrived at the party, their friends had already (leave / left) the party.
(3) She looks (so / even) younger than her age.
(4) Why don't you try much (hard / harder)?
(5) You need to be (a lot / lots of) nicer to the elderly.

13 괄호 안의 단어가 들어갈 수 있는 적절한 위치를 고르시오.

> For me, ① science is ② more ③ difficult ④ than math ⑤. (a lot)

① ② ③ ④ ⑤

서답형

14 다음 괄호 안에 주어진 단어 중 필요한 단어만 골라 바르게 배열하여 문장을 완성하시오.

> 그녀는 자기 딸보다 훨씬 어려 보인다.
> She (many, than, looks, young, even, her daughter, younger, more).

➡ She ______________________________.

서답형

15 주어진 어휘를 활용하여 다음 우리말을 영어로 쓰시오.

> 그녀는 내가 예상한 것보다 훨씬 더 친절하게 행동했다. (behave, kindly, expect)

➡ ______________________________
____

서답형

16 〈보기〉에서 적절한 단어를 골라 빈칸을 알맞은 형태로 완성하시오.

> 보기
> cook fix wash

When Mr. Han came back home,
(1) he found somebody ____________ rice for him.
(2) he was surprised that somebody ____________ his T-shirt.
(3) he was happy that somebody ____________ his chair.

중요

17 빈칸에 공통으로 들어갈 말을 고르시오.

> • Today is ________ colder than yesterday.
> • I have ________ interest in films.

① very ② so ③ much
④ a lot ⑤ even

서답형

18 주어진 어휘를 이용하여 다음 우리말을 영어로 쓰시오.

> 그는 문을 잠그지 않아서 놀랐다. (surprise, that, had, lock)

➡ ______________________________
____

19 다음 중 어법상 <u>어색한</u> 문장을 고르시오.

① Can you run much faster than your dog?
② The bag looks even heavier than the book.
③ My grandfather always gets up much more early than me.
④ Alex works a lot harder than anyone else in his company.
⑤ I can eat even more than my friends.

중요

20 다음 중 밑줄 친 부분의 쓰임이 <u>어색한</u> 것을 고르시오.

① Her hair is <u>much longer</u> than mine.
② This shirt is <u>far cheaper</u> than that one.
③ My bed is <u>a lot more comfortable</u> than yours.
④ This cake tastes <u>even better</u> than that one.
⑤ Dogs are <u>very smarter</u> than birds.

21 다음 중 어법상 <u>어색한</u> 문장의 개수로 알맞은 것은?

> a. Your car is much more expensive than me.
> b. I feel much lonelier than usual.
> c. You look even more lovely than before.
> d. He was very more handsome than I thought.
> e. Is an ostrich a lot faster than a cheetah?

① 1개 ② 2개 ③ 3개 ④ 4개 ⑤ 5개

Grammar 서술형 시험대비

01 중요 과거완료시제를 이용하여 두 문장을 하나로 연결하시오.

(1) • Where did you put the book?
• Did you remember it?
➡ ______________________________
____

(2) • Somebody broke in.
• When I came back home, I found it.
➡ ______________________________
____

(3) • The house was newly painted.
• Did you notice it?
➡ ______________________________
____

(4) • I lost my bag.
• Mom bought it for me.
➡ ______________________________
____

(5) • My teacher already left the classroom.
• When I entered the classroom, I found it.
➡ ______________________________
____

02 우리말과 같은 뜻이 되도록 빈칸에 알맞은 말을 쓰시오.

그녀는 어제보다 훨씬 더 아름답게 춤을 추었다. → She danced ____________ than yesterday.

➡ ____________________

03 다음 그림을 보고 괄호 안의 단어를 바르게 배열하여 문장을 완성하시오.

(1)

A: Look at these shoes. Which one do you like? B: I like the sneakers. They ________. (comfortable, than, others, the, more, look, much)

➡ ______________________________

(2)

A: Which one will you buy? B: I'll buy the backpack. It is ________. (cheaper, the, than, hand bag, much)

➡ ______________________________

04 중요 주어진 문장의 밑줄 친 부분을 괄호 안의 단어로 바꾸어 문장을 다시 쓰시오.

(1) Eric played the violin very <u>well</u>. (better)
➡ ______________________________

(2) You should work very <u>hard</u>. (harder)
➡ ______________________________

05 다음 우리말을 주어진 어휘를 이용하여 영어로 옮기시오.

(1) 어제보다 훨씬 더 비가 심하게 오는 중이다.
(raining, lot, harder)
➡ ______________________
____

(2) 너의 책은 다른 어떤 것보다 읽기에 훨씬 쉽다.
(even, to read, anything)
➡ ______________________
____

(3) 이 책은 저것보다 훨씬 더 어려워 보인다.
(much, difficult, one)
➡ ______________________
____

06 다음 빈칸에 괄호 안의 단어를 알맞은 형태로 바꾸어 쓰시오.

중요

She ________ New York until she became 20 years old. (never, visit)

➡ ______________

07 〈보기〉를 참고하여 주어진 두 문장을 한 문장으로 바르게 바꾸시오.

보기

Mina wrote a letter to Jenny.
+ Jenny read the letter.
→ Jenny read the letter that Mina had written to her.

(1) Jack sent a gift to Tony.
+ Tony threw away the gift by mistake.
➡ ______________________
____

(2) Yuna showed me the notebook.
+ She wrote down a poem on the notebook.
➡ ______________________
____

08 잘못된 부분을 바르게 고쳐 문장을 다시 쓰시오.

(1) Jack lost the umbrella that his friend has lent to him.
➡ ______________________
____

(2) When I called her, she has already gone to sleep.
➡ ______________________
____

(3) Before I get to the theater, the movie had already finished.
➡ ______________________
____

(4) When I arrived at the airport, the plane was already left.
➡ ______________________
____

(5) Did you eat the pie that Dad has baked?
➡ ______________________
____

09 괄호 안의 단어를 빈칸에 알맞은 형태로 쓰시오.

중요

(1) When Mr. Han came back home, he found somebody ________ his house. (clean)
(2) I think sandwiches are much ________ than *gimbap*. (healthy)
(3) When he ________, I had already eaten lunch. (call)
(4) He couldn't open the door because he ________ his key. (lose)
(5) He got up late because he ________ to bed late. (go)

교과서

Reading

Green Thumbs

I complained the whole day. My parents were making me work on the neighborhood project, but I had far better things to do. I didn't understand why we were working on this place. It was just the ugly, old, empty lot across from Johnny's Shop. It was full of wild plants, fast food wraps, old newspapers, broken glass, and every other kind of dirty trash you can imagine. As I looked at it that first morning, I thought, "I bet there are snakes in there, too."

온종일 / 사역동사(making)+목적어+원형부정사 / 비교급 강조(훨씬) / to부정사의 형용사적 용법 / 간접의문문: 의문사+주어+동사 / ~ 맞은편의 / = was filled with / = imaginable / 그 첫날 아침에 / = I'm sure[certain] that: 틀림없이 …이다

There were twenty of us — all ages and sizes — ready to work that day. I didn't think that we could clean up this awful mess and turn it into a garden. We were all wondering where to begin. Then Mr. Hernandez said, "The only way to do it is just to start." Then, he divided the lot into four parts with string and assigned five people to each part.

turn A into B: A를 B로 바꾸다 / = we should. '의문사 to부정사'는 '의문사+주어+should'로 바꿔 쓸 수 있다. / to부정사의 형용사적 용법 / to부정사의 명사적 용법 / divide A into B: A를 B로 나누다

By lunchtime, I was hot, sweaty, and glad my dad had made me wear gloves. We filled fifty trash bags with waste and were ready to pull wild plants. As we pulled and pulled, dust filled the air and made us sneeze. At the end of the day, I had to admit the lot looked much better.

아빠가 장갑을 끼게 시키신 것이 점심때보다 더 먼저 일어난 일이므로 과거완료로 썼다. / fill A with B: A를 B로 채우다 / 사역동사(made)+목적어+원형부정사 / 비교급 강조(훨씬)

green thumb 원예의 재능(식물을 잘 키우는 사람)
neighborhood 이웃
wrap 포장지; 포장하다
ugly 불쾌한, 볼품없는
empty 텅 빈
lot 지역, 부지
be full of …으로 가득 차다
newspaper 신문
bet …이 틀림없다, 확신하다
snake 뱀
awful 끔찍한, 지독한
mess 쓰레기 더미, 혼잡
divide ... into ~ …를 ~로 나누다
string 끈, 줄
assign 맡기다, 배정하다
sweaty 땀에 젖은, 땀이 나는
fill …을 채우다
trash bag 쓰레기 봉투
be ready to …할 준비가 되어 있다
dust 먼지
sneeze 재채기하다
admit 인정하다

확인문제

- 다음 문장이 본문의 내용과 일치하면 T, 일치하지 않으면 F를 쓰시오.

1 The writer complained the whole day. ☐
2 The neighborhood project was working on the town garden across from Johnny's Shop. ☐
3 The place was full of wild plants, fast food wraps, old newspapers, broken glass, etc. ☐
4 Mr. Hernandez divided the lot into four parts with chalk. ☐
5 By lunchtime, the writer was hot and sweaty. ☐
6 The writer filled fifty trash bags with wild plants. ☐

That first day was the toughest. On the weekends that followed, we made rows, planted flower and vegetable seeds, and watered them. After about two weeks, I stopped complaining when I found the plants had started popping up! First, the lettuce and then the beans and the tomatoes. They grew so fast. I couldn't believe it! The bean plants grew an inch, and the tomatoes doubled in size in just a few days.

최상급 / V1 / V2 / V3 / stop ~ing: ~하는 것을 그만두다, to complain(×) / = to pop, start는 목적어로 동명사와 to부정사를 쓸 수 있다. / the lettuce, the beans and the tomatoes / 단지 며칠 만에

Now, two months later, I like to go there every day to see what new flowers are ready to pop up. Lots of people in the neighborhood meet there to enjoy the sights and to talk together.

to부정사의 부사적 용법(목적) / to부정사의 부사적 용법(형용사 수식) / to부정사의 부사적 용법(목적) / to부정사의 부사적 용법(목적)

Tonight, it suddenly hit me — what a good thing we did! I'm proud I have been a part of it. I'm in charge of picking flowers for the nursing home on Fourth Street. The vegetables will go to every kitchen in our town. But even better, an ugly and dirty lot that people didn't like has become a pretty garden for everyone.

= occurred to = struck: ~에게 생각이 떠올랐다 / be in charge of: ~을 담당하다, ~을 책임지고 있다 / 비교급 강조(훨씬) / = which(관계대명사 목적격)

tough 힘든, 질긴
row 열, 줄
pop up 갑자기 나오다
lettuce 상추
bean 콩
complain 불평하다
suddenly 갑자기
double 두 배가 되다
hit (생각 등이 불현듯) 떠오르다
in charge of …을 맡아서, 담당해서
nursing home 양로원
kitchen 부엌, 주방

확인문제

● 다음 문장이 본문의 내용과 일치하면 T, 일치하지 않으면 F를 쓰시오.

1 That first day was the toughest. ☐
2 After about two weeks, the writer kept complaining. ☐
3 The lettuce, the beans and the tomatoes grew so fast. ☐
4 The bean plants doubled in size in just a few days. ☐
5 The writer is in charge of picking flowers for the nursing home on Fourth Street. ☐
6 The vegetables will go to the participants in the project. ☐

Reading 교과서 확인학습 A

• 우리말을 참고하여 빈칸에 알맞은 말을 쓰시오.

1 Green ________

2 I ________ the whole day.

3 My parents were making me ________ on the neighborhood project, but I had ________ ________ things to do.

4 I didn't understand ________ ________ ________ ________ on this place.

5 It was just the ugly, old, empty lot ________ ________ Johnny's Shop.

6 It ________ ________ ________ wild plants, fast food wraps, old newspapers, broken glass, and every other kind of dirty trash ________ ________ ________.

7 As I looked at it that first morning, I thought, "________ ________ there are snakes in there, too."

8 There were twenty of us — ________ ________ ________ ________ — ready to work that day.

9 I didn't think that we could clean up ________ ________ ________ and turn it into a garden.

10 We were all wondering ________ ________ ________.

11 Then Mr. Hernandez said, "The only way to do it is ________ ________ ________."

12 Then, he ________ the lot ________ four parts with string and ________ five people ________ each part.

13 ________ ________, I was hot, sweaty, and glad my dad had made me ________ gloves.

14 We ________ fifty trash bags ________ waste and ________ ________ ________ pull wild plants.

15 As we pulled and pulled, dust filled the air and ________ ________ ________.

1 식물을 잘 키우는 사람들
2 나는 온종일 불평했다.
3 우리 부모님은 나를 이웃 프로젝트에서 일하게 하셨지만, 나에게는 훨씬 더 나은 할 일들이 있었다.
4 나는 우리가 왜 이곳에서 일하고 있어야 하는지 이해하지 못했다.
5 그곳은 그저 Johnny's Shop 건너편에 있는 볼품없고, 오래되고, 텅 빈 지역이었다.
6 그곳은 잡초와 패스트푸드 포장지와 낡은 신문, 깨진 유리, 그리고 상상할 수 있는 모든 다른 종류의 더러운 쓰레기로 가득 차 있었다.
7 그 첫날 아침에 그곳을 보았을 때, 나는 "틀림없이 저 안에는 뱀들도 있을 거야."라고 생각했다.
8 그날 일할 준비가 된 —모든 연령대와 몸집을 가진 — 우리 20명이 있었다.
9 나는 이 끔찍하게 더러운 곳을 청소하여 정원으로 바꿀 수 있다고 생각하지 않았다.
10 우리는 모두 어디서부터 시작해야 할지 궁금해 하고 있었다.
11 그때 Hernandez 씨가 "그것을 할 유일한 방법은 그냥 시작하는 것입니다."라고 말했다.
12 그러고 나서, 그는 그 지역을 끈으로 네 구역으로 나누고, 5명을 각 구역에 배치했다.
13 점심 무렵, 나는 덥고, 땀이 났으며, 아버지가 나에게 장갑을 끼도록 한 것이 기뻤다.
14 우리는 쓰레기 봉투 50개를 쓰레기로 채웠고, 잡초를 뽑을 준비가 되어 있었다.
15 우리가 뽑으면 뽑을수록, 먼지가 공기를 가득 메워서 재채기가 나왔다.

16 ________ ________ ________ ________ the day, I had to admit the lot looked much better.

17 That first day was ________ ________.

18 On the weekends that followed, we ________ ________, planted flower and vegetable seeds, and watered them.

19 After about two weeks, I ________ ________ when I found the plants had started popping up!

20 ________, ________ ________ and then the beans and the tomatoes.

21 They grew ________ ________.

22 I ________ ________ it!

23 The bean plants grew an inch, and the tomatoes doubled ________ ________ ________ ________ ________ ________ ________.

24 Now, two months later, I like to go there every day to see ________ ________ ________ ________ ________ to pop up.

25 Lots of people in the neighborhood meet there to ________ ________ ________ and to talk together.

26 Tonight, it suddenly ________ ________ — what a good thing we did!

27 I'm proud I ________ ________ ________ ________ of it.

28 ________ ________ ________ ________ picking flowers for the nursing home on Fourth Street.

29 The vegetables ________ ________ ________ every kitchen in our town.

30 But ________ ________, an ugly and dirty lot ________ people didn't like has become a pretty garden for everyone.

16 그날이 끝날 무렵, 나는 그 지역이 훨씬 더 나아 보인다는 것을 인정해야 했다.

17 그 첫날이 가장 힘들었다.

18 그다음 주말에 우리는 열을 만들고, 꽃과 채소 씨앗을 심고, 물을 주었다.

19 약 2주 뒤, 나는 식물들이 자라나기 시작한 것을 발견했을 때 불평하는 것을 멈추었다!

20 처음에는 상추, 그러고 나서, 콩과 토마토.

21 그것들은 아주 빨리 자랐다.

22 나는 믿을 수가 없었다!

23 콩 식물은 1인치 자라났고, 토마토는 며칠 만에 크기가 두 배가 되었다.

24 두 달이 지난 지금, 나는 매일 어떤 새로운 꽃들이 피어날 준비가 되었는지 보러 그곳에 가는 것을 좋아한다.

25 이웃의 많은 사람이 그곳에서 만나 풍경을 즐기고 함께 이야기를 나눈다.

26 오늘 밤, 갑자기 생각났다 — 우리가 얼마나 좋은 일을 했는가!

27 나는 내가 그 일의 일부였다는 것이 자랑스럽다.

28 나는 'Fourth Street'에 있는 양로원을 위해 꽃을 따는 일을 맡았다.

29 채소들은 우리 마을의 모든 부엌으로 갈 것이다.

30 하지만 훨씬 더 좋은 것은, 사람들이 좋아하지 않았던 볼품없고 더러운 지역이 모두를 위한 예쁜 정원이 되었다는 것이다.

Reading 교과서 확인학습 B

• 우리말을 참고하여 본문을 영작하시오.

1 식물을 잘 키우는 사람들

➡ ______________________________

2 나는 온종일 불평했다.

➡ ______________________________

3 우리 부모님은 나를 이웃 프로젝트에서 일하게 하셨지만, 나에게는 훨씬 더 나은 할 일들이 있었다.

➡ ______________________________

4 나는 우리가 왜 이곳에서 일하고 있어야 하는지 이해하지 못했다.

➡ ______________________________

5 그곳은 그저 Johnny's Shop 건너편에 있는 볼품없고, 오래되고, 텅 빈 지역이었다.

➡ ______________________________

6 그곳은 잡초와 패스트푸드 포장지와 낡은 신문, 깨진 유리, 그리고 상상할 수 있는 모든 다른 종류의 더러운 쓰레기로 가득 차 있었다.

➡ ______________________________

____

7 그 첫날 아침에 그곳을 보았을 때, 나는 "틀림없이 저 안에는 뱀들도 있을 거야."라고 생각했다.

➡ ______________________________

8 그날 일할 준비가 된 —모든 연령대와 몸집을 가진 — 우리 20명이 있었다.

➡ ______________________________

9 나는 이 끔찍하게 더러운 곳을 청소하여 정원으로 바꿀 수 있다고 생각하지 않았다.

➡ ______________________________

10 우리는 모두 어디서부터 시작해야 할지 궁금해 하고 있었다.

➡ ______________________________

11 그때 Hernandez 씨가 "그것을 할 유일한 방법은 그냥 시작하는 것입니다."라고 말했다.

➡ ______________________________

12 그러고 나서, 그는 그 지역을 끈으로 네 구역으로 나누고, 5명을 각 구역에 배치했다.

➡ ______________________________

13 점심 무렵, 나는 덥고, 땀이 났으며, 아버지가 나에게 장갑을 끼도록 한 것이 기뻤다.

➡ ______________________________

14 우리는 쓰레기 봉투 50개를 쓰레기로 채웠고, 잡초를 뽑을 준비가 되어 있었다.

➡ ______________________________

15 우리가 뽑으면 뽑을수록, 먼지가 공기를 가득 메워서 재채기가 나왔다.

➡ ______________________________

16 그날이 끝날 무렵, 나는 그 지역이 훨씬 더 나아 보인다는 것을 인정해야 했다.

➡ ______________________________

17 그 첫날이 가장 힘들었다.

➡ ______________________________

18 그다음 주말에 우리는 열을 만들고, 꽃과 채소 씨앗을 심고, 물을 주었다.

➡ ______________________________

19 약 2주 뒤, 나는 식물들이 자라나기 시작한 것을 발견했을 때 불평하는 것을 멈추었다!

➡ ______________________________

20 처음에는 상추, 그러고 나서, 콩과 토마토.

➡ ______________________________

21 그것들은 아주 빨리 자랐다.

➡ ______________________________

22 나는 믿을 수가 없었다!

➡ ______________________________

23 콩 식물은 1인치 자라났고, 토마토는 며칠 만에 크기가 두 배가 되었다.

➡ ______________________________

24 두 달이 지난 지금, 나는 매일 어떤 새로운 꽃들이 피어날 준비가 되었는지 보러 그곳에 가는 것을 좋아한다.

➡ ______________________________

25 이웃의 많은 사람이 그곳에서 만나 풍경을 즐기고 함께 이야기를 나눈다.

➡ ______________________________

26 오늘 밤, 갑자기 생각났다 — 우리가 얼마나 좋은 일을 했는가!

➡ ______________________________

27 나는 내가 그 일의 일부였다는 것이 자랑스럽다.

➡ ______________________________

28 나는 'Fourth Street'에 있는 양로원을 위해 꽃을 따는 일을 맡았다.

➡ ______________________________

29 채소들은 우리 마을의 모든 부엌으로 갈 것이다.

➡ ______________________________

30 하지만 훨씬 더 좋은 것은, 사람들이 좋아하지 않았던 볼품없고 더러운 지역이 모두를 위한 예쁜 정원이 되었다는 것이다.

➡ ______________________________

[01~03] 다음 글을 읽고 물음에 답하시오.

I (A)[complained / complained about] the whole day. My parents were making me work on the neighborhood project, but I had far better things to do. I didn't understand why we were working on ①this place. ②It was just the ugly, old, empty lot across from ③ Johnny's Shop. ⓐIt was full of wild plants, fast food wraps, old newspapers, (B)[breaking / broken] glass, and every other (C)[kind / kinds] of dirty trash you can imagine. As I looked at ④it that first morning, I thought, "I bet there are snakes in ⑤there, too."

서답형

01 위 글의 괄호 (A)~(C)에서 어법상 알맞은 낱말을 골라 쓰시오.

➡ (A) ________ (B) ________ (C) ________

중요

02 밑줄 친 ①~⑤ 중에서 가리키는 대상이 나머지 넷과 다른 것은?

① ② ③ ④ ⑤

서답형

03 위 글의 밑줄 친 ⓐ를 다음과 같이 바꿔 쓸 때 빈칸에 들어갈 알맞은 말을 두 단어로 쓰시오.

➡ It was ____________ wild plants

[04~07] 다음 글을 읽고 물음에 답하시오.

There were twenty of us — all ages and sizes — ready to work that day. (A)I didn't think that we could clean up this terrific mess and turn it into a garden. We were all wondering where to begin. Then Mr. Hernandez said, "(B)The only way to do it is just to start." Then, he divided the lot into four parts with string and assigned ___ⓐ___ people to each part.

서답형

04 위 글의 빈칸 ⓐ에 들어갈 알맞은 단어를 쓰시오.

➡ ____________________

서답형

05 위 글의 밑줄 친 (A)에서 흐름상 어색한 부분을 찾아 고치시오.

____________ ➡ ____________

중요

06 위 글의 밑줄 친 (B)에 어울리는 속담으로 가장 알맞은 것을 고르시오.

① Look before you leap.
② Well begun is half done.
③ Too many cooks spoil the broth.
④ Make hay while the sun shines.
⑤ It never rains but it pours.

07 본문의 내용과 일치하도록 다음 빈칸 (A)~(C)에 알맞은 단어를 쓰시오.

When the twenty people were (A)________ where they should begin, Mr. Hernandez (B)________ the lot into four parts with string and (C)________ five people to each part.

[08~11] 다음 글을 읽고 물음에 답하시오.

That first day was the toughest. (①) On the weekends ⓐthat followed, we made rows, planted flower and vegetable seeds, and watered them. (②) After about two weeks, I stopped complaining when I found the plants had started popping up! (③) First, the lettuce and then the beans and the tomatoes. (④) They grew so fast. (⑤) The bean plants grew an inch, and the tomatoes ⓑ며칠 만에 크기가 두 배가 되었다.

서답형

08 위 글의 흐름으로 보아, 주어진 문장이 들어가기에 가장 적절한 곳은?

I couldn't believe it!

① ② ③ ④ ⑤

09 위 글의 제목으로 알맞은 것을 고르시오.

① The Toughest Day in a Week
② Unbelievable! I have a Green Thumb!
③ The Difficulty of Growing Vegetables
④ How to Plant Flower Seeds
⑤ A Shortcut to Grow Vegetables!

10 아래 <보기>에서 위 글의 밑줄 친 ⓐthat과 문법적 쓰임이 같은 것의 개수를 고르시오.

보기
① It's the best novel that I've ever read.
② The watch that you gave me keeps perfect time.
③ I am glad that I found you.
④ I'm so tired that I cannot do my homework.
⑤ Where's the letter that came yesterday?

① 1개 ② 2개 ③ 3개 ④ 4개 ⑤ 5개

서답형

11 위 글의 밑줄 친 ⓑ의 우리말에 맞게 주어진 어휘를 이용하여 8 단어로 영작하시오.

doubled, just a few

➡ ______________________

[12~13] 다음 글을 읽고 물음에 답하시오.

Tonight, it suddenly hit me — what a good thing we did! I'm proud I have been a part of it. I'm in ⓐcharge of picking flowers for the nursing home on Fourth Street. The vegetables will go to every kitchen in our town. But even better, an ugly and dirty lot that people didn't like has become a pretty garden for everyone.

12 위 글의 밑줄 친 ⓐcharge와 같은 의미로 쓰인 것을 고르시오.

① He took charge of the farm then.
② Delivery is free of charge.
③ What did they charge for the repairs?
④ She rejected the charge that the story was untrue.
⑤ They began to charge the enemy.

중요

13 According to the passage, which is NOT true?

① Tonight, it suddenly occurred to the writer that they did a very good thing.
② The writer was proud of having been a part of it.
③ The writer was in charge of picking flowers for the nursing home.
④ The writer brought the vegetables to every kitchen in their town.
⑤ People didn't like the ugly and dirty lot before it became a pretty garden for everyone.

[14~16] 다음 글을 읽고 물음에 답하시오.

I complained the whole day. My parents were making me work on the neighborhood project, but ⓐI had far good things to do. I didn't understand why we were working on this place. It was just the ugly, old, empty lot across from Johnny's Shop. It was full of wild plants, fast food wraps, old newspapers, broken glass, and every other kind of dirty trash you can imagine. ⓑAs I looked at it that first morning, I thought, "I bet there are snakes in there, too."

서답형

14 위 글의 밑줄 친 ⓐ에서 어법상 틀린 부분을 찾아 고치시오.

______ ➡ ______

중요

15 위 글의 마지막 부분 ⓑ에서 알 수 있는 'I'의 심경으로 가장 알맞은 것을 고르시오.

① ashamed
② excited
③ reluctant
④ willing
⑤ calm

16 According to the passage, which is NOT true?

① The writer was full of complaints the whole day.
② The writer's parents had the writer work on the neighborhood project.
③ The writer didn't figure out why they were working on the neighborhood project.
④ The place was just the ordinary empty lot across from Johnny's Shop.
⑤ The place was full of wild plants, fast food wraps, old newspapers, etc.

[17~19] 다음 글을 읽고 물음에 답하시오.

That first day was the toughest. On the weekends that followed, we made ⓐrows, planted flower and vegetable seeds, and watered them. After about two weeks, I stopped complaining ⓑwhen I found the plants had started popping up! First, the lettuce and then the beans and the tomatoes. They grew so fast. I couldn't believe it! The bean plants grew an inch, and the tomatoes doubled in size in just a few days.

중요

17 위 글의 주제로 어울리는 속담을 고르시오.

① The more the better.
② Prevention is better than cure.
③ Haste makes waste.
④ Sweet after bitter.
⑤ It never rains but it pours.

18 위 글의 밑줄 친 ⓐrows와 같은 의미로 쓰인 것을 모두 고르시오.

① He rows around the island.
② She rows against the flood.
③ The vegetables were planted in neat rows.
④ There were endless rows of identical houses.
⑤ The fisherman rows them back to the shore.

서답형

19 위 글의 밑줄 친 ⓑ를 다음과 같이 바꿔 쓸 때 빈칸에 들어갈 알맞은 말을 두 단어로 쓰시오.

➡ when I found the plants had started ______ ______ up

[20~22] 다음 글을 읽고 물음에 답하시오.

(A)There were twenty of us — all ages and sizes — ready to work that day. I didn't think that we could clean up this awful mess and turn it ___ⓐ___ a garden. We were all wondering where to begin. Then Mr. Hernandez said, "The only way to do it is just (B)to start." Then, he divided the lot into four parts with string and assigned five people ___ⓑ___ each part.

20 위 글의 빈칸 ⓐ와 ⓑ에 들어갈 전치사가 바르게 짝지어진 것은?

ⓐ ⓑ	ⓐ ⓑ
① for – to	② into – on
③ to – from	④ for – on
⑤ into – to	

서답형

21 위 글의 밑줄 친 (A)를 다음과 같이 바꿔 쓸 때 빈칸에 들어갈 알맞은 단어를 철자 d로 시작하여 쓰시오.

➡ There were twenty of us who were ready to work that day, and our ages and our sizes were all ________.

중요

22 위 글의 밑줄 친 (B)to start와 to부정사의 용법이 다른 것을 모두 고르시오.

① Give me something hot to drink.
② To get up early is good for your health.
③ I'm pleased to meet you again.
④ I took a subway to get there on time.
⑤ We decided to go to the museum.

[23~25] 다음 글을 읽고 물음에 답하시오.

Tonight, ⓐit suddenly hit me — what a good thing we did! I'm proud I have been a part of it. I'm in charge of picking flowers for the nursing home on Fourth Street. The vegetables will go to every kitchen in our town. But ⓑeven better, ⓒ사람들이 좋아하지 않았던 볼품없고 더러운 지역이 모두를 위한 예쁜 정원이 되었다.

23 위 글의 밑줄 친 ⓐ와 바꿔 쓸 수 없는 말을 고르시오.

① I suddenly hit on it
② it suddenly occurred to me
③ a light suddenly went on in my room
④ it suddenly struck me
⑤ I suddenly came up with it

중요

24 위 글의 밑줄 친 ⓑeven과 같은 의미로 쓰인 것을 고르시오.

① Even a child can understand it.
② Our scores are now even.
③ 4, 6, 8, 10 are all even numbers.
④ You need an even surface to work on.
⑤ You know even less about it than I do.

서답형

25 위 글의 밑줄 친 ⓒ의 우리말에 맞게 주어진 어휘를 알맞게 배열하시오.

has become / that / a pretty garden / for everyone / didn't like / an ugly and dirty lot / people

➡ ______________________________

____

[01~03] 다음 글을 읽고 물음에 답하시오.

I complained the whole day. My parents were making me work on the neighborhood project, but ⓐ나에게는 훨씬 더 나은 할 일들이 있었다. I didn't understand why we were working on this place. It was just the ugly, old, empty lot across from Johnny's Shop. It was full of wild plants, fast food wraps, old newspapers, broken glass, and every other kind of dirty trash you can imagine. As I looked at it that first morning, I thought, "ⓑI bet there are snakes in there, too."

중요

01 위 글의 밑줄 친 ⓐ의 우리말에 맞게 주어진 어휘를 이용하여 7 단어로 영작하시오.

far

➡ ____________________

고난이도

02 위 글의 밑줄 친 ⓑ를 다음과 같이 바꿔 쓸 때 빈칸에 들어갈 알맞은 단어를 쓰시오.

➡ There ________ be snakes in there, too.
= I'm ________ that there are snakes in there, too.

03 다음 문장에서 위 글의 내용과 다른 부분을 찾아서 고치시오.

The writer was willing to work on the neighborhood project.

____________ ➡ ____________

[04~06] 다음 글을 읽고 물음에 답하시오.

There were twenty of us — all ages and sizes — ready to work that day. I didn't think that we could clean up this awful (A)[mass / mess] and turn it into a garden. We were all (B)[wandering / wondering] ⓐwhere to begin. Then Mr. Hernandez said, "The only way to do it is just to start." Then, he (C) [decided / divided] the lot into four parts with string and assigned five people to each part.

중요

04 위 글의 괄호 (A)~(C)에서 문맥상 알맞은 낱말을 골라 쓰시오.

➡ (A) ________ (B) ________ (C) ________

05 위 글의 밑줄 친 ⓐ를 다음과 같이 바꿔 쓸 때 빈칸에 들어갈 알맞은 말을 두 단어로 쓰시오.

➡ where ________ ________ begin.

06 주어진 영영풀이에 해당하는 단어를 본문에서 찾아 쓰시오.

gave someone some work to do

➡ ____________________

[07~09] 다음 글을 읽고 물음에 답하시오.

By lunchtime, I was hot, sweaty, and glad my dad ___ⓐ___ me wear gloves. We filled fifty trash bags with waste and were ready to pull wild plants. As we pulled and pulled, ⓑdust filled the air and made us sneeze. At the end of the day, I had to admit the lot looked much better.

중요

07 위 글의 빈칸 ⓐ에 make를 알맞은 형태로 쓰시오.

➡ ____________________

08 위 글의 밑줄 친 ⓑ를 다음과 같이 바꿔 쓸 때 빈칸에 들어갈 알맞은 말을 of를 포함하여 두 단어로 쓰시오.

➡ we sneezed ________ ________ the dust which filled the air

중요

09 본문의 내용과 일치하도록 다음 빈칸 (A)와 (B)에 공통으로 들어갈 알맞은 단어를 쓰시오.

After the people filled fifty trash bags with waste, they pulled and pulled wild plants. At the end of the day, the writer had to admit the (A)________ looked a (B)________ better.

[10~12] 다음 글을 읽고 물음에 답하시오.

That first day was the toughest. On the weekends that followed, we ___ⓐ___ rows, ___ⓑ___ flower and vegetable seeds, and ___ⓒ___ them. After about two weeks, I stopped complaining when I found the plants had started popping up! First, the lettuce and then the beans and the tomatoes. ⓓ They grew so fast. I couldn't believe it! The bean plants grew an inch, and the tomatoes doubled in size in just a few days.

중요

10 위 글의 빈칸 ⓐ~ⓒ에 make, plant, water를 각각 알맞은 형태로 쓰시오.

➡ ⓐ ________ ⓑ ________ ⓒ ________

11 위 글의 밑줄 친 ⓓThey가 가리키는 것을 본문에서 찾아 쓰시오.

➡ ________________________________

고난이도

12 What made the writer stop complaining after about two weeks? Fill in the blank with a suitable word.

The sight of the ________ that had popped up made the writer stop complaining.

[13~16] 다음 글을 읽고 물음에 답하시오.

Tonight, it suddenly hit me — what ⓐa good thing we did! ⓑI'm proud I have been a part of it. ⓒI'm in charge of picking flowers for the nursing home on Fourth Street. The vegetables will go to every kitchen in our town. ⓓBut even better, an ugly and dirty lot that people didn't like has become a pretty garden for everyone.

13 위 글의 밑줄 친 ⓐ의 구체적인 내용을 본문에서 찾아 쓰시오.

➡ ________________________________

____

고난이도

14 위 글의 밑줄 친 ⓑ를 동명사를 사용하여 고치시오.

➡ ________________________________

중요

15 위 글의 밑줄 친 ⓒ를 다음과 같이 바꿔 쓸 때 빈칸에 들어갈 알맞은 말을 두 단어로 쓰시오.

➡ I'm ________ ________ picking flowers for the nursing home on Fourth Street.

16 위 글의 밑줄 친 ⓓ에서 생략할 수 있는 말을 생략하고 문장을 다시 쓰시오.

➡ ________________________________

____

교과서

구석구석

After You Read A

June 17

I visited the town garden after school. Some people were talking while they were looking at the beautiful garden. I picked some flowers and took them to the nursing home. I'm proud that we made a pretty garden for everyone.

(visited: visited to(×) / after school: 방과 후에 / while: ~하는 동안 / them: = some flowers / that: 접속사: [원인 · 이유] …이므로, …이기 때문에)

구문해설 • visit: 방문하다 • pick: 꺾다 • nursing home: 양로원

해석

6월 17일

나는 방과 후에 마을 정원을 방문했다. 몇몇 사람들이 아름다운 정원을 보면서 이야기하고 있었다. 나는 꽃을 몇 송이 꺾어서 양로원에 가지고 갔다. 우리가 모두를 위한 예쁜 정원을 만든 것이 자랑스럽다.

Do It Yourself

Our Town Symbol

This is Oksig, which I drew as a symbol of my town. I designed this after I had taken pictures of many different kinds of corn. Oksig is much cuter than real corn. I hope everybody likes it.

(which: 관계대명사의 계속적 용법 / as: ~으로(전치사) / designed: 과거 / had taken: 과거완료 (두 동사 간의 시간의 순서를 알려준다.) / much: 비교급 강조 (= still/far/even/a lot) / it: Oksig)

구문해설 • symbol: 상징 • design: 디자인하다 • take pictures of : ~를 사진 찍다

우리 동네 상징

이것은 Oksig이고, 내가 나의 동네 상징으로 그렸습니다. 나는 많은 다양한 종류의 옥수수 사진을 찍은 후에 이것을 디자인했습니다. Oksig은 진짜 옥수수보다 훨씬 더 귀엽습니다. 나는 모든 사람들이 이것을 좋아하길 바랍니다.

Link to the World

• Kampong Ayer is the largest "water village" in the world. It is made up of about 40 small villages.
(the largest "water village" in the world: the+최상급+단수명사+in+단수 명사(범위/장소) / is made up of: ~로 구성되다(= consists of = is composed of))

• All the houses are built over the water.
(are built: 수동태: 지어지다)

• There are schools, police stations, gas stations, and post offices.
(There are: There are+복수명사: ~가 있다)

• It is much more beautiful than you think. It is called the Venice of Asia.
(much: 비교급 강조: 훨씬(= even, still, far, a lot) / is called: 수동태: ~라 불리다)

구문해설 • village 마을 • be made up of ~로 이루어져 있다 • gas station 주유소 • Venice 베니스

• 캄퐁 아에르는 세상에서 가장 큰 '수상 마을'이다. 그것은 40개의 작은 마을들로 이루어져 있다.
• 모든 집은 물 위에 지어져 있다.
• 학교, 경찰서, 주유소, 우체국이 있다.
• 그곳은 여러분이 생각하는 것보다 훨씬 더 아름답다. 그곳은 아시아의 베니스라고 불린다.

영역별 핵심문제

Words & Expressions

01 다음 주어진 두 단어의 관계가 같도록 빈칸에 알맞은 단어를 쓰시오.

fill – empty : wonderful – a________

02 다음 문장의 빈칸 (a)와 (b)에 들어갈 단어가 바르게 짝지어진 것은?

- John wasn't invited to the party, so we were surprised when he (a)__________.
- The (b)________ of the mountains was so beautiful that she cried.

① didn't come – sight
② didn't come – top
③ was delivered – hillside
④ popped up – seed
⑤ popped up – sight

[03~04] 다음 영영풀이에 해당하는 것을 고르시오.

03

to offer to do something that you do not have to do

① fill ② volunteer
③ hang ④ represent
⑤ suggest

04

a line of things or people next to each other

① row ② law
③ low ④ raw
⑤ lot

05 다음 대화의 빈칸에 들어갈 말을 〈영영풀이〉에 맞게 두 단어로 쓰시오.

A: Hi, Molly. Are you good with plants?
B: Not really.
A: Do you know someone?
B: Ask Susan. She has a ____________.
A: Thanks.

<영영풀이> considerable talent or ability to grow plants

➡ ____________________

06 다음 밑줄 친 부분의 뜻이 잘못된 것은?

① I don't use plastic wrap. (포장지)
② She cut the lettuce and made a salad. (상추)
③ My mother often makes rice mixed with beans. (콩)
④ Do not complain about small things. (배정하다)
⑤ Kevin is always late, so I bet that he will be late today. (확신하다)

Conversation

07 다음 대화의 빈칸에 들어갈 말로 문법상 적절하지 않은 것은?

B: Let's talk about what we can do for our town.
G: ______________ on the dirty walls?
B: Sounds good. Anything else?

① How about drawing pictures
② What about drawing pictures
③ What do you say to draw pictures
④ Why don't we draw pictures
⑤ Shall we draw pictures

08 다음 대화의 순서를 바르게 배열한 것은?

(A) I like it, too. It is a very popular place among the students.
(B) I like the corner under the tree most. The Science Club cleaned around the corner and planted the tree.
(C) Thank you for coming, everyone. Let's talk about the Clean School Project.

① (A) – (B) – (C)
② (B) – (A) – (C)
③ (C) – (A) – (B)
④ (C) – (B) – (A)
⑤ (A) – (C) – (B)

09 다음 짝지어진 대화 중 <u>어색한</u> 것은?

① A: Who will make posters for school flea market?
B: I will. I can do it well.
② A: Thank you for taking care of my dog.
B: My pleasure.
③ A: Thank you for teaching me how to ride a bike.
B: No problem.
④ A: How about hanging some pictures?
B: Good.
⑤ A: Let's talk about our club room this time. Any ideas?
B: Great idea!

[10~11] 다음 대화를 읽고 물음에 답하시오.

G1: Let's talk about how we can make our town better.
B: ①<u>Let me tell</u> you first. There's too much trash at the bus stop.
G2: I agree. ②<u>Why don't we cleaning</u> the place together?
B: Good. We can put a bench there, too.
G1: Great idea. It'll be helpful for ③<u>the elderly</u>.
G2: ④<u>How about putting</u> some flower pots around the bench? They'll make the bus stop more beautiful.
G1: Thank you ⑤<u>for suggesting</u> great ideas, everyone. Then, shall we start tomorrow?
G2, B: No problem.

10 위 대화의 제목으로 가장 적절한 것은?

① Making the Bus Stop More Beautiful
② How to Choose Flower Pots
③ Meeting for Making Our Town Better.
④ How to Suggest a Great Idea
⑤ The Influence of Trash at the Bus Stop on the Town

11 위 대화의 밑줄 친 ①~⑤ 중 어법상 <u>어색한</u> 것은?

① ② ③ ④ ⑤

12 다음 대화의 밑줄 친 우리말 해석에 맞게 주어진 단어를 알맞게 배열하여 쓰시오.

> G: Seho, we need something on the wall, too. Don't you think so?
> B1: You're right. Let's talk about it together.
> G: I think we need to put the club member list there. <u>그것은 우리가 신입 회원들의 이름을 알게 되는 데 도움이 될 거야.</u>
> B2: That's a good idea.

(learn / new / helpful / us / to / the / members' / for / be / names)

➡ It'll ______________________

______________.

Grammar

13 다음 중 어법상 <u>어색한</u> 문장을 <u>모두</u> 고르시오.

① Skiing is much more difficult than it looks.
② Driving a car is far more easy than I think.
③ Today is more worse than yesterday.
④ The giraffe is much taller than the deer.
⑤ A whale is still bigger than a dolphin.

14 다음 글에서 어법상 <u>어색한</u> 부분을 찾아 바르게 고치시오.

> **Our Town Symbol**
> This is Oksig, which I drew as a symbol of my town. I designed this after I had taken pictures of many different kinds of corn. Oksig is very cuter than real corn. I hope everybody likes it.

➡ ______________________

15 다음 두 문장을 한 문장으로 바르게 옮긴 것은?

> • I missed the bus.
> • So, I was late for school.

① Because I was late for school, I had missed the bus.
② Because I had been late for school, I missed the bus.
③ Because I missed the bus, I had been late for school.
④ Because I had missed the bus, I had been late for school.
⑤ Because I had missed the bus, I was late for school.

16 괄호 안의 단어를 알맞은 형태로 쓰시오.

> A: The class leaders set up the board and put some posters. We can know (1)(a lot, much) about school events than before.
> B: Right! They did a good job. Let's thank the class leaders.
>
> A: The Green Club cleaned the pond and put some fish into it.
> B: Right! Thanks to the Green Club, this place looks (2)(much, good) than before.
>
> A: The Art Club drew flowers and wings on this wall.
> B: Right! Thanks to the Art Club, this place is (3)(much, popular) than before.

➡ (1) ____________ (2) ____________
(3) ____________

17 다음 빈칸에 공통으로 알맞은 말을 쓰시오.

- Unfortunately, we do not have ________ information on this accident.
- You look ________ better than before.

➡ ____________________

18 다음 우리말을 주어진 어휘를 이용하여 영어로 옮기시오.

(1) Bill Gates는 나보다 훨씬 더 부자이다. (much, rich)

➡ ____________________

(2) 이 책이 저 책보다 훨씬 인기 있다. (even, popular)

➡ ____________________

(3) 너는 나보다 훨씬 더 우아하게 춤을 춘다. (far, gracefully)

➡ ____________________

Reading

[19~20] 다음 글을 읽고 물음에 답하시오.

I complained the whole day. ⓐMy parents were making me to work on the neighborhood project, but I had far better things to do. I didn't understand why we were working on this place. It was just the ugly, old, empty ⓑ lot across from Johnny's Shop. It was full of wild plants, fast food wraps, old newspapers, broken glass, and every other kind of dirty trash you can imagine. As I looked at it that first morning, I thought, "I bet there are snakes in there, too."

19 위 글의 밑줄 친 ⓐ에서 어법상 틀린 부분을 찾아 고치시오.

____________ ➡ ____________

20 위 글의 밑줄 친 ⓑlot과 같은 의미로 쓰인 것을 고르시오.

① A lot of people are coming to the meeting.
② She felt dissatisfied with her lot.
③ I like him quite a lot.
④ You have to find a parking lot there.
⑤ They choose a person by lot.

[21~23] 다음 글을 읽고 물음에 답하시오.

By lunchtime, I was hot, sweaty, and glad my dad had made me wear gloves. We filled fifty trash bags with (A)waste and were ready to pull wild plants. As we pulled and pulled, dust filled the air and made us sneeze. At the end of the day, I had to admit the lot looked ____ⓐ____ better.

21 위 글의 빈칸 ⓐ에 들어갈 수 없는 말을 고르시오.

① even ② still
③ very ④ much
⑤ far

22 위 글의 밑줄 친 (A)waste와 같은 의미로 쓰인 것을 고르시오.

① It's a waste of money to do such a thing.
② Don't waste a good opportunity.
③ Use your waste talents.
④ I have no time to waste.
⑤ Don't throw industrial waste into the river.

23 본문의 내용과 일치하도록 다음 빈칸에 들어갈 두 단어를 쓰시오.

> Before the people pulled wild plants, they ________ ________ fifty trash bags with waste.

[24~26] 다음 글을 읽고 물음에 답하시오.

> **Let's Change the Dirty Lot ___ⓐ___ a Pretty Garden!**
>
> • When: Apr. 17
> • Where: at the empty lot across from Johnny's Shop
> • What to do: to pull wild plants and clean the lot
> • What to bring: gloves, trash bags
> • How: We'll divide the lot ___ⓑ___ four parts. Five people will clean each part.
>
> *If you have any questions, call Mr. Hernandez.*

24 위 글의 빈칸 ⓐ와 ⓑ에 공통으로 들어갈 알맞은 전치사를 고르시오.

① for ② from
③ into ④ in
⑤ to

25 위 글의 종류로 알맞은 것을 고르시오.

① article ② notice
③ catalog ④ review
⑤ advertisement

26 위 글을 읽고 알 수 없는 것을 고르시오.

① 모임 시기 ② 모임 장소
③ 모임 활동 내용 ④ 준비물
⑤ 참가 가능 연령

[27~28] 다음 글을 읽고 물음에 답하시오.

> June 17
>
> I visited the town garden after school. Some people were talking while they were looking at the beautiful garden. I picked some flowers and took ⓐthem to the nursing home. I'm proud that we made a pretty garden for everyone.

27 위 글의 밑줄 친 ⓐ가 가리키는 것을 본문에서 찾아 쓰시오.

➡ ____________________

28 What is the writer proud of? Fill in the blanks with suitable words.

> The writer is proud of having made a ________ ________ for everyone.

단원별 예상문제

출제율 90%

01 다음 짝지어진 단어의 관계가 같도록 빈칸에 알맞은 말을 쓰시오.

remember – forget : partial – ________

출제율 95%

02 다음 영영풀이에 해당하는 단어는?

to make something twice as much or many

① hang ② double ③ second
④ mess ⑤ two

출제율 85%

03 다음 대화를 읽고 B의 말에 대한 A의 대답을 <조건>에 맞게 쓰시오.

보기
- 감사의 표현을 사용할 것.
- 본문에 나오는 한 단어를 활용할 것.

A: Let's talk about the volunteer work for our town. Who will play with the children?
B: I will. I can do it well.
A: ____________________

➡ ____________________

[04~05] 다음 대화를 읽고 물음에 답하시오.

G: Seho, we need something on the wall, too. Don't you think so? (①)
B1: You're right. Let's talk about it together.
G: (②) I think we need to put the club member list there. (③) It'll be helpful for us to learn the new members' names.
B2: That's a good idea. (④)
G: Right! That'll really help us remember important school events. (⑤)
B1: Thank you for suggesting great ideas, everyone. We are a good team.

출제율 100%

04 위 대화의 (①)~(⑤) 중 주어진 문장이 들어갈 위치로 알맞은 것은?

We also need our plan for this school year on the wall.

① ② ③ ④ ⑤

출제율 90%

05 위 대화를 읽고 Seho와 그의 친구들이 할 일 두 가지 내용을 영어로 쓰시오. (to부정사로 시작하여 쓸 것)

➡ ____________________ and their plan ____________________ on the wall

출제율 95%

06 다음 대화의 빈칸에 들어갈 말로 어색한 것은?

A: Thank you for taking care of my dog.
B: ____________

① My pleasure.
② No problem.
③ Don't worry about it.
④ Don't mention it.
⑤ Not at all.

출제율 95%

07 다음 대화의 빈칸 (A)에 들어갈 문장을 주어진 어휘를 배열하여 완성하시오.

B: How about hanging some pictures?
G: Good. Why don't you bring one of your pictures? You're good at painting, Seho.
B: ________(A)________ (you / saying / thank / that / for). I'll bring one of mine.

➡ ____________________

출제율 90%

08 다음 대화의 빈칸 (A)와 (B)에 들어갈 표현으로 알맞은 것은?

> B: Let's talk about what we can do for our town.
> G: ______ (A) ______
> B: Sounds good. Anything else?
> G: Let me help you fix the bench.
> M: Please hold this tight. ______ (B) ______

① (A) Why don't we do a funny dance?
(B) Thank you for your idea.

② (A) How about drawing pictures on the dirty walls?
(B) Thank you for helping me.

③ (A) Let's talk about the town party.
(B) Wonderful.

④ (A) Who will make posters for school flea market?
(B) My pleasure.

⑤ (A) I can do it well.
(B) Thank you for volunteering.

[09~10] 다음 대화를 읽고 물음에 답하시오.

> G1: Let's talk about how we can make our town better.
> B: Let me tell you first. There's too much trash at the bus stop.
> (A) Great idea. It'll be helpful for the elderly.
> (B) Good. We can put a bench there, too.
> (C) How about putting some flower pots around the bench? They'll make the bus stop more beautiful.
> (D) I agree. Why don't we clean the place together?
> G1: Thank you for suggesting great ideas, everyone. Then, shall we start tomorrow?
> G2, B: No problem.

출제율 95%

09 위 대화의 (A)~(D)를 알맞은 순서로 배열하시오.

➡ ____________________

출제율 100%

10 위 대화의 내용과 일치하지 않는 것은?

① There is too much trash at the bus stop.
② All of them will clean the place together.
③ They will put a bench there for the elderly.
④ They will put some flower pots around the bench.
⑤ They will start working right now.

출제율 95%

11 다음 문장에서 어법상 어색한 부분을 찾아 바르게 고치시오.

> When my brother came back home, I have already done the dishes.

____________ ➡ ____________

출제율 90%

12 다음 글에서 밑줄 친 우리말을 괄호 안에 주어진 단어를 사용하여 영어로 옮기시오.

> **Our Town Symbol**
> This is Oksig, which I drew as a symbol of my town. I designed this (1) 많은 다양한 종류의 옥수수 사진을 찍은 후에 (had, different). (2)Oksig은 진짜 옥수수보다 훨씬 더 귀엽습니다.(cuter, real) I hope everybody likes it.

➡ (1) ____________________
(2) ____________________

출제율 90%

13 잘못된 부분을 바르게 고쳐 문장을 다시 쓰시오.

(1) When we visited her, she said she studied music for 5 years in Paris.

➡ ______________________________

(2) It was strange that he didn't remember the movie that we have watched the other day.

➡ ______________________________

(3) Walking is much helpful for your health than running.

➡ ______________________________

(4) The building is very larger than I expected.

➡ ______________________________

[14~15] 다음 글을 읽고 물음에 답하시오.

I ___ⓐ___ the whole day. My parents were making me work on the neighborhood project, but I had far better things to do. I didn't understand why we were working on ⓑthis place. It was just the ugly, old, empty lot across from Johnny's Shop. It was full of wild plants, fast food wraps, old newspapers, broken glass, and every other kind of dirty trash you can imagine. As I looked at it that first morning, I thought, "I bet there are snakes in there, too."

출제율 90%

14 위 글의 빈칸 ⓐ에 들어갈 알맞은 말을 고르시오.

① apologized ② complimented
③ complained ④ rewarded
⑤ offered

출제율 95%

15 다음 빈칸 (A)와 (B)에 서로 상반되는 의미의 단어를 넣어 ⓑthis place에 대한 소개를 완성하시오.

It was just the (A)________ lot which was (B)________ of wild plants, fast food wraps, old newspapers, broken glass, and every other sort of dirty trash imaginable.

[16~17] 다음 글을 읽고 물음에 답하시오.

That first day was the toughest. On the weekends that followed, we made rows, planted flower and vegetable seeds, and watered them. After about two weeks, I stopped complaining when I found the plants ⓐhad started popping up! First, the lettuce and then the beans and the tomatoes. They grew so fast. I couldn't believe it! The bean plants grew an inch, and the tomatoes doubled in size in just a few days.

출제율 90%

16 위 글의 밑줄 친 ⓐhad started와 과거완료의 용법이 같은 것을 고르시오.

① I did not tell her at first, for I had never seen her before.
② I lost the pen that I had bought yesterday.
③ When I met her, she had been ill for two weeks.
④ He said he had been to New York twice.
⑤ He had lived there for ten years when his father died.

출제율 100%

17 According to the passage, which is NOT true?

① That first day was the hardest day for the writer.
② After about two weeks, the writer stopped complaining.
③ The tomatoes popped up first.

④ The lettuce, the beans and the tomatoes grew so fast.

⑤ The tomatoes doubled in size in just a few days.

[18~19] 다음 글을 읽고 물음에 답하시오.

Now, two months later, I like ①to go there every day ②to see what new flowers are ready ③to pop up. ⓐLots of people in the neighborhood meet there ④to enjoy the sights and ⑤to talk together.

출제율 100%

18 밑줄 친 ①~⑤ 중에서 to부정사의 용법이 나머지 넷과 다른 것은?

① ② ③ ④ ⑤

출제율 90%

19 위 글의 밑줄 친 ⓐLots of와 바꿔 쓸 수 있는 말을 두 개 쓰시오.

➡ ________, ________

[20~21] 다음 글을 읽고 물음에 답하시오.

Tonight, ⓐit suddenly hit me — what a good thing we did! I'm proud I have been a part of it. I'm in charge of picking flowers for the nursing home on Fourth Street. The vegetables will go to every kitchen in our town. But even better, an ugly and dirty lot that people didn't like has become a pretty garden for everyone.

출제율 90%

20 위 글의 밑줄 친 ⓐit이 가리키는 것을 본문에서 찾아 쓰시오.

➡ ________________

출제율 90%

21 다음 빈칸 (A)와 (B)에 알맞은 단어를 넣어 글쓴이의 감상문을 완성하시오.

At first, people didn't like the ugly and dirty lot, but it became (A)________ ________ ________ for everyone, and the writer is proud of himself because he has been (B)________ ________ of such a good thing.

[22~23] 다음 글을 읽고 물음에 답하시오.

The Art Club drew wings on this wall. Before that, they ___ⓐ___ flowers. Thanks to the Art Club, this place is much more popular than before.

• the Green Club
Apr. 1: clean it
Apr. 5: put some fish into it

• the Art Club
Mar. 15: draw flowers
Mar. 17: draw wings

The Green Club put some fish into this pond. Before that, they ___ⓑ___ the pond. Thanks to the Green Club, this place is much more popular than before.

출제율 90%

22 위 글의 빈칸 ⓐ와 ⓑ에 draw와 clean을 각각 알맞은 형태로 쓰시오.

➡ ⓐ ________ ⓑ ________

출제율 90%

23 본문의 내용과 일치하도록 다음 빈칸 (A)와 (B)에 알맞은 단어를 쓰시오.

Thanks to the (A)________ ________ and the (B)________ ________, the environment of the town has changed for the better.

서술형 실전문제

01 다음 대화의 빈칸 (A)와 (B)에 주어진 〈조건〉의 어구와 우리 말을 이용하여 알맞은 말을 쓰시오.

B: What do we need in our club room? Let's talk about it.
G: Sure. Well, ______ (A) ______? They'll make our room prettier.
B: That's a good idea. Thank you, Jiu.

B: Let's talk about the corner this time. Any ideas?
G: How about making a small library in the corner of the club room? I will bring some books tomorrow.
B: Great idea! ______ (B) ______, Minju.

조건
(A) • how about / the windows / put / flower pots / by / some
(B) • 감사 표현 / for / suggest / it

➡ (A) ______________________
(B) ______________________

02 다음 대화의 빈칸에 들어갈 문장을 〈조건〉에 맞게 쓰시오.

A: ______________________
Who will cook for the elderly?
B: I will. I can do it well.
A: Thank you for volunteering.

조건
• 주제는 '마을(our town)을 위한 자원봉사'에 관한 것으로 Let's를 이용하여 대화의 주제를 소개하는 문장을 쓰시오.

➡ ______________________

03 다음 대화를 읽고 물음에 영어로 답하시오.

G1: Let's talk about how we can make our town better.
B: Let me tell you first. There's too much trash at the bus stop.
G2: I agree. Why don't we clean the place together?
B: Good. We can put a bench there, too.
G1: Great idea. It'll be helpful for the elderly.
G2: How about putting some flower pots around the bench? They'll make the bus stop more beautiful.
G1: Thank you for suggesting great ideas, everyone. Then, shall we start tomorrow?
G2, B: No problem.

(1) What is the problem in the town?
➡ ______________________

(2) What are they going to do after cleaning the bus stop?
➡ ______________________

04 다음 글에서 어법상 틀린 곳의 기호를 쓰고 바르게 고치시오.

Our Town Symbol
This is Oksig, ⓐthat I drew as a symbol of my town. I designed this after I ⓑhave taken pictures of many different ⓒkinds of corn. Oksig is ⓓmuch cuter than real corn. I hope everybody likes ⓔthem.

➡ (1) __________ (2) __________
(3) __________

05 〈보기〉에 주어진 단어 중 의미상 적절한 것을 골라 다음 문장의 빈칸 하나에 한 단어씩 알맞은 형태로 써 넣으시오.

보기

live see tell have go

(1) We ________ ________ a good time before Mom came home.

(2) Yesterday I found out that my friend ________ ________ a lie to me.

(3) Mark ________ ________ with his family before he got married to Irene.

[06~08] 다음 글을 읽고 물음에 답하시오.

I complained the whole day. My parents were making me work on the neighborhood project, but I had far better things to do. I didn't understand (A)우리가 왜 이곳에서 일하고 있어야 하는지. It was just the ugly, old, empty lot across from Johnny's Shop. It was full of wild plants, fast food wraps, old newspapers, broken glass, and (B)every other kind of dirty trash you can imagine. As I looked at it that first morning, I thought, "____ⓐ____ there are snakes in there, too."

06 다음과 같은 뜻이 되도록 위 글의 빈칸 ⓐ에 들어갈 알맞은 말을 쓰시오. (2 단어)

It is certain that

➡ ____________________

07 위 글의 밑줄 친 (A)의 우리말에 맞게 주어진 어휘를 알맞게 배열하시오.

working / place / were / this / we / why / on

➡ ____________________

08 위 글의 밑줄 친 (B)에 생략된 한 단어를 넣어 다시 쓰시오.

➡ ____________________
____

[09~10] 다음 글을 읽고 물음에 답하시오.

That first day was the toughest. On the weekends that followed, we made rows, planted flower and vegetable seeds, and watered them. ⓐAfter about two weeks, I stopped to complain when I found the plants had started popping up! First, the lettuce and then the beans and the tomatoes. ⓑThey grew so fast. I couldn't believe it! The bean plants grew an inch, and the tomatoes doubled in size in just a few days.

09 위 글의 밑줄 친 ⓐ에서 어법상 틀린 부분을 찾아 고치시오.

____________ ➡ ____________

10 위 글의 밑줄 친 ⓑ의 예를 본문에서 찾아 우리말로 쓰시오.

➡ 콩 식물은 ____________________
____________________.

창의사고력 서술형 문제

01 아래 표의 (A)와 (B)는 학교 행사 준비에 필요한 일들을 적어둔 것이다. 제시된 〈보기〉의 문장처럼 주제 소개와 감사의 표현을 쓰시오.

(A)	(B)
• class party	• make sandwiches
• class field trip	• take pictures of our activities
• club festival	• make posters
• sports day	• run a 100 meter race

보기

A: Let's talk about the class party. Who will make sandwiches?

B: I will. I can do it well.

A: Thank you for volunteering.

02 과거완료시제를 이용하여 주어진 문장의 원인을 자유롭게 쓰시오.

(1) I didn't do well on the test this morning because ______________________.

(2) He lost some weight because ______________________.

(3) Jen needed to buy new shoes because ______________________.

(4) Sera felt bored during the movie because ______________________.

03 다음 내용을 바탕으로 교내 환경의 변화된 모습을 알리는 홍보문을 쓰시오.

• **the Art Club**	• **the Green Club**
Mar. 15: draw flowers	Apr. 1: clean it
Mar. 17: draw wings	Apr. 5: put some fish into it

The Art Club (A)______________ on this wall. Before that, they (B)______________. Thanks to the Art Club, this place is much more popular than before.
The Green Club (C)______________ into this pond. Before that, they (D)______________ the pond. Thanks to the Green Club, this place is much more popular than before.

단원별 모의고사

01 다음 단어에 대한 영어 설명이 어색한 것은?

① suggest: to give a particular job or piece of work to someone
② empty: not containing any things or people
③ tough: difficult to do or to deal with
④ hang: to put something in a position so that the top part is fixed or supported, and the bottom part is free to move and does not touch the ground
⑤ sweaty: covered in sweat or smelling of sweat

02 다음 짝지어진 단어의 관계가 같도록 빈칸에 알맞은 말을 쓰시오.

complain – moan : disgusting – a________

03 다음 영영풀이에 해당하는 단어를 고르시오.

to mention an idea, possible plan, or action for other people to consider

① volunteer ② admit
③ suggest ④ fill
⑤ sneeze

04 다음 중 짝지어진 대화가 어색한 것은?

① A: Let's talk about the corner. What do you think of it?
B: I like it very much.
② A: Shall we start working tomorrow?
B: No problem.
③ A: Bread is very popular.
B: I think *gimbap* is much more popular than bread.
④ A: Let's talk about the town party.
B: Okay. Why don't we play the ukulele?
⑤ A: Let's talk about the volunteer work for our town. Who will guide visitors?
B: How about going to the national park?

[05~06] 다음 대화의 빈칸에 들어갈 말로 알맞은 것을 고르시오.

05

B: How about hanging some pictures?
G: Good. ________________
You're good at painting, Seho.
B: Thank you for saying that. I'll bring one of mine.

① How about making a small library in the corner of the club room?
② Thank you for teaching me how to ride a bike.
③ Who will take pictures of our activities?
④ Why don't you bring one of your pictures?
⑤ How about drawing pictures on the dirty walls?

06

A: ________________ Who will paint the dirty wall?
B: I will. I can do it well.
A: Thank you for volunteering.

① Let's talk about the class field trip.
② Let's talk about the volunteer work for our town.
③ Let's talk about the club festival.
④ Let's talk about the town sports day.
⑤ Let's talk about the pond.

[07~08] 다음 대화를 읽고 물음에 답하시오.

G: Seho, we need something on the wall, too. ①Don't you think so?
B1: You're right. ②Let's talk about it together.
G: I think we need to put the club member list there. (A)It'll be helpful ③for us to learn the new members' names.
B2: That's a good idea. We also need our plan for this school year on the wall.
G: Right! That'll really help us ④remember important school events.
B1: Thank you for ⑤suggest great ideas, everyone. We are a good team.

07 위 대화의 밑줄 친 ①~⑤ 중 어법상 어색한 것은?

① ② ③ ④ ⑤

08 위 대화의 밑줄 친 (A)의 'It'이 가리키는 말을 찾아 영어로 쓰시오. (9 단어로 답할 것)

➡ ____________________

[09~10] 다음 대화를 읽고 물음에 답하시오.

G1: ①Let's talk about how we can make our town better.
B: ②Let me tell you first. There's too much trash at the bus stop.
G2: I agree. ③Why don't we clean the place together?
B: Good. We can put a bench there, too.
G1: Great idea. (A)그것은 어르신들에게 도움이 될 거야.
G2: ④How about putting some flower pots around the bench? They'll make the bus stop more beautiful.
G1: Thank you for suggesting great ideas, everyone. Then, ⑤shall we start tomorrow?
G2, B: No problem.

09 위 대화의 밑줄 (A)의 우리말에 맞게 주어진 단어를 활용하여 영작하시오.

(it / be / help / for / elderly)

➡ ____________________

10 위 대화의 밑줄 친 ①~⑤ 중 의도가 다른 것은?

① ② ③ ④ ⑤

11 다음 중 어법상 올바른 문장을 고르시오.

① Their baby was crying much loudly than usual.
② My health is far more important than my wealth.
③ Your car looks much more cheap than mine.
④ Russia is very bigger than my country.
⑤ We need to spend our allowance much wiser.

12 다음 두 문장을 한 문장으로 바르게 옮긴 것은?

• Mom remembered his name.
• Mom saw him before.

① Mom had remembered his name because she saw him before.
② Mom remembered his name because she saw him before.
③ Mom remembered his name because she had seen him before.
④ Mom remembered his name because she has seen him before.
⑤ Mom had remembered his name because she had seen him before.

13 다음 우리말을 영어로 바르게 옮긴 것은?

> 그녀는 나보다 훨씬 더 부지런하게 일한다.

① She works more diligent than me.
② She works much more diligent than me.
③ She works more diligently than me.
④ She works much diligently than me.
⑤ She works much more diligently than me.

14 〈보기〉에서 내용의 흐름상 적절한 문장을 골라 알맞은 형태로 대화를 완성하시오.

보기
- They draw flowers.
- They clean the pond.
- They set up the board.

A: The class leaders put some posters. Before that, (1)________________. We can know a lot more about school events.
B: Right! They did a good job. Let's thank the class leaders.
A: The Green Club put some fish into the pond. Before that, (2)________________ __________.
B: Right! Thanks to the Green Club, this place looks much better than before.
A: The Art Club drew wings on this wall. Before that, (3)________________ __________.
B: Right! Thanks to the Art Club, this place is much more popular than before.

15 두 문장의 의미가 같도록 주어진 동사를 활용하여 빈칸에 알맞은 말을 쓰시오.

> Jihoo visited the zoo for the first time last month.
> = Jihoo ________ ________ ________ the zoo before last month.

[16~17] 다음 글을 읽고 물음에 답하시오.

> I complained the whole day. My parents were making me work on the neighborhood project, but I had far better things ⓐto do. I didn't understand why we were working on this place. It was just the ugly, old, empty lot across from Johnny's Shop. It was full of wild plants, fast food wraps, old newspapers, broken glass, and every other kind of dirty trash ⓑyou can imagine. As I looked at it that first morning, I thought, "I bet there are snakes in there, too."

16 아래 〈보기〉에서 위 글의 밑줄 친 ⓐto do와 to부정사의 용법이 같은 것의 개수를 고르시오.

보기
① I think it wrong to do such a thing.
② He was the last man to do it.
③ It is time for me to do the dishes.
④ It was impossible for him to do the work.
⑤ She must be mad to do such a thing.

① 1개 ② 2개 ③ 3개 ④ 4개 ⑤ 5개

17 위 글의 밑줄 친 ⓑ를 한 단어의 형용사로 고치시오.

➡ ________________

[18~19] 다음 글을 읽고 물음에 답하시오.

There were twenty of us — all ages and sizes — ready to work that day. ⓐ나는 우리가 이 끔찍하게 더러운 곳을 청소하여 정원으로 바꿀 수 있다고 생각하지 않았다. We were all wondering where to begin. Then Mr. Hernandez said, "The only way to do it is just to start." Then, he divided the lot into four parts with string and assigned five people to each part.

18 위 글의 밑줄 친 ⓐ의 우리말에 맞게 주어진 어휘를 알맞게 배열하시오.

this / mess / a garden / could / awful / clean up / we / and / into / didn't think / turn / that / I / it / .

➡ ______________________________
____

19 According to the passage, which is NOT true?

① Twenty people gathered at the place.
② The ages and sizes of the people were all different.
③ The people didn't know where to begin.
④ Mr. Hernandez divided the lot into five parts with string.
⑤ Mr. Hernandez assigned five people to each part.

[20~21] 다음 글을 읽고 물음에 답하시오.

That first day was the toughest. On the weekends that followed, we made rows, planted flower and vegetable seeds, and watered ⓐthem. After ⓑabout two weeks, I stopped complaining when I found the plants had started popping up! First, the lettuce and then the beans and the tomatoes. They grew so fast. I couldn't believe it! The bean plants grew an inch, and the tomatoes doubled in size in just a few days.

20 위 글의 밑줄 친 ⓐ가 가리키는 것을 본문에서 찾아 쓰시오.

➡ ______________________________

21 위 글의 밑줄 친 ⓑabout과 같은 의미로 쓰인 것을 고르시오.

① What's she so angry about?
② They are about to cross the street.
③ She is about my age.
④ He walked about the room.
⑤ She wore a shawl about her shoulders.

[22~23] 다음 글을 읽고 물음에 답하시오.

Tonight, it suddenly hit me — what a good thing we did! I'm ___ⓐ___ I have been a part of it. I'm in charge of picking flowers for the nursing home on Fourth Street. The vegetables will go to every kitchen in our town. ⓑBut even worse, an ugly and dirty lot that people didn't like has become a pretty garden for everyone.

22 위 글의 빈칸 ⓐ에 들어갈 알맞은 말을 고르시오.

① ashamed
② disappointed
③ nervous
④ proud
⑤ upset

23 위 글의 밑줄 친 ⓑ에서 흐름상 어색한 부분을 찾아 고치시오.

______________ ➡ ______________

Lesson 3

Laugh First and Then Think

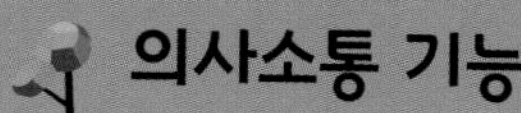

의사소통 기능

- 기대 표현하기
  I'm looking forward to seeing you at the race.
- 기원하기
  I'll keep my fingers crossed!

언어 형식

- enough to
  Is this research project good **enough to** win a Nobel Prize?
- not only ~ but also ...
  Not only the winners' fun studies **but also** the ceremony makes people laugh.

교과서

Words & Expressions

Key Words

- □ **accept** [æksépt] 동 받아들이다
- □ **actually** [ǽktʃuəli] 부 실제로, 사실은
- □ **afraid** [əfréid] 형 두려운
- □ **award** [əwɔ́ːrd] 동 수여하다 명 상
- □ **backward** [bǽkwərd] 부 뒤로 형 뒤의
- □ **bomb** [bɑm] 명 폭탄
- □ **brave** [breiv] 형 용감한
- □ **ceremony** [sérəmòuni] 명 의식, 식
- □ **cheer** [tʃiər] 동 응원하다
- □ **cross** [krɔːs] 동 교차하다 명 십자가
- □ **discovery** [diskʌ́vəri] 명 발견
- □ **eager** [íːgər] 형 열렬한, 간절히 바라는
- □ **economics** 명 경제학
- □ **feeder** [fíːdər] 명 모이통
- □ **field trip** 명 현장 학습, 수학여행
- □ **float** [flout] 동 뜨다
- □ **guess** [ges] 동 추측하다
- □ **honor** [ɑ́nər] 동 존중하다 명 명예
- □ **imaginative** [imǽdʒənətiv] 형 창의적인, 상상력이 풍부한
- □ **interest** [íntərəst] 명 관심
- □ **invent** [invént] 동 발명하다
- □ **invention** [invénʃən] 명 발명, 발명품
- □ **join** [dʒɔin] 동 참가하다
- □ **laughable** [lǽfəbl] 형 웃기는
- □ **live** [laiv] 형 살아 있는
- □ **lovely** [lʌ́vli] 형 귀여운
- □ **magnet** [mǽgnit] 명 자석
- □ **maybe** [méibiː] 부 아마도
- □ **mistake** [mistéik] 명 실수
- □ **navy** [néivi] 명 해군
- □ **nervous** [nə́ːrvəs] 형 긴장한, 초조한
- □ **opening** [óupəniŋ] 명 개막
- □ **peace** [piːs] 명 평화
- □ **perform** [pərfɔ́ːrm] 동 공연하다
- □ **practice** [prǽktis] 동 연습하다 명 연습
- □ **present** [prizént] 동 수여하다
- □ **prize** [praiz] 명 상
- □ **project** [prɑ́dʒekt] 명 과제
- □ **race** [reis] 명 경주, 달리기
- □ **receive** [risíːv] 동 받다
- □ **repeatedly** [ripíːtidli] 부 반복적으로
- □ **research** [risə́ːrtʃ] 명 연구, 조사 동 조사하다
- □ **sailor** [séilər] 명 선원
- □ **solve** [sɑlv] 동 풀다, 해결하다
- □ **store** [stɔːr] 동 저장하다
- □ **study** [stʌ́di] 명 연구
- □ **tradition** [trədíʃən] 명 전통
- □ **trillion** [tríljən] 명 1조
- □ **university** [jùːnəvə́ːrsəti] 명 대학, 대학교
- □ **unusual** [ənjúːʒuəl] 형 드문, 특이한
- □ **useful** [júːsfəl] 형 유용한
- □ **while** [hwail] 접 ~하는 동안, ~인 반면에
- □ **winner** [wínər] 명 수상자
- □ **worth** [wəːrθ] 명 가치 형 ~의 가치가 있는

Key Expressions

- □ **a number of** 얼마간의, 다수의
- □ **be eager to** ~을 (열렬히) 하고 싶어 하다
- □ **be filled with** ~로 가득 차다
- □ **can't wait for** ~를 몹시 기다리다
- □ **closing speech** 폐막 연설
- □ **get bored** 지루해지다
- □ **get out of** ~에서 떠나다, 나가다
- □ **How about ~?** ~하는 것이 어때?
- □ **instead of** ~ 대신에
- □ **keep A from -ing** A가 ~하지 못하게 하다
- □ **keep -ing** 계속 ~하다
- □ **keep one's fingers crossed** 행운을 빌다
- □ **laugh out loud** 큰 소리로 웃다
- □ **less than** ~ 이하, ~보다 적은
- □ **look forward to** ~을 기대하다
- □ **run away** 달아나다
- □ **sense of humor** 유머 감각
- □ **succeed in** ~에 성공하다
- □ **take part in** ~에 참여하다
- □ **talent show** 장기 자랑

Word Power

※ 서로 비슷한 뜻을 가진 어휘

- □ **accept** 받다 : **obtain** 얻다
- □ **cheer** 응원하다 : **encourage** 장려하다
- □ **actually** 실제로 : **really** 사실은
- □ **imaginative** 상상력이 풍부한 : **original** 독창적인

※ 서로 반대의 뜻을 가진 어휘

- □ **accept** 받다 ↔ **reject** 거절하다
- □ **backward** 뒤로 ↔ **forward** 앞으로
- □ **opening** 개막 ↔ **closing** 폐막
- □ **usual** 일상적인 ↔ **unusual** 드문, 특이한
- □ **float** 뜨다 ↔ **sink** 가라앉다
- □ **nervous** 불안한 ↔ **calm** 차분한
- □ **present** 수여하다 ↔ **receive** 받다
- □ **useful** 유용한 ↔ **useless** 쓸모없는

※ 형용사 – 명사

- □ **dark** 어두운 – **darkness** 어두움
- □ **happy** 행복한 – **happiness** 행복
- □ **sad** 슬픈 – **sadness** 슬픔
- □ **eager** 열렬한 – **eagerness** 열망
- □ **kind** 친절한 – **kindness** 친절
- □ **soft** 부드러운 – **softness** 부드러움

English Dictionary

□ **accept** 받아들이다
→ to take something offered 제안된 어떤 것을 취하다

□ **award** 수여하다
→ to give a prize 상을 주다

□ **backward** 뒤의
→ looking or facing in the direction that is behind you
뒤쪽 방향을 보거나 향하고 있는

□ **discovery** 발견
→ the act of finding something for the first time
처음으로 어떤 것을 발견하는 행위

□ **eager** 열렬한, 간절히 바라는
→ wanting very much to do or have something
어떤 것을 하거나 갖기를 매우 원하는

□ **float** 뜨다, 띄우다
→ to be on a liquid and not sink
액체의 위에 있고 가라앉지 않다

□ **honor** (명) 명예
→ something you are proud to do
하기를 자랑스러워하는 어떤 것
(동) 존경하다
→ to show great respect for someone, esp. in public
특히 공공연히 누군가에 대한 대단한 존경을 보여주다

□ **imaginative** 창의적인, 상상력이 풍부한
→ having or showing new and exciting ideas
새롭고 흥미로운 생각을 갖거나 보여주는

□ **invent** 발명하다
→ to make, design, or think of a new type of thing
새로운 것을 만들거나 디자인하거나 생각해 내다

□ **live** 살아 있는
→ not dead 죽지 않은

□ **magnet** 자석
→ a piece of metal that attracts other iron
다른 철을 끌어당기는 금속 조각

□ **navy** 해군
→ a military force made up of boats and ships
배와 함선으로 이루어진 군대

□ **research** 연구, 조사
→ the study of something to discover new facts
새로운 사실들을 발견하기 위한 어떤 것의 연구

□ **sailor** 선원
→ someone who works on a ship 배에서 일하는 사람

□ **trillion** 1조
→ the number 1,000,000,000,000
1,000,000,000,000이라는 수

□ **university** 대학
→ an educational institution at the highest level, where you study for a degree
학위를 받기 위해서 공부하는 가장 높은 수준의 교육 기관

Words & Expressions **시험대비 실력평가** Step2

서답형

01 다음 글의 빈칸에 <영어 설명>에 알맞은 단어를 쓰시오.

> Finding the new land was an amazing ________.
> <영어 설명> the act of finding something for the first time

중요

02 다음 빈칸에 공통으로 들어갈 말로 가장 적절한 것은?

> • The friendship between the cat and the dog is quite ________.
> • Some people keep ________ pets such as pigs, iguanas, and even snakes.

① ugly ② unusual
③ popular ④ useful
⑤ wonderful

[03~04] 다음 영어 설명에 해당하는 단어를 고르시오.

03

> an educational institution at the highest level, where you study for a degree

① navy ② honor
③ bomb ④ university
⑤ research

04

> someone who works on a boat or ship

① sail ② peace
③ nurse ④ navy
⑤ sailor

서답형

05 다음 우리말에 맞게 주어진 단어를 이용하여 쓰시오.

> 아이들은 어서 수업을 마치고 놀기 시작하고 싶어 했다. (eager / finish)

➡ The children ________________________ class and start playing.

06 다음 빈칸에 공통으로 들어갈 말로 알맞은 것은?

> (A) On July 16, the Korean ________ contest was held in California, U.S.
> (B) The boy gave a ________ in front of the class.

① research ② science
③ speech ④ trillion
⑤ ceremony

서답형

07 다음 짝지어진 단어의 관계가 같도록 알맞은 말을 쓰시오.

> sad – sadness : dark – ________

중요

08 다음 빈칸에 들어갈 말이 바르게 짝지어진 것은?

> (A) The gate ________ people from entering the park.
> (B) The paintings of Leonardo da Vinci are ________ a lot of money.

① keeps – worth
② keeps – eager
③ receives – worth
④ gets – unusual
⑤ gets – eager

중요
01 〈보기〉에서 알맞은 단어를 선택하여 문장의 빈칸을 완성하시오. (필요하면 변형하여 쓰시오.)

보기
receive repeated bore number

(1) Bring games on an airplane not to get ________.
(2) The kids sang their favorite song ________.
(3) ________ of students failed the test.
(4) He ________ a special card from his grandfather last Christmas.

02 대화의 빈칸에 〈영영 풀이〉에 해당하는 단어를 쓰시오.

B: Minji, you're a happy girl. I think you'll get the Ms. Cheerful ________. I'll keep my fingers crossed!
G: Oh, thank you, Jiho.

<영영 풀이> a prize or other marks of recognition given in honor of an achievement

➡ ________________

고난이도
03 영영 풀이에 해당하는 단어를 〈보기〉에서 찾아 첫 번째 빈칸에 쓰고, 두 번째 빈칸에는 우리말 뜻을 쓰시오.

보기
ceremony magnet invent navy

(1) ________: a military force made up of boats and ships: ________
(2) ________: a piece of metal that attracts other iron: ________
(3) ________: to make, design, or think of a new type of thing: ________
(4) ________: a formal public event with special traditions: ________

중요
04 다음 우리말에 맞게 주어진 글의 빈칸에 알맞은 단어를 쓰시오.

이것은 '커피 애호가를 위한 우산'입니다. 당신은 그것을 우산뿐만 아니라 컵 걸이로도 사용할 수 있습니다. 이 발명품은 당신의 삶을 훨씬 더 편안하게 할 정도로 충분히 유용합니다.

➡ This is the Umbrella for Coffee Lovers. You can use it ____________ as an umbrella ____________ as a cup holder. This ____________ is ____________ to make your life much easier.

중요
05 다음 글의 빈칸에 주어진 철자로 시작하는 알맞은 단어를 쓰시오.

(1) The workers at this company didn't a________ any gifts from customers.
(2) I think I have a good sense of h________.
(3) I will study e________ at university to become a banker.
(4) The large box is f________ with warm clothes for the poor.
(5) The writer of the children's story is very i________.

교과서

Conversation

1 기대 표현하기

• I'm looking forward to seeing you at the race. 나는 경기에서 너를 보기를 기대해.

■ 앞으로 일어날 일이나 하고 싶은 일에 대한 기대를 표현할 때 '~을 기대한다'의 의미로 'I'm looking forward to ~.'나 'I look forward to ~.'의 표현을 사용한다. '빨리 ~하고 싶다, ~을 너무 하고 싶다.'의 뜻으로 'I can't wait for ~.', 'I am dying to ~.', 'I'm expecting to ~.'라고 하기도 한다.

■ '~을 기대하다'라는 의미의 'look forward to'에서 to가 전치사이기 때문에 그 뒤에 명사나 동명사가 온다. 'I can't wait for ~.'는 원하던 일이 다가오고 있어 빨리하고 싶은 기대감을 나타내는 표현이며, 직역의 의미는 '~하는 것을 기다릴 수 없다.'이고, 보통 '당장 ~하고 싶다, 빨리 ~했으면 좋겠다.'로 해석한다. to 뒤에는 동사원형의 형태가 오는데, 뒤에 명사구가 올 경우에는 'I can't wait for+명사[명사구]'의 형태로 쓰기도 한다.

■ '기대하다'라는 의미의 expect를 써서 'I'm expecting to 동사원형 ~.'이라고 하거나 '열망하다'라는 의미의 동사 long을 써서 'I'm longing to+동사원형', 'I'm longing for+명사'라고 하거나, 형용사 eager(열망하는)를 써서 'I'm eager to+동사원형', 'I'm eager for+명사'의 형태로 나타내기도 한다.

기대 표현하기

- I'm looking forward to+명사(구) (~을 기대한다.)
- I can't wait for+명사/to+동사원형 (빨리 ~했으면 좋겠다.)
- I am expecting to+동사원형 (~하기를 기대한다.)
- I am longing for+명사/to+동사원형 (~하기를 열망한다.)
- I am eager for+명사/to+동사원형 (~하기를 기대한다.)

핵심 Check

1. 다음 우리말과 일치하도록 주어진 단어를 포함하여 적절한 형태로 빈칸에 알맞은 말을 쓰시오.

A: We're going on a field trip next Tuesday. What are you going to do in the talent show, Jimin?

B: I'm going to talk like our teachers do in class and tell some jokes.

A: Wow! ____________________. (나는 정말로 그것이 기대가 돼.) (be, really, forward, it)

B: Will everyone like my show? I'm not sure.

➡ ______________________________

2 기원하기

- I'll keep my fingers crossed. 행운을 빌어.

- 상대가 하는 일이 잘 되기를 기원하면서 '행운을 빌어!'라고 할 때 'I'll keep my finger's crossed (for you)!'라고 한다. 'keep one's fingers crossed'란 집게손가락 위에 가운데 손가락을 교차시켜서 소원이 이루어지도록(= hope for something) 행운을 비는 동작을 묘사한 말로 '기도하다, 좋은 결과나 행운을 빌어준다'라는 의미이다.
- 흔히 상대에게 행운을 비는 말은 'Good luck!'이고, 'Have a nice ~!'도 상대에게 행운을 기원하는 말이다. 기원이나 기대를 나타내는 wish, expect, hope, pray를 사용하여 행운을 기원하기도 한다. 'Break a leg!(행운을 빌어!)'라는 표현은 주로 공연이나 행사, 경기 등을 앞두고 있는 사람에게 '행운을 빌어!' 라고 격려할 때 자주 쓰인다.
- 긴장한 상대에게 긴장을 풀어주는 표현 'Don't worry.', 'Don't be worried.', 'Just relax.', 'Take it easy.', 'Loosen up.', 'Don't be too nervous.'(긴장 풀어. 너무 긴장하지 마.)에 이어서 행운을 빌어주는 표현을 쓰는 경우가 많다. '기원하다'라는 의미의 'wish'는 'wish+명사, wish+주어+동사'의 형태이다.

기대 표현하기

- I'll keep my fingers crossed (for you)! (행운을 빌게!)
- Let's keep our fingers crossed for you. (행운을 빌어.)
- Good luck! / Good luck to you! (행운을 빌어!)
- I wish you luck! (행운이 함께 하기를 빌어!)
- Break a leg! (행운을 빌어!)
- I wish/hope/pray ~. (나는 ~하길 바란다.)
- I wish you all the best. (행운이 있기를 빌어.)
- I hope everything goes well with you. / Everything will be okay. (다 잘 될 거야.)

핵심 Check

2. 다음 주어진 말에 이어지는 대화의 순서를 바르게 배열하시오.

W: Soyun, are you going to take part in any races on the sports day?
(A) Just do your best. I'll keep my fingers crossed!
(B) Wow, I'm looking forward to seeing you at the race.
(C) But, Mom, I'm not sure I'll win the race.
(D) Sure. I'm going to run a 100 meter race at the end of the day.

➡ ______________________

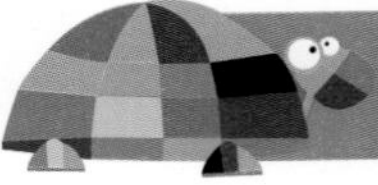

Conversation 교과서 대화문 익히기

Step Up – Real-life Scene

Miso: We're going on a field trip next Tuesday. ❶What are you going to do in the talent show, Jimin?
Jimin: I'm going to talk like our teachers ❷do in class and tell some jokes.
Miso: Wow! I'm really ❸looking forward to it.
Jimin: Will everyone like my show? I'm not sure.
Miso: Don't worry. I'm sure you'll do great. I'll ❹keep my fingers crossed!
Jimin: Thank you, Miso. ❺Let me show you one part of my act. Guess who? "Goood Jooob!"
Miso: Ha-ha, you sound like our English teacher.
Jimin: Do I? I'm going to show you more at the show.
Miso: Great! You always ❻make us laugh out loud.

미소: 다음 주 화요일에 수학여행을 갈 거야. 지민아, 너는 장기 자랑에서 뭘 할 거니?
지민: 나는 수업 시간에 선생님들이 말하는 것을 흉내 내고 농담도 할 거야.
미소: 와! 정말 기대되는데.
지민: 모든 사람이 나의 쇼를 좋아할까? 잘 모르겠어.
미소: 걱정하지 마. 나는 네가 잘 할 거라고 확신해. 행운을 빌어 줄게!
지민: 고마워, 미소야. 내가 나의 연기의 한 부분을 보여 줄게. 누군지 맞힐 수 있겠니? "잘~ 했어~요!"
미소: 하하. 우리 영어 선생님처럼 들리는데.
지민: 그래? 장기 자랑에서 더 많이 보여 줄게.
미소: 멋지다! 너는 항상 우리를 웃게 만들어.

❶ 미래의 계획을 물을 때 사용하는 표현으로 "무엇을 할 예정이니?"의 의미이다.
❷ 앞 문장의 'talk'을 대신하는 대동사이다.
❸ 앞으로 일어날 일이나 하고 싶은 일에 대한 기대를 표현하는 말로, 'look forward to+명사/동명사' 형태이다.
❹ 행운을 빌어줄 때 사용하는 표현으로 '동사(keep)+목적어(my fingers)+목적보어(crossed: 과거분사)'의 5형식 구문이다.
❺ 'let+목적어+동사원형'은 '…가 ~하게 하다'라는 의미이다.
❻ 'make(사역동사)+목적어+목적보어(동사원형)' 구문으로 '…가 ~하게 하다'라는 의미이다.

Check(√) True or False

(1) Miso is looking forward to Jimin's show. T ☐ F ☐

(2) Miso is not sure whether Jimin will do great. T ☐ F ☐

Start Off – Listen & Talk A 1

G: Mom, ❶I can't wait for the sports day.
W: What are you going to do on that day, Minji?
G: I'm going to play basketball for my class. ❷We've practiced hard for a few weeks.
W: Oh, I'm looking forward to your game.
G: Actually, ❸I'm a little worried. I'm afraid I'll make a mistake.
W: Don't worry. You'll do a good job. I'll keep my fingers crossed!

G: 엄마, 체육 대회가 정말 기다려져요.
W: 민지야, 너는 그날 무엇을 할 거니?
G: 저는 학급을 대표해서 농구를 할 거예요. 우리는 몇 주간 열심히 연습해 왔어요.
W: 오, 너의 경기가 기대되는구나.
G: 사실은, 전 조금 걱정이 돼요. 제가 실수를 할까봐 겁나요.
W: 걱정하지 마. 넌 잘할 거야. 행운을 빌어 줄게!

❶ '~이 정말 기다려져'의 뜻으로 기대를 표현할 때 사용한다.
❷ 현재완료(have practiced)는 기간을 나타내는 for a few weeks와 함께 사용되어 과거부터 현재까지의 계속적인 일을 나타낸다.
❸ '걱정하다'라는 표현으로 'be worried'를 사용한다. a little은 '약간, 조금'의 의미로 과거분사 worried를 수식한다.

Check(√) True or False

(3) Minji is looking forward to the sports day. T ☐ F ☐

(4) Minji's mother is afraid Minji will make a mistake. T ☐ F ☐

Start Off – Listen & Talk B

G: Mom, ❶are you coming to the sports day?
W: Sure. I'm going to play the game Kick a Shoe. This will be the first time ❷for me to try it.
G: Don't worry. I'm sure you'll ❸do great. I'll keep my fingers crossed for you!
W: Thank you. I'm also going to perform a funny dance with some other mothers.
G: ❹That sounds fun. I'm looking forward to watching you on the stage.

G: 엄마, 체육 대회에 오실 거예요?
W: 물론이지. 나는 'Kick a Shoe' 게임에 참가할 거야. 이번에 처음 해 보는 거야.
G: 걱정하지 마세요. 엄마는 잘 하실 거예요. 행운을 빌어 드릴게요!
W: 고맙다. 나는 다른 엄마들과 코믹 댄스도 할 거야.
G: 재밌겠네요. 무대에 선 엄마 모습을 보는 것이 기대돼요.

❶ 'are coming(현재진행형)'은 미래 시점과 사용이 될 때 미래의 일을 나타낼 수 있다.
❷ 'for me(for+목적격)'는 to부정사의 의미상의 주어로 '내가'로 해석한다. to부정사 'to try it'은 'the first time'을 수식하는 형용사 용법이다. it = the game Kick a Shoe
❸ do great: 잘하다
❹ 'sound+형용사'로 '~처럼 들리다'라는 뜻이다.

Check(√) True or False

(5) The girl's mom have played the game Kick a Shoe before. T ☐ F ☐
(6) The girl is looking forward to watching her mom on the stage. T ☐ F ☐

Fun Time

A: I'm going to travel to Jejudo next week.
B: Wow! That sounds great.
A: Yeah, I'm really looking forward to it.

A: I'm going to ❶enter the dance contest next week, but ❷I'm worried about it.
B: Don't worry. You'll do great. I'll keep my fingers crossed.
A: Thank you.

A: 나는 다음 주에 제주도를 여행할 거야.
B: 와! 멋지다.
A: 응, 난 그것이 정말 기대돼.

A: 난 다음 주에 춤 대회에 나갈 건데, 걱정이 된다.
B: 걱정하지 마. 넌 잘할 거야. 행운을 빌어 줄게.
A: 고마워.

❶ enter는 타동사이므로 전치사 없이 목적어를 취한다.
❷ 'be worried about ~'은 '~에 관해 걱정하다'라는 뜻이다.

Check(√) True or False

(7) A will travel to Jejudo next week. T ☐ F ☐
(8) B hopes A will do great at the dance contest next week. T ☐ F ☐

Get Ready 2

(1) G: You solved ❶a lot of problems in class. I'm sure you'll win the Class Brain award.
B: Do you really think so?
G: Of course. I'll keep my fingers crossed for you, Sangjun!

(2) B: The winner of the Oh So Sweet award will get some candies.
G: Oh, I ❷want to get the prize.
B: ❸I'm sure you'll get the prize this time. Good luck, Jiu!

(3) B: ❹I'm looking forward to the Best Joker award this time.
G: Ha-ha. You always ❺make us laugh out loud. So you'll get the prize, Yunki. Good luck.
B: Thank you.

(4) B: Minji, you're a happy girl. I think you'll get the Ms. Cheerful award. I'll keep my fingers crossed!
G: Oh, thank you, Jiho.

❶ 여기서 'a lot of'는 'many'의 의미로 'lots of, plenty of'로 바꾸어 쓸 수 있다.
❷ 'want'는 목적어로 'to-V'를 취한다.
❸ '~을 확신하다'라는 표현으로 'I'm sure (that)+주어+동사 ~'를 사용한다.
❹ 앞으로 일어날 일에 대한 기대를 표현하는 말로 'to'는 전치사로 뒤에 명사나 동명사가 온다.
❺ 'make(사역동사)+목적어+목적보어(동사원형)' 구문으로 '…가 ~하게 하다'라는 의미이다.

Start Off – Listen & Talk A 2

W: Soyun, ❶are you going to take part in any races on the sports day?
G: Sure. ❷I'm going to run a 100 meter race at the end of the day.
W: Wow, ❸I'm looking forward to seeing you at the race.
G: But, Mom, I'm not sure I'll win the race.
W: Just do your best. I'll keep my fingers crossed!

❶ 'take part in ~'은 '~에 참가하다'라는 의미이고, 의문문에서는 '어떤'의 의미로 'any'를 사용한다.
❷ 'be going to+동사원형'은 '~할 예정이다'라는 미래의 일을 나타낼 때 사용한다.
❸ 'look forward to+동명사(seeing)'는 '~을 기대하다'라는 뜻이다.

Start Off – Speak Up

A: I'm looking forward to the model airplane contest tomorrow. Are you ready?
B: Well, ❶I think so, but I'm nervous.
A: You will do well. ❷I'll keep my fingers crossed!

❶ I think so = I think (that) I'm ready
❷ 상대가 하는 일이 잘 되기를 기원하면서 "행운을 빌어!"라고 할 때 사용하는 표현이다.

Express Yourself A

1. G: Can you tell me something about your invention?
B: They are ❶a pair of special shoes. You can also clean the floor with them.
G: Great! I'm sure you'll win a prize. I'll keep my fingers crossed!

2. B: This ❷looks interesting. Is this a cutting board or a bird feeder?
G: It is ❸not only a cutting board but also a bird feeder. You can do two things ❹at the same time.
B: That's a great idea!
G: Do you really think so?
B: Yes. ❺I'm really looking forward to using it.

❶ '신발 한 켤레'를 나타낼 때는 'a pair of shoes'를 쓴다.
❷ 'look+형용사'로 '~처럼 보이다'라는 의미이다.
❸ 'not only A but also B'는 'A뿐만 아니라 B도'의 의미이다.
❹ at the same time: 동시에
❺ 'look forward to+동명사(using)'는 '~을 기대하다'라는 뜻이다.

Conversation 교과서 확인학습

• 다음 우리말과 일치하도록 빈칸에 알맞은 말을 쓰시오.

Get Ready 2

(1) G: You ________ ________ ________ ________ problems in class. ________ ________ you'll win the Class Brain ________.
B: Do you really ________ ________?
G: Of course. I'll ________ my fingers ________ for you, Sangjun!

(2) B: The ________ of the Oh So Sweet ________ will get some candies.
G: Oh, I want ________ ________ the ________.
B: ________ ________ you'll get the prize this time. ________ ________, Jiu!

(3) B: I'm ________ ________ ________ the Best Joker award this time.
G: Ha-ha. You always ________ us ________ out loud. So you'll ________ ________ ________, Yunki. Good luck.
B: Thank you.

(4) B: Minji, you're a happy girl. I think you'll get the Ms. Cheerful award. I'll ________ ________ ________ ________!
G: Oh, thank you, Jiho.

해석

(1) G: 너는 수업 중 많은 문제를 해결했잖아. 나는 네가 'Class Brain'상을 탈 거라고 확신해.
B: 정말 그렇게 생각하니?
G: 물론이야. 행운을 빌게, 상준아!
(2) B: 'Oh So Sweet'상 수상자는 사탕을 받을 거야.
G: 오, 그 상을 받고 싶다.
B: 네가 이번에는 그 상을 탈 거라고 확신해. 행운을 빌어, 지우야!
(3) B: 난 이번에 'Best Joker'상을 받기를 기대해.
G: 하하. 너는 항상 우리를 웃게 하잖아. 그러니 네가 그 상을 탈 거야, 윤기야. 행운을 빌어.
B: 고마워.
(4) B: 민지야, 너는 쾌활한 아이야. 나는 네가 'Ms. Cheerful'상을 탈 거라고 생각해. 행운을 빌게!
G: 오, 고마워, 지호야.

Start Off – Listen & Talk A

1. G: Mom, I ________ ________ ________ the sports day.
W: ________ are you ________ ________ ________ on that day, Minji?
G: I'm going to play basketball for my class. We've ________ hard ________ a few weeks.
W: Oh, I'm ________ ________ ________ your game.
G: ________, I'm ________ ________ ________. I'm ________ I'll ________ a ________.
W: ________ ________. You'll ________ a good ________. I'll keep ________ ________ ________!

2. W: Soyun, are you going to ________ ________ ________ any races on the sports day?
G: Sure. I'________ ________ ________ run a 100 meter race at the ________ of the day.
W: Wow, I'm looking ________ to ________ you at the race.
G: But, Mom, I'm not ________ I'll ________ the race.
W: Just ________ ________ ________. I'll ________ ________ ________ ________!

1. G: 엄마, 체육 대회가 정말 기다려져요.
W: 민지야, 너는 그날 무엇을 할 거니?
G: 저는 학급을 대표해서 농구를 할 거예요. 우리는 몇 주간 열심히 연습해 왔어요.
W: 오, 너의 경기가 기대되는구나.
G: 사실은, 전 조금 걱정이 돼요. 제가 실수를 할까봐 겁나요.
W: 걱정하지 마. 넌 잘할 거야. 행운을 빌어줄게!

2. W: 소윤아, 넌 체육 대회에서 경주에 참가하니?
G: 물론이죠. 전 그날 마지막에 있는 100 미터 달리기를 뛸 거예요.
W: 와, 네가 경주에서 달리는 모습을 보는 것이 기대되는구나.
G: 하지만 엄마, 전 경주에서 이길지 잘 모르겠어요.
W: 그냥 최선을 다하렴. 행운을 빌어 줄게!

Start Off – Listen & Talk B

G: Mom, ________ ________ ________ to the sports day?

W: Sure. I'm ________ to play the game Kick a Shoe. This will be the first time ________ ________ ________ ________ it.

G: Don't worry. I'm ________ you'll ________ ________. I'll ________ my fingers ________ for you!

W: Thank you. I'm also going to ________ a funny dance with some ________ mothers.

G: That ________ ________. I'm ________ ________ to ________ you on the ________.

해석

G: 엄마, 체육 대회에 오실 거예요?
W: 물론이지. 나는 'Kick a Shoe' 게임에 참가할 거야. 이번에 처음 해 보는 거야.
G: 걱정하지 마세요. 엄마는 잘하실 거예요. 행운을 빌어 드릴게요!
W: 고맙다. 나는 다른 엄마들과 코믹 댄스도 할 거야.
G: 재밌겠네요. 무대에 선 엄마 모습을 보는 것이 기대돼요.

Start Off – Speak Up

A: I'm ________ ________ ________ the ________ airplane contest tomorrow. Are you ________?

B: Well, I think ________, but I'm ________.

A: You will ________ ________. I'll ________ my fingers ________!

B: 나는 내일 모형 비행기 대회가 기대돼. 너는 준비됐니?
G: 음, 그런 것 같아, 하지만 긴장돼.
B: 너는 잘할 거야. 내가 행운을 빌어 줄게!

Step Up – Real-life Scene

Miso: We're going on a ________ ________ next Tuesday. What are you going to do in the ________ ________, Jimin?

Jimin: I'm going to talk ________ our teachers ________ in class and tell some ________.

Miso: Wow! I'm really ________ ________ ________ ________.

Jimin: Will everyone like my ________? I'm not ________.

Miso: Don't ________. I'm sure you'll ________ ________. I'll ________ ________ ________ ________!

Jimin: Thank you, Miso. ________ me ________ you one part of my act. ________ who? "Goood Jooob!"

Miso: Ha-ha, you ________ ________ our English teacher.

Jimin: Do I? I'm going to ________ you more at the show.

Miso: Great! You always ________ us ________ ________ ________.

미소: 다음 주 화요일에 수학여행을 갈 거야. 지민아, 너는 장기 자랑에서 뭘 할 거니?
지민: 나는 수업 시간에 선생님들이 말하는 것을 흉내 내고 농담도 할 거야.
미소: 와! 정말 기대되는데.
지민: 모든 사람이 나의 쇼를 좋아할까? 잘 모르겠어.
미소: 걱정하지 마. 나는 네가 잘할 거라고 확신해. 행운을 빌어 줄게!
지민: 고마워, 미소야. 내가 나의 연기의 한 부분을 보여 줄게. 누군지 맞힐 수 있겠니? "잘~ 했어~요!"
미소: 하하. 우리 영어 선생님처럼 들리는데.
지민: 그래? 장기 자랑에서 더 많이 보여 줄게.
미소: 멋지다! 너는 항상 우리를 웃게 만들어.

Fun Time

A: I'________ ________ ________ travel to Jejudo next week.

B: Wow! That ________ ________.

A: Yeah, I'________ ________ ________ ________ ________ it.

A: I'm going to ________ the dance contest next week, but I'________ ________ ________ it.

B: Don't worry. You'll do great. I'll ________ ________ ________ ________.

A: Thank you.

해석

A: 나는 다음 주에 제주도를 여행할 거야.
B: 와! 멋지다.
A: 응, 난 그것이 정말 기대돼.

A: 난 다음 주에 춤 대회에 나갈 건데, 걱정이 된다.
B: 걱정하지 마. 넌 잘할 거야. 행운을 빌어 줄게.
A: 고마워.

Express Yourself A

1. G: ________ ________ ________ ________ something about your ________?

   B: They are ________ ________ ________ ________ shoes. You can also ________ the ________ with them.

   G: Great! I'm sure you'll ________ ________ ________. I'll ________ my fingers crossed!

2. B: This looks ________. Is this a ________ ________ or a bird ________?

   G: It is ________ ________ a cutting ________ ________ ________ a bird ________. You can do two things ________ ________ ________ ________.

   B: That's a great ________!

   G: Do you really think so?

   B: Yes. I'm really ________ ________ to ________ it.

1. G: 너의 발명품에 관해 이야기를 좀 해 줄래?
   B: 그것은 특별한 신발이야. 너는 그것으로 바닥을 청소할 수도 있어.
   G: 멋지다! 네가 상을 탈 거라고 확신해. 행운을 빌게!

2. B: 이것은 흥미로워 보여. 도마니, 아니면 새 모이통이니?
   G: 그것은 도마일 뿐만 아니라 새 모이통이기도 해. 너는 동시에 두 가지를 할 수 있어.
   B: 멋진 아이디어야!
   G: 정말 그렇게 생각하니?
   B: 응. 난 그것을 사용해 보는 게 정말 기대가 되는 걸.

01 다음 우리말에 맞도록 주어진 단어를 활용하여 4단어로 쓰시오.

행운을 빌어. (keep, fingers, cross)

➡ I'll ______________________.

02 다음 대화의 빈칸에 들어갈 말로 알맞은 것은?

> B: I'm looking forward to the Best Joker award this time.
> G: Ha-ha. ______________ So you'll get the prize, Yunki. Good luck.
> B: Thank you.

① We've practiced hard for a few weeks.
② I'm looking forward to seeing your photos.
③ You always make us laugh out loud.
④ That sounds great.
⑤ Joker is my favorite movie of all.

03 다음 대화의 빈칸에 들어갈 말로 적절한 것은?

> B: The winner of the Oh So Sweet award will get some candies.
> G: Oh, I want to get the prize.
> B: ______________ Good luck, Jiu!

① Eating too many candies isn't good for your teeth.
② I'm sure you'll like the candies.
③ Why don't you bring some sweets to your classmates?
④ I don't think so.
⑤ I'm sure you'll get the prize this time.

04 다음 대화의 빈칸에 들어갈 말로 알맞은 것은?

> A: I'm looking forward to the model airplane contest tomorrow. Are you ready?
> B: Well, I think so, but I'm _________.
> A: You will do well.

① proud ② nervous ③ funny
④ cheerful ⑤ useful

[01~02] 다음 대화를 읽고 물음에 답하시오.

W: Soyun, are you going to take part in any races on the sports day?
G: Sure. I'm going to run a 100 meter race at the end of the day.
W: Wow, I'm looking forward to ___(A)___ (see) you at the race.
G: But, Mom, I'm not sure I'll win the race.
W: Just do your best. I'll keep my fingers ___(B)___ (cross)!

서답형

01 위 대화의 빈칸 (A)와 (B)에 주어진 단어를 알맞은 형태로 고치시오.

➡ (A) ____________ (B) ____________

중요

02 위 대화의 내용과 일치하지 않는 것은?

① They are talking about the sports day.
② Soyun is going to run a 100 meter race.
③ Soyun's mom wants to run the race.
④ Soyun is not sure she'll win the race.
⑤ Soyun's mom hopes that Soyun will do her best.

[03~05] 다음 대화를 읽고 물음에 답하시오.

G: Mom, are you coming to the sports day?
W: Sure. I'm going ⓐto play the game Kick a Shoe. This will be the first time ⓑfor me to try it.
G: Don't worry. I'm sure you'll ⓒdo great. (A) I'll keep my fingers crossed for you!
W: Thank you. I'm also going to perform a funny dance with some ⓓother mothers.
G: That sounds fun. I'm looking forward ⓔto watch you on the stage.

중요

03 위 대화의 밑줄 친 ⓐ~ⓔ 중 어법상 어색한 것은?

① ⓐ ② ⓑ ③ ⓒ ④ ⓓ ⑤ ⓔ

04 위 대화의 밑줄 친 (A)와 바꾸어 사용할 수 없는 표현은?

① Let's keep our fingers crossed for you.
② Good luck to you!
③ I wish you all the best.
④ Don't be worried. Just relax.
⑤ Break a leg!

서답형

05 위 대화를 읽고 다음 질문에 영어로 답하시오.

Q: What is Mom going to take part in?
➡ She is going to take part in ____________
____
______________________________.

[06~07] 다음 대화를 읽고 물음에 답하시오.

B: This looks interesting. Is this a cutting board or a bird feeder?
G: ___________(A)___________ You can do two things at the same time.
B: That's a great idea!
G: Do you really think so?
B: Yes. (B)난 그것을 사용해 보는 게 정말 기대가 되는 걸.

06 위 대화의 빈칸 (A)에 들어갈 말로 알맞은 것은?

① It is either a cutting board or a bird feeder.
② You can use it only as a bird feeder.
③ It is neither a cutting board nor a bird feeder.
④ It is only a cutting board.
⑤ It is not only a cutting board but also a bird feeder.

서답형

07 위 대화의 밑줄 친 (B)의 우리말에 맞게 주어진 단어를 활용하여 영어로 쓰시오.

be, really, forward, use, it

➡ ______________________

[08~09] 다음 대화를 읽고 물음에 답하시오.

Miso: We're going on a field trip next Tuesday. What are you going to do in the talent show, Jimin? (①)

Jimin: I'm going to talk like our teachers do in class and tell some jokes. (②)

Miso: Wow! I'm really looking forward to it.

Jimin: Will everyone like my show? I'm not sure.

Miso: Don't worry. (③) I'm sure you'll do great. I'll keep my fingers crossed!

Jimin: Thank you, Miso. (④) Guess who? "Goood Jooob!" (⑤)

Miso: Ha-ha, you sound like our English teacher.

Jimin: Do I? I'm going to show you more at the show.

Miso: Great! You always make us laugh out loud.

08 위 대화의 (①)~(⑤) 중 주어진 문장이 들어갈 위치로 알맞은 것은?

Let me show you one part of my act.

① ② ③ ④ ⑤

09 위 대화를 읽고 답할 수 없는 질문은?

① What are Jimin and Miso talking about?
② When is the field trip?
③ What is Jimin going to do in the talent show?
④ Why is Miso looking forward to Jimin's show?
⑤ How many times has Jimin ever taken part in a talent show?

[10~11] 다음 대화를 읽고 물음에 답하시오.

G: Mom, ____________(A)____________

W: What are you going to do on that day, Minji?

G: I'm going to play basketball for my class. We've practiced hard for a few weeks.

W: Oh, (B)너의 경기가 기대되는구나.

G: Actually, I'm a little worried. I'm afraid I'll make a mistake.

W: Don't worry. You'll do a good job. I'll keep my fingers crossed!

중요

10 위 대화의 빈칸 (A)에 들어갈 말로 알맞은 것은?

① are you going to take part in any races on the sports day?
② are you coming on the sports day?
③ I think I'll get the Ms. Cheerful award.
④ I can't wait for the sports day.
⑤ are you ready?

서답형

11 위 대화의 밑줄 친 (B)의 우리말에 맞게 주어진 단어를 활용하여 영작하시오.

(be / look / to / your game)

➡ ______________________

[01~02] 다음 대화를 읽고 물음에 답하시오.

Miso: We're going on a field trip next Tuesday. What are you going to do in the talent show, Jimin?
Jimin: I'm going to talk like our teachers do in class and tell some jokes.
Miso: Wow! ______(A)______
Jimin: Will everyone like my show? I'm not sure.
Miso: Don't worry. I'm sure you'll do great. ______(B)______
Jimin: Thank you, Miso. Let me show you one part of my act. Guess who? "Goood Jooob!"
Miso: Ha-ha, you sound like our English teacher.
Jimin: Do I? I'm going to show you more at the show.
Miso: Great! You always make us laugh out loud.

중요

01 위 대화의 빈칸 (A)와 (B)에 들어갈 말을 〈조건〉에 맞게 영어로 쓰시오.

조건

(A) • 기대를 표현하는 말을 쓸 것.
• 현재진행형과 대명사 'it'을 사용할 것.
(B) • 기원을 표현하는 말을 쓸 것.
• 'keep'과 'cross'를 활용할 것.

➡ (A) ________________________
(B) ________________________

02 위 대화를 읽고 다음 물음에 영어로 답하시오.

Who did Jimin talk like in the dialog?

➡ ________________________

03 다음 대화의 밑줄 친 부분과 같은 의미가 되도록 주어진 단어를 써서 문장을 다시 쓰시오.

B: This looks interesting. Is this a cutting board or a bird feeder?
G: It is a bird feeder as well as a cutting board.(only, also) You can do two things at the same time.
B: That's a great idea!
G: Do you really think so?
B: Yes. I'm really looking forward to using it.

➡ ________________________

[04~05] 다음 대화를 읽고 물음에 답하시오.

G: Mom, (a)체육 대회가 정말 기다려져요.
W: What are you going to do on that day, Minji?
G: I'm going to play basketball for my class. We've practiced hard for a few weeks.
W: Oh, I'm looking forward to your game.
G: Actually, I'm a little worried. ______(A)______
W: Don't worry. You'll do a good job.

중요

04 위 대화의 흐름상 빈칸 (A)에 들어갈 말을 주어진 단어를 이용하여 영작하시오.

(afraid, a mistake)

➡ ________________________

05 위 대화의 밑줄 친 (a)의 우리말을 주어진 〈조건〉을 이용하여 영작하시오.

조건

• 'wait'을 이용할 것.
• the sports day

➡ ________________________

교과서

Grammar

1 enough to

- Is this research project good **enough to** win a Nobel Prize?
  이 연구 과제는 노벨상을 받을 정도로 훌륭할까?

■ 형태: 형용사/부사+enough to+동사원형
의미: '~할 만큼 충분히 ~한/하게'

■ 'enough'는 형용사/부사 뒤에 위치한다.

- My bag is big **enough to** hold as many as 5 books.
  나의 가방은 책을 5권이나 담을 수 있을 만큼 충분히 크다.

■ to부정사의 의미상 주어가 문장의 주어와 다를 경우 to부정사 앞에 'for+목적격'을 쓴다.

- The weather was warm **enough for the kids to play** outside.
  날씨가 아이들이 밖에 나가서 놀 수 있을 만큼 충분히 따뜻했다.

■ 'so+형용사/부사+that+주절의 주어(또는 의미상 주어)+can+동사원형(+목적어)'으로 바꾸어 쓸 수 있다.

- She is **smart enough to understand** the difficult question.
  = She is **so smart that she can understand** the difficult question.
  그녀는 그 어려운 문제를 이해할 만큼 충분히 똑똑하다.
- This soup tastes **good enough for me to enjoy**.
  = This soup tastes **so good that I can enjoy it**.
  이 수프는 내가 즐기기에 충분히 맛이 좋다.

핵심 Check

1. 다음 괄호 안에서 알맞은 것을 고르시오.
   (1) I'm (enough strong / strong enough) to carry the big box.
   (2) Did you work hard enough (winning / to win) the contest?
   (3) This textbook is easy enough (for young students / of young students) to read.

2 not only ~ but also ...

- **Not only** the winners' fun studies **but also** the ceremony makes people laugh.
  수상자들의 재밌는 연구들뿐만 아니라 시상식도 또한 사람들을 웃게 만든다.

■ 형태: not only ~ but also …
의미: ~뿐만 아니라 …도

■ 두 단어가 짝을 이루어 하나의 접속사 역할을 하는 상관접속사로, 상관접속사로 연결되는 두 어구의 형태를 일치시킨다.

- Jack is **not only** kind **but also** smart. (형용사)
  Jack은 친절할 뿐만 아니라 똑똑하기도 하다.
- We can **not only** meet the singer **but also** take a picture with him. (동사원형)
  우리는 그 가수를 만날 수 있을 뿐만 아니라 그와 사진을 찍을 수도 있다.

■ '… as well as ~'로 바꾸어 쓸 수 있다.

- This coffee **not only** tastes fresh **but also** has rich aromas.
  = This coffee has rich aromas **as well as** tastes fresh.
  이 커피는 맛이 신선할 뿐만 아니라 풍부한 향을 가지고 있다.

■ 'Not only ~ but also …'가 주어로 쓰일 경우 수의 일치는 'but also'와 쓰인 주어에 맞춘다.

- **Not only** Jenny **but also** her parents were born in New Zealand.
  Jenny뿐만 아니라 그녀의 부모님들도 뉴질랜드에서 태어났다.

핵심 Check

2. 다음 괄호 안에서 알맞은 것을 고르시오.
   (1) The dancers performed not only beautifully but also (intense / intensely).
   (2) This vegetable is not only nutritious (and / but) also delicious.
   (3) Not only (they are / are they) dangerous but also they can harm the environment.

01 다음 우리말에 맞게 괄호 안에 주어진 단어를 이용하여 문장을 완성하시오.

(1) 그 밴드는 상을 수상할 정도로 충분히 인기 있다. (popular, win, award)
➡ The band is ________________________________.

(2) 우리의 노래들은 부르기에 충분히 쉽다. (easy, sing)
➡ Our songs ________________________________.

(3) 그는 용감할 뿐만 아니라 매우 친절하다. (brave, nice)
➡ He is not only ________________________________.

(4) Ann은 사랑스러울 뿐만 아니라 똑똑하다. (lovely, smart)
➡ Ann ________________________________.

02 다음 문장에서 어법상 어색한 부분을 바르게 고쳐 쓰시오.

(1) Their music is enough great to make their fans excited.
➡ ________________________________

(2) Their fans are excited enough crying out.
➡ ________________________________

(3) Pinocchio is not only popular but also very nicely.
➡ ________________________________

(4) I know not only the meaning of "eager" but also "eagerness".
➡ ________________________________

03 다음 〈보기〉의 문장을 참고하여 주어진 두 문장을 한 문장으로 바꾸어 쓰시오.

보기
My mom is brave. She can climb the high mountain.
→ My mom is brave enough to climb the high mountain.

(1) The singer is tall. She can reach the shelf.
➡ ________________________________

(2) The flower is big. It can cover the woman's face.
➡ ________________________________

01 다음 빈칸에 'enough'가 들어갈 수 없는 하나를 고르시오.

① She is rich ________ to have a fancy car.
② Ann is brave ________ to catch the bug.
③ I have ________ time to meet you.
④ Do we have ________ paint for the wall?
⑤ Leslie is ________ shy to raise her hand.

중요
02 다음 두 문장을 한 문장으로 바르게 바꾸면?

> • I teach German to the students.
> • Oliver teaches German to the students, too.

① Either I or Oliver teaches German to the students.
② Not only I but also Oliver teach German to the students.
③ Oliver as well as I teaches German to the students.
④ Neither I nor Oliver teaches German to the students.
⑤ Both I and Oliver teaches German to the students.

03 다음 빈칸에 들어갈 말로 적절한 것은?

> It was warm ________ for children to play soccer outside.

① so ② very ③ too
④ enough ⑤ as

중요
04 다음 중 어법상 어색한 문장을 고르시오.

① He is not only kind but also intelligent.
② I like to play soccer as well as basketball.
③ Not only Tom but also Susie will take part in the contest.
④ You as well as he have a sister.
⑤ He enjoys not only cooking but also to eat.

05 다음 문장의 뜻이 나머지 넷과 다른 것은?

① Because it was so cold, we stayed in the classroom.
② It was so cold that we stayed in the classroom.
③ It was very cold, so we stayed in the classroom.
④ It was cold enough for us to stay in the classroom.
⑤ It was too cold for us to stay in the classroom.

중요
06 빈칸에 들어갈 말을 순서대로 바르게 연결한 것은?

> • The movie was ________ touching that I almost cried.
> • She was ________ sad to go to the party.

① so – so
② so – enough
③ so – too
④ enough – too
⑤ enough – so

서답형

07 다음 괄호 안에 주어진 어구를 바르게 배열하여 문장을 다시 쓰시오.

The room is (enough, up to 100 people, to accommodate, big).

➡ ______________________________

08 다음 문장과 같은 뜻을 가진 것은?

She is so tall that she can reach the ceiling.

① She is tall enough that she can reach the ceiling.
② She is too tall to reach the ceiling.
③ She is enough tall to reach the ceiling.
④ She is tall enough to reach the ceiling.
⑤ She is so tall to reach the ceiling.

서답형

09 다음 문장에서 어법상 어색한 것을 바르게 고쳐 다시 쓰시오.

(1) He was so diligent that he can finish the work.
➡ ______________________________

(2) Tom as well as his parents are eating chicken.
➡ ______________________________

서답형

10 다음 두 문장을 'enough to'를 사용하여 한 문장으로 바꿔 쓰시오.

• The puzzle was so easy. • I could solve it.

➡ ______________________________

11 다음 중 어법상 어색한 문장을 고르시오.

① Not only my dad but also my uncle are going to quit smoking.
② Harry as well as you is very famous now.
③ Not only children but also adults like the movie *Frozen*.
④ Not only you but also he was interested in the game.
⑤ Not only the teacher but also her students try their best.

서답형

12 다음 괄호 안에서 알맞은 말을 고르시오.

(1) The girl was (enough nice / nice enough) to help the poor.
(2) The box is (too / enough) big to put in the car.
(3) The princess was brave enough (to fight / fighting) the monster.
(4) This coat is so warm that I (wear / wear it) in winter.
(5) The computer is so fast that (to run / it can run) the program.

13 다음 밑줄 친 우리말을 영어로 바르게 옮긴 것은? (2개)

Mary뿐만 아니라 John도 joined the drama club.

① Not only Mary but also John
② Not John but Mary
③ Neither Mary nor John
④ John as well as Mary
⑤ Either John or Mary

서답형

14 다음 괄호 안에 주어진 어구를 바르게 배열하여 문장을 다시 쓰시오.

This building (to survive / is / strong / a heavy storm / enough).

➡ ________________________________

____

서답형

15 주어진 어휘를 이용하여 다음 우리말을 영어로 쓰시오.

그 책은 여러 번 읽을 만큼 충분히 흥미롭다. (interesting, several times)

➡ ________________________________

____

16 다음 중 내용상 어색한 문장을 고르시오.

① He was so young that he couldn't go to school.
② It was so hot that we went to the pool.
③ She was brave enough to stand up for the truth.
④ He was too strong to carry all the books.
⑤ The box is light enough for a young child to lift up.

17 빈칸에 들어갈 말을 순서대로 바르게 연결한 것은?

• Both Tom and Ann ________ late.
• I'm hungry ________ to eat all the food.

① were – too
② was – enough
③ were – so
④ was – too
⑤ were – enough

서답형

18 주어진 어휘를 이용하여 다음 우리말을 영어로 쓰시오.

그 강은 거대한 배가 항해할 수 있을 만큼 충분히 깊다. (a huge ship, enough, sail on, deep)

➡ ________________________________

____

19 다음 두 문장을 한 문장으로 바르게 옮긴 것은?

• He is very smart.
• He can put a 500-piece puzzle together.

① He is too smart to put a 500-piece puzzle together.
② He is so smart to put a 500-piece puzzle together.
③ He is smart enough to put a 500-piece puzzle together.
④ He is smart so that he can put a 500-piece puzzle together.
⑤ He is smart so that he can't put a 500-piece puzzle together.

서답형

20 대화의 빈칸에 적절한 말을 주어진 단어를 알맞은 형태로 바꾸어 써 넣으시오.

(1) A: I think Winnie the Pooh is very heavy. What do you think?
B: He is not only heavy but also very ________. (love)

(2) A: I think Hong Gildong is very fast. What do you think?
B: He is not only fast but also very ________. (strength)

Grammar 서술형 시험대비

중요

01 'not only ~ but also ...'를 이용하여 두 문장을 한 문장으로 쓰시오.

(1) • Eric is kind.
• Eric is smart.
➡ ______________________

(2) • Jake is a student.
• You are a student.
➡ ______________________

(3) • She was hardworking.
• She was honest.
➡ ______________________

(4) • You run fast.
• He runs fast.
➡ ______________________

(5) • You are going to join our club.
• He is going to join our club.
➡ ______________________

02 다음 우리말을 주어진 어휘를 이용하여 영어로 옮기시오.

(1) 이 발명품은 너의 삶을 훨씬 쉽게 만들어 줄 만큼 충분히 유용하다. (invention, useful, enough, make, much easier)
➡ ______________________
____

(2) 너의 미소는 교실을 밝혀줄 만큼 충분히 환하다. (smile, bright, enough, light up)
➡ ______________________
____

(3) 너는 우리를 행복하게 만들 뿐만 아니라 우리가 잘 지내도록 도와준다. (not only, make, help, get along well)
➡ ______________________
____

고난이도

03 다음 문장을 괄호 안의 어구를 써서 문장을 다시 쓰시오.

(1) You can use it not only as a door but also as a table for playing table tennis. (as well as)
➡ ______________________
____

(2) She was so kind that she showed me how to use chopsticks. (enough to)
➡ ______________________
____

04 잘못된 부분을 바르게 고쳐 문장을 다시 쓰시오.

(1) Mark visited not only his mother also his friends.
➡ ______________________
____

(2) This building is strong enough surviving a heavy storm.
➡ ______________________
____

(3) He is enough tall to touch the ceiling.
➡ ______________________
____

(4) They sell not only eggs but also to milk.
➡ ______________________
____

(5) The box is too heavy for the girl to move it.
➡ ______________________
____

05 다음 두 문장을 'enough to부정사'를 이용하여 한 문장으로 바르게 바꿔 쓰시오.

• The water is very clean. • We can drink it.

➡ ______________________________

06 다음 그림을 보고 괄호 안의 단어를 활용하여 문장을 완성하시오.

(1)

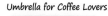

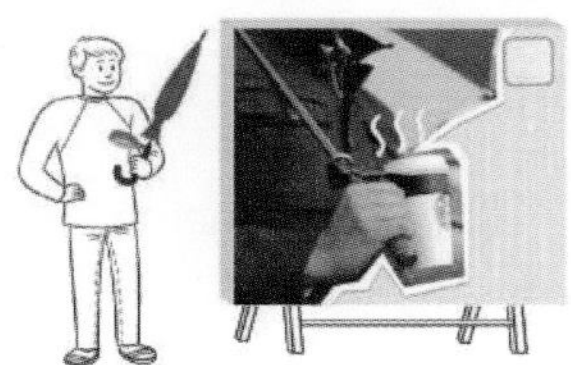

This is the Umbrella for Coffee Lovers. You can use it not only as an umbrella ______________. (but also, cup holder)

(2)

Magic Stairs

These are Magic Stairs. You can use them not only for going up and down ______________. (but also, store, things)

(3)

LED Shoes

These are LED Shoes. You can use them not only as shoes ______________. (but also, lights)

07 다음 (A), (B) 문장을 괄호 안의 지시대로 바꿔 쓰시오.

(A) He is not only a teacher but also a painter. (as well as를 써서) (B) She looks wise as well as friendly. (not only ~ but also를 써서)

➡ (A) ______________________________

(B) ______________________________

고난이도

08 다음 문장을 어법에 맞게 고쳐 쓰시오.

(1) He is tall very to be a basketball player.

➡ ______________________________

(2) Sumin ran enough fast to get there on time.

➡ ______________________________

(3) The girl was brave too to speak in front of many people.

➡ ______________________________

(4) It is warm enough plays outside.

➡ ______________________________

(5) He's cheerful enough making us feel happy.

➡ ______________________________

교과서

Reading

The Ig Nobel Prize

"What happens when you walk backward while you are carrying a cup of coffee?" Han Jiwon, a Korean high school student, did research on this topic in 2015. Is this research project good enough to win a Nobel Prize? Maybe not. But how about an Ig Nobel Prize? He won one in 2017 for this fun research.

to부정사의 부사적 용법(부사 수식 용법). ~ enough to = so ~ that ... can
Maybe not. = Maybe this research project is not good enough to win a Nobel Prize.

The Ig Nobel Prizes are awarded for discoveries that "first make one laugh and then think." They were started in 1991 by *AIR* magazine to increase people's interest in science by honoring the unusual and the imaginative.

= which / makes(×) / The Ig Nobel Prizes / to부정사의 부사적 용법(목적) / = unusual people / = imaginative people: the+형용사 = 복수 보통명사

The prizes are presented by real Nobel winners in Sanders Theater at Harvard University. The room is usually filled with people who are eager to cheer for the brave scientists with their "laughable" research.

= awarded / be eager[anxious/dying] to 동사원형: ~하고 싶은 생각이 간절하다

The U.K. Navy won the Ig Nobel Prize for Peace in 2000. To save money, the Navy made its sailors shout, "Bang!" instead of using real bombs. Is that funny enough for you to laugh out loud?

사역동사(made)+목적어+목적격보어(동사원형)

Andre Geim also won an award that year. He succeeded in floating a live frog in the air by using magnets. "In my experience, if people don't have a sense of humor, they are usually not very good scientists," he said when he accepted his award.

succeed in ~ing: ~하는 데 성공하다 / = Unless people have

magnet 자석
float 뜨다, 띄우다
research 연구, 조사
award 상; 수여하다
discovery 발견
increase 증가시키다, 늘리다
honor 명예; 존경하다
unusual 특이한, 색다른
imaginative 창의적인, 상상력이 풍부한
university 대학교
be filled with …로 가득 차다
eager 열렬한, 간절히 바라는
be eager to …을 (열렬히) 하고 싶어 하다
peace 평화
sailor 선원
instead of … 대신에
bomb 폭탄
navy 해군
succeed 성공하다
sense 감각
humor 유머, 익살
accept 받아들이다

● 다음 문장이 본문의 내용과 일치하면 T, 일치하지 않으면 F를 쓰시오.

1 Han Jiwon won an Ig Nobel Prize in 2017 for this fun research. ☐
2 The Ig Nobel Prizes are awarded for discoveries that "first make one think and then laugh." ☐
3 *AIR* magazine started the Ig Nobel Prizes in 1991. ☐
4 The Ig Nobel Prizes are presented by former Ig Nobel winners. ☐
5 The U.K. Navy won the Ig Nobel Prize for Peace in 2000. ☐

If that still does not bring a smile to your face, how about this?
= what about
In 2005, Gauri Nanda won the Ig Nobel Prize in Economics
in: [성질 · 능력 · 기예 등의 분야를 한정하여] …에서
for inventing an alarm clock. It keeps running away until the sleeper
for: [이유 · 원인] … 때문에, …으로 (인하여) keep ~ing: 계속해서 ~하다
finally gets out of bed.
= at last

Not only the winners' fun studies but also the ceremony for the Ig
not only A but also B = B as well as A: A뿐만 아니라 B도
Nobel Prizes makes people laugh. There are a number of interesting
make(×) a number of: 많은, the number of: ~의 수
things that keep people from getting bored. The opening and closing
keep/stop/prevent/prohibit A from ~ing: A가 ~하지 못하게 하다
speeches are just two words each: "Welcome. Welcome." and "Goodbye. Goodbye." If someone talks for too long, an eight-year-old girl called Miss Sweetie Poo shouts repeatedly, "Please stop! I'm
called 앞에 주격 관계대명사 who와 be동사가 생략되어 있다. = over and over (again)
bored." Each winner receives ten trillion Zimbabwean dollars, which
boring(×)
is worth less than one U.S. dollar. Throwing paper planes is another
be worth: ~의 가치가 있다 동명사 주어 are(×)
fun tradition.

The Ig Nobel Prize ceremony ends with the words, "If you didn't
end with: …으로 끝나다 = Unless you won
win a prize — and if you did — better luck next year!" The winners do
'won a prize'를 대신하는 대동사
not receive lots of money. And the awards are not great honors like the
= much …와 (똑)같이[마찬가지로]
Nobel Prizes. But the Ig Nobel Prizes make science a lot more fun!
비교급을 강조

economics 경제학
get out of …에서 떠나다, 나가다
ceremony 의식, 식
a number of 얼마간의, 다수의
keep ... from …가 ~하지 못하게 하다
get bored 지루해지다
speech 연설, 담화
repeatedly 반복적으로
receive 받다
trillion 1조
worth …의 가치가 있는

확인문제

- 다음 문장이 본문의 내용과 일치하면 T, 일치하지 않으면 F를 쓰시오.

1 In 2005, Gauri Nanda won the Ig Nobel Prize in Economics for inventing an alarm clock. ☐

2 The alarm clock keeps running after the sleeper until the sleeper finally gets out of bed. ☐

3 The ceremony for the Ig Nobel Prizes as well as the winners' fun studies makes people laugh. ☐

4 There are a number of things that keep people bored. ☐

5 The opening and closing speeches are just two words each. ☐

6 Ten trillion Zimbabwean dollars is worth more than one U.S. dollar. ☐

Reading 교과서 확인학습 A

• 우리말을 참고하여 빈칸에 알맞은 말을 쓰시오.

1 The ________ ________ Prize

2 "What ________ when you walk ________ while you are carrying a cup of coffee?"

3 Han Jiwon, a Korean high school student, ________ ________ on this topic in 2015.

4 Is this research project good ________ ________ win a Nobel Prize?

5 ________ not.

6 But ________ ________ an Ig Nobel Prize?

7 He won ________ in 2017 for this fun research.

8 The Ig Nobel Prizes ________ ________ ________ discoveries that "first make one ________ and then ________."

9 They were started in 1991 by *AIR* magazine to increase people's interest in science ________ ________ ________ ________ and ________ ________.

10 The prizes ________ ________ ________ real Nobel winners in Sanders Theater at Harvard University.

11 The room ________ usually ________ ________ people who are eager to cheer for the brave scientists with their "________" research.

12 The U.K. Navy won the Ig Nobel Prize ________ Peace in 2000.

13 ________ ________ money, the Navy made its sailors shout, "Bang!" ________ ________ using real bombs.

14 Is that funny enough for you to ________ ________ ________?

15 Andre Geim also ________ ________ ________ that year.

16 He ________ ________ ________ a live frog in the air by using magnets.

1 이그노벨상

2 "당신이 커피 한 잔을 들고 가면서 뒤로 걸을 때 무슨 일이 일어날까?"

3 한국의 한 고등학생인 한지원은 2015년에 이 주제에 관해 연구했다.

4 이 연구 과제는 노벨상을 받을 정도로 훌륭할까?

5 아마도 아닐 것이다.

6 하지만 이그노벨상은 어떤가?

7 그는 이 재미있는 연구로 2017년에 상을 탔다.

8 이그노벨상은 '먼저 웃기고 나서 다음에 생각하게 하는' 발견에 수여된다.

9 그것은 특이하고 창의적인 사람들을 높이 평가함으로써 과학에 대한 사람들의 흥미를 늘리기 위해 AIR 잡지에 의해 1991년에 시작되었다.

10 그 상들은 하버드 대학의 Sanders 극장에서 진짜 노벨상 수상자들에 의해 수여된다.

11 그 방은 대개 '웃기는' 연구를 한 용감한 과학자들을 열렬히 격려하고자 하는 사람들로 가득 찬다.

12 영국 해군은 2000년에 이그노벨 평화상을 탔다.

13 돈을 아끼기 위해, 해군에서는 선원들에게 진짜 폭탄을 사용하는 대신에 "쾅!"이라고 소리치게 했다.

14 그것이 당신이 큰 소리로 웃을 정도로 우스운가?

15 Andre Geim도 그해에 상을 탔다.

16 그는 자석을 이용해서 살아 있는 개구리를 공중에 띄우는 데 성공했다.

17 "In my experience, if people don't have ________ ________ ________ ________, they are usually not very good scientists," he said when he accepted his award.

18 If that still does not ________ a smile ________ your face, how about this?

19 In 2005, Gauri Nanda won the Ig Nobel Prize ________ Economics ________ inventing an alarm clock.

20 It ________ ________ ________ until the sleeper finally gets out of bed.

21 ________ ________ the winners' fun studies ________ ________ the ceremony for the Ig Nobel Prizes ________ people laugh.

22 There are ________ ________ ________ interesting things that ________ people ________ ________ ________.

23 The opening and closing speeches are just ________ ________ ________: "Welcome. Welcome." and "Goodbye. Goodbye."

24 If someone talks for too long, ________ ________ ________ ________ Miss Sweetie Poo shouts repeatedly, "Please stop! I'm bored."

25 Each winner receives ten trillion Zimbabwean dollars, which is ________ ________ ________ one U.S. dollar.

26 ________ paper planes ________ another fun tradition.

27 The Ig Nobel Prize ceremony ________ ________ the words, "If you didn't win a prize — and if you ________ — better luck next year!"

28 The winners ________ ________ ________ lots of money.

29 And the awards are not ________ ________ ________ the Nobel Prizes.

30 But the Ig Nobel Prizes make science ________ ________ ________ ________!

17 그는 상을 받을 때, "내 경험상, 사람들이 유머 감각이 없다면, 그들은 대개 별로 훌륭한 과학자가 아니다."라고 말했다.

18 그것이 아직도 당신의 얼굴에 미소를 띠게 하지 않는다면, 이것은 어떤가?

19 2005년에 Gauri Nanda는 자명종을 발명해서 이그노벨 경제학상을 받았다.

20 그것은 잠자는 사람이 결국 침대 밖으로 나올 때까지 계속 도망을 다닌다.

21 수상자들의 재미있는 연구뿐만 아니라 이그노벨상 시상식도 또한 사람들을 웃게 만든다.

22 사람들이 지루해하지 않도록 하는 재미있는 것들이 많이 있다.

23 개회사와 폐회사는 단지 두 마디이다: "환영합니다. 환영합니다."와 "안녕. 안녕."

24 만일 누군가가 너무 오랫동안 말을 하면, Miss Sweetie Poo 라고 하는 여덟 살짜리 여자아이가 "제발 멈춰요! 지루해요." 라고 계속 외친다.

25 각 수상자는 10조의 짐바브웨 달러를 받는데, 그것은 미국의 1달러보다 가치가 낮다.

26 종이비행기를 날리는 것은 또 다른 재미있는 전통이다.

27 이그노벨상 시상식은 "만일 당신이 상을 타지 못했다면 – 그리고 만일 탔다면 – 내년에는 좀 더 많은 행운이 있기를!"이라는 말로 끝이 난다.

28 수상자들은 많은 상금을 받지 않는다.

29 그리고 그 상은 노벨상같이 훌륭한 영광은 아니다.

30 하지만 이그노벨상은 과학을 훨씬 더 재미있게 만든다!

Reading 교과서 확인학습 B

• 우리말을 참고하여 본문을 영작하시오.

1 이그노벨상

➡ ____________________

2 "당신이 커피 한 잔을 들고 가면서 뒤로 걸을 때 무슨 일이 일어날까?"

➡ ____________________

3 한국의 한 고등학생인 한지원은 2015년에 이 주제에 관해 연구했다.

➡ ____________________

4 이 연구 과제는 노벨상을 받을 정도로 훌륭할까?

➡ ____________________

5 아마도 아닐 것이다.

➡ ____________________

6 하지만 이그노벨상은 어떤가?

➡ ____________________

7 그는 이 재미있는 연구로 2017년에 상을 탔다.

➡ ____________________

8 이그노벨상은 '먼저 웃기고 나서 다음에 생각하게 하는' 발견에 수여된다.

➡ ____________________

9 그것은 특이하고 창의적인 사람들을 높이 평가함으로써 과학에 대한 사람들의 흥미를 늘리기 위해 AIR 잡지에 의해 1991년에 시작되었다.

➡ ____________________

____

10 그 상들은 하버드 대학의 Sanders 극장에서 진짜 노벨상 수상자들에 의해 수여된다.

➡ ____________________

11 그 방은 대개 '웃기는' 연구를 한 용감한 과학자들을 열렬히 격려하고자 하는 사람들로 가득 찬다.

➡ ____________________

____

12 영국 해군은 2000년에 이그노벨 평화상을 탔다.

➡ ____________________

13 돈을 아끼기 위해, 해군에서는 선원들에게 진짜 폭탄을 사용하는 대신에 "쾅!"이라고 소리치게 했다.

➡ ____________________

14 그것이 당신이 큰 소리로 웃을 정도로 우스운가?

➡ ____________________

15 Andre Geim도 그해에 상을 탔다.

➡ ____________________

16 그는 자석을 이용해서 살아 있는 개구리를 공중에 띄우는 데 성공했다.

➡ ______________________________

17 그는 상을 받을 때, "내 경험상, 사람들이 유머 감각이 없다면, 그들은 대개 별로 훌륭한 과학자가 아니다."라고 말했다.

➡ ______________________________

____

18 그것이 아직도 당신의 얼굴에 미소를 띠게 하지 않는다면, 이것은 어떤가?

➡ ______________________________

19 2005년에 Gauri Nanda는 자명종을 발명해서 이그노벨 경제학상을 받았다.

➡ ______________________________

20 그것은 잠자는 사람이 결국 침대 밖으로 나올 때까지 계속 도망을 다닌다.

➡ ______________________________

21 수상자들의 재미있는 연구뿐만 아니라 이그노벨상 시상식도 또한 사람들을 웃게 만든다.

➡ ______________________________

22 사람들이 지루해하지 않도록 하는 재미있는 것들이 많이 있다.

➡ ______________________________

23 개회사와 폐회사는 단지 두 마디이다: "환영합니다. 환영합니다."와 "안녕. 안녕."

➡ ______________________________

24 만일 누군가가 너무 오랫동안 말을 하면, Miss Sweetie Poo라고 하는 여덟 살짜리 여자아이가 "제발 멈춰요! 지루해요."라고 계속 외친다.

➡ ______________________________

____

25 각 수상자는 10조의 짐바브웨 달러를 받는데, 그것은 미국의 1달러보다 가치가 낮다.

➡ ______________________________

26 종이비행기를 날리는 것은 또 다른 재미있는 전통이다.

➡ ______________________________

27 이그노벨상 시상식은 "만일 당신이 상을 타지 못했다면 – 그리고 만일 탔다면 – 내년에는 좀 더 많은 행운이 있기를!"이라는 말로 끝이 난다.

➡ ______________________________

____

28 수상자들은 많은 상금을 받지 않는다.

➡ ______________________________

29 그리고 그 상은 노벨상같이 훌륭한 영광은 아니다.

➡ ______________________________

30 하지만 이그노벨상은 과학을 훨씬 더 재미있게 만든다!

➡ ______________________________

Reading 시험대비 실력평가

[01~03] 다음 글을 읽고 물음에 답하시오.

"What happens when you walk backward while you are carrying a cup of coffee?" (①) Han Jiwon, a Korean high school student, did research ___ⓐ___ this topic in 2015. (②) Is this research project good enough to win a Nobel Prize? (③) But how about an Ig Nobel Prize? (④) He won one in 2017 ___ⓑ___ this fun research. (⑤)

The Ig Nobel Prizes are awarded for discoveries that "first make one laugh and then think." They were started in 1991 by *AIR* magazine to increase people's interest in science by honoring the unusual and the imaginative.

01 위 글의 빈칸 ⓐ와 ⓑ에 들어갈 전치사가 바르게 짝지어진 것은?

ⓐ ⓑ
① on – in
② about – of
③ about – in
④ at – for
⑤ on – for

02 위 글의 흐름으로 보아, 주어진 문장이 들어가기에 가장 적절한 곳은?

Maybe not.

① ② ③ ④ ⑤

03 According to the passage, which is NOT true?

① Han Jiwon was a Korean high school student.
② Han Jiwon studied about the topic "What happens when you walk backward while you are carrying a cup of coffee?"
③ Han Jiwon won an Ig Nobel Prize in 2017.
④ The Ig Nobel Prizes are awarded for discoveries that "first make one think and then laugh."
⑤ The Ig Nobel Prizes were started in 1991 by *AIR* magazine.

[04~06] 다음 글을 읽고 물음에 답하시오.

The prizes are presented by real Nobel winners in Sanders Theater at Harvard University. The room is usually filled with people who (A)<u>are eager to cheer</u> for the brave scientists with their "laughable" research.

The U.K. Navy won the Ig Nobel Prize for Peace in 2000. (B)<u>To save money, the Navy made its sailors shouting, "Bang!"</u> instead of using ___ⓐ___. Is that funny enough for you to laugh out loud?

04 위 글의 빈칸 ⓐ에 들어갈 알맞은 말을 고르시오.

① real knives
② fake blows
③ fake bombs
④ artificial knives
⑤ real bombs

05 위 글의 밑줄 친 (A)와 바꿔 쓸 수 <u>없는</u> 말을 고르시오.

① are anxious to cheer
② long to cheer
③ are anxious about cheering
④ long for cheering
⑤ are dying to cheer

서답형

06 위 글의 밑줄 친 (B)에서 어법상 틀린 부분을 찾아 고치시오.

__________ ➡ __________

[07~09] 다음 글을 읽고 물음에 답하시오.

The U.K. Navy won the Ig Nobel Prize for Peace in 2000. To save money, the Navy made its sailors shout, "Bang!" instead of using real bombs. ⓐIs that __________ out loud?

Andre Geim also won an award that year. He succeeded in floating a ⓑlive frog in the air by using magnets. "In my experience, if people don't have a sense of humor, they are usually not very good scientists," he said when he accepted his award.

서답형

07 위 글의 문장 ⓐ의 빈칸에 알맞은 단어를 넣어 다음 문장과 같은 뜻이 되도록 하시오. (여섯 단어)

> Is that so funny that you can laugh out loud?

➡ __________

서답형

08 When did Andre Geim win the Ig Nobel Prize? Answer in English in a full sentence. (5 words)

➡ __________

09 위 글의 밑줄 친 ⓑlive와 같은 의미로 쓰인 것을 고르시오.

① The doctors said he only had six months to live.
② The show is going out live.
③ We saw a real live rattlesnake!
④ The club has live music most nights.
⑤ Their names live in our memory.

[10~12] 다음 글을 읽고 물음에 답하시오.

Not only the winners' fun studies but also the ceremony for the Ig Nobel Prizes makes people laugh. There are a number of interesting things that keep people from getting bored. The opening and closing speeches are just two words each: "Welcome. Welcome." and "Goodbye. Goodbye." If someone talks for too long, an eight-year-old girl called Miss Sweetie Poo shouts ⓐrepeatedly, "Please stop! I'm bored." ⓑEach winner receives ten trillion Zimbabwean dollars, which are worth less than one U.S. dollar. Throwing paper planes is another fun tradition.

10 위 글의 밑줄 친 ⓐrepeatedly와 바꿔 쓸 수 없는 말을 모두 고르시오.

① again and again
② over and over
③ all of a sudden
④ all at once
⑤ over and over again

서답형

11 위 글의 밑줄 친 ⓑ에서 어법상 틀린 부분을 찾아서 고치시오.

__________ ➡ __________

중요

12 다음 중 이그노벨상 시상식의 재미있는 전통에 해당하지 않는 것은?

① The opening speech is "Welcome. Welcome."
② The closing speech is "Goodbye. Goodbye."
③ The winners must give a long speech.
④ Miss Sweetie Poo is an eight-year-old girl.
⑤ The prize money is ten trillion Zimbabwean dollars.

[13~15] 다음 글을 읽고 물음에 답하시오.

The Ig Nobel Prize ceremony ends with the words, "If you didn't win a prize — and if you (A)did — better luck next year!" The winners do not receive lots of money. And the awards are not great honors (B)like the Nobel Prizes. But the Ig Nobel Prizes make science ___ⓐ___ more fun!

13 위 글의 빈칸 ⓐ에 들어갈 수 없는 말을 고르시오.

① much ② very ③ even
④ a lot ⑤ still

서답형

14 위 글의 밑줄 친 (A)did와 바꿔 쓸 수 있는 말을 쓰시오. (세 단어)

➡ ______________________

중요

15 위 글의 밑줄 친 (B)like와 같은 의미로 쓰인 것을 고르시오.

① How did you like the movie?
② She responded in like manner.
③ I don't like the way he's looking at me.
④ He ran like the wind.
⑤ Like I said, you're always welcome to stay.

[16~18] 다음 글을 읽고 물음에 답하시오.

The prizes are (A)presented by real Nobel winners in Sanders Theater at Harvard University. The room is usually filled with people who are eager to cheer for the brave scientists with their "laughable" research.

The U.K. Navy won the Ig Nobel Prize for Peace in 2000. To save money, the Navy made its sailors shout, "Bang!" ___ⓐ___ using real bombs. Is that funny enough for you to laugh out loud?

16 위 글의 빈칸 ⓐ에 들어갈 알맞은 말을 고르시오.

① besides ② instead of
③ along with ④ in spite of
⑤ in addition to

서답형

17 위 글의 밑줄 친 (A)presented와 바꿔 쓸 수 있는 단어를 철자 a로 시작하여 쓰시오.

➡ ______________________

중요

18 위 글을 읽고 'the Ig Nobel Prize'에 대해 알 수 없는 것을 고르시오.

① 상의 수여자 ② 시상식 장소
③ 시상식 참여자 ④ 시상식 시기
⑤ 2000년 수상자

[19~21] 다음 글을 읽고 물음에 답하시오.

Andre Geim also won an award that year. He succeeded in floating a live frog in the air by using magnets. "In my experience, if people don't have a sense of humor, they are usually not very good scientists," he said when he accepted his award.

If that still does not bring ___ⓐ___ to your face, how about this? In 2005, Gauri Nanda won the Ig Nobel Prize in Economics for inventing an alarm clock. It keeps ___ⓑ___ away until the sleeper finally gets out of bed.

중요

19 위 글의 빈칸 ⓐ에 들어갈 가장 알맞은 말을 고르시오.

① some comfort ② your regret
③ some respect ④ inner peace
⑤ a smile

서답형

20 위 글의 빈칸 ⓑ에 run을 알맞은 형태로 쓰시오.

➡ ________________

서답형

21 How did Andre Geim succeed in floating a live frog in the air? Fill in the blanks with suitable words.

He accomplished it by ________ ________.

[22~24] 다음 글을 읽고 물음에 답하시오.

The Ig Nobel Prize ceremony ends (A)[up / with] the words, "(A)If you didn't win a prize — and if you (B)[did / were] — better luck next year!" The winners do not receive lots of money. And the awards are not great honors (C)[alike / like] the Nobel Prizes. But the Ig Nobel Prizes make science a lot more fun!

서답형

22 위 글의 괄호 (A)~(C)에서 문맥이나 어법상 알맞은 낱말을 골라 쓰시오.

➡ (A) ________ (B) ________ (C) ________

서답형

23 위 글의 밑줄 친 (A)를 Unless를 사용하여 고치시오.

➡ ________________

서답형

24 본문의 내용과 일치하도록 다음 빈칸 (A)~(C)에 알맞은 단어를 쓰시오. (한 칸에 두 단어도 가능)

Though the prize money of the (A)________ Prize is not big and the winners don't gain great honors like the (B)________ Prize winners, the (C)________ Prizes make science much more fun.

[25~27] 다음 글을 읽고 물음에 답하시오.

"What happens when you walk backward while you are carrying a cup of coffee?" Han Jiwon, a Korean high school student, did research on this topic in 2015. Is this research project good enough ⓐto win a Nobel Prize? Maybe not. But how about an Ig Nobel Prize? He won one in 2017 for this fun research.

The Ig Nobel Prizes are awarded for discoveries that "first make one laugh and then think." ⓑThey were started in 1991 by *AIR* magazine to increase people's interest in science by honoring ⓒthe unusual and ⓓthe imaginative.

25 위 글의 밑줄 친 ⓐto win과 to부정사의 용법이 같은 것을 고르시오.

① He cannot be a gentleman to do such a thing.
② She is studying English to get a good job.
③ He worked too slowly to finish it in time.
④ He left his native country never to return.
⑤ She smiled to see the monkey.

서답형

26 위 글의 밑줄 친 ⓑThey가 가리키는 것을 본문에서 찾아 쓰시오.

➡ ________________

서답형

27 위 글의 밑줄 친 ⓒthe unusual, ⓓthe imaginative와 바꿔 쓸 수 있는 말을 각각 두 단어로 쓰시오.

➡ ⓒ ________________ ⓓ ________________

[01~03] 다음 글을 읽고 물음에 답하시오.

"What happens when you walk backward while you are carrying a cup of coffee?" Han Jiwon, a Korean high school student, did research on this topic in 2015. ⓐ이 연구 과제는 노벨상을 받을 정도로 훌륭할까? Maybe not. But how about an Ig Nobel Prize? He won one in 2017 for this fun research.

The Ig Nobel Prizes are (A)[awarded / rewarded] for discoveries that "first make one laugh and then think." They were started in 1991 by *AIR* magazine to increase people's interest in science by (B)[honoring / ignoring] the unusual and the imaginative.

중요

01 위 글의 괄호 (A)~(B)에서 문맥상 알맞은 낱말을 골라 쓰시오.

➡ (A) ____________ (B) ____________

02 위 글의 밑줄 친 ⓐ의 우리말에 맞게 주어진 어휘를 알맞게 배열하시오.

a Nobel Prize / enough / research project / good / this / to win / is / ?

➡ ________________________________

____

03 다음 빈칸 (A)와 (B)에 알맞은 단어를 넣어 Han Jiwon에 대한 소개를 완성하시오.

He was a Korean high school student and won an (A)_______ _______ _______ in 2017 because of the (B)_______ research that he had done in 2015.

[04~06] 다음 글을 읽고 물음에 답하시오.

ⓐThe prizes are presented by real Nobel winners in Sanders Theater at Harvard University. The room is usually filled with people who are eager to cheer for the brave scientists with their "laughable" research.

The U.K. Navy won the Ig Nobel Prize for Peace in 2000. To save money, the Navy made its sailors shout, "Bang!" instead of using real bombs. Is ⓑthat funny enough for you to laugh out loud?

04 위 글의 밑줄 친 ⓐ를 능동태로 고치시오.

➡ ________________________________

____

05 Why did the U.K. Navy make its sailors shout, "Bang!" instead of using real bombs? Fill in the blanks with suitable words.

Because it wanted to _______ _______.

중요

06 위 글의 밑줄 친 ⓑthat이 가리키는 것을 본문에서 찾아 쓰시오.

➡ ________________________________

____

[07~08] 다음 글을 읽고 물음에 답하시오.

Andre Geim also won an Ig Nobel Prize that year. He succeeded in floating a live frog in the air by using magnets. "In my experience, ⓐif people don't have a sense of humor, they are usually not very good scientists," he said when he accepted his award.

07 위 글의 밑줄 친 ⓐ를 unless를 사용하여 고치시오.

➡ ______________________________

고난이도

08 다음 빈칸 (A)와 (B)에 알맞은 단어를 넣어 Andre Geim에 대한 소개를 완성하시오.

> Andre Geim was successful in (A)_______ a live frog in the air by using magnets, and won an Ig Nobel Prize. In his acceptance speech, he referred to (B)_______ _______ _______ _______ as an essential qualification of a good scientist.

[09~10] 다음 글을 읽고 물음에 답하시오.

> ⓐNot only the winners' fun studies but also the ceremony for the Ig Nobel Prizes makes people laugh. There are ⓑa number of interesting things that keep people from getting bored. The opening and closing speeches are just two words each: "Welcome. Welcome." and "Goodbye. Goodbye." If someone talks for too long, an eight-year-old girl called Miss Sweetie Poo shouts repeatedly, "Please stop! I'm bored." Each winner receives ten trillion Zimbabwean dollars, which is worth less than one U.S. dollar. Throwing paper planes is another fun tradition.

09 위 글의 밑줄 친 ⓐ를 as well as을 사용하여 고치시오.

➡ ______________________________

____

중요

10 위 글의 밑줄 친 ⓑ에 해당하는 것을 우리말로 쓰시오. (네 가지)

➡ ______________________________

____

____

____

____

[11~12] 다음 글을 읽고 물음에 답하시오.

> "What happens when you walk backward while you are carrying a cup of coffee?" Han Jiwon, a Korean high school student, did research on this topic in 2015. Is this research project good enough to win a Nobel Prize? ⓐ Maybe not. But how about an Ig Nobel Prize? He won one in 2017 for this fun research.
>
> The Ig Nobel Prizes are awarded for discoveries that "first make one laugh and then think." They were started in 1991 by *AIR* magazine to increase people's interest in science by honoring the unusual and the imaginative.

고난이도

11 위 글의 밑줄 친 ⓐ에 생략된 부분을 넣어 완전한 문장으로 쓰시오.

➡ ______________________________

____

12 Why did *AIR* magazine start the Ig Nobel Prizes? Fill in the blanks with suitable words.

> *AIR* magazine started them to increase people's _______ _______ _______ by honoring the unusual and the imaginative.

교과서

구석구석

해석

Self-study Guide

- New words again!
- He showed great eagerness to learn new things.
  명사를 수식하는 형용사 용법
- Oh, I get the meaning of "-ness."
  = understand
- Now I know not only the meaning of "eager" but also the meaning of "eagerness."

- 또 새 단어네!
- 그는 새로운 것들을 배우고자 하는 열정을 보여주었다.
- 오, 나는 '-ness'의 의미를 알았어.
- 이제 나는 'eager'의 뜻뿐만 아니라 'eagerness'의 뜻도 알아.

구문해설 • eagerness: 열정 • meaning: 의미 • not only A but also B: A뿐만 아니라 B도 • eager: 열렬한, 간절히 바라는

Express Yourself C

Magic Stairs

These are Magic Stairs. You can use them not only for going up and down but also for storing things. This invention is useful enough to make your life much easier.

not only A but also B = B as well as A: A뿐만 아니라 B도 / going: 동명사 / storing: 동명사 / ~ enough to = so ~ that ... can / much: 비교급 강조(훨씬)

마법의 계단

이것은 '마법의 계단'입니다. 당신은 그것을 올라가고 내려가기 위해서 뿐만 아니라 물건을 보관하기 위해서도 사용할 수 있습니다. 이 발명품은 당신의 삶을 훨씬 더 편안하게 할 정도로 충분히 유용합니다.

구문해설 • stair: 계단 • store: 저장[보관]하다 • invention: 발명

Link to the World

The Nobel Prize

The Nobel Prize was named after Alfred Nobel, a Swedish scientist. It is awarded to people who have done great work for the world.

be named after: ~의 이름을 따서 짓다 / Alfred Nobel, a Swedish scientist: 동격 / is awarded: 수동태 / who: 주격 관계대명사

Of all the winners, Malala Yousafzai is the youngest. She won the Nobel Prize at the age of 17 because she had fought for women's and children's rights.

Of: ~ 중에서 / at the age of: ~의 나이에 / had fought: 과거완료

The Curie family received the Nobel Prize three times. Not only Marie Curie but also her daughter was awarded the Nobel Prize.

= Her daughter as well as Marie Curie

노벨상

노벨상은 스웨덴 과학자인 Alfred Nobel의 이름을 따서 지었다. 그 상은 세계를 위해 위대한 일을 행한 사람들에게 수여된다.

모든 수상자들 중에서, Malala Yousafzai가 최연소이다. 그녀는 여성과 어린이의 권리를 위해서 싸웠기 때문에 17세의 나이에 노벨상을 수상했다.

Curie 가족은 노벨상을 3번 수상했다. Marie Curie뿐만 아니라 그녀의 딸도 노벨상을 수상했다.

구문해설 • be named after: ~의 이름을 따서 짓다 • Swedish: 스웨덴의 • award: 수여하다 • right: 권리

영역별 핵심문제

Words & Expressions

01 다음 주어진 두 단어의 관계가 같도록 빈칸에 알맞은 단어를 쓰시오.

useful – useless : usual – ________

02 다음 문장의 빈칸 (a)와 (b)에 들어갈 단어가 바르게 짝지어진 것은?

- We had to ____(a)____ the swimming pool as it rained.
- The nation's president hoped to end the war and bring __(b)__.

① wait for – peace
② get into – discovery
③ get out of – peace
④ get out of – discovery
⑤ wait for – honor

03 다음 대화의 빈칸에 들어갈 말을 〈영영 풀이〉를 참고하여 대화에 나오는 한 단어를 이용하여 쓰시오.

A: I'm going to enter the dance contest next week, but I'm ________ about it.
B: Don't worry. You'll do great. I'll keep my fingers crossed.
A: Thank you.

<영영 풀이> unhappy because you are thinking about problems or unpleasant things that might happen

➡ ____________________

[04~05] 다음 영영 풀이에 해당하는 것을 고르시오.

04

to be on a liquid and not sink

① fill ② volunteer
③ hang ④ represent
⑤ float

05

something you are proud to do

① honor ② humor
③ sense ④ trillion
⑤ sailor

06 다음 중 밑줄 친 부분의 뜻이 잘못된 것은?

① Everyone went underground before the bomb went off. (폭탄)
② He wanted to join the navy instead of the army. (해군)
③ The student did research on the Internet to learn about King Sejong. (조사)
④ The writer of the children's story is very imaginative. (가상의)
⑤ The store increased the price of toys. (증가시키다, 늘리다)

Conversation

07 다음 대화에서 어법상 어색한 부분을 찾아 바르게 고치시오.

B: I'm looking forward to the Best Joker award this time.
G: Ha-ha. You always make us laughing out loud. So you'll get the prize, Yunki. Good luck.
B: Thank you.

____________ ➡ ____________

08 다음 짝지어진 대화 중 어색한 것은?

① A: What kind of prize did Han Jiwon win in 2017?
B: He won an Ig Nobel Prize.

② A: I'm going to travel to Jejudo next week.
B: Wow! That sounds great.

③ A: I'm going to enter the speech contest tomorrow.
B: Me, too. I'm looking forward to it.

④ A: I'm going to join the dance contest next Friday.
B: Are you? I'm looking forward to watching you dance.

⑤ A: I'm looking forward to the funny dance contest tomorrow. Are you ready?
B: Well, I think so, but I'm confident.

[09~11] 다음 대화를 읽고 물음에 답하시오.

Miso: We're going on a field trip next Tuesday. What are you going to do in the talent show, Jimin?
Jimin: I'm going to talk like our teachers do in class and tell some jokes.
Miso: Wow! I'm really ⓐlooking forward to it.
Jimin: Will everyone like my show? I'm not sure.
Miso: Don't worry. I'm sure you'll do great. I'll ⓑkeep my fingers crossed!
Jimin: Thank you, Miso. ⓒLet me to show you one part of my act. Guess who? "Goood Jooob!"
Miso: Ha-ha, you ⓓsound like our English teacher.
Jimin: Do I? I'm going to show you more at the show.
Miso: Great! You always make us ⓔlaugh out loud.

09 위 대화의 밑줄 친 부분 중 어법상 틀린 것은?

① ⓐ ② ⓑ ③ ⓒ ④ ⓓ ⑤ ⓔ

10 위 대화의 제목으로 가장 적절한 것은?

① Difficulty of Imitating Teachers' Voice
② Doing the Show Which Everyone likes
③ Choosing the Place of a Field Trip
④ Looking Forward to the Talent Show
⑤ Making Others Laugh out Loud

11 위 대화의 내용과 일치하지 않는 것을 고르시오.

① They are talking about the talent show.
② The field trip is next Tuesday.
③ Miso is going to talk like the teachers do in class and tell some jokes.
④ Jimin always makes Miso laugh out loud.
⑤ Jimin talked like his English teacher.

Grammar

12 주어진 문장의 밑줄 친 that과 용법이 같은 것은?

The dinner at that famous restaurant was so nice that I couldn't forget it.

① I hope that I can see your face.
② The report shows that we need to have healthier food.
③ The money that you saved will be used to buy a bike.
④ That is the jacket that my aunt made for me.
⑤ The old lady is so wise that we always get advice from her.

13 다음 글에서 어법상 어색한 부분을 찾아 바르게 고치시오.

> The Curie family received the Nobel Prize three times. Not only Marie Curie but also her daughter were awarded the Nobel Prize.

➡ ______________________

____

14 다음 주어진 우리말과 의미가 다른 하나를 고르시오.

> 방이 너무 어두워서 나는 책을 읽을 수 없었다.

① It was so dark in the room that I couldn't read books.
② Because it was so dark in the room, I couldn't read books.
③ It was dark enough in the room for me to read books.
④ It was too dark in the room for me to read books.
⑤ It was very dark in the room, so I wasn't able to read books.

15 다음 중 어법상 어색한 문장의 개수로 알맞은 것은?

> a. Kate not only runs fast but also jump high.
> b. Mike drinks a lot as well as eats a lot.
> c. She is such smart that she can make those decisions.
> d. This is not only an umbrella but also a coffee holder.
> e. It is useful enough making my life much easier.
> f. He was clever enough to understand the question.

① 1개 ② 2개 ③ 3개 ④ 4개 ⑤ 5개

16 주어진 문장과 같은 뜻이 되도록 'as well as'를 써서 바꿔 쓸 때 빈칸에 알맞은 말을 쓰시오.

> We communicate not only on the phone but also by email.
> = We communicate ______________.

➡ ______________________

17 다음 우리말을 주어진 어휘를 이용하여 영어로 옮기시오.

(1) Ted는 나의 가방을 들어줄 만큼 충분히 친절했다. (kind, enough, carry)
➡ ______________________

(2) Vivian은 많은 돈을 저축할 만큼 충분히 열심히 일했다. (hard, to save, lots)
➡ ______________________

(3) 그 마당은 매우 커서 우리 모두 자전거를 탈 수 있다. (yard, so big, bikes, in)
➡ ______________________

18 다음 우리말을 영어로 바르게 옮긴 것은?

> Mary는 불을 끌 수 있을 정도로 키가 크다.

① Mary is tall enough to turn on the light.
② Mary is tall enough to turn off the light.
③ Mary is so tall that she can't turn off the light.
④ Mary is so tall that she can turn on the light.
⑤ Mary is too tall not to turn off the light.

Reading

[19~20] 다음 글을 읽고 물음에 답하시오.

Not only the winners' fun studies but also the ceremony for the Ig Nobel Prizes makes people laugh. There are a number of interesting things that keep people from getting bored. The opening and closing speeches are just two words each: "Welcome. Welcome." and "Goodbye. Goodbye." If someone talks for too long, an eight-year-old girl ⓐcalled Miss Sweetie Poo shouts repeatedly, "Please stop! I'm bored." Each winner receives ten trillion Zimbabwean dollars, which is worth less than one U.S. dollar. ⓑThrowing paper planes is another fun tradition.

19 위 글의 밑줄 친 ⓐcalled 앞에 생략된 말을 쓰시오.

➡ ________________

20 아래 〈보기〉에서 위 글의 밑줄 친 ⓑThrowing과 문법적 쓰임이 같은 것의 개수를 고르시오.

보기
① We stopped throwing paper planes.
② They are throwing paper planes.
③ Do you know the boys throwing paper planes?
④ They are fond of throwing paper planes.
⑤ I saw them throwing paper planes.

① 1개 ② 2개 ③ 3개 ④ 4개 ⑤ 5개

[21~23] 다음 글을 읽고 물음에 답하시오.

"What happens when you walk backward while you are carrying a cup of coffee?" Han Jiwon, a Korean high school student, did research on this topic in 2015. (A)Is this research project good enough to win a Nobel Prize? Maybe not. But how about an Ig Nobel Prize? He won (B)one in 2017 for this fun research.

The Ig Nobel Prizes are awarded for discoveries that "first make (C)one laugh and then think." They were started in 1991 ___ⓐ___ *AIR* magazine to increase people's interest in science ___ⓑ___ honoring the unusual and the imaginative.

21 위 글의 빈칸 ⓐ와 ⓑ에 공통으로 들어갈 알맞은 전치사를 쓰시오.

➡ ________________

22 다음 빈칸에 알맞은 단어를 넣어 위 글의 밑줄 친 (A)를 복문으로 고치시오.

➡ Is this research project ________ good ________ it ________ win a Nobel Prize?

23 아래 〈보기〉에서 위 글의 밑줄 친 (B)one, (C)one과 같은 의미로 쓰인 것을 각각 고르시오.

보기
① One must obey one's parents.
② I'd like an ice cream. Are you having one, too?
③ One can be glad and sorry at the same time.
④ I don't have a pen. Can you lend me one?
⑤ Do you have a watch? — Yes, I have one.

➡ (B) one: ________ (C) one: ________

[24~25] 다음 글을 읽고 물음에 답하시오.

Andre Geim also won an award that year. He succeeded in floating a live frog in the air by using magnets. "In my experience, if people don't have a sense of humor, they are usually not very good scientists," he said when he accepted his award.

If that still does not bring a smile to your face, how about this? In 2005, Gauri Nanda won the Ig Nobel Prize in Economics for inventing an alarm clock. It keeps running away until the sleeper ⓐfinally gets out of bed.

24 위 글의 밑줄 친 ⓐfinally와 바꿔 쓸 수 없는 말을 모두 고르시오.

① at last ② in the end
③ above all ④ at least
⑤ in the long run

25 다음 중 위 글에 대한 설명을 바르게 하지 못한 사람을 고르시오.

① 형규: Andre Geim은 자석을 사용해서 살아 있는 개구리를 공중에 띄울 수 있었어.
② 수희: Andre Geim에 따르면, 대체로 아주 훌륭한 과학자가 되려면 유머 감각이 필요하다고 해.
③ 민수: 2005년에 Gauri Nanda가 이그노벨상을 탔어.
④ 세진: 응, 자명종을 발명해서 이그노벨 경제학상을 받은 거야.
⑤ 나리: 그 자명종은 잠자는 사람이 깨어날 때까지 쫓아다닌대.

[26~28] 다음 글을 읽고 물음에 답하시오.

Umbrella for Coffee Lovers

This is the Umbrella for Coffee Lovers. You can use it not only ⓐas an umbrella but also as a cup holder. ⓑThis invention is useful enough to make your life much easier.

Magic Stairs

These are Magic Stairs. ⓒYou can use them not only for going up and down but also for storing things. This invention is useful enough to make your life much easier.

26 위 글의 밑줄 친 ⓐas와 같은 의미로 쓰인 것을 고르시오.

① As he is honest, he is trusted by everyone.
② This box will serve as a table.
③ Susan is not as pretty as Jane.
④ As I entered the room, they cried.
⑤ Her anger grew as she talked.

27 위 글의 밑줄 친 ⓑ를 복문으로 고치시오.

➡ ______________________________
____

28 다음 중 위 글의 밑줄 친 문장 ⓒ와 의미가 같지 않은 문장을 고르시오.

① You can use them not just for going up and down but also for storing things.
② You can use them not simply for going up and down but also for storing things.
③ You can use them for storing things as well as for going up and down.
④ You can use them not for going up and down but for storing things.
⑤ You can use them not only for going up and down but for storing things as well.

단원별 예상문제

출제율 90%

01 다음 짝지어진 단어의 관계가 같도록 빈칸에 알맞은 말을 쓰시오.

backward – forward : sink – ________

출제율 95%

02 다음 영영 풀이에 해당하는 단어는?

a weapon made of material that will explode

① magnet ② navy ③ bomb
④ army ⑤ science

출제율 100%

03 다음 대화를 읽고 B의 빈칸에 들어갈 말을 〈조건〉에 맞게 쓰시오.

보기
- 행운을 빌어주는 표현을 쓸 것.
- 'leg'를 사용할 것.

A: I'm going to enter the dance contest next week, but I'm worried about it.
B: Don't worry. You'll do great. ________!
A: Thank you.

➡ ____________________

[04~05] 다음 대화를 읽고 물음에 답하시오.

Miso: We're going on a field trip next Tuesday. What are you going to do in the talent show, Jimin?
Jimin: I'm going to talk like our teachers do in class and tell some jokes.

(A) Will everyone like my show? I'm not sure.
(B) Thank you, Miso. Let me show you one part of my act. Guess who? "Goood Jooob!"
(C) Ha-ha, you sound like our English teacher.
(D) Don't worry. I'm sure you'll do great. I'll keep my fingers crossed!
(E) Wow! I'm really looking forward to it.

Jimin: Do I? I'm going to show you more at the show.
Miso: Great! You always make us laugh out loud.

출제율 100%

04 위 대화의 (A)~(E) 중 흐름상 네 번째 위치할 대화는?

① (A) ② (B) ③ (C) ④ (D) ⑤ (E)

출제율 90%

05 위 대화를 읽고 다음 질문에 영어로 답하시오.

Q: What is Jimin going to do in the talent show?

➡ ____________________
____

출제율 95%

06 다음 대화의 빈칸에 들어갈 말로 어색한 것은?

A: I'm looking forward to the model airplane contest tomorrow. Are you ready?
B: Well, I think so, but I'm nervous.
A: You will do well. ____________

① I'll keep my fingers crossed!
② Good luck!
③ Don't give up!
④ I wish you all the best.
⑤ Don't be worried.

출제율 95%

07 대화에서 단어의 쓰임이 어색한 곳을 찾아 바르게 고치시오. (2개)

> B: This looks interesting. Is this a cutting board and a bird feeder?
> G: It is not only a cutting board but also a bird feeder. You can do one thing at the same time.
> B: That's a great idea!
> G: Do you really think so?
> B: Yes. I'm really looking forward to using it.

________ ➡ ________, ________ ➡ ________

[08~09] 다음 대화를 읽고 물음에 답하시오.

> G: Mom, I can't wait for the sports day.
> W: What are you going to do on that day, Minji?
> G: I'm going to play basketball for my class. We've practiced hard for a few weeks.
> W: Oh, I'm looking forward to your game.
> G: Actually, I'm a little worried. I'm afraid I'll make a mistake.
> W: Don't worry. You'll do a good job. ________(A)________!

출제율 95%

08 위 대화의 빈칸 (A)에 들어갈 알맞은 말을 주어진 단어를 이용하여 쓰시오.

(keep, fingers, crossed)

➡ ________________

출제율 100%

09 위 대화의 내용과 일치하지 않는 것은?

① They are talking about the sports day.
② Minji will play basketball for her class.
③ Minji is looking forward to the sports days.
④ Minji's mom is expecting to play basketball.
⑤ Minji is afraid she'll make a mistake.

출제율 95%

10 다음 대화의 빈칸에 들어갈 말로 어색한 것은?

> (A) B: The winner of the Oh So Sweet award will get some candies.
> G: Oh, I want to get the prize.
> B: I'm sure you'll get the prize this time. ____________, Jiu!
> (B) B: I'm looking forward to the Best Joker award this time.
> G: Ha-ha. You always make us laugh out loud. So you'll get the prize, Yunki. ____________.
> B: Thank you.

① Good luck
② I knock on wood for you
③ I hope everything goes well with you
④ I'll keep my fingers crossed for you
⑤ I can't wait to get the prize

출제율 95%

11 다음 문장에서 어법상 어색한 부분을 찾아 바르게 고치시오.

> You can use it not only putting on your back but also for controlling the TV.

____________ ➡ ____________

출제율 100%

12 다음 빈칸에 들어갈 말로 적절하지 않은 것을 고르시오.

> He gave me not ________ clothes but also money.

① only ② just ③ rather
④ simply ⑤ merely

출제율 90%

13 우리말과 같은 뜻이 되도록 괄호 안에 주어진 말과 'not only ~ but also ...'를 사용하여 한 문장으로 쓰시오.

(1) Tommy는 힘이 셀뿐만 아니라 현명하기도 해. (strong, wise)
➡ ________________

(2) 그녀는 지식뿐만 아니라 용기도 가지고 있다. (knowledge, courage)
➡ ________________

(3) 나는 춤추는 것뿐만 아니라 노래도 잘한다. (good at, dancing, singing)
➡ ________________

(4) 너뿐만 아니라 그도 그 영화를 보고 싶어 한다. (want, see the movie)
➡ ________________

[14~16] 다음 글을 읽고 물음에 답하시오.

"What happens when you walk backward while you are carrying a cup of coffee?" Han Jiwon, a Korean high school student, did research on ⓐthis topic in 2015. Is this research project good enough to win a Nobel Prize? Maybe not. But how about an Ig Nobel Prize? He won one in 2017 for this fun research.

The Ig Nobel Prizes are awarded for discoveries ⓑthat "first make one laugh and then think." ⓒThey were started in 1991 by *AIR* magazine to increase people's interest in science by honoring the unusual and the imaginative.

출제율 90%

14 위 글의 밑줄 친 ⓐthis topic이 가리키는 것을 본문에서 찾아 쓰시오.

➡ ________________
____

출제율 95%

15 위 글의 밑줄 친 ⓑthat과 문법적 쓰임이 같은 것을 모두 고르시오.

① Look at that man over there.
② Who was the first man that came here?
③ The trouble is that we are short of money.
④ This is my sister and that is my cousin.
⑤ Is this the farm that they spoke of?

출제율 90%

16 위 글의 밑줄 친 ⓒ를 능동태로 고치시오.

➡ ________________

[17~18] 다음 글을 읽고 물음에 답하시오.

Andre Geim also won an award that year. He (A)succeeded in floating a live frog in the air by using magnets. "In my experience, if people don't have a sense of humor, they are usually not very good scientists," he said when he accepted his award.

If that still does not bring a smile to your face, how about this? In 2005, Gauri Nanda won the Ig Nobel Prize __ⓐ__ Economics __ⓑ__ inventing an alarm clock. It keeps running away until the sleeper finally gets out of bed.

출제율 95%

17 위 글의 빈칸 ⓐ와 ⓑ에 들어갈 전치사가 바르게 짝지어진 것은?

ⓐ ⓑ
① for – at
② in – at
③ in – for
④ to – by
⑤ to – for

출제율 90%

18 위 글의 밑줄 친 (A)를 다음과 같이 바꿔 쓸 때, 빈칸에 들어갈 알맞은 단어를 쓰시오.

➡ was ________ in floating

[19~21] 다음 글을 읽고 물음에 답하시오.

> Since 1991
> First make one laugh and then think
>
> The 27th Ig Nobel Prize Ceremony
>
> Thursday, September 14, 2017 6:00 PM
> in Sanders Theater at Harvard University
> Join us for the awarding of 10 new Ig Nobel Prizes
> Winners of 2017:
> Han Jiwon, Korea
> "How to Carry Your Coffee"

출제율 100%

19 위 글의 종류로 알맞은 것을 고르시오.

① diary ② summary ③ article
④ invitation ⑤ advertisement

출제율 90%

20 To win an Ig Nobel Prize, which is more important, making one laugh or making one think? Fill in the blanks (A) and (B) with suitable words.

> To win an Ig Nobel Prize, making one (A)________ is more important than making one (B)________.

출제율 95%

21 위 글을 읽고 답할 수 없는 질문을 고르시오.

① When was the Ig Nobel Prize started?
② What is the condition of winning the prize?
③ When will the ceremony be held?
④ Where will the ceremony be held?
⑤ Who will present the prizes?

[22~24] 다음 글을 읽고 물음에 답하시오.

> Not only the winners' fun studies but also the ceremony for the Ig Nobel Prizes makes people laugh. There are a number of interesting things that ⓐkeep people from getting bored. The opening and closing speeches are just two words each: "Welcome. Welcome." and "Goodbye. Goodbye." If someone talks for too long, an eight-year-old girl called Miss Sweetie Poo shouts repeatedly, "Please stop! I'm bored." Each winner receives ten trillion Zimbabwean dollars, which is worth less than one U.S. dollar. ⓑThrowing paper planes is another fun tradition.

출제율 90%

22 위 글의 밑줄 친 ⓐkeep과 바꿔 쓸 수 있는 말을 모두 고르시오.

① stop ② prevent ③ prohibit
④ allow ⑤ encourage

출제율 95%

23 밑줄 친 ⓑ를 다음과 같이 바꿔 쓸 때 빈칸에 들어갈 알맞은 말을 두 단어로 쓰시오.

➡ It is another fun tradition ________ ________ paper planes.

출제율 100%

24 According to the passage, which is NOT true?

① The winners' fun studies make people laugh.
② The ceremony for the Ig Nobel Prizes also makes people laugh.
③ There are many interesting things that keep people interested.
④ The opening speeches are just four words: "Welcome. Welcome." and "Goodbye. Goodbye."
⑤ Miss Sweetie Poo is eight years old.

서술형 실전문제

01 다음 대화의 우리말에 맞게 주어진 단어를 활용하여 영어로 쓰시오.

G: Mom, are you coming to the sports day?
W: Sure. I'm going to play the game Kick a Shoe. This will be the first time for me to try it.
G: Don't worry. I'm sure you'll do great. I'll keep my fingers crossed for you!
W: Thank you. I'm also going to perform a funny dance with some other mothers.
G: That sounds fun. 무대에 선 엄마 모습을 보는 것이 기대돼요. (I'm / look / watch / on the stage)

➡ ______________________________

02 다음 대화를 읽고 요약문을 완성하시오.

A: We're going on a field trip next Tuesday. What are you going to do in the talent show, Jimin?
B: I'm going to talk like our teachers do in class and tell some jokes.
A: Wow! I'm really looking forward to it.
B: Will everyone like my show? I'm not sure.
A: Don't worry. I'm sure you'll do great. I'll keep my fingers crossed!
B: Thank you, Miso. Let me show you one part of my act. Guess who? "Goood Jooob!"
A: Ha-ha, you sound like our English teacher.
B: Do I? I'm going to show you more at the show.
A: Great! You always make us laugh out loud.

Jimin and Miso are talking about the ____________. Jimin is going to ____________ their teachers do in class and ____________. Miso is ____________ his show.

03 대화의 흐름상 빈칸에 들어갈 문장을 〈조건〉에 맞게 쓰시오.

W: Soyun, are you going to take part in any races on the sports day?
G: Sure. I'm going to run a 100 meter race at the end of the day.
W: Wow, ______________________
G: But, Mom, I'm not sure I'll win the race.
W: Just do your best. I'll keep my fingers crossed!

조건
- 진행형을 이용하여 '기대를 표현하는 말'을 쓸 것.
- look / see / you / at the race를 사용할 것.

➡ ______________________________

04 다음 글에서 어법상 틀린 곳의 기호를 쓰고 바르게 고쳐 쓰시오. (3개)

The Nobel Prize

The Nobel Prize (a)named after Alfred Nobel, a Swedish scientist. It (b)is awarded to people who (c)has done great work for the world.

The Curie family (d)received the Nobel Prize three times. Not only Marie Curie but also her daughter (e)were awarded the Nobel Prize.

➡ ______________________________

[05~07] 다음 글을 읽고 물음에 답하시오.

"What happens when you walk backward while you are carrying a cup of coffee?" Han Jiwon, a Korean high school student, did research on this topic in 2015. Is this research project good enough to win a Nobel Prize? Maybe not. ⓐBut how about an Ig Nobel Prize? He won one in 2017 for this fun research.

The Ig Nobel Prizes are awarded for discoveries that "first make one laugh and then think." They were started in 1991 by *AIR* magazine to increase people's interest in science by honoring ⓑ특이하고 창의적인 사람들.

05 위 글의 밑줄 친 ⓐ를 다음과 같이 바꿔 쓸 때 빈칸에 들어갈 알맞은 말을 두 단어로 쓰시오.

➡ But is this research project ________ ________ to win an Ig Nobel Prize?

06 위 글의 밑줄 친 ⓑ의 우리말에 맞게 주어진 단어를 사용하여 5 단어로 영작하시오. (unusual, imaginative)

➡ ______________________________

07 다음 빈칸 (A)와 (B)에 알맞은 단어를 넣어 the Ig Nobel Prizes에 대한 소개를 완성하시오.

> *AIR* magazine started them in 1991 for the purpose of increasing people's interest in science. If a discovery first makes one (A)________ and then (B)________, it can award the prize.

[08~10] 다음 글을 읽고 물음에 답하시오.

Not only the winners' fun studies but also the ceremony for the Ig Nobel Prizes (A)[make / makes] people laugh. ⓐ사람들이 지루해하지 않도록 하는 재미있는 것들이 많이 있다. The opening and closing speeches are just two words each: "Welcome. Welcome." and "Goodbye. Goodbye." If someone talks for too long, an eight-year-old girl called Miss Sweetie Poo shouts repeatedly, "Please stop! I'm bored." Each winner receives ten trillion Zimbabwean dollars, which (B)[is / are] worth less than one U.S. dollar. Throwing paper planes (C)[is / are] another fun tradition.

08 위 글의 괄호 (A)~(C)에서 어법상 알맞은 낱말을 골라 쓰시오.

➡ (A) ________ (B) ________ (C) ________

09 위 글의 밑줄 친 ⓐ의 우리말에 맞게 주어진 어휘를 이용하여 13 단어로 영작하시오.

> a number of, keep, bored

➡ ______________________________
____

10 What is the closing speech of the Ig Nobel Prizes? Answer in English in a full sentence. (4 words)

➡ ______________________________

창의사고력 서술형 문제

01 〈보기〉의 (A)는 기대를 표현하는 대화이고, (B)는 기원을 표현하는 대화이다. 〈보기〉를 보고 (A), (B)의 표현을 써서 대화를 완성하시오.

(A)	(B)
• travel to Jejudo	• have a basketball game
• go camping with my parents	• enter the dance contest
• club festival	• join the invention contest
• see a musical	• have an important meeting

보기

(A) **A:** I'm going to travel to Jejudo next week.
B: Wow! That sounds great.
A: Yeah, I'm really looking forward to it.

(B) **A:** I'm going to enter the dance contest next week, but I'm worried about it.
B: Don't worry. You'll do great. I'll keep my fingers crossed.
A: Thank you.

02 〈보기〉에 주어진 표현을 사용하여 'not only ~ but also ...' 또는 'enough to부정사'의 문장을 쓰시오.

보기

understand the novel　　buy the building　　speak English　　speak Chinese
interested in basketball　　interested in volleyball　　watch the drama　　play the game

rich　clever　young　old　careful　foolish　cheap　expensive

(1) ____________________
(2) ____________________
(3) ____________________
(4) ____________________

단원별 모의고사

01 다음 단어에 대한 영어 설명이 어색한 것은?

① backward: looking or facing in the direction that is behind you
② imaginative: having or showing new and exciting ideas
③ live: not dead
④ million: the number 1,000,000,000,000
⑤ university: an educational institution of learning of the highest level

02 다음 짝지어진 단어의 관계가 같도록 빈칸에 알맞은 말을 쓰시오.

happy – happiness : eager – ________

03 다음 영영풀이에 해당하는 단어를 고르시오.

to achieve something that you planned to do

① reach ② accept ③ succeed
④ fill ⑤ throw

[04~05] 다음 대화의 빈칸에 들어갈 말로 알맞은 것을 고르시오.

04

A: I'm going to enter the dance contest next week, but I'm worried about it.
B: ________________ I'll keep my fingers crossed.
A: Thank you.

① Why don't you practice dancing hard?
② Don't worry. You'll do great.
③ Who will take part in the dance contest?
④ I'm looking forward to it.
⑤ Wow! That sounds great.

05

B: ________________ award this time.
G: Ha-ha. You always make us laugh out loud. So you'll get the prize, Yunki. Good luck.
B: Thank you.

① I'm looking forward to the Best Joker
② I'm looking forward to the Class Brain
③ I'm looking forward to Oh So Sweet
④ I'm looking forward to the Ms. Cheerful
⑤ I'm looking forward to the Best Note Keeper

06 다음 중 짝지어진 대화가 어색한 것은?

① A: These are special shoes. I hope to win a prize with this invention.
B: I'm sure you will.
② A: I'm looking forward to the funny dance contest tomorrow. Are you ready?
B: Well, I think so, but I'm nervous.
③ A: I'm going to enter the photo contest tomorrow.
B: Are you? I'll keep my fingers crossed!
④ A: I'm going to go camping with my parents next week.
B: Wow! That sounds great.
⑤ A: Minho always makes us laugh out loud.
B: Don't worry. You'll do great. I'll keep my fingers crossed.

07 대화의 흐름상 밑줄 친 ①~⑤ 중 어휘의 쓰임이 어색한 것은?

G: Mom, I ①can't wait for the sports day.
W: What are you going to do on that day, Minji?
G: I'm going to play basketball for my class. We've ②practiced hard for a few weeks.
W: Oh, ③I'm looking forward to your game.
G: Actually, ④I'm little worried. I'm afraid I'll make a mistake.
W: Don't worry. You'll do a good job. I'll ⑤keep my fingers crossed!

① ② ③ ④ ⑤

[08~09] 다음 대화를 읽고 물음에 답하시오.

G: Mom, are you coming to the sports day?
W: Sure. I'm going to play the game Kick a Shoe. (①) This will be the first time for me to try it. (②)
G: Don't worry. I'm sure you'll do great. I'll keep my fingers ___(A)___ (cross) for you! (③)
W: Thank you. (④)
G: That sounds fun. (⑤) I'm looking forward to ___(B)___ (watch) you on the stage.

08 위 대화의 (①)~(⑤) 중 주어진 문장이 들어갈 위치로 알맞은 곳은?

I'm also going to perform a funny dance with some other mothers.

① ② ③ ④ ⑤

09 위 대화의 (A)와 (B)에 주어진 단어를 알맞은 형태로 쓰시오.

➡ (A) ____________ (B) ____________

[10~12] 다음 대화를 읽고 물음에 답하시오.

Miso: We're going on a field trip next Tuesday. What are you going to do in the talent show, Jimin?
Jimin: I'm going to talk like our teachers (A)do in class and tell some jokes.
Miso: Wow! I'm really looking forward to it.
Jimin: Will everyone like my show? I'm not sure.
Miso: Don't worry. I'm sure you'll do great. I'll keep my fingers crossed!
Jimin: Thank you, Miso. Let me show you one part of my act. Guess who? "Goood Jooob!"
Miso: Ha-ha, you sound like our English teacher.
Jimin: (B)Do I? I'm going to show you more at the show.
Miso: Great! You always make us laugh out loud.

10 위 대화의 내용과 일치하도록 Jimin의 장기 자랑 계획을 영어로 쓰시오. (to부정사로 문장을 시작하시오.)

➡ Jimin's Plan for the Talent Show
(1) ______________________________
(2) ______________________________

11 위 대화의 밑줄 친 (A)의 'do'가 의미하는 바로 알맞은 것은?

① teach ② like ③ talk
④ make ⑤ go

12 위 대화의 밑줄 친 (B)의 'Do I?'를 완전한 문장으로 쓰시오.

➡ ____________________

[13~15] 괄호 안에 주어진 표현을 사용하여 우리말을 영어로 완성하시오.

13 (as well as, nice)

A: I think Pinocchio is very popular. What do you think?

B: 그는 매우 친절할 뿐만 아니라 인기 있어.

➡ ____________________

14 (both ~ and ..., lovely)

A: I think Rapunzel is very beautiful. What do you think?

B: 그녀는 예쁘고 사랑스러워.

➡ ____________________

15 (neither ~ nor ⋯, creative)

A: I think Ms. Marple is very smart. What do you think?

B: 그녀는 똑똑하지도 창의적이지도 않아.

➡ ____________________

16 다음 중 어법상 어색한 문장을 고르시오.

① This hall is big enough to hold 1,000 people.
② Mr. Kim is old enough to drive a car.
③ Jimin was smart enough to solve the difficult problem.
④ Sue sings not only beautifully but also happy.
⑤ He teaches not just English but science.

17 다음 두 문장을 한 문장으로 바르게 옮긴 것을 모두 고르시오.

• The lake is deep.
• You can't swim in the lake.

① The lake is so deep that you can't swim in the lake.
② The lake is so deep for you to swim in the lake.
③ The lake is too deep for you to swim in the lake.
④ The lake is too deep for you to swim in.
⑤ The lake is so deep that you can't swim in.

18 다음 중 어법상 어색한 문장의 개수로 알맞은 것은?

a. You can use it not only for holding paper but also to put your phone on it.
b. She not only sang well but also dance perfectly.
c. The cat was not only tired but also hungry.
d. This water is so clean that we could drink it.
e. Her voice was loud enough to wake the boy up.

① 1개 ② 2개 ③ 3개 ④ 4개 ⑤ 5개

[19~22] 두 문장이 같은 뜻이 되도록 괄호 안의 어구를 사용하여 문장을 쓰시오.

19 We were so brave that we faced the strong enemy. (enough to)

➡ ______________________________
____

20 Ted is old enough to talk about the topic. (so ... that ~ can)

➡ ______________________________
____

21 He has experience as well as knowledge. (not only ~ but also ...)

➡ ______________________________
____

22 I must not only feed the animals but also look after the children. (as well as)

➡ ______________________________
____

23 다음 문장에서 밑줄 친 우리말을 영어로 옮기시오.

You can use it not only for (1)피자를 자르기 (2)피자 한 조각을 집기 위해서도.

➡ (1) ______________________________
(2) ______________________________

24 주어진 〈보기〉를 참고하여 두 문장을 하나의 문장으로 쓰시오.

보기

You like the movie.
\+ Eric likes the movie, too.
→ Not only you but also Eric likes the movie.

(1) She has to leave here.
\+ You have to leave here, too.
➡ ______________________________
____

(2) I like to play with dogs.
\+ My brothers like to play with dogs, too.
➡ ______________________________
____

(3) I am from Busan.
\+ My best friend is from Busan, too.
➡ ______________________________
____

[25~26] 다음 글을 읽고 물음에 답하시오.

"What happens when you walk backward while you are carrying a cup of coffee?" Han Jiwon, a Korean high school student, did research on this topic in 2015. Is this research project good enough to win a Nobel Prize? Maybe not. But how about an Ig Nobel Prize? He won ⓐone in 2017 for ⓑthis fun research.

ⓒThe Ig Nobel Prizes are awarded for discoveries that "first makes one laugh and then think." They were started in 1991 by *AIR* magazine to increase people's interest in science by honoring the unusual and the imaginative.

25 위 글의 밑줄 친 ⓐone이 가리키는 것을 본문에서 찾아 쓰고, ⓑthis fun research의 조사 내용을 우리말로 쓰시오.

➡ ⓐ ______________________

ⓑ ______________________

26 위 글의 밑줄 친 ⓒ에서 어법상 틀린 부분을 찾아 고치시오.

____________ ➡ ____________

[27~28] 다음 글을 읽고 물음에 답하시오.

The prizes are presented by real Nobel winners in Sanders Theater at Harvard University. The room is usually filled with people who are eager ⓐto cheer for the brave scientists with their "laughable" research.

The U.K. Navy won the Ig Nobel Prize for Peace in 2000. To save money, the Navy made its sailors shout, "Bang!" instead of using real bombs. Is that funny enough for you to laugh out loud?

27 아래 <보기>에서 위 글의 밑줄 친 ⓐto cheer와 to부정사의 용법이 같은 것의 개수를 고르시오.

보기

① To hear him talk, you would take him for a fool.

② My plan is to go to the movies tonight.

③ The mother was pleased to see her son well.

④ He didn't live to see the work finished.

⑤ What a fool she is to believe such a thing!

① 1개 ② 2개 ③ 3개 ④ 4개 ⑤ 5개

28 According to the passage, which is NOT true?

① The prizes are presented by real Ig Nobel winners.

② The prizes are presented in Sanders Theater at Harvard University.

③ People who are eager to cheer for the brave scientists with their "laughable" research usually fill the room.

④ The U.K. Navy won the Ig Nobel Prize for Peace in 2000.

⑤ To save money, the Navy made its sailors shout, "Bang!" instead of using real bombs.

[29~30] 다음 글을 읽고 물음에 답하시오.

Andre Geim also won an award that year. He succeeded in floating a live frog in the air by using magnets. "In my experience, if people don't have a sense of humor, they are usually not very good scientists," he said when he accepted his award.

If that still does not bring a smile to your face, how about this? In 2005, Gauri Nanda won the Ig Nobel Prize in Economics for inventing an alarm clock. It keeps running away until the sleeper finally gets out of bed.

29 본문의 내용과 일치하도록 다음 빈칸에 알맞은 단어들을 쓰시오.

According to Andre Geim, _______ _______ _______ _______ is usually a necessary condition to be a very good scientist.

30 다음 빈칸 (A)와 (B)에 알맞은 단어를 넣어 Gauri Nanda에 대한 소개를 완성하시오.

Gauri Nanda won the Ig Nobel Prize in Economics in 2005 because she invented (A)_______ _______ _______ which the sleeper can stop only after he or she finally (B)_______ _______ _______ _______.

[31~32] 다음 글을 읽고 물음에 답하시오.

Not only the winners' fun studies but also the ceremony for the Ig Nobel Prizes makes people laugh. ⓐThere are the number of interesting things that keeps people from getting bored. The opening and closing speeches are just two words each: "Welcome. Welcome." and "Goodbye. Goodbye." If someone talks for too long, an eight-year-old girl called Miss Sweetie Poo shouts repeatedly, "Please stop! I'm bored." Each winner receives ten trillion Zimbabwean dollars, ⓑ그것은 미국의 1달러보다 가치가 낮다. Throwing paper planes is another fun tradition.

31 위 글의 밑줄 친 ⓐ에서 어법상 틀린 부분을 찾아 고치시오. (두 군데)

_______ ➡ _______

_______ ➡ _______

32 위 글의 밑줄 친 ⓑ의 우리말에 맞게 주어진 어휘를 알맞게 배열하시오.

one U.S. dollar / worth / than / which / less / is

➡ _______________

교과서 파헤치기

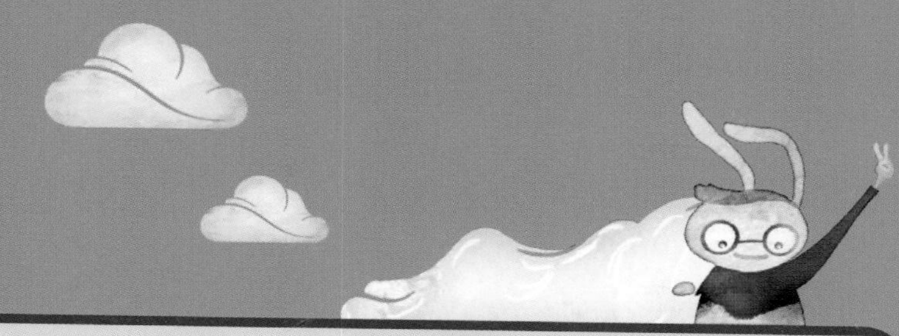

단어 Test

Step1

※ 다음 영어를 우리말로 쓰시오.

01 healthy ________
02 joke ________
03 book ________
04 deliver ________
05 miss ________
06 available ________
07 nervous ________
08 expression ________
09 written ________
10 gentleman ________
11 actually ________
12 guess ________
13 present ________
14 human ________
15 various ________
16 tone ________
17 break wind ________
18 visually ________
19 popular ________
20 whole ________
21 chance ________

22 facial ________
23 lunch break ________
24 since ________
25 wonder ________
26 finally ________
27 promise ________
28 laughter ________
29 represent ________
30 even ________
31 letter ________
32 meaningful ________
33 tear ________
34 move ________
35 keep in touch ________
36 such as ________
37 care for ________
38 stand for ________
39 laugh out loud ________
40 grow+비교급 ________
41 the same ~ as ________
42 can't wait for ________
43 with+명사+형용사~ ________

단어 Test

Step2

※ 다음 우리말을 영어로 쓰시오.

01 농담 ____________
02 실제로 ____________
03 막대기, 나뭇가지 ____________
04 의미 있는 ____________
05 전달하다 ____________
06 표현 ____________
07 웃음 ____________
08 신사 ____________
09 드디어, 마지막으로 ____________
10 구할 수 있는, 이용할 수 있는 ____________
11 예매하다, 예약하다 ____________
12 건강에 좋은 ____________
13 완전한, 전체의 ____________
14 인간적인, 인간의 ____________
15 약속하다; 약속 ____________
16 어조, 말투 ____________
17 그리워하다 ____________
18 얼굴의 ____________
19 글로 쓴, 글로 표현된 ____________
20 시각적으로 ____________
21 초조한 ____________
22 인기 있는 ____________
23 선물 ____________
24 꽤 ____________
25 나타내다, 대표하다 ____________
26 이사하다 ____________
27 추측하다, 짐작하다 ____________
28 궁금해 하다 ____________
29 기회, 가능성 ____________
30 눈물 ____________
31 다양한 ____________
32 문자 ____________
33 찬장 ____________
34 기름에 튀긴 ____________
35 큰 소리로 웃다 ____________
36 ~을 몹시 기다리다 ____________
37 ~을 의미하다, 상징하다 ____________
38 ~와 같은 … ____________
39 ~을 좋아하다 ____________
40 계속해서 연락하다 ____________
41 어느 때보다 행복한 ____________
42 ~을 보다 ____________
43 ~에 대해 걱정하다 ____________

단어 Test

Step3

※ 다음 영영풀이에 알맞은 단어를 <보기>에서 골라 쓴 후, 우리말 뜻을 쓰시오.

1 __________: having many different features: __________

2 __________: a type or variety of something: __________

3 __________: involving writing rather than speaking: __________

4 __________: able to be bought or used: __________

5 __________: in a way that is connected with seeing or sight: __________

6 __________: from a time in the past until a later past time or until now: __________

7 __________: to write something using a computer or typewrite: __________

8 __________: to bring goods, letter, etc. to the proper person: __________

9 __________: a man who is polite, well educated and has excellent manners: __________

10 __________: to be accepted as meaning a certain thing: __________

11 __________: an informal talk involving a small group of people or only two: __________

12 __________: a sign, shape, or object that is used to represent something else: __________

13 __________: to arrange to have a seat, room, performer, etc. at a particular time in the future: __________

14 __________: a short set of keyboard symbols that represents the facial expression used in email, etc. to show feelings: __________

15 __________: being, relating to, or belonging to a person or to people as opposed to animals: __________

16 __________: to give an answer to a particular question when you do not have all the facts and so cannot be certain if you are correct: __________

보기

book	since	form	conversation
available	gentleman	various	deliver
human	symbol	written	visually
guess	represent	emoticon	type

※ 다음 우리말과 일치하도록 빈칸에 알맞은 말을 쓰시오.

Get Ready 2

(1) **B:** You don't ________ ________. Are you all ________?

G: No, I'm ________ ________. My dog is ________. He won't eat ________ ________.

B: ________ ________ ________.

(2) **B:** It'll ________ a ________ ________ today! ________ ________ ________ at today's lunch menu.

G: Wow! I'm ________ ________ ________ fried chicken! I ________ ________ ________ ________ ________.

(3) **W:** Good morning, Mr. Lee. ________ are you ________?

M: I'm ________ very happy this morning. Some students are ________ me ________ the school.

W: I'm________ ________ ________ ________.

(4) **G:** You look ________. Are you ________ ________?

B: My mom won't ________ me ________ soccer ________ ________.

G: ________ ________ ________ ask her one more time?

(1) **B:** 기분이 좋아 보이지 않는구나. 너 괜찮니?

G: 아니, 나 정말 슬퍼. 내 개가 아파. 그는 아무것도 안 먹으려고 해.

B: 정말 안됐구나.

(2) **B:** 오늘은 좋은 날이 될 거야! 오늘 점심 메뉴 좀 봐.

G: 와! 닭튀김을 먹게 되어 기뻐! 점심시간이 무척 기다려져.

(3) **W:** 안녕하세요, 이 선생님. 기분이 어떠세요?

M: 오늘 아침에는 기분이 아주 좋습니다. 몇몇 학생들이 학교 청소하는 것을 돕고 있어요.

W: 그 말을 들으니 기쁘군요.

(4) **G:** 기분이 언짢아 보인다. 너 괜찮니?

B: 엄마가 방과 후에 축구하는 것을 허락하지 않으셔.

G: 한 번 더 말씀드려 보지 그러니?

Start Off – Listen & Talk A

1. **G:** Jihun, you're ________ to ________ ________ next week. ________ are you ________?

B: I'm ________ ________ go to a ________ new world, Yunju.

G: I'm glad ________ ________ that. I ________ ________ ________ you.

B: ________, I'm sad, too. I'll ________ all of you ________ ________.

G: Let's ________ ________ ________ online.

B: Okay. ________ ________ video chats often.

2. **G:** Minsu, Jihun ________ ________ to Abu Dhabi in the UAE next week. ________ are you ________?

B: I'm sad. I'm ________ ________ ________ him a lot.

G: I'm sad, too, but I'm also happy. We can visit Abu Dhabi. He ________ ________ to ________ us. He ________.

B: That's great! I'm ________ ________ ________ a ________ to ________ to a new country.

1. **G:** 지훈아, 너 다음 주에 다른 나라로 이사가지. 기분이 어때?

B: 완전히 새로운 나라에 가게 되어 흥분돼, 윤주야.

G: 그 말을 들으니 기쁘구나. 나는 너를 걱정했어.

B: 사실, 슬프기도 해. 너희 모두를 많이 그리워할 거야.

G: 온라인으로 계속 연락하자.

B: 좋아. 자주 화상 채팅하자.

2. **G:** 민수야, 지훈이가 다음 주에 아랍에미리트의 아부다비로 이사 간대. 기분이 어떠니?

B: 슬퍼. 그 애가 많이 보고 싶을 거야.

G: 나도 슬퍼, 하지만 기쁘기도 해. 우리는 아부다비를 방문할 수 있잖아. 그가 우리를 초대할 거야. 약속했어.

B: 그거 굉장하다! 새로운 나라로 여행할 기회를 얻게 되어 기뻐.

Start Off – Listen & Talk B

B: Yena, ________ ________ ________ ________?

G: I'm ________ very ________, Seho. My best friend Jihun is ________ ________.

B: Really? I'm ________. But ________ ________ so sad. You two can have ________ ________ online.

G: You're right.

B: ________ ________ ________ make him a photo book ________ a ________ ________?

G: Great idea. I'm glad to give him ________ ________.

B: 예나야, 기분이 어떠니?
G: 아주 슬퍼, 세호야. 내 가장 친한 친구인 지훈이가 이사 간대.
B: 정말? 유감이구나. 하지만 너무 슬퍼하지 마. 너희 둘은 온라인으로 화상 채팅을 할 수 있잖아.
G: 네 말이 맞아.
B: 우리 이별 선물로 그에게 사진책을 만들어 주는 게 어때?
G: 좋은 생각이야. 그에게 뭔가 의미 있는 것을 준다니 기뻐.

Start Off – Speak Up – Mission

A: ________ ________ ________ feeling today?

B: I'm ________ happy. Today's lunch is great.

A: I'm ________ ________ ________ ________.

A: 오늘 기분이 어떠니?
B: 기분이 좋아. 오늘 점심이 훌륭해.
A: 그 말을 들으니 기쁘구나.

Step Up – Real-life Scene

I Like Their Emojis

Nari: Hi, Jiho. ________ are you ________?

Jiho: I'm ________ than ________, Nari.

Nari: I know ________. You did it, ________ ________?

Jiho: Yes. I finally ________ four tickets for the VTS concert!

Nari: Good job. Did you tell Minsu and Yujin ________ that?

Jiho: Sure. Oh, I just ________ ________ from them. They said they are really happy. Look.

Nari: ________ ________! I like their ________. They will ________ ________ ________ and a nice camera.

Jiho: ________ ________ ________ ________ ________. We're going to have ________ ________ ________!

나는 그들의 이모지가 마음에 들어

나리: 안녕, 지호. 기분이 어떠니?
지호: 어떤 때보다 행복해, 나리야.
나리: 왜 그런지 알겠다. 너 해냈구나, 그렇지?
지호: 그래. 내가 마침내 VTS 콘서트 표를 4장 예매했어!
나리: 잘했어. 민수와 유진이에게도 그것에 대해 말했니?
지호: 물론이지. 오, 그들에게서 방금 메시지를 받았어. 그 애들도 정말 기쁘다고 말했어. 봐.
나리: 정말 귀엽구나! 나는 그들의 이모지가 마음에 들어. 그 애들은 광선 막대기와 멋진 카메라를 가져올 거야.
지호: 그 말을 들으니 기쁘다. 우리는 정말 재미있을 거야!

Fun Time

A: ________ are you ________?

B: I'm ________. I ________ ________ ________ my math homework. ________ ________ you feeling?

A: I'm ________, ________. I have a math test tomorrow. I'm ________ ________ ________ someone ________ ________ the same.

B: Me, ________.

A: 기분이 어떠니?
B: 나는 초조해. 수학 숙제 가져오는 걸 잊어버렸어. 너는 기분이 어떠니?
A: 나도 초조해. 내일 수학 시험이 있어. 같은 감정을 가진 사람을 찾아서 기뻐.
B: 나도 그래.

A: ________ are you feeling?

B: I'm ________. I ________ a good ________. How are you feeling?

A: I'm ________. Someone ________ my glasses.

A: 기분이 어떠니?
B: 나는 기분이 좋아. 좋은 점수를 받았어. 너는 기분이 어떠니?
A: 나는 화가 나. 누군가가 내 안경을 망가뜨렸어.

Express Yourself A 1

G: ________ ________ you feeling today?

B: I'm really ________ ________ ________ ________ ________ for my birthday.

G: What is the ________?

B: It's this drone, ________ our grandpa ________ ________ my birthday.

G: Wow! I ________ ________ ________ it ________ ________.

B: ________ ________ ________ you.

G: Thanks.

G: 넌 오늘 기분이 어때?
B: 생일 선물을 받아서 정말 기뻐.
G: 선물이 뭔데?
B: 이 드론인데, 우리 할아버지가 내 생일에 보내 주셨어.
G: 와! 그게 얼마나 높이 날 수 있는지 궁금하다.
B: 내가 보여 줄게.
G: 고마워.

Express Yourself A 2

G: ________ are you ________?

M: I'm really glad ________ ________ my ________ food.

G: I want ________ ________ ________ ________ ________.

M: It's *japchae*, ________ is ________ and ________.

G: I want ________ ________ some.

M: Okay. ________ ________ 30 ________!

G: 기분이 어떠세요?
M: 내가 가장 좋아하는 음식을 요리해서 정말 기뻐.
G: 그게 뭔지 알고 싶은데요.
M: 그건 잡채인데, 맛있고 건강에도 좋아.
G: 저도 좀 먹어 보고 싶어요.
M: 좋아. 30분만 기다려!

Check Yourself – Listen & Speak 1

G: Minsu, ________ ________ ________ ________?

B: I'm really ________, Miso. We ________ a new student ________ ________ ________. His name is Kim Kihun.

G: So ________ are you ________?

B: He was a soccer player ________ his school ________. ________ ________ ________, my team ________ a player.

G: ________ ________ ________ ________ that. I ________ he ________ your team.

B: Thanks a lot.

G: 민수야, 기분이 어떠니?
B: 나 정말 신나, 미소야. 우리 반에 새 학생이 한 명 왔어. 이름은 김기훈이야.
G: 그래서 네가 왜 신나는데?
B: 그는 학교 팀 축구 선수였대. 너도 알다시피, 우리 팀은 선수가 한 명 필요하잖아.
G: 그 말을 들으니 기뻐. 그가 너희 팀에 합류하길 바랄게.
B: 고마워.

대화문 Test

※ 다음 우리말에 맞도록 대화를 영어로 쓰시오.

Get Ready 2

(1) B: ______

G: ______

B: ______

(2) B: ______

G: ______

(3) W: ______

M: ______

______

W: ______

(4) G: ______

B: ______

G: ______

(1) B: 기분이 좋아 보이지 않는구나. 너 괜찮니?
G: 아니, 나 정말 슬퍼. 내 개가 아파. 그는 아무것도 안 먹으려고 해.
B: 정말 안됐구나.

(2) B: 오늘은 좋은 날이 될 거야! 오늘 점심 메뉴 좀 봐.
G: 와! 닭튀김을 먹게 되어 기뻐! 점심시간이 무척 기다려져.

(3) W: 안녕하세요, 이 선생님. 기분이 어떠세요?
M: 오늘 아침에는 기분이 아주 좋습니다. 몇몇 학생들이 학교 청소하는 것을 돕고 있어요.
W: 그 말을 들으니 기쁘군요.

(4) G: 기분이 언짢아 보인다. 너 괜찮니?
B: 엄마가 방과 후에 축구하는 것을 허락하지 않으셔.
G: 한 번 더 말씀드려 보지 그러니?

Start Off – Listen & Talk A

1. G: ______

B: ______

G: ______

B: ______

G: ______

B: ______

2. G: ______

______

B: ______

G: ______

______

B: ______

1. G: 지훈아, 너 다음 주에 다른 나라로 이사가지. 기분이 어때?
B: 완전히 새로운 나라에 가게 되어 흥분돼, 윤주야.
G: 그 말을 들으니 기쁘구나. 나는 너를 걱정했어.
B: 사실, 슬프기도 해. 너희 모두를 많이 그리워할 거야.
G: 온라인으로 계속 연락하자.
B: 좋아. 자주 화상 채팅하자.

2. G: 민수야, 지훈이가 다음 주에 아랍에미리트의 아부다비로 이사 간대. 기분이 어떠니?
B: 슬퍼. 그 애가 많이 보고 싶을 거야.
G: 나도 슬퍼, 하지만 기쁘기도 해. 우리는 아부다비를 방문할 수 있잖아. 그가 우리를 초대할 거야. 약속했어.
B: 그거 굉장하다! 새로운 나라로 여행할 기회를 얻게 되어 기뻐.

Start Off – Listen & Talk B

B: ______________________________

G: ______________________________

B: ______________________________

G: ______________________________

B: ______________________________

G: ______________________________

B: 예나야, 기분이 어떠니?
G: 아주 슬퍼, 세호야. 내 가장 친한 친구인 지훈이가 이사 간대.
B: 정말? 유감이구나. 하지만 너무 슬퍼하지 마. 너희 둘은 온라인으로 화상 채팅을 할 수 있잖아.
G: 네 말이 맞아.
B: 우리 이별 선물로 그에게 사진책을 만들어 주는 게 어때?
G: 좋은 생각이야. 그에게 뭔가 의미 있는 것을 준다니 기뻐.

Start Off – Speak Up – Mission

A: ______________________________

B: ______________________________

A: ______________________________

A: 오늘 기분이 어떠니?
B: 기분이 좋아. 오늘 점심이 훌륭해.
A: 그 말을 들으니 기쁘구나.

Step Up – Real-life Scene

I Like Their Emojis

Nari: ______________________________

Jiho: ______________________________

Nari: ______________________________

Jiho: ______________________________

Nari: ______________________________

Jiho: ______________________________

____

Nari: ______________________________

Jiho: ______________________________

나는 그들의 이모지가 마음에 들어
나리: 안녕, 지호. 기분이 어떠니?
지호: 어떤 때보다 행복해, 나리야.
나리: 왜 그런지 알겠다. 너 해냈구나, 그렇지?
지호: 그래. 내가 마침내 VTS 콘서트 표를 4장 예매했어!
나리: 잘했어. 민수와 유진이에게도 그것에 대해 말했니?
지호: 물론이지. 오, 그들에게서 방금 메시지를 받았어. 그 애들도 정말 기쁘다고 말했어. 봐.
나리: 정말 귀엽구나! 나는 그들의 이모지가 마음에 들어. 그 애들은 광선 막대기와 멋진 카메라를 가져올 거야.
지호: 그 말을 들으니 기쁘다. 우리는 정말 재미있을 거야!

Fun Time

A: ______________________________

B: ______________________________

A: ______________________________

____

B: ______________________________

A: ______________________________

B: ______________________________

A: ______________________________

A: 기분이 어떠니?
B: 나는 초조해. 수학 숙제 가져오는 걸 잊어버렸어. 너는 기분이 어떠니?
A: 나도 초조해. 내일 수학 시험이 있어. 같은 감정을 가진 사람을 찾아서 기뻐.
B: 나도 그래.

A: 기분이 어떠니?
B: 나는 기분이 좋아. 좋은 점수를 받았어. 너는 기분이 어떠니?
A: 나는 화가 나. 누군가가 내 안경을 망가뜨렸어.

Express Yourself A 1

G: ____________________

B: ____________________

G: ____________________

B: ____________________

G: ____________________

B: ____________________

G: ____________________

G: 넌 오늘 기분이 어때?
B: 생일 선물을 받아서 정말 기뻐.
G: 선물이 뭔데?
B: 이 드론인데, 우리 할아버지가 내 생일에 보내 주셨어.
G: 와! 그게 얼마나 높이 날 수 있는지 궁금하다.
B: 내가 보여 줄게.
G: 고마워.

Express Yourself A 2

G: ____________________

M: ____________________

G: ____________________

M: ____________________

G: ____________________

M: ____________________

G: 기분이 어떠세요?
M: 내가 가장 좋아하는 음식을 요리해서 정말 기뻐.
G: 그게 뭔지 알고 싶은데요.
M: 그건 잡채인데, 맛있고 건강에도 좋아.
G: 저도 좀 먹어 보고 싶어요.
M: 좋아. 30분만 기다려!

Check Yourself – Listen & Speak 1

G: ____________________

B: ____________________

____

G: ____________________

B: ____________________

____

G: ____________________

B: ____________________

G: 민수야, 기분이 어떠니?
B: 나 정말 신나, 미소야. 우리 반에 새 학생이 한 명 왔어. 이름은 김기훈이야.
G: 그래서 네가 왜 신나는데?
B: 그는 학교 팀 축구 선수였대. 너도 알다시피, 우리 팀은 선수가 한 명 필요하잖아.
G: 그 말을 들으니 기뻐. 그가 너희 팀에 합류하길 바랄게.
B: 고마워.

※ 다음 우리말과 일치하도록 빈칸에 알맞은 것을 골라 쓰시오.

1 ________ Do You "Ha-Ha" ________ Your ________?
A. Texts B. How C. in

2 ________ is ________.
A. human B. laughter

3 We ________ ________ ________ when we hear a ________, see something funny, or feel happy.
A. out B. joke C. loud D. laugh

4 We laugh ________ in our ________, such ________ emails or texts, as we do in our ________.
A. writings B. even C. as D. conversations

5 ________ do ________ do ________?
A. that B. we C. how

6 "Ha-ha" is a ________ of ________ ________.
A. written B. form C. laughter

7 Everyone knows ________ ________ ________.
A. it B. what C. means

8 Actually, it ________ ________ ________ ________ long ago.
A. been B. since C. has D. used

9 ________ Shakespeare used "ha-ha" ________ his ________.
A. works B. even C. in

10 **DOGBERRY**: Ha, ha, ha! Well, ________, ________ ________.
A. good B. gentlemen C. night

11 And if ________ ________ ________, find me and ________ me know.
A. important B. let C. happens D. anything

12 (Shakespeare, ________ *Ado About Nothing* ________ 3, ________ 3, Page 4)
A. Act B. Much C. Scene

13 ________ form of ________ ________ is LOL.
A. written B. another C. laughter

14 It ________ ________ "Laughing ________ ________."
A. for B. Loud C. stands D. Out

15 People also use ROFL ________ often, which means "________ ________ the Floor ________."
A. on B. Laughing C. quite D. Rolling

1 글에서는 어떻게 "하하"라고 웃나요?

2 웃음은 인간 고유의 것이다.

3 우리는 농담을 듣거나 우스운 것을 보거나 행복감을 느끼면 소리 내어 웃는다.

4 우리는 이메일이나 문자 메시지 같은 글 속에서조차 대화에서 하듯이 웃는다.

5 어떻게 그렇게 하는가?

6 "하하"는 문자로 된 웃음의 한 형태이다.

7 모두가 그것이 무엇을 의미하는지 안다.

8 실제로 그것은 오래전부터 사용되어 왔다.

9 셰익스피어조차도 "하하"를 자신의 작품에 사용하였다.

10 DOGBERRY: 하하하! 자, 신사분들, 좋은 밤 보내시오.

11 그리고 만일 뭔가 중요한 일이 일어난다면 나를 찾아서 알려 주시오.

12 (셰익스피어, 헛소동, 3막 3장 4쪽)

13 또 다른 형태의 문자로 된 웃음은 LOL이다.

14 그것은 '크게 소리 내어 웃기'를 상징한다.

15 사람들은 또한 ROFL도 꽤 자주 사용하는데, 그것은 '바닥을 구르면서 웃기'를 의미한다.

16 These ________ have become ________ because they can ________ ________ quite quickly.

A. popular B. expressions C. typed D. be

17 A: ________ a ________ ________ 2mrw.

A. trip B. safe C. have

18 ________ ________ u ________ ________ me too much. LOL

A. miss B. sure C. don't D. make

19 B: OK. I'll ________ to make ________ I don't ________ u. LOL

A. miss B. sure C. try

20 Thanks ________ ________ me a ________ ________.

A. wishing B. for C. trip D. safe

21 XD also ________ ________ in ________.

A. text B. represents C. laughter

22 It shows a laughing face ________ a mouth ________ and eyes ________ ________.

A. open B. with C. tightly D. closed

23 XD is ________ ________ ________.

A. not B. word C. a

24 It's an emoticon, which is a group of letters or symbols ________ to ________ a ________ ________.

A. represent B. expression C. used D. facial

25 The ________ XD ________ our happy ________ more ________ than ha-ha and LOL do.

A. visually B. emoticon C. feelings D. expresses

26 I ________ ________ ________ go to Disneyland. XD

A. to B. can't C. wait

27 These days, people use 😂 — a "face ________ ________ ________ ________."

A. tears B. joy C. of D. with

28 This is a ________ picture ________ an "________."

A. emoji B. small C. called

29 Lots of ________ emojis are ________ to use online, so people can express their ________ in ________ ways.

A. available B. various C. laughter D. laughing

30 A: I ________ my ________ on the ________.

A. cupboard B. hit C. head

31 B: Oh, my! ________ you ________?

A. okay B. are

16 이 표현들은 상당히 빠르게 타자를 칠 수 있어서 인기를 얻었다.

17 A: 내일 안전한 여행을 해.

18 나를 너무 많이 그리워하지 않도록 해. LOL

19 B: 좋아. 너를 그리워하지 않도록 할게. LOL

20 안전한 여행을 기원해 줘서 고마워.

21 XD 또한 문자 메시지에서 웃음을 나타낸다.

22 그것은 입을 벌리고 눈을 질끈 감은 채 웃는 얼굴을 보여 준다.

23 XD는 단어가 아니다.

24 그것은 이모티콘이고, 얼굴 표정을 나타내기 위해 사용되는 한 무리의 문자나 상징이다.

25 이모티콘 XD는 우리의 행복한 감정을 하하와 LOL보다 더 시각적으로 표현한다.

26 나는 디즈니랜드에 가는 게 몹시 기다려져. XD

27 요즘 사람들은 '기쁨의 눈물을 흘리는 얼굴'인 😂를 사용한다.

28 이것은 '이모지'라고 불리는 작은 그림이다.

29 많은 웃는 이모지가 온라인에서 사용될 수 있고, 그래서 사람들은 다양한 방식으로 자신들의 웃음을 표현할 수 있다.

30 A: 찬장에 머리를 부딪쳤어.

31 B: 오, 이런! 너 괜찮니?

32 A: I ________ my ________ on the ________.

A. head B. cupboard C. hit

33 B: Uh-oh! ________ the ________ ________?

A. okay B. cupboard C. is

34 Some emojis ________ ________ bigger, and some even move or make ________ ________.

A. grown B. sounds C. have D. laughing

35 A: So yesterday, I was in a restaurant, and I really ________ ________ ________ ________.

A. break B. wind C. to D. needed

36 B: And ...

37 A: Well, the music was really ________, ________ I ________ ________ it.

A. so B. loud C. did D. just

38 B: And ...

39 A: And then I ________ I was ________ to music ________ my ________.

A. with B. realized C. listening D. earphones

40 Laughing marks can represent our ________ ________ and deliver our ________ ________.

A. tones B. expressions C. voice D. facial

41 ________ using various laughing marks, we can show our friends how much we ________ ________ them or how happy we are ________ them.

A. care B. for C. by D. with

42 ________, even in ________ ________, ________ your friends will laugh with you.

A. written B. and C. laugh D. forms

43 Me ________ it's ________ ________

A. out B. when C. cold

44 This ________ ________ ________

A. yesterday B. was C. me

32 A: 찬장에 머리를 부딪쳤어.

33 B: 어 어! 찬장 괜찮니?

34 어떤 이모지들은 크기가 커졌고, 또 어떤 것들은 심지어 움직이거나 웃음소리를 내기까지 한다.

35 A: 그래서 어제 나는 식당에 있었는데 정말 방귀를 뀌어야 했어.

36 B: 그리고 …

37 A: 음, 음악이 정말 시끄럽길래 나는 그냥 뀌어 버렸어.

38 B: 그리고 …

39 A: 그리고 그때 나는 내가 이어폰을 끼고 음악을 듣고 있다는 걸 깨달았지.

40 웃음 표시는 우리의 얼굴 표정을 나타내고 우리의 목소리 어조를 전달할 수 있다.

41 다양한 웃음 표시를 사용함으로써, 우리는 친구들을 얼마나 좋아하는지 또는 그들과 함께 있어서 얼마나 행복한지를 그들에게 보여 줄 수 있다.

42 웃어라, 문자로 된 형태로라도. 그러면 친구들도 여러분과 함께 웃을 것이다.

43 추울 때 내 모습이네.

44 이건 어제의 나야.

본문 Test

※ 다음 우리말과 일치하도록 빈칸에 알맞은 것을 골라 쓰시오.

1 ________ Do You "Ha-Ha" in Your ________?

2 ________ is ________.

3 We ________ ________ ________ when we hear a joke, see ________ ________, or feel happy.

4 We ________ ________ ________ ________ ________, such as emails or texts, ________ we do in our conversations.

5 ________ do we do ________?

6 "Ha-ha" is a ________ of ________ ________.

7 Everyone knows ________ ________ ________.

8 Actually, it ________ ________ ________ ________ long ago.

9 Even Shakespeare used "ha-ha" ________ ________ ________.

10 **DOGBERRY**: Ha, ha, ha! Well, ________, ________ night.

11 And if ________ ________ happens, find me and let me know.

12 (Shakespeare, *Much Ado About Nothing* ________ 3, ________ 3, Page 4)

13 ________ form of ________ ________ is LOL.

14 It ________ ________ "________ Out ________."

15 People also use ROFL quite often, which means "________ ________ ________ ________ ________."

16 These ________ have become popular ________ they ________ ________ ________ quite quickly.

17 A: ________ ________ ________ ________ 2mrw.

18 ________ ________ u don't ________ me too much. LOL

19 B: OK. I'll try to make sure I don't ________ ________. LOL

20 Thanks for ________ ________ ________ ________ ________.

21 XD also ________ ________ in text.

22 It shows a ________ ________ ________ a mouth ________ and eyes ________ ________.

---

1 글에서는 어떻게 "하하"라고 웃나요?
2 웃음은 인간 고유의 것이다.
3 우리는 농담을 듣거나 우스운 것을 보거나 행복감을 느끼면 소리 내어 웃는다.
4 우리는 이메일이나 문자 메시지 같은 글 속에서조차 대화에서 하듯이 웃는다.
5 어떻게 그렇게 하는가?
6 "하하"는 문자로 된 웃음의 한 형태이다.
7 모두가 그것이 무엇을 의미하는지 안다.
8 실제로 그것은 오래전부터 사용되어 왔다.
9 셰익스피어조차도 "하하"를 자신의 작품에 사용하였다.
10 DOGBERRY: 하하하! 자, 신사분들, 좋은 밤 보내시오.
11 그리고 만일 뭔가 중요한 일이 일어난다면 나를 찾아서 알려 주시오.
12 (셰익스피어, 헛소동, 3막 3장 4쪽)
13 또 다른 형태의 문자로 된 웃음은 LOL이다.
14 그것은 '크게 소리 내어 웃기'를 상징한다.
15 사람들은 또한 ROFL도 꽤 자주 사용하는데, 그것은 '바닥을 구르면서 웃기'를 의미한다.
16 이 표현들은 상당히 빠르게 타자를 칠 수 있어서 인기를 얻었다.
17 A: 내일 안전한 여행을 해.
18 나를 너무 많이 그리워하지 않도록 해. LOL
19 B: 좋아. 너를 그리워하지 않도록 할게. LOL.
20 안전한 여행을 기원해 줘서 고마워.
21 XD 또한 문자 메시지에서 웃음을 나타낸다.
22 그것은 입을 벌리고 눈을 질끈 감은 채 웃는 얼굴을 보여 준다.

23 XD is not ________ ________.

24 It's an emoticon, ________ is a group of letters or symbols ________ ________ ________ ________ ________ ________.

25 The emoticon XD ________ our happy feelings ________ ________ than ha-ha and LOL do.

26 I ________ ________ ________ go to Disneyland. XD

27 ________ ________, people use 😂 — a "________ ________ ________ ________ ________."

28 This is a small picture ________ an "emoji."

29 Lots of laughing emojis are ________ ________ ________ online, so people can express their laughter in ________ ________.

30 A: I ________ ________ ________ on the cupboard.

31 B: Oh, my! Are you ________?

32 A: I ________ my head ________ ________ ________. 😂

33 B: Uh-oh! Is the cupboard ________? 😂

34 Some emojis ________ ________ ________, and some ________ ________ or make ________ ________.

35 A: So yesterday, I was in a restaurant, and I really ________ ________ ________ ________.

36 B: And ...

37 A: Well, the music was really ________, ________ I ________ ________ ________.

38 B: And ...

39 A: And then I ________ I was ________ ________ music ________ ________ ________.

40 Laughing marks can ________ our ________ ________ and ________ our ________ ________.

41 ________ ________ various laughing marks, we can show our friends how much we ________ ________ them or how happy we are ________ ________.

42 ________, even in ________ ________, ________ your friends will ________ with you.

43 Me when it's ________ ________

44 ________ ________ me yesterday

23 XD는 단어가 아니다.
24 그것은 이모티콘이고, 얼굴 표정을 나타내기 위해 사용되는 한 무리의 문자나 상징이다.
25 이모티콘 XD는 우리의 행복한 감정을 하하와 LOL보다 더 시각적으로 표현한다.
26 나는 디즈니랜드에 가는 게 몹시 기다려져. XD
27 요즘 사람들은 '기쁨의 눈물을 흘리는 얼굴'인 😂를 사용한다.
28 이것은 '이모지'라고 불리는 작은 그림이다.
29 많은 웃는 이모지가 온라인에서 사용될 수 있고, 그래서 사람들은 다양한 방식으로 자신들의 웃음을 표현할 수 있다.
30 A: 찬장에 머리를 부딪쳤어.
31 B: 오, 이런! 너 괜찮니?
32 A: 찬장에 머리를 부딪쳤어. 😂
33 B: 어 어! 찬장 괜찮니? 😂
34 어떤 이모지들은 크기가 커졌고, 또 어떤 것들은 심지어 움직이거나 웃음소리를 내기까지 한다.
35 A: 그래서 어제 나는 식당에 있었는데 정말 방귀를 뀌어야 했어.
36 B: 그리고 …
37 A: 음, 음악이 정말 시끄럽길래 나는 그냥 뀌어 버렸어.
38 B: 그리고 …
39 A: 그리고 그때 나는 내가 이어폰을 끼고 음악을 듣고 있다는 걸 깨달았지.
40 웃음 표시는 우리의 얼굴 표정을 나타내고 우리의 목소리 어조를 전달할 수 있다.
41 다양한 웃음 표시를 사용함으로써, 우리는 친구들을 얼마나 좋아하는지 또는 그들과 함께 있어서 얼마나 행복한지를 그들에게 보여 줄 수 있다.
42 웃어라, 문자로 된 형태로라도. 그러면 친구들도 여러분과 함께 웃을 것이다.
43 추울 때 내 모습이네.
44 이건 어제의 나야.

본문 Test

※ 다음 문장을 우리말로 쓰시오.

1 How Do You "Ha-Ha" in Your Texts?

➡ ______________________________

2 Laughter is human.

➡ ______________________________

3 We laugh out loud when we hear a joke, see something funny, or feel happy.

➡ ______________________________

4 We laugh even in our writings, such as emails or texts, as we do in our conversations.

➡ ______________________________

5 How do we do that?

➡ ______________________________

6 "Ha-ha" is a form of written laughter.

➡ ______________________________

7 Everyone knows what it means.

➡ ______________________________

8 Actually, it has been used since long ago.

➡ ______________________________

9 Even Shakespeare used "ha-ha" in his works.

➡ ______________________________

10 DOGBERRY: Ha, ha, ha! Well, gentlemen, good night.

➡ ______________________________

11 And if anything important happens, find me and let me know.

➡ ______________________________

12 (Shakespeare, Much Ado About Nothing Act 3, Scene 3, Page 4)

➡ ______________________________

13 Another form of written laughter is LOL.

➡ ______________________________

14 It stands for "Laughing Out Loud."

➡ ______________________________

15 People also use ROFL quite often, which means "Rolling on the Floor Laughing."

➡ ______________________________

16 These expressions have become popular because they can be typed quite quickly.

➡ ______________________________

17 A: Have a safe trip 2mrw.

➡ ______________________________

18 Make sure u don't miss me too much. LOL

➡ ______________________________

19 B: OK. I'll try to make sure I don't miss u. LOL.

➡ ______________________________

20 Thanks for wishing me a safe trip.

➡ ______________________________

21 XD also represents laughter in text.

➡ ______________________________

22 It shows a laughing face with a mouth open and eyes closed tightly.

➡ ______________________________

23 XD is not a word.

➡ ______________________________

24 It's an emoticon, which is a group of letters or symbols used to represent a facial expression.

➡ ______________________________

25 The emoticon XD expresses our happy feelings more visually than ha-ha and LOL do.

➡ ______________________________

26 I can't wait to go to Disneyland. XD

➡ ______________________________

27 These days, people use 😂 — a "face with tears of joy."

➡ ______________________________

28 This is a small picture called an "emoji."

➡ ______________________________

29 Lots of laughing emojis are available to use online, so people can express their laughter in various ways.

➡ ______________________________

30 A: I hit my head on the cupboard.

➡ ______________________________

31 B: Oh, my! Are you okay?

➡ ______________________________

32 A: I hit my head on the cupboard.😂

➡ ______________________________

33 B: Uh-oh! Is the cupboard okay?😂

➡ ______________________________

34 Some emojis have grown bigger, and some even move or make laughing sounds.

➡ ______________________________

35 A: So yesterday, I was in a restaurant, and I really needed to break wind.

➡ ______________________________

36 B: And ...

➡ ______________________________

37 A: Well, the music was really loud, so I just did it.

➡ ______________________________

38 B: And ...

➡ ______________________________

39 A: And then I realized I was listening to music with my earphones.

➡ ______________________________

40 Laughing marks can represent our facial expressions and deliver our voice tones.

➡ ______________________________

41 By using various laughing marks, we can show our friends how much we care for them or how happy we are with them.

➡ ______________________________

____

42 Laugh, even in written forms, and your friends will laugh with you.

➡ ______________________________

43 Me when it's cold out

➡ ______________________________

44 This was me yesterday

➡ ______________________________

본문 Test

Step4

※ 다음 괄호 안의 단어들을 우리말에 맞도록 바르게 배열하시오.

1 (Do / How / "Ha-Ha" / You / in / Texts? / Your)
➡ ____________________

2 (is / Laughter / human.)
➡ ____________________

3 (laugh / we / loud / out / we / when / hear / joke, / a / see / funny, / something / or / happy. / feel)
➡ ____________________
____

4 (laugh / we / in / even / writings, / our / as / such / or / emails / texts, / we / as / do / our / in / conversations.)
➡ ____________________
____

5 (do / how / do / we / that?)
➡ ____________________

6 (is / "ha-ha" / form / a / written / of / laughter.)
➡ ____________________

7 (knows / everyone / it / what / means.)
➡ ____________________

8 (it / actually, / has / used / been / long / since / ago.)
➡ ____________________

9 (Shakespeare / even / "ha-ha" / used / in / works. / his)
➡ ____________________

10 (DOGBERRY: / ha, / ha! / ha, / gentlemen, / well, / night. / good)
➡ ____________________

11 (if / and / anything / happens, / important / me / find / and / me / let / know.)
➡ ____________________

12 ((Much / Shakespeare, / Ado / Nothing / About / 3, / Act / Scene / 4 / 3, / Page)
➡ ____________________

13 (form / another / written / of / is / laughter / LOL.)
➡ ____________________

14 (stands / it / for / Out / "Laughing / Loud.")
➡ ____________________

15 (also / people / FOFL / use / often, / quite / means / which / on / "Rolling / the / Laughing." / Floor)
➡ ____________________
____

1 글에서는 어떻게 "하하"라고 웃나요?

2 웃음은 인간 고유의 것이다.

3 우리는 농담을 듣거나 우스운 것을 보거나 행복감을 느끼면 소리 내어 웃는다.

4 우리는 이메일이나 문자 메시지 같은 글 속에서조차 대화에서 하듯이 웃는다.

5 어떻게 그렇게 하는가?

6 "하하"는 문자로 된 웃음의 한 형태이다.

7 모두가 그것이 무엇을 의미하는지 안다.

8 실제로 그것은 오래전부터 사용되어 왔다.

9 셰익스피어조차도 "하하"를 자신의 작품에 사용하였다.

10 DOGBERRY: 하하하! 자, 신사분들, 좋은 밤 보내시오.

11 그리고 만일 뭔가 중요한 일이 일어난다면 나를 찾아서 알려 주시오.

12 (셰익스피어, 헛소동, 3막 3장 4쪽)

13 또 다른 형태의 문자로 된 웃음은 LOL이다.

14 그것은 '크게 소리 내어 웃기'를 상징한다.

15 사람들은 또한 ROFL도 꽤 자주 사용하는데, 그것은 '바닥을 구르면서 웃기'를 의미한다.

16 (expressions / these / become / have / because / popular / can / they / typed / be / quickly. / quite)

➡ ______________________________

____

17 (A: / a / have / safe / 2mrw. / trip)

➡ ______________________________

18 (sure / make / don't / u / me / miss / much. / too / LOL)

➡ ______________________________

19 (B: / OK. // try / I'll / make / to / I / sure / miss / don't / u. / LOL.)

➡ ______________________________

20 (for / thanks / me / wishing / safe / a / trip.)

➡ ______________________________

21 (also / XD / laughter / represents / text. / in)

➡ ______________________________

22 (shows / it / laughing / a / with / face / mouth / a / open / eyes / and / tightly. / closed)

➡ ______________________________

23 (is / XD / a / not / word.)

➡ ______________________________

24 (an / it's / emoticon, / is / which / group / a / letters / of / or / uesed / symbols / represent / to / facial / a / expression.)

➡ ______________________________

____

25 (emoticon / the / expresses / XD / happy / our / more / feelings / than / visually / ha-ha / LOL / and / do.)

➡ ______________________________

____

26 (can't / I / to / wait / to / go / XD / Disneyland.)

➡ ______________________________

27 (days, / these / use / people / 😂 / – / "face / a / tears / with / joy." / of)

➡ ______________________________

28 (is / small / this / picture / a / called / "emoji." / an)

➡ ______________________________

29 (of / lots / emojis / laughing / available / are / use / to / online, / people / so / express / can / laughter / their / various / in / ways.)

➡ ______________________________

____

30 (A: / hit / I / head / my / on / cupboard. / the)

➡ ______________________________

31 (B: / my! / oh, // you / are / okay?)

➡ ______________________________

16 이 표현들은 상당히 빠르게 타자를 칠 수 있어서 인기를 얻었다.

17 A: 내일 안전한 여행을 해.

18 나를 너무 많이 그리워하지 않도록 해. LOL

19 B: 좋아. 너를 그리워하지 않도록 할게. LOL

20 안전한 여행을 기원해 줘서 고마워.

21 XD 또한 문자 메시지에서 웃음을 나타낸다.

22 그것은 입을 벌리고 눈을 질끈 감은 채 웃는 얼굴을 보여 준다.

23 XD는 단어가 아니다.

24 그것은 이모티콘이고, 얼굴 표정을 나타내기 위해 사용되는 한 무리의 문자나 상징이다.

25 이모티콘 XD는 우리의 행복한 감정을 하하와 LOL보다 더 시각적으로 표현한다.

26 나는 디즈니랜드에 가는 게 몹시 기다려져. XD

27 요즘 사람들은 '기쁨의 눈물을 흘리는 얼굴'인 😂를 사용한다.

28 이것은 '이모지'라고 불리는 작은 그림이다.

29 많은 웃는 이모지가 온라인에서 사용될 수 있고, 그래서 사람들은 다양한 방식으로 자신들의 웃음을 표현할 수 있다.

30 A: 찬장에 머리를 부딪쳤어.

31 B: 오, 이런! 너 괜찮니?

32 (A: / hit / I / head / my / the / on / cupboard. / 😂)

➡ ____________________

33 (B: /uh-oh! / the / is / okay? / cupboard/ 😂)

➡ ____________________

34 (emojis / some / grown / have / bigger, / some / and / move / even / make / or / sounds. / laughing)

➡ ____________________

____

35 (A: yesterday, / so / was / I / in / restaurant, / a / and / really / I / to / needed / wind. / break /)

➡ ____________________

____

36 (B: / ... / and)

➡ ____________________

37 (A: / the / well, / music / really / was / so / loud, / just / I / it. / did)

➡ ____________________

38 (B: / ... / and)

➡ ____________________

39 (A: / then / and / I / realized / I / listening / was / music / to / my / with / earphones.)

➡ ____________________

40 (marks / laughing / represent / can / facial / our / expressions / and / our / deliver / tones. / voice)

➡ ____________________

____

41 (using / by / laughing / various / marks, / can / we / our / show / friends / much / how / care / we / for / or / them / happy / how / are / we / them. / with)

➡ ____________________

____

42 (even / laugh, / written / in / forms, / your / and / will / friends / with / laugh / you.)

➡ ____________________

43 (when / me / cold / it's / out)

➡ ____________________

44 (was / this / yesterday / me)

➡ ____________________

32 A: 찬장에 머리를 부딪쳤어. 😂

33 B: 어 어! 찬장 괜찮니? 😂

34 어떤 이모지들은 크기가 커졌고, 또 어떤 것들은 심지어 움직이거나 웃음소리를 내기까지 한다.

35 A: 그래서 어제 나는 식당에 있었는데 정말 방귀를 뀌어야 했어.

36 B: 그리고 …

37 A: 음, 음악이 정말 시끄럽길래 나는 그냥 뀌어 버렸어.

38 B: 그리고 …

39 A: 그리고 그때 나는 내가 이어폰을 끼고 음악을 듣고 있다는 걸 깨달았지.

40 웃음 표시는 우리의 얼굴 표정을 나타내고 우리의 목소리 어조를 전달할 수 있다.

41 다양한 웃음 표시를 사용함으로써, 우리는 친구들을 얼마나 좋아하는지 또는 그들과 함께 있어서 얼마나 행복한지를 그들에게 보여 줄 수 있다.

42 웃어라, 문자로 된 형태로라도. 그러면 친구들도 여러분과 함께 웃을 것이다.

43 추울 때 내 모습이네.

44 이건 어제의 나야.

본문 Test

※ 다음 우리말을 영어로 쓰시오.

1 글에서는 어떻게 "하하"라고 웃나요?

➡ ______________________________

2 웃음은 인간 고유의 것이다.

➡ ______________________________

3 우리는 농담을 듣거나 우스운 것을 보거나 행복감을 느끼면 소리 내어 웃는다.

➡ ______________________________

4 우리는 이메일이나 문자 메시지 같은 글 속에서조차 대화에서 하듯이 웃는다.

➡ ______________________________

5 어떻게 그렇게 하는가?

➡ ______________________________

6 "하하"는 문자로 된 웃음의 한 형태이다.

➡ ______________________________

7 모두가 그것이 무엇을 의미하는지 안다.

➡ ______________________________

8 실제로 그것은 오래전부터 사용되어 왔다.

➡ ______________________________

9 셰익스피어조차도 "하하"를 자신의 작품에 사용하였다.

➡ ______________________________

10 DOGBERRY: 하하하! 자, 신사분들, 좋은 밤 보내시오.

➡ ______________________________

11 그리고 만일 뭔가 중요한 일이 일어난다면 나를 찾아서 알려 주시오.

➡ ______________________________

12 (셰익스피어. 헛소동. 3막 3장 4쪽)

➡ ______________________________

13 또 다른 형태의 문자로 된 웃음은 LOL이다.

➡ ______________________________

14 그것은 '크게 소리 내어 웃기'를 상징한다.

➡ ______________________________

15 사람들은 또한 ROFL도 꽤 자주 사용하는데. 그것은 '바닥을 구르면서 웃기'를 의미한다.

➡ ______________________________

16 이 표현들은 상당히 빠르게 타자를 칠 수 있어서 인기를 얻었다.

➡ ______________________________

17 A: 내일 안전한 여행을 해.

➡ ______________________________

18 나를 너무 많이 그리워하지 않도록 해. LOL

➡ ______________________________

19 B: 좋아. 너를 그리워하지 않도록 할게. LOL

➡ ______________________________

20 안전한 여행을 기원해 줘서 고마워.

➡ ______________________________

21 XD 또한 문자 메시지에서 웃음을 나타낸다.

➡ ______________________________

22 그것은 입을 벌리고 눈을 질끈 감은 채 웃는 얼굴을 보여 준다.

➡ ______________________________

23 XD는 단어가 아니다.

➡ ______________________________

24 그것은 이모티콘이고, 얼굴 표정을 나타내기 위해 사용되는 한 무리의 문자나 상징이다.

➡ ______________________________

25 이모티콘 XD는 우리의 행복한 감정을 하하와 LOL보다 더 시각적으로 표현한다.

➡ ______________________________

26 나는 디즈니랜드에 가는 게 몹시 기다려져. XD

➡ ______________________________

27 요즘 사람들은 '기쁨의 눈물을 흘리는 얼굴'인 😂를 사용한다.

➡ ______________________________

28 이것은 '이모지'라고 불리는 작은 그림이다.

➡ ______________________________

29 많은 웃는 이모지가 온라인에서 사용될 수 있고, 그래서 사람들은 다양한 방식으로 자신들의 웃음을 표현할 수 있다.

➡ ______________________________

30 A: 찬장에 머리를 부딪쳤어.

➡ ______________________________

31 B: 오. 이런! 너 괜찮니?

➡ ______________________________

32 A: 찬장에 머리를 부딪쳤어. 😂

➡ ______________________________

33 B: 어 어! 찬장 괜찮니? 😂

➡ ______________________________

34 어떤 이모지들은 크기가 커졌고, 또 어떤 것들은 심지어 움직이거나 웃음소리를 내기까지 한다.

➡ ______________________________

35 A: 그래서 어제 나는 식당에 있었는데 정말 방귀를 뀌어야 했어.

➡ ______________________________

36 B: 그리고 …

➡ ______________________________

37 A: 음, 음악이 정말 시끄럽길래 나는 그냥 뀌어 버렸어.

➡ ______________________________

38 B: 그리고 …

➡ ______________________________

39 A: 그리고 그때 나는 내가 이어폰을 끼고 음악을 듣고 있다는 걸 깨달았지.

➡ ______________________________

40 웃음 표시는 우리의 얼굴 표정을 나타내고 우리의 목소리 어조를 전달할 수 있다.

➡ ______________________________

41 다양한 웃음 표시를 사용함으로써, 우리는 친구들을 얼마나 좋아하는지 또는 그들과 함께 있어서 얼마나 행복한지를 그들에게 보여 줄 수 있다.

➡ ______________________________

42 웃어라, 문자로 된 형태로라도. 그러면 친구들도 여러분과 함께 웃을 것이다.

➡ ______________________________

43 추울 때 내 모습이네.

➡ ______________________________

44 이건 어제의 나야.

➡ ______________________________

구석구석 지문 Test

Step1

※ 다음 우리말과 일치하도록 빈칸에 알맞은 말을 쓰시오.

Self-study Guide

1. A: Can you tell me ________ ________ ________?
2. B: Sure. I ________ ________ Mokpo.
3. A: ________ ________ tell me ________ ________ ________ ________ ________ ________?
4. B: Sure. It will come ________ ________ ________.

1. A: 당신이 어디에 사는지 제게 말해 줄 수 있나요?
2. B: 물론이죠. 저는 목포에 살아요.
3. A: 다음 버스가 언제 올지 제게 말씀해 주실 수 있으신가요?
4. B: 물론이죠. 그건 10분 후에 올 겁니다.

Link to the World

1. Do you know ________ ________ ________ ________ ________.
2. • This is the uniform of the Reds, ________ ________ ________ the Korean soccer team. Red ________ "power" on this uniform.
3. • Red on a ________ ________ means "stop."
4. • ________ ________ ________ ________ of red, "love" is my favorite. "Love ________ ________."

1. 빨간색이 무엇을 의미하는지 알고 있니?
2. • 이것은 붉은 악마들의 유니폼인데, 그들은 한국 축구팀을 응원한다. 이 유니폼에서 빨간색은 "힘"을 의미한다.
3. • 교통 신호등의 빨간색은 "멈추시오"라는 뜻이다.
4. • 빨간색의 여러 의미 중에서, '사랑'이 나는 가장 좋다. "사랑은 절대 실패하지 않는다."

Express Yourself C

1. Yeji: Can you ________ ________ ________ ________ ________ for his birthday?
2. He ________ a drone ________ our grandpa, ________ ________ ________ Busan.

1. 예지: 내 남동생이 그의 생일 선물로 무엇을 받았는지 추측할 수 있니?
2. 그는 우리 할아버지로부터 드론을 받았는데, 할아버지는 부산에 사셔.

구석구석 지문 Test

Step2

※ 다음 우리말을 영어로 쓰시오.

Self-study Guide

1. A: 당신이 어디에 사는지 제게 말해 줄 수 있나요?
➡ ______________________________

2. B: 물론이죠. 저는 목포에 살아요.
➡ ______________________________

3. A: 다음 버스가 언제 올지 제게 말씀해 주실 수 있으신가요?
➡ ______________________________

4. B: 물론이죠. 그건 10분 후에 올 겁니다.
➡ ______________________________

Link to the World

1. 빨간색이 무엇을 의미하는지 알고 있니?
➡ ______________________________

2. • 이것은 붉은 악마들의 유니폼인데, 그들은 한국 축구팀을 응원한다. 이 유니폼에서 빨간색은 "힘"을 의미한다.
➡ ______________________________
____

3. • 교통 신호등의 빨간색은 "멈추시오"라는 뜻이다.
➡ ______________________________

4. • 빨간색의 여러 의미 중에서, '사랑'이 나는 가장 좋다. "사랑은 절대 실패하지 않는다."
➡ ______________________________

Express Yourself C

1. 예지: 내 남동생이 그의 생일 선물로 무엇을 받았는지 추측할 수 있니?
➡ ______________________________

2. 그는 우리 할아버지로부터 드론을 받았는데, 할아버지는 부산에 사셔.
➡ ______________________________

단어 Test

Step1

※ 다음 영어를 우리말로 쓰시오.

01 awful ____________
02 sweaty ____________
03 class leader ____________
04 dirty ____________
05 double ____________
06 activity ____________
07 else ____________
08 empty ____________
09 suggest ____________
10 sneeze ____________
11 pleasure ____________
12 trash bag ____________
13 hang ____________
14 string ____________
15 tough ____________
16 fill ____________
17 complain ____________
18 fix ____________
19 admit ____________
20 dust ____________
21 lettuce ____________
22 neighborhood ____________
23 among ____________
24 trash ____________
25 wrap ____________
26 imagine ____________
27 bean ____________
28 helpful ____________
29 wonder ____________
30 mess ____________
31 assign ____________
32 sight ____________
33 tight ____________
34 popular ____________
35 work on ____________
36 in charge of ____________
37 set up ____________
38 take care of ____________
39 fill A with B ____________
40 divide A into B ____________
41 turn A into B ____________
42 be ready to-V ____________
43 pop up ____________

단어 Test

Step2

※ 다음 우리말을 영어로 쓰시오.

01 끔찍한, 지독한 ____________

02 더러운 ____________

03 제안하다 ____________

04 두 배가 되다 ____________

05 채우다 ____________

06 불평하다, 투덜거리다 ____________

07 수리하다 ____________

08 쓰레기 봉투 ____________

09 먼지 ____________

10 도움이 되는, 유용한 ____________

11 (생각이) ~에게 떠오르다 ____________

12 끈, 줄 ____________

13 배정하다, 배치하다, 맡기다 ____________

14 상상하다 ____________

15 단단히, 꽉 ____________

16 텅 빈, 비어 있는 ____________

17 기쁨 ____________

18 인정하다, 시인하다 ____________

19 ~ 중에, ~ 사이에 ____________

20 포장지 ____________

21 땀투성이의, 땀에 젖은 ____________

22 콩 ____________

23 재채기하다 ____________

24 걸다, 매달다 ____________

25 힘든 ____________

26 인기 있는 ____________

27 열, 줄 ____________

28 광경 ____________

29 쓰레기 ____________

30 상추 ____________

31 쓰레기 더미, 지저분함 ____________

32 이웃, 인근 주민 ____________

33 양로원 ____________

34 무거운 ____________

35 ~로 가득 차다 ____________

36 ~을 돌보다 ____________

37 설치하다, 마련하다 ____________

38 A를 B로 바꾸다 ____________

39 ~에 공들이다[애쓰다] ____________

40 ~할 준비가 되다 ____________

41 A를 B로 나누다 ____________

42 ~ 맞은편에 ____________

43 ~을 맡아, ~을 담당하여 ____________

단어 Test

Step3

※ 다음 영영풀이에 알맞은 단어를 <보기>에서 골라 쓴 후, 우리말 뜻을 쓰시오.

1 __________: an area of land: __________

2 __________: to repair something: __________

3 __________: to make or become full: __________

4 __________: extremely bad or unpleasant: __________

5 __________: difficult to do or to deal with: __________

6 __________: covered in sweat or smelling of sweat: __________

7 __________: not containing any things or people: __________

8 __________: to offer to do something that you do not have to do: __________

9 __________: to say that something is wrong or not satisfactory: __________

10 __________: to make something twice as much or many: __________

11 __________: to agree that something is true, especially unwillingly: __________

12 __________: to give a particular job or piece of work to someone: __________

13 __________: to tell someone your ideas about what they should do, where they should go etc.: __________

14 __________: dry dirt in the form of powder that covers surfaces inside a building, or very small dry pieces of soil, sand, or other substances: __________

15 __________: a place where very old people who are ill live and receive medical treatment and care: __________

16 __________: to put something in a position so that the top part is fixed or supported, and the bottom part is free to move and does not touch the ground: __________

보기

dust	admit	empty	volunteer
hang	tough	lot	awful
suggest	assign	nursing home	double
fill	complain	fix	sweaty

대화문 Test

Step1

※ 다음 우리말과 일치하도록 빈칸에 알맞은 말을 쓰시오.

Get Ready 2

(1) B: The ________ ________ looks ________. ________ ________ help you, Ms. Min?

W: You're so ________. ________ ________ very much.

(2) G: ________ ________ ________ you ________ the bench.

M: Please ________ this ________. Thank you ________ ________ me.

(3) B: ________ ________ ________ what we can do ________ our town.

G: ________ ________ ________ pictures on the ________ walls?

B: ________ good. ________ ________?

(1) B: 화분이 무거워 보여요. 민 선생님, 도와드릴까요?

W: 아주 친절하구나. 정말 고마워.

(2) G: 제가 의자 고치시는 걸 도와 드릴게요.

M: 이걸 좀 꽉 잡아 다오. 도와줘서 고맙구나.

(3) B: 우리가 마을을 위해 무엇을 할 수 있는지 이야기해 보자.

G: 지저분한 벽에 그림을 그리는 게 어떠니?

B: 좋아. 또 다른 건?

Start Off – Listen & Talk A

1. B: What do we ________ in our club room? ________ talk about it.

G: Sure. Well, ________ ________ ________ some ________ ________ ________ the windows? They'll ________ our room ________.

B: That's a ________ ________. Thank you, Jiu.

2. B: ________ ________ ________ some pictures?

G: Good. ________ ________ ________ ________ one of your pictures? You're ________ ________ ________, Seho.

B: ________ you ________ ________ that. I'll ________ one of ________.

3. B: Let's talk ________ the ________ this time. ________ ideas?

G: ________ ________ ________ a small library in the ________ of the club room? I will ________ some books tomorrow.

B: Great idea! Thank you ________ ________ it, Minju.

1. B: 우리 동아리실에 무엇이 필요할까? 그것에 대해 이야기해 보자.

G: 좋아. 음, 창가에 몇 개의 화분을 두는 게 어때? 그것들은 우리 동아리실을 더 예쁘게 할 거야.

B: 좋은 생각이야. 지우야, 고마워.

2. B: 그림을 좀 거는 게 어때?

G: 좋아. 네 그림 중의 하나를 가져오는 게 어때? 세호야, 넌 그림을 잘 그리잖아.

B: 그렇게 말해 주니 고마워. 내가 내 그림 중에서 하나를 가져올게.

3. B: 이번에는 모퉁이에 대해 이야기해 보자. 의견 있니?

G: 동아리실 모퉁이에 작은 도서관을 만드는 게 어때? 내가 내일 책 몇 권을 가져올게.

B: 좋은 생각이야! 민주야, 제안해 줘서 고마워.

Start Off – Listen & Talk B

G: Seho, we need something on the wall, too. ________ you think so?

B1: You're ________. ________ ________ about it ________.

G: I think we ________ ________ ________ the club ________ list there. It'll be ________ ________ ________ ________ ________ the new ________ names.

B2: That's a good idea. We ________ ________ our ________ for this ________ ________ on the wall.

G: Right! That'll really ________ us ________ important school events.

B1: Thank you for ________ great ideas, everyone. We are a good team.

G: 세호야, 우리는 벽에도 뭔가 필요해. 그렇게 생각하지 않니?

B1: 네 말이 맞아. 그것에 대해서 함께 이야기해 보자.

G: 내 생각에는 거기에 동아리 회원 목록을 붙일 필요가 있는 것 같아. 그것은 우리가 신입 회원들의 이름을 알게 되는 데 도움이 될 거야.

B2: 좋은 생각이야. 이번 학년도의 우리 계획도 벽에 필요해.

G: 맞아! 그러면 우리가 중요한 학교 행사를 기억하는 데 정말 도움이 될 거야.

B1: 모두 좋은 의견을 내줘서 고마워. 우린 좋은 팀이야.

Step Up – Real-life Scene

G1: Let's ________ ________ how we can make our town ________.

B: ________ ________ ________ you first. There's too much ________ at the ________ ________.

G2: I ________. ________ ________ ________ clean the place together?

B: Good. We ________ ________ a ________ there, ________.

G1: Great idea. It'll be ________ for ________ ________.

G2: ________ ________ ________ some flower pots ________ the bench? They'll ________ the bus stop ________ ________.

G1: Thank you ________ ________ great ideas, everyone. Then, ________ ________ start tomorrow?

G2, B: No ________.

G1: 우리 마을을 어떻게 하면 더 좋게 만들 수 있을지를 이야기해 보자.
B: 내가 먼저 말할게. 버스 정류장에 쓰레기가 너무 많아.
G2: 동의해. 그 장소를 함께 치우는 게 어때?
B: 좋아. 우리가 거기에 벤치를 놓을 수도 있을 것 같아.
G1: 좋은 생각이야. 그것은 어르신들에게 도움이될 거야.
G2: 벤치 주변에 화분도 좀 놓는 게 어때? 그것들은 버스 정류장을 더 아름답게 할 거야.
G1: 모두 좋은 의견을 내줘서 고마워. 그러면, 내일 시작하는 게 어때?
G2, B: 좋아.

Fun Time

A: ________ ________ about the ________ ________.

B: Okay. ________ ________ ________ ________ *bibimbap*?

A: Wonderful. ________ you ________ your idea.

A: 마을 파티에 대해 이야기해 보자.
B: 좋아. 우리 비빔밥을 요리하는 게 어때?
A: 훌륭해. 의견을 내줘서 고마워.

Express Yourself A

1. **M1:** Thank you ________ ________, everyone. Let's ________ ________ the Clean School Project.

   W: I like the corner ________ the tree ________. The Science Club ________ ________ the corner and ________ the tree.

   M2: I like it, too. It is a very ________ ________ ________ the students.

2. **M1:** ________ ________ about the ________ ________ this time. ________ ________ ________ ________ ________ it?

   W: The class ________ ________ ________ the board and ________ ________ some posters. We can know ________ ________ ________ about school ________.

   M2: Right! They did a good job. ________ ________ the ________ ________.

1. **M1:** 모두 와 주셔서 감사합니다. '깨끗한 학교 프로젝트'에 대해 이야기해 봅시다.
   W: 저는 나무 아래의 모퉁이가 가장 마음에 듭니다. '과학 동아리'가 모퉁이 주변을 청소하고 나무를 심었어요.
   M2: 저도 마음에 듭니다. 그곳은 학생들 사이에 아주 인기 있습니다.
2. **M1:** 이번에는 학교 정문에 관해 이야기해 봅시다. 그것에 대해 어떻게 생각하나요?
   W: 학급 반장들이 판을 설치하고 몇 개의 포스터를 붙였어요. 우리가 학교 행사에 관해 훨씬 더 많이 알 수 있죠.
   M2: 맞아요! 정말 잘했어요. 학급 반장들에게 감사합니다.

대화문 Test

Step2

※ 다음 우리말에 맞도록 대화를 영어로 쓰시오.

Get Ready 2

(1) B: ______

W: ______

(2) G: ______

M: ______

(3) B: ______

G: ______

B: ______

(1) B: 화분이 무거워 보여요. 민 선생님, 도와드릴까요?
W: 아주 친절하구나. 정말 고마워.

(2) G: 제가 의자 고치시는 걸 도와 드릴게요.
M: 이걸 좀 꽉 잡아 다오. 도와줘서 고맙구나.

(3) B: 우리가 마을을 위해 무엇을 할 수 있는지 이야기해 보자.
G: 지저분한 벽에 그림을 그리는 게 어떠니?
B: 좋아. 또 다른 건?

Start Off – Listen & Talk A

1. B: ______

G: ______

______

B: ______

2. B: ______

G: ______

______

B: ______

3. B: ______

G: ______

______

B: ______

1. B: 우리 동아리실에 무엇이 필요할까? 그것에 대해 이야기해 보자.
G: 좋아. 음, 창가에 몇 개의 화분을 두는 게 어때? 그것들은 우리 동아리실을 더 예쁘게 할 거야.
B: 좋은 생각이야. 지우야, 고마워.

2. B: 그림을 좀 거는 게 어때?
G: 좋아. 네 그림 중의 하나를 가져오는 게 어때? 세호야, 넌 그림을 잘 그리잖아.
B: 그렇게 말해 주니 고마워. 내가 내 그림 중에서 하나를 가져올게.

3. B: 이번에는 모퉁이에 대해 이야기해 보자. 의견 있니?
G: 동아리실 모퉁이에 작은 도서관을 만드는 게 어때? 내가 내일 책 몇 권을 가져올게.
B: 좋은 생각이야! 민주야, 제안해 줘서 고마워.

Start Off – Listen & Talk B

G: ______

B1: ______

G: ______

______

B2: ______

G: ______

B1: ______

G: 세호야, 우리는 벽에도 뭔가 필요해. 그렇게 생각하지 않니?
B1: 네 말이 맞아. 그것에 대해서 함께 이야기해 보자.
G: 내 생각에는 거기에 동아리 회원 목록을 붙일 필요가 있는 것 같아. 그것은 우리가 신입 회원들의 이름을 알게 되는 데 도움이 될 거야.
B2: 좋은 생각이야. 이번 학년도의 우리 계획도 벽에 필요해.
G: 맞아! 그러면 우리가 중요한 학교 행사를 기억하는 데 정말 도움이 될 거야.
B1: 모두 좋은 의견을 내줘서 고마워. 우린 좋은 팀이야.

Step Up – Real-life Scene

G1: ______________________

B: ______________________

G2: ______________________

B: ______________________

G1: ______________________

G2: ______________________

____

G1: ______________________

G2, B: ______________________

G1: 우리 마을을 어떻게 하면 더 좋게 만들 수 있을지를 이야기해 보자.
B: 내가 먼저 말할게. 버스 정류장에 쓰레기가 너무 많아.
G2: 동의해. 그 장소를 함께 치우는 게 어때?
B: 좋아. 우리가 거기에 벤치를 놓을 수도 있을 것 같아.
G1: 좋은 생각이야. 그것은 어르신들에게 도움이될 거야.
G2: 벤치 주변에 화분도 좀 놓는 게 어때? 그것들은 버스 정류장을 더 아름답게 할 거야.
G1: 모두 좋은 의견을 내줘서 고마워. 그러면, 내일 시작하는 게 어때?
G2, B: 좋아.

Fun Time

A: ______________________

B: ______________________

A: ______________________

A: 마을 파티에 대해 이야기해 보자.
B: 좋아. 우리 비빔밥을 요리하는 게 어때?
A: 훌륭해. 의견을 내줘서 고마워.

Express Yourself A

1. M1: ______________________

W: ______________________

____

M2: ______________________

2. M1: ______________________

W: ______________________

____

M2: ______________________

1. M1: 모두 와 주셔서 감사합니다. '깨끗한 학교 프로젝트'에 대해 이야기해 봅시다.
W: 저는 나무 아래의 모퉁이가 가장 마음에 듭니다. '과학 동아리'가 모퉁이 주변을 청소하고 나무를 심었어요.
M2: 저도 마음에 듭니다. 그곳은 학생들 사이에 아주 인기 있습니다.

2. M1: 이번에는 학교 정문에 관해 이야기해 봅시다. 그것에 대해 어떻게 생각하나요?
W: 학급 반장들이 판을 설치하고 몇 개의 포스터를 붙였어요. 우리가 학교 행사에 관해 훨씬 더 많이 알 수 있죠.
M2: 맞아요! 정말 잘했어요. 학급 반장들에게 감사합시다.

본문 Test

Step1

※ 다음 우리말과 일치하도록 빈칸에 알맞은 것을 골라 쓰시오.

1 ________ ________
A. Thumbs B. Green

2 I ________ the ________ ________.
A. whole B. complained C. day

3 My parents were making me ________ on the ________ project, but I had ________ ________ things to do.
A. far B. neighborhood C. better D. work

4 I didn't understand ________ ________ ________ ________ on this place.
A. were B. why C. working D. we

5 It was just the________ugly, old, ________ lot ________ ________ Johnny's Shop.
A. across B. ugly C. from D. empty

6 It was ________ of wild plants, fast food ________, old newspapers, broken glass, and every ________ kind of dirty trash you can ________.
A. imagine B. full C. wraps D. other

7 As I looked ________ it that first morning, I thought, "I ________ ________ are snakes in there, ________."
A. bet B. at C. too D. there

8 There were twenty of us — all ________ and ________ — ________ to ________ that day.
A. ages B. ready C. sizes D. work

9 I didn't think that we could clean ________ this ________ ________ and turn it ________ a garden.
A. mess B. up C. awful D. into

10 We were all wondering ________ ________ ________.
A. begin B. to C. where

11 Then Mr. Hernandez said, "The ________ ________ to do it is ________ to ________."
A. way B. start C. only D. just

12 Then, he ________ the lot ________ four parts with string and ________ five people ________ each part.
A. assigned B. into C. divided D. to

13 ________ ________, I was hot, ________, and glad my dad had made me ________ gloves.
A. sweaty B. lunchtime C. wear D. by

14 We ________ fifty trash bags ________ waste and were ________ to ________ wild plants.
A. with B. ready C. filled D. pull

15 As we pulled and pulled, dust ________ the air and ________ ________ ________.
A. sneeze B. filled C. us D. made

1 식물을 잘 키우는 사람들
2 나는 온종일 불평했다.
3 우리 부모님은 나를 이웃 프로젝트에서 일하게 하셨지만, 나에게는 훨씬 더 나은 할 일들이 있었다.
4 나는 우리가 왜 이곳에서 일하고 있어야 하는지 이해하지 못했다.
5 그곳은 그저 Johnny's Shop 건너편에 있는 볼품없고, 오래되고, 텅 빈 지역이었다.
6 그곳은 잡초와 패스트푸드 포장지와 낡은 신문, 깨진 유리, 그리고 상상할 수 있는 모든 다른 종류의 더러운 쓰레기로 가득 차 있었다.
7 그 첫날 아침에 그곳을 보았을 때, 나는 "틀림없이 저 안에는 뱀들도 있을 거야."라고 생각했다.
8 그날 일할 준비가 된 — 모든 연령대와 몸집을 가진 — 우리 20명이 있었다.
9 나는 이 끔찍하게 더러운 곳을 청소하여 정원으로 바꿀 수 있다고 생각하지 않았다.
10 우리는 모두 어디서부터 시작해야 할지 궁금해 하고 있었다.
11 그때 Hernandez 씨가 "그것을 할 유일한 방법은 그냥 시작하는 것입니다."라고 말했다.
12 그러고 나서, 그는 그 지역을 끈으로 네 구역으로 나누고, 5명을 각 구역에 배치했다.
13 점심 무렵, 나는 덥고, 땀이 났으며, 아버지가 나에게 장갑을 끼도록 한 것이 기뻤다.
14 우리는 쓰레기 봉투 50개를 쓰레기로 채웠고, 잡초를 뽑을 준비가 되어 있었다.
15 우리가 뽑으면 뽑을수록, 먼지가 공기를 가득 메워서 재채기가 나왔다.

16 At the ________ of the day, I had to ________ the lot looked ________ ________.

A. much B. admit C. better D. end

17 That ________ day was ________ ________.

A. toughest B. the C. first

18 On the weekends that ________, we made ________, planted flower and vegetable ________, and ________ them.

A. watered B. rows C. seeds D. followed

19 After ________ two weeks, I ________ ________ when I found the plants had started popping ________!

A. complaining B. up C. stopped D. about

20 ________, the ________ and ________ the ________ and the tomatoes.

A. beans B. lettuce C. then D. first

21 They ________ ________ ________.

A. fast B. so C. grew

22 I ________ ________ it!

A. believe B. couldn't

23 The bean plants grew an inch, and the tomatoes ________ in ________ in just a ________ days.

A. few B. doubled C. grew D. size

24 Now, two months ________, I like to go there ________ day to see ________ new flowers are ________ to pop up.

A. what B. later C. ready D. every

25 ________ of people in the neighborhood meet ________ to ________ the ________ and to talk together.

A. sights B. lots C. enjoy D. there

26 Tonight, it ________ ________ me — ________ a good ________ we did!

A. hit B. suddenly C. thing D. what

27 I'm ________ I ________ ________ a ________ of it.

A. part B. been C. proud D. have

28 I'm in ________ of ________ flowers for the ________ ________ on Fourth Street.

A. nursing B. picking C. charge D. home

29 The vegetables ________ ________ ________ every kitchen ________ our town.

A. to B. will C. in D. go

30 But ________ ________, an ugly and dirty lot ________ people didn't like has ________ a pretty garden for everyone.

A. better B. that C. even D. become

16 그날이 끝날 무렵, 나는 그 지역이 훨씬 더 나아 보인다는 것을 인정해야 했다.

17 그 첫날이 가장 힘들었다.

18 그다음 주말에 우리는 열을 만들고, 꽃과 채소 씨앗을 심고, 물을 주었다.

19 약 2주 뒤, 나는 식물들이 자라나기 시작한 것을 발견했을 때 불평하는 것을 멈추었다!

20 처음에는 상추, 그러고 나서, 콩과 토마토.

21 그것들은 아주 빨리 자랐다.

22 나는 믿을 수가 없었다!

23 콩 식물은 1인치 자라났고, 토마토는 며칠 만에 크기가 두 배가 되었다.

24 두 달이 지난 지금, 나는 매일 어떤 새로운 꽃들이 피어날 준비가 되었는지 보러 그곳에 가는 것을 좋아한다.

25 이웃의 많은 사람이 그곳에서 만나 풍경을 즐기고 함께 이야기를 나눈다.

26 오늘 밤, 갑자기 생각났다 — 우리가 얼마나 좋은 일을 했는가!

27 나는 내가 그 일의 일부였다는 것이 자랑스럽다.

28 나는 'Fourth Street'에 있는 양로원을 위해 꽃을 따는 일을 맡았다.

29 채소들은 우리 마을의 모든 부엌으로 갈 것이다.

30 하지만 훨씬 더 좋은 것은, 사람들이 좋아하지 않았던 볼품없고 더러운 지역이 모두를 위한 예쁜 정원이 되었다는 것이다.

※ 다음 우리말과 일치하도록 빈칸에 알맞은 말을 쓰시오.

1 Green ________

2 I ________ the ________ ________.

3 My parents were ________ me ________ on the neighborhood project, but I had ________ ________ things ________ ________.

4 I didn't understand ________ ________ ________ ________ on this place.

5 It was just the ________, old, ________ lot ________ ________ Johnny's Shop.

6 It ________ ________ ________ wild plants, fast food ________, old newspapers, ________ glass, and ________ ________ ________ of dirty trash ________ ________ ________.

7 As I looked at it that first morning, I thought, "________ ________ ________ ________ snakes in there, ________."

8 There were twenty of us — ________ ________ ________ ________ — ________ ________ ________ that day.

9 I didn't think that we could ________ ________ ________ ________ ________ and ________ it ________ a garden.

10 We were all wondering ________ ________ ________.

11 Then Mr. Hernandez said, "The ________ ________ ________ ________ it is ________ ________ ________."

12 Then, he ________ the lot ________ four parts ________ ________ and ________ five people ________ each part.

13 ________ ________, I was hot, ________, and glad my dad had made me ________ ________.

14 We ________ fifty trash bags ________ ________ and ________ ________ ________ ________ wild plants.

15 ________ we pulled and pulled, ________ ________ the air and ________ ________ ________.

1 식물을 잘 키우는 사람들
2 나는 온종일 불평했다.
3 우리 부모님은 나를 이웃 프로젝트에서 일하게 하셨지만, 나에게는 훨씬 더 나은 할 일들이 있었다.
4 나는 우리가 왜 이곳에서 일하고 있어야 하는지 이해하지 못했다.
5 그곳은 그저 Johnny's Shop 건너편에 있는 볼품없고, 오래되고, 텅 빈 지역이었다.
6 그곳은 잡초와 패스트푸드 포장지와 낡은 신문, 깨진 유리, 그리고 상상할 수 있는 모든 다른 종류의 더러운 쓰레기로 가득 차 있었다.
7 그 첫날 아침에 그곳을 보았을 때, 나는 "틀림없이 저 안에는 뱀들도 있을 거야."라고 생각했다.
8 그날 일할 준비가 된 — 모든 연령대와 몸집을 가진 — 우리 20명이 있었다.
9 나는 이 끔찍하게 더러운 곳을 청소하여 정원으로 바꿀 수 있다고 생각하지 않았다.
10 우리는 모두 어디서부터 시작해야 할지 궁금해 하고 있었다.
11 그때 Hernandez 씨가 "그것을 할 유일한 방법은 그냥 시작하는 것입니다."라고 말했다.
12 그러고 나서, 그는 그 지역을 끈으로 네 구역으로 나누고, 5명을 각 구역에 배치했다.
13 점심 무렵, 나는 덥고, 땀이 났으며, 아버지가 나에게 장갑을 끼도록 한 것이 기뻤다.
14 우리는 쓰레기 봉투 50개를 쓰레기로 채웠고, 잡초를 뽑을 준비가 되어 있었다.
15 우리가 뽑으면 뽑을수록, 먼지가 공기를 가득 메워서 재채기가 나왔다.

16 ________ ________ ________ ________ the day, I ________ ________ ________ the lot looked ________ ________.

17 That first day was ________ ________.

18 On the weekends that followed, we ________ ________, planted flower and vegetable seeds, and ________ them.

19 After about two weeks, I ________ ________ when I found the plants had started ________ ________!

20 ________, ________ ________ and then the beans and the tomatoes.

21 They ________ ________ ________.

22 I ________ ________ it!

23 The bean plants grew an inch, and the tomatoes doubled ________ ________ ________ ________ ________ ________ ________.

24 Now, two months ________, I like to go there every day to see ________ ________ ________ ________ ________ to pop up.

25 ________ ________ people in the neighborhood meet there ________ ________ ________ ________ and to talk together.

26 Tonight, it ________ ________ ________ — what a good thing we did!

27 I'm ________ I ________ ________ ________ ________ of it.

28 ________ ________ ________ ________ ________ flowers for the ________ ________ on Fourth Street.

29 The vegetables ________ ________ ________ every kitchen in our town.

30 But ________ ________, an ugly and dirty lot ________ people didn't like ________ ________ a pretty garden for everyone.

16 그날이 끝날 무렵, 나는 그 지역이 훨씬 더 나아 보인다는 것을 인정해야 했다.

17 그 첫날이 가장 힘들었다.

18 그다음 주말에 우리는 열을 만들고, 꽃과 채소 씨앗을 심고, 물을 주었다.

19 약 2주 뒤, 나는 식물들이 자라나기 시작한 것을 발견했을 때 불평하는 것을 멈추었다!

20 처음에는 상추, 그러고 나서, 콩과 토마토.

21 그것들은 아주 빨리 자랐다.

22 나는 믿을 수가 없었다!

23 콩 식물은 1인치 자라났고, 토마토는 며칠 만에 크기가 두 배가 되었다.

24 두 달이 지난 지금, 나는 매일 어떤 새로운 꽃들이 피어날 준비가 되었는지 보러 그곳에 가는 것을 좋아한다.

25 이웃의 많은 사람이 그곳에서 만나 풍경을 즐기고 함께 이야기를 나눈다.

26 오늘 밤, 갑자기 생각났다 — 우리가 얼마나 좋은 일을 했는가!

27 나는 내가 그 일의 일부였다는 것이 자랑스럽다.

28 나는 'Fourth Street'에 있는 양로원을 위해 꽃을 따는 일을 맡았다.

29 채소들은 우리 마을의 모든 부엌으로 갈 것이다.

30 하지만 훨씬 더 좋은 것은, 사람들이 좋아하지 않았던 볼품없고 더러운 지역이 모두를 위한 예쁜 정원이 되었다는 것이다.

본문 Test

Step3

※ 다음 문장을 우리말로 쓰시오.

1 Green Thumbs

➡ ______________________

2 I complained the whole day.

➡ ______________________

3 My parents were making me work on the neighborhood project, but I had far better things to do.

➡ ______________________

4 I didn't understand why we were working on this place.

➡ ______________________

5 It was just the ugly, old, empty lot across from Johnny's Shop.

➡ ______________________

6 It was full of wild plants, fast food wraps, old newspapers, broken glass, and every other kind of dirty trash you can imagine.

➡ ______________________

____

7 As I looked at it that first morning, I thought, "I bet there are snakes in there, too."

➡ ______________________

8 There were twenty of us — all ages and sizes — ready to work that day.

➡ ______________________

9 I didn't think that we could clean up this awful mess and turn it into a garden.

➡ ______________________

10 We were all wondering where to begin.

➡ ______________________

11 Then Mr. Hernandez said, "The only way to do it is just to start."

➡ ______________________

12 Then, he divided the lot into four parts with string and assigned five people to each part.

➡ ______________________

13 By lunchtime, I was hot, sweaty, and glad my dad had made me wear gloves.

➡ ______________________

14 We filled fifty trash bags with waste and were ready to pull wild plants.

➡ ______________________

15 As we pulled and pulled, dust filled the air and made us sneeze.

➡ ______________________

16 At the end of the day, I had to admit the lot looked much better.

➡ ______________________________

17 That first day was the toughest.

➡ ______________________________

18 On the weekends that followed, we made rows, planted flower and vegetable seeds, and watered them.

➡ ______________________________

19 After about two weeks, I stopped complaining when I found the plants had started popping up!

➡ ______________________________

20 First, the lettuce and then the beans and the tomatoes.

➡ ______________________________

21 They grew so fast.

➡ ______________________________

22 I couldn't believe it!

➡ ______________________________

23 The bean plants grew an inch, and the tomatoes doubled in size in just a few days.

➡ ______________________________

24 Now, two months later, I like to go there every day to see what new flowers are ready to pop up.

➡ ______________________________

25 Lots of people in the neighborhood meet there to enjoy the sights and to talk together.

➡ ______________________________

26 Tonight, it suddenly hit me — what a good thing we did!

➡ ______________________________

27 I'm proud I have been a part of it.

➡ ______________________________

28 I'm in charge of picking flowers for the nursing home on Fourth Street.

➡ ______________________________

29 The vegetables will go to every kitchen in our town.

➡ ______________________________

30 But even better, an ugly and dirty lot that people didn't like has become a pretty garden for everyone.

➡ ______________________________

본문 Test

Step4

※ 다음 괄호 안의 단어들을 우리말에 맞도록 바르게 배열하시오.

1 (Thumbs / Green)

➡ ________________________________

2 (complained / I / whole / the / day.)

➡ ________________________________

3 (parents / my / making / were / work / me / on / neighborhood / the / project, / but / had / I / better / far / to / do. / things)

➡ ________________________________

____

4 (didn't / I / why / understand / we / working / were / this / on / place.)

➡ ________________________________

5 (was / it / just / ugly, / the / old, / lot / empty / from / across / Shop. / Johnny's)

➡ ________________________________

6 (was / it / full / wild / of / plants, / food / fast / wraps, / newspapers, / old / glass, / broken / and / other / every / kind / dirty / of / you / trash / imagine. / can)

➡ ________________________________

____

7 (I / as / looked / at / that / it / morning, / first / thought, / I / "I / there / bet / are / in / snakes / there, / too.")

➡ ________________________________

____

8 (were / there / of / us / twenty / – / ages / all / sizes / and / – / to / ready / work / day. / that)

➡ ________________________________

9 (didn't / I / that / think / could / we / clean / this / up / mess / awful / and / it / turn / into / garden. / a)

➡ ________________________________

____

10 (were / we / wondering / all / to / where / begin.)

➡ ________________________________

11 (Mr. / then / Hernandes / said, / "the / way / only / do / to / is / it / to / just / start.")

➡ ________________________________

12 (he / then, / divided / lot / the / four / into / with / parts / string / assinged / and / people / five / each / to / part.)

➡ ________________________________

____

13 (lunchtime, / by / was / I / hot, / and / sweaty, / glad / dad / my / made / had / wear / me / gloves.)

➡ ________________________________

____

14 (filled / we / trash / fifty / with / bags / waste / and / ready / were / pull / to / plants. / wild)

➡ ________________________________

15 (we / as / pulled / and / dust / pulled / filled / air / the / and / us / made / sneeze.)

➡ ________________________________

1 식물을 잘 키우는 사람들

2 나는 온종일 불평했다.

3 우리 부모님은 나를 이웃 프로젝트에서 일하게 하셨지만, 나에게는 훨씬 더 나은 할 일들이 있었다.

4 나는 우리가 왜 이곳에서 일하고 있어야 하는지 이해하지 못했다.

5 그곳은 그저 Johnny's Shop 건너편에 있는 볼품없고, 오래되고, 텅 빈 지역이었다.

6 그곳은 잡초와 패스트푸드 포장지와 낡은 신문, 깨진 유리, 그리고 상상할 수 있는 모든 다른 종류의 더러운 쓰레기로 가득 차 있었다.

7 그 첫날 아침에 그곳을 보았을 때, 나는 "틀림없이 저 안에는 뱀들도 있을 거야."라고 생각했다.

8 그날 일할 준비가 된 — 모든 연령대와 몸집을 가진 — 우리 20명이 있었다.

9 나는 이 끔찍하게 더러운 곳을 청소하여 정원으로 바꿀 수 있다고 생각하지 않았다.

10 우리는 모두 어디서부터 시작해야 할지 궁금해 하고 있었다.

11 그때 Hernandez 씨가 "그것을 할 유일한 방법은 그냥 시작하는 것입니다."라고 말했다.

12 그러고 나서, 그는 그 지역을 끈으로 네 구역으로 나누고, 5명을 각 구역에 배치했다.

13 점심 무렵, 나는 덥고, 땀이 났으며, 아버지가 나에게 장갑을 끼도록 한 것이 기뻤다.

14 우리는 쓰레기 봉투 50개를 쓰레기로 채웠고, 잡초를 뽑을 준비가 되어 있었다.

15 우리가 뽑으면 뽑을수록, 먼지가 공기를 가득 메워서 재채기가 나왔다.

16 (the / at / of / end / day, / the / had / I / admit / to / lot / the / looked / better. / much)

➡ ____________________

17 (first / that / was / day / toughest. / the)

➡ ____________________

18 (the / on / weekends / followed, / that / made / we / rows, / flower / planted / and / seeds, / vegetable / watered / and / them.)

➡ ____________________

19 (about / after / weeks, / two / stopped / I / when / complaining / I / the / found / plants / started / had / up! / popping)

➡ ____________________

20 (the / first, / and / lettuce / then / beans / the / and / tomatoes. / the)

➡ ____________________

21 (grew / they / fast. / so)

➡ ____________________

22 (couldn't / I / it! / believe)

➡ ____________________

23 (bean / the / grew / plants / inch, / an / and / tomatoes / the / in / doubled / size / just / in / few / a / days.)

➡ ____________________

24 (two / now, / later, / months / like / I / go / to / every / there / day / see / to / new / what / flowers / ready / are / pop / to / up.)

➡ ____________________

25 (of / lots / people / the / in / neighborhood / there / meet / enjoy / to / sights / the / to / and / together. / talk)

➡ ____________________

26 (it / tonight, / suddenly / me / hit / – / a / what / thing / good / did! / we)

➡ ____________________

27 (proud / I'm / have / I / been / part / a / it. / of)

➡ ____________________

28 (in / I'm / of / charge / flowers / picking / the / for / home / nursing / on / Street. / Fourth)

➡ ____________________

29 (vegetables / the / go / will / every / to / in / kitchen / our / town.)

➡ ____________________

30 (even / but / better, / ugly / an / and / lot / dirty / that / didn't / people / like / become / has / pretty / a / for / garden / everyone.)

➡ ____________________

16 그날이 끝날 무렵, 나는 그 지역이 훨씬 더 나아 보인다는 것을 인정해야 했다.

17 그 첫날이 가장 힘들었다.

18 그다음 주말에 우리는 열을 만들고, 꽃과 채소 씨앗을 심고, 물을 주었다.

19 약 2주 뒤, 나는 식물들이 자라나기 시작한 것을 발견했을 때 불평하는 것을 멈추었다!

20 처음에는 상추, 그러고 나서, 콩과 토마토.

21 그것들은 아주 빨리 자랐다.

22 나는 믿을 수가 없었다!

23 콩 식물은 1인치 자라났고, 토마토는 며칠 만에 크기가 두 배가 되었다.

24 두 달이 지난 지금, 나는 매일 어떤 새로운 꽃들이 피어날 준비가 되었는지 보러 그곳에 가는 것을 좋아한다.

25 이웃의 많은 사람이 그곳에서 만나 풍경을 즐기고 함께 이야기를 나눈다.

26 오늘 밤, 갑자기 생각났다 — 우리가 얼마나 좋은 일을 했는가!

27 나는 내가 그 일의 일부였다는 것이 자랑스럽다.

28 나는 'Fourth Street'에 있는 양로원을 위해 꽃을 따는 일을 맡았다.

29 채소들은 우리 마을의 모든 부엌으로 갈 것이다.

30 하지만 훨씬 더 좋은 것은, 사람들이 좋아하지 않았던 볼품없고 더러운 지역이 모두를 위한 예쁜 정원이 되었다는 것이다.

본문 Test

Step5

※ 다음 우리말을 영어로 쓰시오.

1 식물을 잘 키우는 사람들

➡ ______________________________

2 나는 온종일 불평했다.

➡ ______________________________

3 우리 부모님은 나를 이웃 프로젝트에서 일하게 하셨지만, 나에게는 훨씬 더 나은 할 일들이 있었다.

➡ ______________________________

4 나는 우리가 왜 이곳에서 일하고 있어야 하는지 이해하지 못했다.

➡ ______________________________

5 그곳은 그저 Johnny's Shop 건너편에 있는 볼품없고, 오래되고, 텅 빈 지역이었다.

➡ ______________________________

6 그곳은 잡초와 패스트푸드 포장지와 낡은 신문, 깨진 유리, 그리고 상상할 수 있는 모든 다른 종류의 더러운 쓰레기로 가득 차 있었다.

➡ ______________________________

____

7 그 첫날 아침에 그곳을 보았을 때, 나는 "틀림없이 저 안에는 뱀들도 있을 거야."라고 생각했다.

➡ ______________________________

8 그날 일할 준비가 된 — 모든 연령대와 몸집을 가진 — 우리 20명이 있었다.

➡ ______________________________

9 나는 이 끔찍하게 더러운 곳을 청소하여 정원으로 바꿀 수 있다고 생각하지 않았다.

➡ ______________________________

10 우리는 모두 어디서부터 시작해야 할지 궁금해 하고 있었다.

➡ ______________________________

11 그때 Hernandez 씨가 "그것을 할 유일한 방법은 그냥 시작하는 것입니다."라고 말했다.

➡ ______________________________

12 그러고 나서, 그는 그 지역을 끈으로 네 구역으로 나누고, 5명을 각 구역에 배치했다.

➡ ______________________________

13 점심 무렵, 나는 덥고, 땀이 났으며, 아버지가 나에게 장갑을 끼도록 한 것이 기뻤다.

➡ ______________________________

14 우리는 쓰레기 봉투 50개를 쓰레기로 채웠고, 잡초를 뽑을 준비가 되어 있었다.

➡ ______________________________

15 우리가 뽑으면 뽑을수록, 먼지가 공기를 가득 메워서 재채기가 나왔다.

➡ ______________________________

16 그날이 끝날 무렵, 나는 그 지역이 훨씬 더 나아 보인다는 것을 인정해야 했다.

➡ ______________________________

17 그 첫날이 가장 힘들었다.

➡ ______________________________

18 그다음 주말에 우리는 열을 만들고, 꽃과 채소 씨앗을 심고, 물을 주었다.

➡ ______________________________

19 약 2주 뒤, 나는 식물들이 자라나기 시작한 것을 발견했을 때 불평하는 것을 멈추었다!

➡ ______________________________

20 처음에는 상추, 그러고 나서, 콩과 토마토.

➡ ______________________________

21 그것들은 아주 빨리 자랐다.

➡ ______________________________

22 나는 믿을 수가 없었다!

➡ ______________________________

23 콩 식물은 1인치 자라났고, 토마토는 며칠 만에 크기가 두 배가 되었다.

➡ ______________________________

24 두 달이 지난 지금, 나는 매일 어떤 새로운 꽃들이 피어날 준비가 되었는지 보러 그곳에 가는 것을 좋아한다.

➡ ______________________________

25 이웃의 많은 사람이 그곳에서 만나 풍경을 즐기고 함께 이야기를 나눈다.

➡ ______________________________

26 오늘 밤, 갑자기 생각났다 — 우리가 얼마나 좋은 일을 했는가!

➡ ______________________________

27 나는 내가 그 일의 일부였다는 것이 자랑스럽다.

➡ ______________________________

28 나는 'Fourth Street'에 있는 양로원을 위해 꽃을 따는 일을 맡았다.

➡ ______________________________

29 채소들은 우리 마을의 모든 부엌으로 갈 것이다.

➡ ______________________________

30 하지만 훨씬 더 좋은 것은, 사람들이 좋아하지 않았던 볼품없고 더러운 지역이 모두를 위한 예쁜 정원이 되었다는 것이다.

➡ ______________________________

구석구석 지문 Test

Step1

※ 다음 우리말과 일치하도록 빈칸에 알맞은 말을 쓰시오.

After You Read A

June 17

1. I ________ the town garden ________ ________.
2. Some people were talking ________ they ________ ________ at the beautiful garden.
3. I ________ some ________ and ________ them ________ the ________ ________.
4. I'm ________ ________ we ________ a pretty garden ________ ________.

6월 17일
1. 나는 방과 후에 마을 정원을 방문했다.
2. 몇몇 사람들이 아름다운 정원을 보면서 이야기하고 있었다.
3. 나는 꽃을 몇 송이 꺾어서 양로원에 가지고 갔다.
4. 우리가 모두를 위한 예쁜 정원을 만든 것이 자랑스럽다.

Do It Yourself

1. ________ Town ________
2. This is Oksig, ________ I ________ ________ a symbol of ________ ________.
3. I ________ this after I ________ ________ pictures of ________ ________ ________ ________ ________.
4. Oksig is ________ ________ ________ real corn.
5. I hope ________ ________ ________.

1. 우리 동네 상징
2. 이것은 Oksig이고, 내가 나의 동네 상징으로 그렸습니다.
3. 나는 많은 다양한 종류의 옥수수 사진을 찍은 후에 이것을 디자인했습니다.
4. Oksig은 진짜 옥수수보다 훨씬 더 귀엽습니다.
5. 나는 모든 사람들이 이것을 좋아하길 바랍니다.

Link to the World

1. • Kampong Ayer is ________ ________ "water village" ________ ________ ________.
2. It ________ ________ ________ ________ about 40 small villages.
3. • All the houses ________ ________ ________ the water.
4. • ________ ________ schools, ________ ________, gas stations, and ________ ________.
5. • It is ________ ________ beautiful ________ you think.
6. It ________ ________ the Venice of Asia.

1. • 캄퐁 아에르는 세상에서 가장 큰 '수상 마을'이다.
2. 그것은 40개의 작은 마을들로 이루어져 있다.
3. • 모든 집은 물 위에 지어져 있다.
4. • 학교, 경찰서, 주유소, 우체국이 있다.
5. • 그곳은 여러분이 생각하는 것보다 훨씬 더 아름답다.
6. 그곳은 아시아의 베니스라고 불린다.

구석구석 지문 Test

Step2

※ 다음 우리말을 영어로 쓰시오.

After You Read A

1. 나는 방과 후에 마을 정원을 방문했다.

➡ ______________________________

2. 몇몇 사람들이 아름다운 정원을 보면서 이야기하고 있었다.

➡ ______________________________

3. 나는 꽃을 몇 송이 꺾어서 양로원에 가지고 갔다.

➡ ______________________________

4. 우리가 모두를 위한 예쁜 정원을 만든 것이 자랑스럽다.

➡ ______________________________

Do It Yourself

1. 우리 동네 상징

➡ ______________________________

2. 이것은 Oksig이고, 내가 나의 동네 상징으로 그렸습니다.

➡ ______________________________

3. 나는 많은 다양한 종류의 옥수수 사진을 찍은 후에 이것을 디자인했습니다.

➡ ______________________________

4. Oksig은 진짜 옥수수보다 훨씬 더 귀엽습니다.

➡ ______________________________

5. 나는 모든 사람들이 이것을 좋아하길 바랍니다.

➡ ______________________________

Link To The World

1. • 캄퐁 아에르는 세상에서 가장 큰 '수상 마을'이다.

➡ ______________________________

2. 그것은 40개의 작은 마을들로 이루어져 있다.

➡ ______________________________

3. • 모든 집은 물 위에 지어져 있다.

➡ ______________________________

4. • 학교, 경찰서, 주유소, 우체국이 있다.

➡ ______________________________

5. • 그곳은 여러분이 생각하는 것보다 훨씬 더 아름답다.

➡ ______________________________

6. 그곳은 아시아의 베니스라고 불린다.

➡ ______________________________

단어 Test

Step1

※ 다음 영어를 우리말로 쓰시오.

01 brave ____________

02 discovery ____________

03 university ____________

04 backward ____________

05 bomb ____________

06 float ____________

07 mistake ____________

08 honor ____________

09 imaginative ____________

10 maybe ____________

11 award ____________

12 opening ____________

13 invention ____________

14 laughable ____________

15 ceremony ____________

16 store ____________

17 worth ____________

18 accept ____________

19 magnet ____________

20 eager ____________

21 repeatedly ____________

22 cheer ____________

23 tradition ____________

24 perform ____________

25 actually ____________

26 economics ____________

27 navy ____________

28 present ____________

29 interest ____________

30 research ____________

31 sailor ____________

32 useful ____________

33 trillion ____________

34 unusual ____________

35 instead of ____________

36 keep -ing ____________

37 succeed in ____________

38 laugh out loud ____________

39 take part in ____________

40 keep A from -ing ____________

41 be eager to ____________

42 get out of ____________

43 keep one's fingers crossed ____________

단어 Test

Step2

※ 다음 우리말을 영어로 쓰시오.

01 받아들이다 ____________

02 개막 ____________

03 뒤로 ____________

04 발견 ____________

05 열렬한, 간절히 바라는 ____________

06 반복적으로 ____________

07 공연하다 ____________

08 경제학 ____________

09 뜨다 ____________

10 평화 ____________

11 존중하다; 명예 ____________

12 폭탄 ____________

13 용감한 ____________

14 수여하다; 상 ____________

15 의식, 식 ____________

16 발명, 발명품 ____________

17 ~하는 동안, ~인 반면에 ____________

18 웃기는 ____________

19 실제로, 사실은 ____________

20 드문, 특이한 ____________

21 해군 ____________

22 자석 ____________

23 아마도 ____________

24 실수 ____________

25 선원 ____________

26 전통 ____________

27 연구, 조사; 조사하다 ____________

28 1조 ____________

29 유용한 ____________

30 가치; ~의 가치가 있는 ____________

31 창의적인, 상상력이 풍부한 ____________

32 관심 ____________

33 대학, 대학교 ____________

34 받다 ____________

35 ~ 이하, ~보다 적은 ____________

36 ~ 대신에 ____________

37 ~에 성공하다 ____________

38 ~에 참여하다 ____________

39 큰 소리로 웃다 ____________

40 계속 ~하다 ____________

41 ~에서 떠나다, 나가다 ____________

42 ~을 (열렬히) 하고 싶어 하다 ____________

43 A가 ~하지 못하게 하다 ____________

단어 Test

Step3

※ 다음 영영풀이에 알맞은 단어를 <보기>에서 골라 쓴 후, 우리말 뜻을 쓰시오.

1 __________: not dead: __________

2 __________: to give a prize: __________

3 __________: someone who works on a ship: __________

4 __________: the number 1,000,000,000,000: __________

5 __________: to take something offered: __________

6 __________: a piece of metal that attracts other iron: __________

7 __________: a military force made up of boats and ships: __________

8 __________: looking or facing in the direction that is behind you: __________

9 __________: the act of finding something for the first time: __________

10 __________: to be on a liquid and not sink: __________

11 __________: the study of something to discover new facts: __________

12 __________: to make, design, or think of a new type of thing: __________

13 __________: wanting very much to do or have something: __________

14 __________: • something you are proud to do: __________
• to show great respect for someone, esp. in public: __________

15 __________: having or showing new and exciting ideas: __________

16 __________: an educational institution at the highest level, where you study for a degree: __________

보기

honor	float	live	sailor
backward	invent	accept	navy
university	award	imaginative	trillion
eager	research	magnet	discovery

대화문 Test

※ 다음 우리말과 일치하도록 빈칸에 알맞은 말을 쓰시오.

Get Ready 2

(1) G: You ________ ________ ________ ________ problems in class. ________ ________ you'll ________ the Class Brain ________.
B: Do you really ________ ________?
G: Of course. I'll ________ my fingers ________ for you, Sangjun!

(2) B: The ________ of the Oh So Sweet ________ will get some candies.
G: Oh, I want ________ ________ the ________.
B: ________ ________ you'll ________ the ________ this time. ________ ________, Jiu!

(3) B: I'm ________ ________ ________ the Best Joker award this time.
G: Ha-ha. You always ________ us ________ ________ ________. So you'll ________ ________ ________, Yunki. Good luck.
B: Thank you.

(4) B: Minji, you're a happy girl. I think you'll ________ the Ms. Cheerful ________. I'll ________ ________ ________ ________!
G: Oh, thank you, Jiho.

(1) G: 너는 수업 중 많은 문제를 해결했잖아. 나는 네가 'Class Brain'상을 탈 거라고 확신해.
B: 정말 그렇게 생각하니?
G: 물론이야. 행운을 빌게, 상준아!
(2) B: 'Oh So Sweet'상 수상자는 사탕을 받을 거야.
G: 오, 그 상을 받고 싶다.
B: 네가 이번에는 그 상을 탈 거라고 확신해. 행운을 빌어, 지우야!
(3) B: 난 이번에 'Best Joker'상을 받기를 기대해.
G: 하하. 너는 항상 우리를 웃게 하잖아. 그러니 네가 그 상을 탈 거야, 윤기야. 행운을 빌어.
B: 고마워.
(4) B: 민지야, 너는 쾌활한 아이야. 나는 네가 'Ms. Cheerful'상을 탈 거라고 생각해. 행운을 빌게!
G: 오, 고마워, 지호야.

Start Off – Listen & Talk A

1. G: Mom, I ________ ________ ________ the sports day.
W: ________ are you ________ ________ ________ on that day, Minji?
G: I'm going to play basketball for my class. We've ________ hard ________ ________ ________ ________.
W: Oh, I'm ________ ________ ________ your game.
G: ________, I'm ________ ________ ________. I'm ________ I'll ________ a ________.
W: ________ ________. You'll ________ a good ________. I'll keep ________ ________ ________!

2. W: Soyun, are you going to ________ ________ ________ any races on the sports day?
G: Sure. I'________ ________ ________ ________ a 100 meter race at the ________ of the day.
W: Wow, I'm ________ ________ to ________ you at the race.
G: But, Mom, I'm not ________ I'll ________ the race.
W: Just ________ ________ ________. I'll ________ ________ ________ ________!

1. G: 엄마, 체육 대회가 정말 기다려져요.
W: 민지야, 너는 그날 무엇을 할 거니?
G: 저는 학급을 대표해서 농구를 할 거예요. 우리는 몇 주간 열심히 연습해 왔어요.
W: 오, 너의 경기가 기대되는구나.
G: 사실은, 전 조금 걱정이 돼요. 제가 실수를 할까봐 겁나요.
W: 걱정하지 마. 넌 잘할 거야. 행운을 빌어줄게!

2. W: 소윤아, 넌 체육 대회에서 경주에 참가하니?
G: 물론이죠. 전 그날 마지막에 있는 100 미터 달리기를 뛸 거예요.
W: 와, 네가 경주에서 달리는 모습을 보는 것이 기대되는구나.
G: 하지만 엄마, 전 경주에서 이길지 잘 모르겠어요.
W: 그냥 최선을 다하렴. 행운을 빌어줄게!

Start Off – Listen & Talk B

G: Mom, ________ ________ ________ to the sports day?

W: Sure. I'm ________ ________ ________ the game Kick a Shoe. This will be the first time ________ ________ ________ ________ it.

G: Don't worry. I'm ________ you'll ________ ________. I'll ________ my ________ ________ for you!

W: Thank you. I'm also ________ ________ ________ a funny dance with some ________ ________.

G: That ________ ________. I'm ________ ________ to ________ you on the ________.

G: 엄마, 체육 대회에 오실 거예요?
W: 물론이지. 나는 'Kick a Shoe' 게임에 참가할 거야. 이번에 처음 해 보는 거야.
G: 걱정하지 마세요. 엄마는 잘하실 거예요. 행운을 빌어 드릴게요!
W: 고맙다. 나는 다른 엄마들과 코믹 댄스도 할 거야.
G: 재밌겠네요. 무대에 선 엄마 모습을 보는 것이 기대돼요.

Start Off – Speak Up

A: I'm ________ ________ ________ the ________ airplane contest tomorrow. Are you ________?

B: Well, I think ________, but I'm ________.

A: You will ________ ________. I'll ________ ________ ________ ________!

B: 나는 내일 모형 비행기 대회가 기대돼. 너는 준비됐니?
G: 음, 그런 것 같아, 하지만 긴장돼.
B: 너는 잘할 거야. 내가 행운을 빌어 줄게!

Step Up – Real-life Scene

Miso: We're going on a ________ ________ next Tuesday. What are you going to do in the ________ ________, Jimin?

Jimin: I'm ________ ________ talk ________ our teachers ________ ________ ________ and tell some ________.

Miso: Wow! I'm really ________ ________ ________ ________.

Jimin: Will everyone like my ________? I'm not ________.

Miso: Don't ________. I'm sure you'll ________ ________. I'll ________ ________ ________ ________!

Jimin: Thank you, Miso. ________ ________ ________ you one part of my ________. ________ who? "Goood Jooob!"

Miso: Ha-ha, you ________ ________ our English teacher.

Jimin: Do I? I'm ________ ________ ________ you more at the show.

Miso: Great! You always ________ us ________ ________ ________.

미소: 다음 주 화요일에 수학여행을 갈 거야. 지민아, 너는 장기 자랑에서 뭘 할 거니?
지민: 나는 수업 시간에 선생님들이 말하는 것을 흉내 내고 농담도 할 거야.
미소: 와! 정말 기대되는데.
지민: 모든 사람이 나의 쇼를 좋아할까? 잘 모르겠어.
미소: 걱정하지 마. 나는 네가 잘할 거라고 확신해. 행운을 빌어 줄게!
지민: 고마워, 미소야. 내가 나의 연기의 한 부분을 보여 줄게. 누군지 맞힐 수 있겠니? "잘~ 했어~요!"
미소: 하하. 우리 영어 선생님처럼 들리는데.
지민: 그래? 장기 자랑에서 더 많이 보여 줄게.
미소: 멋지다! 너는 항상 우리를 웃게 만들어.

Fun Time

A: I'________ ________ ________ ________ to Jejudo next week.

B: Wow! That ________ ________.

A: Yeah, I'________ ________ ________ ________ ________ it.

A: I'm ________ ________ ________ the dance contest next week, but I'________ ________ ________ it.

B: ________ ________. You'll do great. I'll ________ ________ ________ ________.

A: Thank you.

A: 나는 다음 주에 제주도를 여행할 거야.
B: 와! 멋지다.
A: 응, 난 그것이 정말 기대돼.

A: 난 다음 주에 춤 대회에 나갈 건데, 걱정이 된다.
B: 걱정하지 마. 넌 잘할 거야. 행운을 빌어 줄게.
A: 고마워.

Express Yourself A

1. G: ________ ________ ________ ________ something about your ________?

   B: They are ________ ________ ________ ________ shoes. You can also ________ the ________ with them.

   G: Great! I'm sure you'll ________ ________ ________. I'll ________ my fingers ________!

2. B: This ________ ________. Is this a ________ ________ or a bird ________?

   G: It is ________ ________ a cutting ________ ________ ________ a bird ________. You can do two things ________ ________ ________ ________.

   B: That's a great ________!

   G: Do you ________ ________ ________?

   B: Yes. I'm really ________ ________ to ________ it.

1. G: 너의 발명품에 관해 이야기를 좀 해 줄래?
   B: 그것은 특별한 신발이야. 너는 그것으로 바닥을 청소할 수도 있어.
   G: 멋지다! 네가 상을 탈 거라고 확신해. 행운을 빌게!

2. B: 이것은 흥미로워 보여. 도마니, 아니면 새 모이통이니?
   G: 그것은 도마일 뿐만 아니라 새 모이통이기도 해. 너는 동시에 두 가지를 할 수 있어.
   B: 멋진 아이디어야!
   G: 정말 그렇게 생각하니?
   B: 응. 난 그것을 사용해 보는 게 정말 기대가 되는 걸.

※ 다음 우리말에 맞도록 대화를 영어로 쓰시오.

Get Ready 2

(1) G: ______________________________

____

B: ______________________________

G: ______________________________

(2) B: ______________________________

G: ______________________________

B: ______________________________

(3) B: ______________________________

G: ______________________________

____

B: ______________________________

(4) B: ______________________________

____

G: ______________________________

(1) G: 너는 수업 중 많은 문제를 해결했잖아. 나는 네가 'Class Brain'상을 탈 거라고 확신해.
B: 정말 그렇게 생각하니?
G: 물론이야. 행운을 빌게, 상준아!
(2) B: 'Oh So Sweet'상 수상자는 사탕을 받을 거야.
G: 오, 그 상을 받고 싶다.
B: 네가 이번에는 그 상을 탈 거라고 확신해. 행운을 빌어, 지우야!
(3) B: 난 이번에 'Best Joker'상을 받기를 기대해.
G: 하하. 너는 항상 우리를 웃게 하잖아. 그러니 네가 그 상을 탈 거야, 윤기야. 행운을 빌어.
B: 고마워.
(4) B: 민지야, 너는 쾌활한 아이야. 나는 네가 'Ms. Cheerful'상을 탈 거라고 생각해. 행운을 빌게!
G: 오, 고마워, 지호야.

Start Off – Listen & Talk A

1. G: ______________________________
W: ______________________________
G: ______________________________
W: ______________________________
G: ______________________________
W: ______________________________

2. W: ______________________________
G: ______________________________
W: ______________________________
G: ______________________________
W: ______________________________

1. G: 엄마, 체육 대회가 정말 기다려져요.
W: 민지야, 너는 그날 무엇을 할 거니?
G: 저는 학급을 대표해서 농구를 할 거예요. 우리는 몇 주간 열심히 연습해 왔어요.
W: 오, 너의 경기가 기대되는구나.
G: 사실은, 전 조금 걱정이 돼요. 제가 실수를 할까봐 겁나요.
W: 걱정하지 마. 넌 잘할 거야. 행운을 빌어줄게!

2. W: 소윤아, 넌 체육 대회에서 경주에 참가하니?
G: 물론이죠. 전 그날 마지막에 있는 100 미터 달리기를 뛸 거예요.
W: 와, 네가 경주에서 달리는 모습을 보는 것이 기대되는구나.
G: 하지만 엄마, 전 경주에서 이길지 잘 모르겠어요.
W: 그냥 최선을 다하렴. 행운을 빌어 줄게!

Start Off – Listen & Talk B

G: ______________________________

W: ______________________________

____

G: ______________________________

W: ______________________________

G: ______________________________

G: 엄마, 체육 대회에 오실 거예요?
W: 물론이지. 나는 'Kick a Shoe' 게임에 참가할 거야. 이번에 처음 해 보는 거야.
G: 걱정하지 마세요. 엄마는 잘하실 거예요. 행운을 빌어 드릴게요!
W: 고맙다. 나는 다른 엄마들과 코믹 댄스도 할 거야.
G: 재밌겠네요. 무대에 선 엄마 모습을 보는 것이 기대돼요.

Start Off – Speak Up

A: ______________________________

B: ______________________________

A: ______________________________

B: 나는 내일 모형 비행기 대회가 기대돼. 너는 준비됐니?
G: 음, 그런 것 같아. 하지만 긴장돼.
B: 너는 잘할 거야. 내가 행운을 빌어 줄게!

Step Up – Real-life Scene

Miso: ______________________________

____

Jimin: ______________________________

Miso: ______________________________

Jimin: ______________________________

Miso: ______________________________

Jimin: ______________________________

____

Miso: ______________________________

Jimin: ______________________________

Miso: ______________________________

미소: 다음 주 화요일에 수학여행을 갈 거야. 지민아, 너는 장기 자랑에서 뭘 할 거니?
지민: 나는 수업 시간에 선생님들이 말하는 것을 흉내 내고 농담도 할 거야.
미소: 와! 정말 기대되는데.
지민: 모든 사람이 나의 쇼를 좋아할까? 잘 모르겠어.
미소: 걱정하지 마. 나는 네가 잘할 거라고 확신해. 행운을 빌어 줄게!
지민: 고마워, 미소야. 내가 나의 연기의 한 부분을 보여 줄게. 누군지 맞힐 수 있겠니? "잘~ 했어~요!"
미소: 하하. 우리 영어 선생님처럼 들리는데.
지민: 그래? 장기 자랑에서 더 많이 보여 줄게.
미소: 멋지다! 너는 항상 우리를 웃게 만들어.

Fun Time

A: ______________________

B: ______________________

A: ______________________

A: ______________________

B: ______________________

A: ______________________

A: 나는 다음 주에 제주도를 여행할 거야.
B: 와! 멋지다.
A: 응, 난 그것이 정말 기대돼.

A: 난 다음 주에 춤 대회에 나갈 건데, 걱정이 된다.
B: 걱정하지 마. 넌 잘할 거야. 행운을 빌어 줄게.
A: 고마워.

Express Yourself A

1. G: ______________________
   B: ______________________
   G: ______________________

2. B: ______________________
   G: ______________________
   ____
   B: ______________________
   G: ______________________
   B: ______________________

1. G: 너의 발명품에 관해 이야기를 좀 해 줄래?
   B: 그것은 특별한 신발이야. 너는 그것으로 바닥을 청소할 수도 있어.
   G: 멋지다! 네가 상을 탈 거라고 확신해. 행운을 빌게!

2. B: 이것은 흥미로워 보여. 도마니, 아니면 새 모이통이니?
   G: 그것은 도마일 뿐만 아니라 새 모이통이기도 해. 너는 동시에 두 가지를 할 수 있어.
   B: 멋진 아이디어야!
   G: 정말 그렇게 생각하니?
   B: 응. 난 그것을 사용해 보는 게 정말 기대가 되는 걸.

본문 Test

※ 다음 우리말과 일치하도록 빈칸에 알맞은 것을 골라 쓰시오.

1 The ________ ________ ________
A. Prize B. Nobel C. Ig

1 이그노벨상

2 "What ________ when you walk ________ ________ you are ________ a cup of coffee?"
A. backward B. happens C. carrying D. while

2 "당신이 커피 한 잔을 들고 가면서 뒤로 걸을 때 무슨 일이 일어날까?"

3 Han Jiwon, a Korean high school student, ________ ________ ________ this ________ in 2015.
A. research B. on C. did D. topic

3 한국의 한 고등학생인 한지원은 2015년에 이 주제에 관해 연구했다.

4 Is this ________ project good ________ ________ ________ a Nobel Prize?
A. win B. research C. enough D. to

4 이 연구 과제는 노벨상을 받을 정도로 훌륭할까?

5 ________ ________.
A. not B. maybe

5 아마도 아닐 것이다.

6 But ________ ________ an Ig Nobel Prize?
A. about B. how

6 하지만 이그노벨상은 어떤가?

7 He ________ one in 2017 for this ________ ________.
A. fun B. won C. research

7 그는 이 재미있는 연구로 2017년에 상을 탔다.

8 The Ig Nobel Prizes are ________ ________ discoveries that "first make one ________ and then ________."
A. awarded B. laugh C. for D. think

8 이그노벨상은 '먼저 웃기고 나서 다음에 생각하게 하는' 발견에 수여된다.

9 They were started in 1991 by *AIR* magazine to increase people's ________ in science by ________ the ________ and the ________.
A. interest B. imaginative C. honoring D. unusual

9 그것은 특이하고 창의적인 사람들을 높이 평가함으로써 과학에 대한 사람들의 흥미를 늘리기 위해 AIR 잡지에 의해 1991년에 시작되었다.

10 The prizes ________ ________ ________ real Nobel ________ in Sanders Theater at Harvard University.
A. winners B. are C. by D. presented

10 그 상들은 하버드 대학의 Sanders 극장에서 진짜 노벨상 수상자들에 의해 수여된다.

11 The room is usually ________ ________ people who are eager to ________ for the brave scientists with their "________" research.

A. cheer B. with C. laughable D. filled

12 The U.K. Navy ________ the Ig Nobel Prize ________ Peace ________ 2000.

A. for B. won C. in

13 ________ ________ money, the Navy made its sailors shout, "Bang!" ________ ________ using real bombs.

A. of B. save C. to D. instead

14 Is that funny ________ for you to ________ ________ ________?

A. laugh B. loud C. enough D. out

15 Andre Geim ________ ________ an ________ that year.

A. award B. also C. won

16 He ________ ________ ________ a live frog in the air by ________ magnets.

A. using B. succeeded C. floating D. in

17 "In my experience, if people don't have a ________ of ________, they are usually not very good scientists," he said when he ________ his ________.

A. humor B. accepted C. sense D. award

18 If that still does not ________ a smile ________ your ________, ________ about this?

A. to B. bring C. how D. face

19 In 2005, Gauri Nanda won the Ig Nobel Prize ________ Economics ________ ________ an ________ clock.

A. for B. alarm C. inventing D. in

20 It ________ ________ ________ until the sleeper finally gets ________ of bed.

A. away B. out C. running D. keeps

11 그 방은 대개 '웃기는' 연구를 한 용감한 과학자들을 열렬히 격려하고자 하는 사람들로 가득 찬다.

12 영국 해군은 2000년에 이그노벨 평화상을 탔다.

13 돈을 아끼기 위해, 해군에서는 선원들에게 진짜 폭탄을 사용하는 대신에 "쾅!"이라고 소리치게 했다.

14 그것이 당신이 큰 소리로 웃을 정도로 우스운가?

15 Andre Geim도 그해에 상을 탔다.

16 그는 자석을 이용해서 살아 있는 개구리를 공중에 띄우는 데 성공했다.

17 그는 상을 받을 때, "내 경험상, 사람들이 유머 감각이 없다면, 그들은 대개 별로 훌륭한 과학자가 아니다."라고 말했다.

18 그것이 아직도 당신의 얼굴에 미소를 띠게 하지 않는다면, 이것은 어떤가?

19 2005년에 Gauri Nanda는 자명종을 발명해서 이그노벨 경제학상을 받았다.

20 그것은 잠자는 사람이 결국 침대 밖으로 나올 때까지 계속 도망을 다닌다.

21 ________ ________ the winners' fun studies ________ also the ceremony for the Ig Nobel Prizes ________ people laugh.

A. but B. only C. makes D. not

22 There are a ________ of interesting things that ________ people ________ getting ________.

A. from B. number C. bored D. keep

23 The ________ and ________ speeches are just two ________ ________: "Welcome. Welcome." and "Goodbye. Goodbye."

A. each B. closing C. words D. opening

24 If someone talks for too long, an eight-year-old girl ________ Miss Sweetie Poo ________ ________, "Please stop! I'm ________."

A. called B. bored C. repeatedly D. shouts

25 Each winner receives ten ________ Zimbabwean dollars, ________ is ________ ________ than one U.S. dollar.

A. less B. trillion C. worth D. which

26 ________ paper planes ________ ________ fun ________.

A. is B. throwing C. tradition D. another

27 The Ig Nobel Prize ceremony ________ ________ the words, "If you didn't ________ a prize — and if you ________ — better luck next year!"

A. with B. did C. win D. ends

28 The ________ do not ________ ________ ________ money.

A. receive B. lots C. winners D. of

29 And the ________ are not ________ ________ ________ the Nobel Prizes.

A. honors B. awards C. like D. great

30 But the Ig Nobel Prizes make science ________ ________ ________ ________!

A. fun B. a C. more D. lot

21 수상자들의 재미있는 연구뿐만 아니라 이그노벨상 시상식도 또한 사람들을 웃게 만든다.

22 사람들이 지루해하지 않도록 하는 재미있는 것들이 많이 있다.

23 개회사와 폐회사는 단지 두 마디이다: "환영합니다. 환영합니다."와 "안녕. 안녕."

24 만일 누군가가 너무 오랫동안 말을 하면, Miss Sweetie Poo 라고 하는 여덟 살짜리 여자아이가 "제발 멈춰요! 지루해요." 라고 계속 외친다.

25 각 수상자는 10조의 짐바브웨 달러를 받는데, 그것은 미국의 1 달러보다 가치가 낮다.

26 종이비행기를 날리는 것은 또 다른 재미있는 전통이다.

27 이그노벨상 시상식은 "만일 당신이 상을 타지 못했다면 – 그리고 만일 탔다면 – 내년에는 좀 더 많은 행운이 있기를!"이라는 말로 끝이 난다.

28 수상자들은 많은 상금을 받지 않는다.

29 그리고 그 상은 노벨상같이 훌륭한 영광은 아니다.

30 하지만 이그노벨상은 과학을 훨씬 더 재미있게 만든다!

본문 Test

Step2

※ 다음 우리말과 일치하도록 빈칸에 알맞은 말을 쓰시오.

1 The ________ ________ ________

2 "What ________ when you walk ________ ________ you are ________ a cup of coffee?"

3 Han Jiwon, a Korean high school student, ________ ________ on this ________ in 2015.

4 Is this research project ________ ________ ________ ________ a Nobel Prize?

5 ________ not.

6 But ________ ________ an Ig Nobel Prize?

7 He ________ ________ in 2017 for this ________ ________.

8 The Ig Nobel Prizes ________ ________ ________ ________ that "first make one ________ and then ________."

9 They were started in 1991 by *AIR* magazine ________ ________ people's ________ in science ________ ________ ________ ________ and ________ ________.

10 The prizes ________ ________ ________ ________ ________ ________ in Sanders Theater at Harvard University.

1 이그노벨상

2 "당신이 커피 한 잔을 들고 가면서 뒤로 걸을 때 무슨 일이 일어날까?"

3 한국의 한 고등학생인 한지원은 2015년에 이 주제에 관해 연구했다.

4 이 연구 과제는 노벨상을 받을 정도로 훌륭할까?

5 아마도 아닐 것이다.

6 하지만 이그노벨상은 어떤가?

7 그는 이 재미있는 연구로 2017년에 상을 탔다.

8 이그노벨상은 '먼저 웃기고 나서 다음에 생각하게 하는' 발견에 수여된다.

9 그것은 특이하고 창의적인 사람들을 높이 평가함으로써 과학에 대한 사람들의 흥미를 늘리기 위해 AIR 잡지에 의해 1991년에 시작되었다.

10 그 상들은 하버드 대학의 Sanders 극장에서 진짜 노벨상 수상자들에 의해 수여된다.

11 The room ________ usually ________ ________ people who are ________ ________ ________ for the brave scientists with their "________" research.

12 The U.K. Navy ________ the Ig Nobel Prize ________ Peace in 2000.

13 ________ ________ money, the Navy ________ its sailors ________, "Bang!" ________ ________ ________ real bombs.

14 Is that ________ ________ for you to ________ ________ ________?

15 Andre Geim also ________ ________ ________ that year.

16 He ________ ________ ________ a live frog in the air ________ ________ ________.

17 "In my experience, if people don't have ________ ________ ________ ________, they are usually not very good scientists," he said ________ he ________ his ________.

18 If that still does not ________ a smile ________ your face, ________ ________ this?

19 In 2005, Gauri Nanda won the Ig Nobel Prize ________ Economics ________ ________ an alarm clock.

20 It ________ ________ ________ until the sleeper finally ________ ________ ________ bed.

11 그 방은 대개 '웃기는' 연구를 한 용감한 과학자들을 열렬히 격려하고자 하는 사람들로 가득 찬다.

12 영국 해군은 2000년에 이그노벨 평화상을 탔다.

13 돈을 아끼기 위해, 해군에서는 선원들에게 진짜 폭탄을 사용하는 대신에 "쾅!"이라고 소리치게 했다.

14 그것이 당신이 큰 소리로 웃을 정도로 우스운가?

15 Andre Geim도 그해에 상을 탔다.

16 그는 자석을 이용해서 살아 있는 개구리를 공중에 띄우는 데 성공했다.

17 그는 상을 받을 때, "내 경험상, 사람들이 유머 감각이 없다면, 그들은 대개 별로 훌륭한 과학자가 아니다."라고 말했다.

18 그것이 아직도 당신의 얼굴에 미소를 띠게 하지 않는다면, 이것은 어떤가?

19 2005년에 Gauri Nanda는 자명종을 발명해서 이그노벨 경제학상을 받았다.

20 그것은 잠자는 사람이 결국 침대 밖으로 나올 때까지 계속 도망을 다닌다.

21 ________ ________ the winners' fun studies ________ ________ the ceremony for the Ig Nobel Prizes ________ people ________.

22 There are ________ ________ ________ interesting things that ________ people ________ ________ ________.

23 The ________ and ________ ________ are just ________ ________ ________: "Welcome. Welcome." and "Goodbye. Goodbye."

24 If someone talks for too long, ________ ________ ________ ________ Miss Sweetie Poo shouts ________, "Please stop! I'm bored."

25 Each winner receives ________ ________ Zimbabwean dollars, ________ is ________ ________ ________ one U.S. dollar.

26 ________ paper planes ________ another fun ________.

27 The Ig Nobel Prize ceremony ________ ________ the words, "If you didn't ________ a ________ — and if you ________ — better luck next year!"

28 The winners ________ ________ ________ lots of money.

29 And the awards are not ________ ________ ________ the Nobel Prizes.

30 But the Ig Nobel Prizes make science ________ ________ ________ ________!

21 수상자들의 재미있는 연구뿐만 아니라 이그노벨상 시상식도 또한 사람들을 웃게 만든다.

22 사람들이 지루해하지 않도록 하는 재미있는 것들이 많이 있다.

23 개회사와 폐회사는 단지 두 마디이다: "환영합니다. 환영합니다."와 "안녕. 안녕."

24 만일 누군가가 너무 오랫동안 말을 하면, Miss Sweetie Poo 라고 하는 여덟 살짜리 여자아이가 "제발 멈춰요! 지루해요." 라고 계속 외친다.

25 각 수상자는 10조의 짐바브웨 달러를 받는데, 그것은 미국의 1 달러보다 가치가 낮다.

26 종이비행기를 날리는 것은 또 다른 재미있는 전통이다.

27 이그노벨상 시상식은 "만일 당신이 상을 타지 못했다면 – 그리고 만일 탔다면 – 내년에는 좀 더 많은 행운이 있기를!"이라는 말로 끝이 난다.

28 수상자들은 많은 상금을 받지 않는다.

29 그리고 그 상은 노벨상같이 훌륭한 영광은 아니다.

30 하지만 이그노벨상은 과학을 훨씬 더 재미있게 만든다!

본문 Test

※ 다음 문장을 우리말로 쓰시오.

1 The Ig Nobel Prize

➡ ______________________________

2 "What happens when you walk backward while you are carrying a cup of coffee?"

➡ ______________________________

3 Han Jiwon, a Korean high school student, did research on this topic in 2015.

➡ ______________________________

4 Is this research project good enough to win a Nobel Prize?

➡ ______________________________

5 Maybe not.

➡ ______________________________

6 But how about an Ig Nobel Prize?

➡ ______________________________

7 He won one in 2017 for this fun research.

➡ ______________________________

8 The Ig Nobel Prizes are awarded for discoveries that "first make one laugh and then think."

➡ ______________________________

9 They were started in 1991 by AIR magazine to increase people's interest in science by honoring the unusual and the imaginative.

➡ ______________________________

____

10 The prizes are presented by real Nobel winners in Sanders Theater at Harvard University.

➡ ______________________________

11 The room is usually filled with people who are eager to cheer for the brave scientists with their "laughable" research.

➡ ______________________________

12 The U.K. Navy won the Ig Nobel Prize for Peace in 2000.

➡ ______________________________

13 To save money, the Navy made its sailors shout, "Bang!" instead of using real bombs.

➡ ______________________________

14 Is that funny enough for you to laugh out loud?

➡ ______________________________

15 Andre Geim also won an award that year.

➡ ______________________________

Step3

16 He succeeded in floating a live frog in the air by using magnets.

➡ ______________________________

17 "In my experience, if people don't have a sense of humor, they are usually not very good scientists," he said when he accepted his award.

➡ ______________________________

18 If that still does not bring a smile to your face, how about this?

➡ ______________________________

19 In 2005, Gauri Nanda won the Ig Nobel Prize in Economics for inventing an alarm clock.

➡ ______________________________

20 It keeps running away until the sleeper finally gets out of bed.

➡ ______________________________

21 Not only the winners' fun studies but also the ceremony for the Ig Nobel Prizes makes people laugh.

➡ ______________________________

22 There are a number of interesting things that keep people from getting bored.

➡ ______________________________

23 The opening and closing speeches are just two words each: "Welcome. Welcome." and "Goodbye. Goodbye."

➡ ______________________________

24 If someone talks for too long, an eight-year-old girl called Miss Sweetie Poo shouts repeatedly, "Please stop! I'm bored."

➡ ______________________________

____

25 Each winner receives ten trillion Zimbabwean dollars, which is worth less than one U.S. dollar.

➡ ______________________________

26 Throwing paper planes is another fun tradition.

➡ ______________________________

27 The Ig Nobel Prize ceremony ends with the words, "If you didn't win a prize — and if you did — better luck next year!"

➡ ______________________________

____

28 The winners do not receive lots of money.

➡ ______________________________

29 And the awards are not great honors like the Nobel Prizes.

➡ ______________________________

30 But the Ig Nobel Prizes make science a lot more fun!

➡ ______________________________

본문 Test

※ 다음 괄호 안의 단어들을 우리말에 맞도록 바르게 배열하시오.

1 (Ig / The / Prize / Nobel)

➡ ______________________________

2 (happens / "what / you / when / backward / walk / you / while / carrying / are / cup / a / of / coffee?")

➡ ______________________________

____

3 (Jiwon, / Han / Korean / a / school / high / student, / research / did / this / on / topic / 2015. / in)

➡ ______________________________

____

4 (this / is / project / research / enough / good / win / to / a / Prize? / Nobel)

➡ ______________________________

5 (not. / maybe)

➡ ______________________________

6 (how / but / an / about / Nobel / Ig / Prize?)

➡ ______________________________

7 (won / he / in / one / 2017 / this / for / research. / fun)

➡ ______________________________

8 (Ig / The / Prizes / Nobel / awarded / are / discoveries / for / "first / that / one / make / laugh / then / and / think.")

➡ ______________________________

____

9 (were / they / in / started / 1991 / *AIR* / by / to / magazine / interest / people's / increase / in / by / science / the / honoring / unusual / and / imaginative. / the)

➡ ______________________________

____

10 (prizes / the / presented / are / real / by / winners / Nobel / Sanders / in / Theater / Harvard / at / University.)

➡ ______________________________

____

1 이그노벨상

2 "당신이 커피 한 잔을 들고 가면서 뒤로 걸을 때 무슨 일이 일어날까?"

3 한국의 한 고등학생인 한지원은 2015년에 이 주제에 관해 연구했다.

4 이 연구 과제는 노벨상을 받을 정도로 훌륭할까?

5 아마도 아닐 것이다.

6 하지만 이그노벨상은 어떤가?

7 그는 이 재미있는 연구로 2017년에 상을 탔다.

8 이그노벨상은 '먼저 웃기고 나서 다음에 생각하게 하는' 발견에 수여된다.

9 그것은 특이하고 창의적인 사람들을 높이 평가함으로써 과학에 대한 사람들의 흥미를 늘리기 위해 AIR 잡지에 의해 1991년에 시작되었다.

10 그 상들은 하버드 대학의 Sanders 극장에서 진짜 노벨상 수상자들에 의해 수여된다.

11 (room / the / usually / is / with / filled / who / people / eager / are / to / for / cheer / the / scientists / brave / their / with / research. / "laughable")

➡ ______________________________

____

12 (U.K. / the / won / Navy / Ig / the / Prize / Nobel / Peace / in / 2000. / for)

➡ ______________________________

13 (save / to / money, / Navy / the / its / made / sailors / "Bang!" / shout, / of / instead / using / of / bombs. / real)

➡ ______________________________

____

14 (that / is / enough / funny / you / for / laugh / to / loud? / out)

➡ ______________________________

15 (Geim / Andre / won / also / award / an / year. / that)

➡ ______________________________

16 (succeeded / he / floating / in / live / a / in / frog / the / by / air / magnets. / using)

➡ ______________________________

17 (my / "in / experience, / people / if / have / don't / sense / a / of / they / humor, / are / not / usually / very / scientists," / good / said / he / he / when / his / award. / accepted)

➡ ______________________________

____

18 (that / if / does / still / bring / not / smile / a / your / to / face, / about / this? / how)

➡ ______________________________

19 (2005, / in / Nanda / Gauri / the / won / Nobel / Ig / in / Prize / for / Economics / inventing / alarm / an / clock.)

➡ ______________________________

____

20 (keeps / it / away / running / the / until / finally / sleeper / out / gets / bed. / of)

➡ ______________________________

11 그 방은 대개 '웃기는' 연구를 한 용감한 과학자들을 열렬히 격려하고자 하는 사람들로 가득 찬다.

12 영국 해군은 2000년에 이그노벨 평화상을 탔다.

13 돈을 아끼기 위해, 해군에서는 선원들에게 진짜 폭탄을 사용하는 대신에 "쾅!"이라고 소리치게 했다.

14 그것이 당신이 큰 소리로 웃을 정도로 우스운가?

15 Andre Geim도 그해에 상을 탔다.

16 그는 자석을 이용해서 살아 있는 개구리를 공중에 띄우는 데 성공했다.

17 그는 상을 받을 때, "내 경험상, 사람들이 유머 감각이 없다면, 그들은 대개 별로 훌륭한 과학자가 아니다."라고 말했다.

18 그것이 아직도 당신의 얼굴에 미소를 띠게 하지 않는다면, 이것은 어떤가?

19 2005년에 Gauri Nanda는 자명종을 발명해서 이그노벨 경제학상을 받았다.

20 그것은 잠자는 사람이 결국 침대 밖으로 나올 때까지 계속 도망을 다닌다.

21 (only / not / winners' / the / studies / fun / also / but / ceremony / the / the / for / Ig / Prizes / Nobel / people / laugh. / makes)

➡ ______________________________

____

22 (are / there / number / a / interesting / of / that / things / people / keep / from / bored. / getting)

➡ ______________________________

____

23 (opening / the / and / speeches / closing / just / are / words / two / each: / "welcome. / goodbye." / welcome." / and / "goodbye.)

➡ ______________________________

____

24 (someone / if / for / talks / long, / too / eight-year-old / an / called / girl / Sweetie / Miss / shouts / Poo / repeatedly, / stop! / "please / bored." / I'm)

➡ ______________________________

____

25 (winner / each / ten / receives / trillion / dollars, / Zimbabwean / is / which / less / worth / one / than / dollar. / U.S.)

➡ ______________________________

____

26 (paper / throwing / planes / another / is / tradition. / fun)

➡ ______________________________

27 (Ig / The / Prize / ceremony / with / ends / words, / the / you / "if / win / didn't / prize / a / – / if / and / did / you / – / luck / year!" / better / next)

➡ ______________________________

____

28 (winners / the / not / do / lots / receive / money. / of)

➡ ______________________________

29 (the / and / are / awards / great / not / like / honors / the / Prizes. / Nobel)

➡ ______________________________

30 (the / but / Nobel / Ig / make / Prizes / a / science / more / lot / fun!)

➡ ______________________________

21 수상자들의 재미있는 연구뿐만 아니라 이그노벨상 시상식도 또한 사람들을 웃게 만든다.

22 사람들이 지루해하지 않도록 하는 재미있는 것들이 많이 있다.

23 개회사와 폐회사는 단지 두 마디이다: "환영합니다. 환영합니다."와 "안녕. 안녕."

24 만일 누군가가 너무 오랫동안 말을 하면, Miss Sweetie Poo 라고 하는 여덟 살짜리 여자아이가 "제발 멈춰요! 지루해요." 라고 계속 외친다.

25 각 수상자는 10조의 짐바브웨 달러를 받는데, 그것은 미국의 1 달러보다 가치가 낮다.

26 종이비행기를 날리는 것은 또 다른 재미있는 전통이다.

27 이그노벨상 시상식은 "만일 당신이 상을 타지 못했다면 – 그리고 만일 탔다면 – 내년에는 좀 더 많은 행운이 있기를!"이라는 말로 끝이 난다.

28 수상자들은 많은 상금을 받지 않는다.

29 그리고 그 상은 노벨상같이 훌륭한 영광은 아니다.

30 하지만 이그노벨상은 과학을 훨씬 더 재미있게 만든다!

본문 Test

Step5

※ 다음 우리말을 영어로 쓰시오.

1 이그노벨상

➡ ______________________________

2 "당신이 커피 한 잔을 들고 가면서 뒤로 걸을 때 무슨 일이 일어날까?"

➡ ______________________________

3 한국의 한 고등학생인 한지원은 2015년에 이 주제에 관해 연구했다.

➡ ______________________________

4 이 연구 과제는 노벨상을 받을 정도로 훌륭할까?

➡ ______________________________

5 아마도 아닐 것이다.

➡ ______________________________

6 하지만 이그노벨상은 어떤가?

➡ ______________________________

7 그는 이 재미있는 연구로 2017년에 상을 탔다.

➡ ______________________________

8 이그노벨상은 '먼저 웃기고 나서 다음에 생각하게 하는' 발견에 수여된다.

➡ ______________________________

9 그것은 특이하고 창의적인 사람들을 높이 평가함으로써 과학에 대한 사람들의 흥미를 늘리기 위해 AIR 잡지에 의해 1991년에 시작되었다.

➡ ______________________________

____

10 그 상들은 하버드 대학의 Sanders 극장에서 진짜 노벨상 수상자들에 의해 수여된다.

➡ ______________________________

11 그 방은 대개 '웃기는' 연구를 한 용감한 과학자들을 열렬히 격려하고자 하는 사람들로 가득 찬다.

➡ ______________________________

____

12 영국 해군은 2000년에 이그노벨 평화상을 탔다.

➡ ______________________________

13 돈을 아끼기 위해, 해군에서는 선원들에게 진짜 폭탄을 사용하는 대신에 "쾅!"이라고 소리치게 했다.

➡ ______________________________

14 그것이 당신이 큰 소리로 웃을 정도로 우스운가?

➡ ______________________________

15 Andre Geim도 그해에 상을 탔다.

➡ ______________________________

16 그는 자석을 이용해서 살아 있는 개구리를 공중에 띄우는 데 성공했다.

➡ ______________________________

17 그는 상을 받을 때, "내 경험상, 사람들이 유머 감각이 없다면, 그들은 대개 별로 훌륭한 과학자가 아니다."라고 말했다.

➡ ______________________________

____

18 그것이 아직도 당신의 얼굴에 미소를 띠게 하지 않는다면, 이것은 어떤가?

➡ ______________________________

19 2005년에 Gauri Nanda는 자명종을 발명해서 이그노벨 경제학상을 받았다.

➡ ______________________________

20 그것은 잠자는 사람이 결국 침대 밖으로 나올 때까지 계속 도망을 다닌다.

➡ ______________________________

21 수상자들의 재미있는 연구뿐만 아니라 이그노벨상 시상식도 또한 사람들을 웃게 만든다.

➡ ______________________________

22 사람들이 지루해하지 않도록 하는 재미있는 것들이 많이 있다.

➡ ______________________________

23 개회사와 폐회사는 단지 두 마디이다: "환영합니다. 환영합니다."와 "안녕. 안녕."

➡ ______________________________

24 만일 누군가가 너무 오랫동안 말을 하면, Miss Sweetie Poo라고 하는 여덟 살짜리 여자아이가 "제발 멈춰요! 지루해요."라고 계속 외친다.

➡ ______________________________

____

25 각 수상자는 10조의 짐바브웨 달러를 받는데, 그것은 미국의 1달러보다 가치가 낮다.

➡ ______________________________

26 종이비행기를 날리는 것은 또 다른 재미있는 전통이다.

➡ ______________________________

27 이그노벨상 시상식은 "만일 당신이 상을 타지 못했다면 – 그리고 만일 탔다면 – 내년에는 좀 더 많은 행운이 있기를!"이라는 말로 끝이 난다.

➡ ______________________________

____

28 수상자들은 많은 상금을 받지 않는다.

➡ ______________________________

29 그리고 그 상은 노벨상같이 훌륭한 영광은 아니다.

➡ ______________________________

30 하지만 이그노벨상은 과학을 훨씬 더 재미있게 만든다!

➡ ______________________________

구석구석 지문 Test

※ 다음 우리말과 일치하도록 빈칸에 알맞은 말을 쓰시오.

Self-study Guide

1. New ________ again!
2. He ________ great ________ ________ ________ new things.
3. Oh, I ________ the ________ of "-ness."
4. Now I know ________ ________ the meaning of "eager" ________ ________ the meaning of "eagerness."

1. 또 새 단어네!
2. 그는 새로운 것들을 배우고자 하는 열정을 보여주었다.
3. 오, 나는 '-ness'의 의미를 알았어.
4. 이제 나는 'eager'의 뜻뿐만 아니라 'eagerness'의 뜻도 알아.

Express Yourself C

1. Magic ________
2. ________ are ________ Stairs.
3. You can use them ________ ________ for ________ up and down ________ ________ for ________ things.
4. This invention is ________ ________ ________ ________ your life ________ ________.

1. 마법의 계단
2. 이것은 '마법의 계단'입니다.
3. 당신은 그것을 올라가고 내려가기 위해서 뿐만 아니라 물건을 보관하기 위해서도 사용할 수 있습니다.
4. 이 발명품은 당신의 삶을 훨씬 더 편안하게 할 정도로 충분히 유용합니다.

Link to the World

1. The ________ ________
2. The Nobel Prize was ________ ________ Alfred Nobel, a ________ ________.
3. It ________ ________ ________ people ________ have done ________ ________ for the world.
4. Of ________ ________ ________, Malala Yousafzai is ________ ________.
5. She won the Nobel Prize ________ ________ ________ ________ 17 because she ________ ________ for women's and ________ ________.
6. The Curie family ________ the Nobel Prize ________ ________.
7. ________ ________ Marie Curie ________ ________ her daughter ________ ________ the Nobel Prize.

1. 노벨상
2. 노벨상은 스웨덴 과학자인, Alfred Nobel의 이름을 따서 지었다.
3. 그 상은 세계를 위해 위대한 일을 행한 사람들에게 수여된다.
4. 모든 수상자들 중에서, Malala Yousafzai가 최연소이다.
5. 그녀는 여성과 어린이의 권리를 위해서 싸웠기 때문에 17세의 나이에 노벨상을 수상했다.
6. Curie 가족은 노벨상을 3번 수상했다.
7. Marie Curie뿐만 아니라 그녀의 딸도 노벨상을 수상했다.

구석구석 지문 Test

Step2

※ 다음 우리말을 영어로 쓰시오.

Self-study Guide

1. 또 새 단어네!
➡ ______________________________

2. 그는 새로운 것들을 배우고자 하는 열정을 보여주었다.
➡ ______________________________

3. 오, 나는 '-ness'의 의미를 알았어.
➡ ______________________________

4. 이제 나는 'eager'의 뜻뿐만 아니라 'eagerness'의 뜻도 알아.
➡ ______________________________

Express Yourself C

1. 마법의 계단
➡ ______________________________

2. 이것은 '마법의 계단'입니다.
➡ ______________________________

3. 당신은 그것을 올라가고 내려가기 위해서 뿐만 아니라 물건을 보관하기 위해서도 사용할 수 있습니다.
➡ ______________________________

4. 이 발명품은 당신의 삶을 훨씬 더 편안하게 할 정도로 충분히 유용합니다.
➡ ______________________________

Link to the World

1. 노벨상
➡ ______________________________

2. 노벨상은 스웨덴 과학자인, Alfred Nobel의 이름을 따서 지었다.
➡ ______________________________

3. 그 상은 세계를 위해 위대한 일을 행한 사람들에게 수여된다.
➡ ______________________________

4. 모든 수상자들 중에서, Malala Yousafzai가 최연소이다.
➡ ______________________________

5. 그녀는 여성과 어린이의 권리를 위해서 싸웠기 때문에 17세의 나이에 노벨상을 수상했다.
➡ ______________________________

6. Curie 가족은 노벨상을 3번 수상했다.
➡ ______________________________

7. Marie Curie뿐만 아니라 그녀의 딸도 노벨상을 수상했다.
➡ ______________________________

MEMO

MEMO

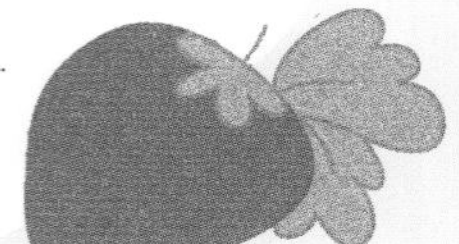

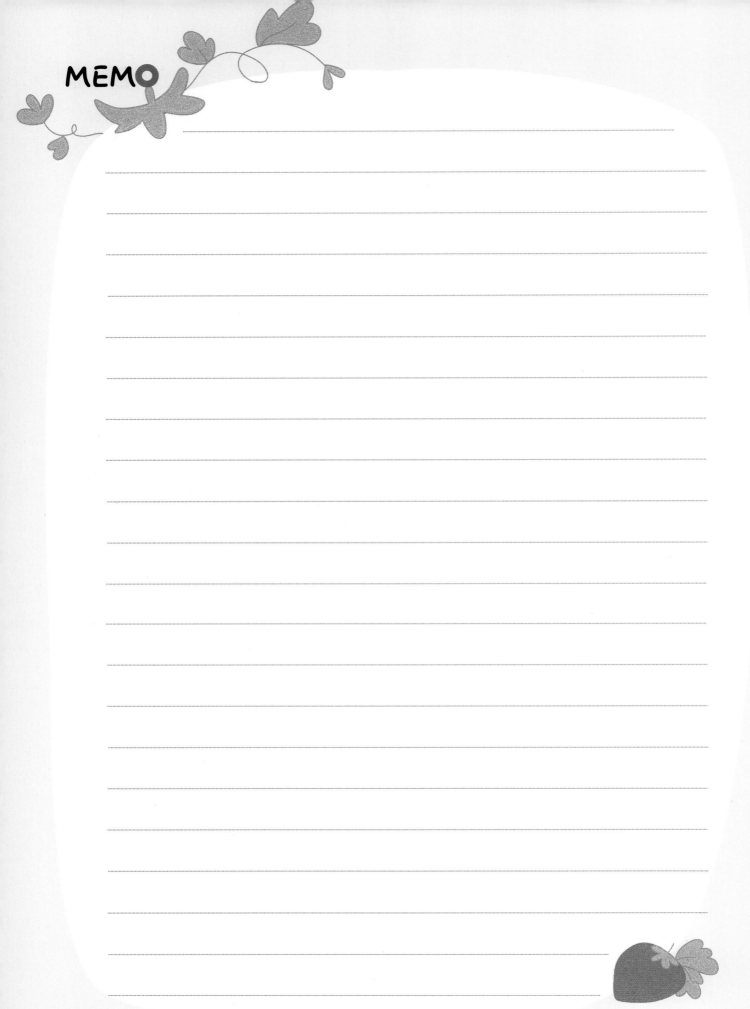

영어 기출 문제집

적중100

중 3

적중100

영어 기출 문제집

적중100

중3

적중100

Lesson 1

Express Your Feelings

시험대비 실력평가 p.08

01 book	02 ④	03 ⑤	04 ①
05 stands for	06 ③	07 (f)inally	08 ④

01 '미래의 특정 시간에 좌석, 방, 공연자 등을 갖도록 준비하다'라는 의미로 'book(예약하다)'가 적절하다.

02 우리가 농담을 듣거나 우스운 것을 보거나 행복감을 느끼면 소리 내어 웃는다는 내용으로 보아 '웃음(laughter)'에 관한 것임을 알 수 있다.

03 '구입되거나 사용될 수 있는'의 뜻으로 available이 적절하다.

04 소수의 사람들 또는 단지 두 명의 사람들이 관여한 비공식적인 이야기

05 'stand for'는 '…을 상징하다'라는 뜻으로, 주어가 3인칭 단수이므로 stand에 -s를 붙인다.

06 (A) 이모티콘 XD는 우리의 행복한 감정을 하하와 LOL보다 더 시각적으로 표현한다(express). (B) 급행열차(express)는 정시에 런던을 출발했다.

07 유의어 관계다. 기회 - 마침내

08 (A) 사람들이 이모지를 사용하고 있다는 말 다음에 많은 웃는 이모지가 온라인에서 사용될 수 있다는 말이 적절하다. (B) 그래서 사람들이 다양한 방식으로 웃음을 표현한다.

서술형 시험대비 p.09

01 written, means, since
02 (1) Actually (2) meaningful (3) facial
03 (1) various (2) emojis (3) typed
04 (1) guess, 추측하다 (2) tone, 어조, 말투
(3) human, 인간의, 인간적인
05 (t)ext

01 "하하"는 문자로 된 웃음의 한 형태이다. 모두가 그것이 무엇을 의미하는지 알고 있다. 실제로 그것은 오래전부터 사용되어 왔다. 셰익스피어조차도 "하하"를 자신의 작품에 사용하였다.

02 (1) '사실, 슬퍼. 너희 모두를 그리워할 거야.' actual은 형용사로 -ly를 붙여 부사로 만들어 주어야 한다. (2) '그에게 뭔가 의미 있는 것을 준다니 기뻐.' -thing으로 끝나는 대명사는 형용사가 뒤에서 수식한다. 동사 mean을 형용사 meaningful로 바꾸어 준다. (3) '웃음 표시는 우리의 얼굴 표정을 나타내고 우리의 목소리 어조를 전달할 수 있다.' 명사 expression을 수식하는 형용사가 필요하다. face의 형용사 형태인 facial이 적절하다.

03 (1) 다양한: various (2) 이모지: emoji (3) 타자 치다: type, 문장은 수동태로 과거분사 typed로 바꾸어야 한다.

04 (1) '모든 사실을 가지고 있지 않아서 당신이 옳은지 확신할 수 없을 때 특정 질문에 대답을 하다'라는 의미로 '추측하다(guess)'가 적절하다. (2) '특히 특정한 감정을 표현하는 누군가의 목소리의 특질'이란 의미로 '어조, 말투(tone)'를 나타낸다. (3) '동물과는 반대로 사람 또는 사람에 관계되거나 소속되어 있는'의 뜻으로 '인간의(human)'가 적절하다.

05 text: 글, 문자 메시지

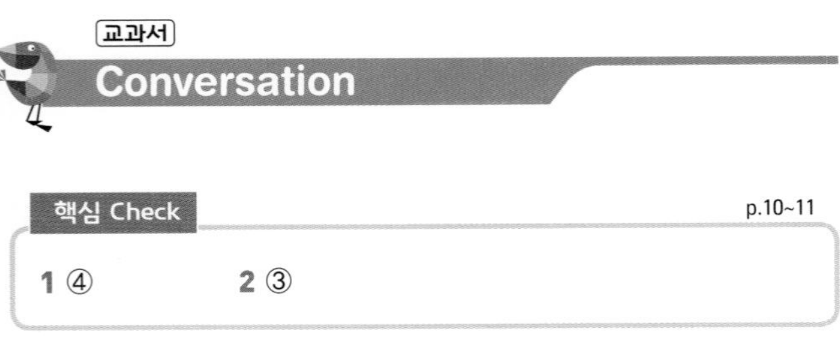

교과서

Conversation

핵심 Check p.10~11

1 ④ 2 ③

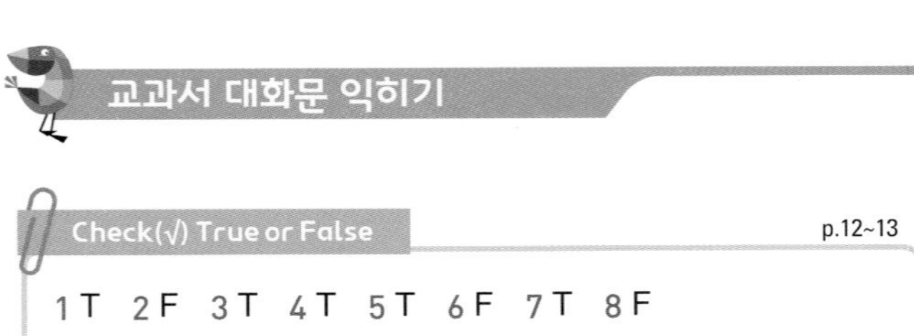

교과서 대화문 익히기

Check(√) True or False p.12~13

1 T 2 F 3 T 4 T 5 T 6 F 7 T 8 F

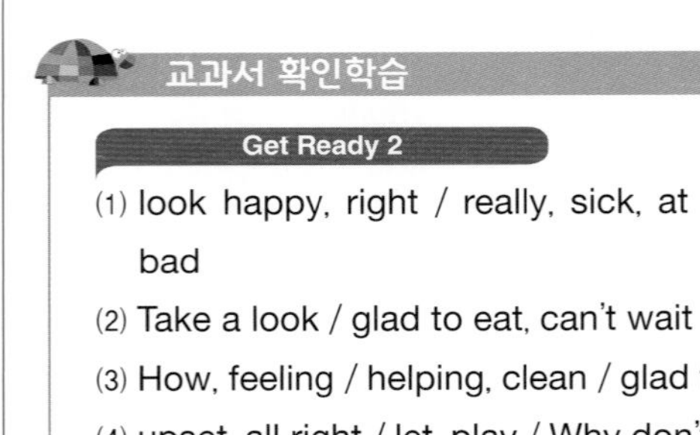

교과서 확인학습 p.15~17

Get Ready 2

(1) look happy, right / really, sick, at all / That's too bad
(2) Take a look / glad to eat, can't wait for
(3) How, feeling / helping, clean / glad to hear that
(4) upset, all right / let, play / Why don't you

Start Off – Listen & Talk A

1. moving, How / excited, whole / to hear, was worried about / Actually, miss / keep in touch / have
2. is moving / miss / is going, invite, promised / glad to have, chance

Start Off – Listen & Talk B

how are you feeling / moving away / sorry, don't be / Why don't we, as / something meaningful

Start Off – Speak Up – Mission

How are you / feeling / glad to hear that

Step Up – Real-life Scene

How / happier, ever / why, didn't / booked / about / got messages / How cute, emojis, bring, sticks / I'm glad to hear that, fun

Fun Time

feeling / nervous, forgot to bring, How are / nervous, who feels / How / happy, got / angry, broke

Express Yourself A 1

How are / get a present / present / which / wonder how high / Let me show

Express Yourself A 2

How, feeling / to cook, favorite / what it is / which, delicious, healthy / to try / Wait for

Check Yourself – Listen & Speak 1

how are you feeling / excited, have, in / why, excited / on, team, As you know, needs / I'm glad to hear, hope, joins

시험대비 기본평가

p.18

01 How are you feeling today?
02 ⑤ 03 ④ 04 was worried about

01 How are you feeling?은 '기분이 어떠니?'라는 뜻으로 상대방의 기쁨이나 슬픔 등의 감정에 대해 물을 때 사용하는 표현이다.

02 몇몇 학생들이 학교 청소하는 것을 돕고 있어서 아침에 기분이 아주 좋다는 말에 대한 응답으로 그 말을 들으니 기쁘다는 말이 적절하다.

03 G가 정말로 슬프다고 말하고 있으므로 '닭튀김을 먹게 되어 기뻐!'라고 말하는 ④번은 자연스럽지 못하다.

04 '~에 관해 걱정하다'는 의미로 'be worried about'을 사용한다.

시험대비 실력평가

p.19~20

01 ② 02 ④ 03 I'm sorry to hear that.
04 ① 05 I wonder how high it can fly.
06 ⑤ 07 ① 08 ④
09 (n)ervous 10 ④ 11 ③

01 G의 두 번째 말에서 '그 말을 들으니 기쁘구나.'라고 말하는 것으로 보아 Jihun은 새로운 나라로 가게 되어 슬픈 것이 아니라 기쁘거나 신나 있다는 것을 짐작할 수 있다. sad를 'happy' 또는 'excited'로 바꾸어야 한다.

02 B의 '좋아. 자주 화상 채팅하자.'는 마지막 말로 미루어 보아 빈칸에는 '온라인으로 계속 연락하자.'는 말이 자연스럽다.

03 상대방의 말에 대해 유감을 나타내는 표현으로 'I'm sorry to hear that.'을 사용한다. 여기서 to hear는 '~해서'의 의미를 가지는 부정사의 부사적 용법이다.

04 B가 '생일 선물을 받아서 정말 기뻐.'라고 말하는 것으로 보아 빈칸에는 B의 기분을 묻는 말이 자연스럽다.

05 동사 wonder의 목적어 자리에 사용된 간접의문문으로 'how+형용사/부사+주어+동사' 어순으로 써야 한다.

06 'I'm sorry to hear that.'은 상대방으로부터 좋지 않은 소식을 들은 후, '그것 참 안됐구나.'라고 유감이나 동정을 표현하는 말이다.

07 than이 있으면 앞 문장에는 비교급 형태가 있어야 한다. happy를 happier로 바꾸어야 한다.

08 지호가 VTS 콘서트 표를 어떻게 예매하게 되었는지는 대화에 언급되어 있지 않다.

09 '어떤 것에 대해 걱정하거나 두려워하고, 긴장을 풀지 못하는'의 뜻으로 'nervous(초조한)'가 적절하다.

10 감정을 묻는 말에 (C) 가장 좋아하는 음식을 요리하게 되어 기쁘다는 말이 오고 → (D) 그것이 무엇인지 알고 싶다는 말에 → (B) 잡채라는 답이 오고 → (A) 좀 먹어 보고 싶다는 말에 좋다며 30분 동안 기다리라는 말이 적절하다.

11 친한 친구가 외국으로 떠난다는 말에 '그 말을 들으니 기뻐.'라고 답하는 ③번은 적절하지 않다.

서술형 시험대비

p.21

01 She thinks they are cute.
02 I'm happier than ever
03 (A) how are you feeling?
(B) Really? I'm sorry.
(C) Why don't we make him a photo book as a goodbye gift?
04 this drone, which our grandpa sent for my birthday
05 I can't wait for lunch break.

01 질문: '나리는 이모지에 대해 어떻게 생각하는가?' - '나리는 그것이 귀엽다고 생각한다.'

02 '어느 때보다'라는 의미로 비교급이 적절하다. happy의 비교급 happier than ever를 사용한다.

04 계속적 용법의 관계대명사는 콤마(comma)를 관계대명사 앞에 사용한다. 목적격 관계대명사이므로 뒤에 '주어+동사'를 사용한다.

05 대화의 흐름상 '점심시간이 무척 기다려져.'라는 의미가 되도록 'can't wait for ~'를 사용한다.

교과서

Grammar

핵심 Check

p.22~23

1 (1) who he is (2) where he comes from
(3) how old he is
2 (1) who (2) which (3) who

시험대비 기본평가

p.24

01 (1) Tell me what the name of your school is.
(2) I'd like to know where your English teacher comes from.
(3) Can you tell me how much this bag is?
(4) I'd like to know why you are feeling sad.
02 (1) where → which (2) that → which
(3) where did Ann spend her vacation → where Ann spent her vacation
(4) why was he → why he was
03 (1) Tell me when your birthday is.
(2) I didn't know what she majored in.
(3) Do you know what the most famous online game is these days?

01 간접의문문은 '의문사+주어+동사'의 순서로 쓴다.
02 (1) 주격 관계대명사가 계속적 용법으로 쓰인 문장이므로 which를 쓰는 것이 적절하다. (2) 관계대명사의 계속적 용법에서는 'that'은 사용되지 않는다. (3), (4) 간접의문문은 '의문사+주어+동사'의 순서로 쓴다.
03 간접의문문은 '의문사+주어+동사'의 순서로 쓰고, 반드시 의문사를 제외한 문장의 주어와 동사는 평서문의 형태로 되돌려야 한다. these days: 요즘

시험대비 실력평가

p.25~27

01 ② 02 ④ 03 ② 04 ③
05 ⑤ 06 ⑤
07 whom Amy met after a big soccer game
08 ④
09 (1) I wonder how many books you need.
(2) Tell me why he invented the machine.
10 I'm going to show you the photo, which my friend, Amy, sent to me.
11 ④ 12 (1) they (2) which (3) which
(4) which (5) which
13 how many pencils we need to bring for the next class
14 Can you tell me why you want to become a scientist?
15 I have an older sister, who is studying music in New York.
16 ④ 17 ② 18 ② 19 ②
20 (1) Do you know? What does the color red mean?
(2) My best friends are Ken and Mary. They are nice and smart.
(3) I wonder. How often does Mary meet Ken?
21 ③

01 'what time'이 하나의 의문사구이다. 그러므로 'Can you tell me what time it is?'로 쓰는 것이 적절하다.
02 'Can you tell me' 다음에 의문사구 'how many hours'를 함께 쓰고 나머지 부분을 평서문의 형태로 바꿔야 한다. 이 경우는 의문사를 맨 앞으로 보내지 않는다.
03 계속적 용법으로 쓰인 주격 관계대명사 자리이고 선행사가 사람이므로 'who'를 쓴다.
04 모두 관계대명사 'who'가 적절하지만 ③번은 선행사가 앞의 절 전체이므로 'which'를 쓴다.
05 첫 번째 문장에서는 그가 필통을 놓은 장소를 묻는 의문사 'where'가 적절하고, 두 번째 문장에서는 동사 got의 목적어가 필요하므로 'what'이 쓰여야 한다.
06 ①~④번은 의문사 'who'이다. ⑤는 계속적 용법으로 사용된 관계대명사이다.
07 '관계대명사+주어+동사'의 어순으로 쓴다.
08 'Do you know?'의 목적어로 간접의문문을 쓴다. 의문사가 없는 의문문은 whether+주어+동사의 어순으로 쓴다.
09 (1) 'how many books'가 하나의 의문사구이다. (2) 간접의문문이므로 '의문사+주어+동사'의 어순이 된다.
10 선행사 'the photo'를 설명하는 계속적 용법의 관계대명사 'which'를 사용하여 두 문장을 하나로 연결한다.
11 I wonder의 목적어로는 간접의문문을 쓰는 것이 자연스럽다. 의문사가 없는 간접의문문이 적절하므로 'that' 대신 'whether'를 쓴다.t to eat이 적절하다.
12 (1) 두 절을 연결하는 접속사 'and'가 있으므로 'who'를 쓰지 않는다. (2) 선행사가 'a song'이므로 who가 아닌 which가 적절하다. (3) 주어 역할을 하는 관계대명사가 필요하므로 which를 쓴다. (4) 선행사가 앞의 절 전체이므로, 'which'를 사용한 관계대명사의 계속적 용법으로 문장을 쓴다. (5) 계속적 용법의 관계대명사를 쓸 때는 'that'을 쓰지 않는다.
13 간접의문문 how many pencils(의문사구), we(주어), need to bring(동사) 순서로 쓴다.
14 Can you tell me의 목적어로 간접의문문을 '의문사+주어+동사'의 순서로 쓴다.
15 an older sister를 계속적 용법의 관계대명사를 사용하여 부연

설명한다.

16 관계대명사가 부연 설명하는 것이 June이 아니라 a camera이므로, 'who'가 아닌 'which'로 써야 한다.

17 첫 번째 문장에서는 Nancy를 설명하는 계속적 용법의 관계대명사 'who'를 써야 한다. 두 번째 문장에서는 your parents' favorite food를 질문하는 의문사 'what'을 써야 한다.

18 선행사 'Nancy'를 관계사절 'who will throw a birthday party tomorrow'가 꾸며 주는 형태가 자연스럽다.

19 ②에서 관계대명사가 설명하는 내용은 앞의 절 전체이므로 관계대명사 'which'를 써야 한다.

20 (1), (3) '의문사+주어+동사' 순서의 간접의문문을 직접의문문의 어순인 '의문사+동사+주어'로 바꾼다. (2) 계속적 용법의 '관계대명사는 접속사와 선행사의 대명사로 이루어져 있다.

21 첫 번째 빈칸은 의문사구 'how high'가 필요하고, 두 번째 빈칸은 this drone을 설명하는 계속적 용법의 관계대명사 'which'가 적절하다.

서술형 시험대비

p.28~29

01 (1) Do you know why Mira is smiling?
(2) What do you think my dad is cooking?
(3) How do you guess she found out the answer?
(4) I want to know what made him happy.
(5) I wonder how much time they spend studying.

02 (1) I wonder how you made the doll.
(2) Do you know when the movie starts?
(3) Can you tell me what you said to her?

03 (1) Minsu got a drone from his grandpa, who lives in Busan.
(2) He is cooking *japchae*, which he likes the most.

04 (1) Do you know how old he is?
(2) The girl is Amy, who enjoys cooking.
(3) Look at this guitar, which I gave to Amy for her birthday.
(4) The cute dog is Lucky, which likes catching balls.
(5) Do you know when he came to Korea?

05 I want to learn what he does in his free time.

06 (1) tell me where you live
(2) when the next bus will come

07 c. it → which / d. who → which / e. tells → tell

08 (1) She met my sister, who lives in Hawaii.
(2) He is dancing with Nancy, who is 20 years old.
(3) He is happy to get a cat, Milky, which is white like milk.
(4) Do you know why the boy is happy?
(5) What do you guess Mr. Lee is doing?

09 (1) When does the game start?
(2) I want to know where she went last night.
(3) I wonder who broke the glasses.
(4) Can you tell me what color you like?

01 (1), (5) 주절 뒤에 간접의문문을 '의문사+주어+동사'의 어순으로 쓴다. (2), (3) 주절이 'Do you think[guess]'인 경우 간접의문문의 의문사는 문두로 보내진다. (4) 의문사가 주어인 경우에는 의문사 뒤에 바로 동사가 이어진다.

02 (1), (2), (3) 의문사가 있는 간접의문문은 '의문사+주어+동사'의 순서로 쓴다.

03 (1) 접속사 and와 대명사 he를 결합하여 선행사 his grandpa를 설명해 주는 관계대명사절 'who lives in Busan'으로 쓴다. (2) 접속사 and와 대명사 it을 결합하여 선행사 japchae를 설명해 주는 관계대명사절 'which he likes the most'로 쓴다.

04 (1) 의문사구 'how old'를 함께 써야 한다. (2) 관계대명사의 계속적 용법에서는 'that'은 쓰지 않는다. (3) 목적격 관계대명사가 사용된 문장이므로 관계사절에 목적어 'it'은 쓰지 않는다. (4) 선행사가 단수 명사이므로 주격 관계대명사 뒤에 이어지는 동사는 선행사의 수에 맞추어야 한다. (5) 간접의문문은 '의문사+주어+동사'의 어순으로 쓴다. 조동사 'did'는 사용하지 않는다.

05 직접의문문이 간접의문문이 될 때 의문사를 쓴 후 조동사 do(does/did)를 없애고 평서문의 형태로 써야 한다.

06 (1), (2) Can you tell me 다음에 목적어로 간접의문문을 '의문사+주어+동사'의 어순으로 배열한다.

07 c. 한 문장에서 두 개의 절이 사용되었으므로, 두 개의 절을 연결하는 접속사 또는 접속사와 대명사 it을 결합한 관계대명사 'which'를 써야 한다. d. 관계대명사가 설명하는 것이 Mary가 아닌 Mt. Halla이므로 관계대명사 'which'를 써야 한다. e. 선행사가 'those guys'이므로 관계대명사 다음에 이어지는 동사는 'tell'로 써야 한다.

08 (1) 선행사가 my sister이므로 관계대명사 다음에 이어지는 동사를 'lives'로 써야 한다. (2) 한 문장에 두 개의 절이 사용될 경우, 두 개의 절을 연결하는 접속사 또는 접속사와 대명사를 결합한 관계대명사를 써야 한다. (3) 계속적 용법의 관계대명사로는 'that'을 사용하지 않는다. (4) 간접의문문이므로 '의문사+주어+동사'의 어순이 되어야 한다. (5) 'Do you think[suppose, guess, believe]'에 뒤따르는 간접의문문은 의문사를 문두로 보내야 한다.

09 간접의문문은 '의문사+주어+동사'의 순서로, 직접의문문은 '의문사+동사+주어'의 어순으로 쓴다. 이때 직접의문문에서 일반동사가 쓰인 경우 '의문사+조동사 do(does/did)+주어+동사원형'을 써야 한다. 간접의문문은 그 반대로 조동사 do(does/did)를 없애고 평서문의 형태로 써야 한다.

교과서 Reading

확인문제 p.30

1 T 2 F 3 F 4 T 5 F

확인문제 p.31

1 T 2 F 3 T 4 F 5 T 6 F

교과서 확인학습 A p.32~33

01 How, Texts
02 human
03 laugh out loud
04 laugh even in our writings
05 How
06 written laughter
07 what it means
08 has been used
09 in his works
10 gentlemen, good
11 anything important
12 Act, Scene
13 written laughter
14 stands for
15 Rolling on the Floor Laughing
16 can be typed
17 Have a safe trip
18 Make sure
19 miss u
20 wishing me a safe trip
21 represents
22 with, open, closed tightly
23 a word
24 used to represent a facial expression
25 more visually
26 can't wait to
27 face with tears of joy
28 called
29 available to use, various ways
30 hit my head
31 okay
32 on the cupboard
33 okay
34 have grown, laughing sounds
35 break wind
37 just did it
39 with my earphones
40 facial expressions, voice tones
41 care for, with them
42 Laugh, and
43 cold out
44 This was

교과서 확인학습 B p.34~35

1 How Do You "Ha-Ha" in Your Texts?
2 Laughter is human.
3 We laugh out loud when we hear a joke, see something funny, or feel happy.
4 We laugh even in our writings, such as emails or texts, as we do in our conversations.
5 How do we do that?
6 "Ha-ha" is a form of written laughter.
7 Everyone knows what it means.
8 Actually, it has been used since long ago.
9 Even Shakespeare used "ha-ha" in his works.
10 DOGBERRY: Ha, ha, ha! Well, gentlemen, good night.
11 And if anything important happens, find me and let me know.
12 (Shakespeare, Much Ado About Nothing Act 3, Scene 3, Page 4)
13 Another form of written laughter is LOL.
14 It stands for "Laughing Out Loud."
15 People also use ROFL quite often, which means "Rolling On the Floor Laughing."
16 These expressions have become popular because they can be typed quite quickly.
17 A: Have a safe trip 2mrw.
18 Make sure u don't miss me too much. LOL
19 B: OK. I'll try to make sure I don't miss u. LOL.
20 Thanks for wishing me a safe trip.
21 XD also represents laughter in text.
22 It shows a laughing face with a mouth open and eyes closed tightly.
23 XD is not a word.
24 It's an emoticon, which is a group of letters or symbols used to represent a facial expression.
25 The emoticon XD expresses our happy feelings more visually than ha-ha and LOL do.
26 I can't wait to go to Disneyland. XD
27 These days, people use 😂 — a "face with tears of joy."
28 This is a small picture called an "emoji."
29 Lots of laughing emojis are available to use online, so people can express their laughter in various ways.
30 A: I hit my head on the cupboard.
31 B: Oh, my! Are you okay?
32 A: I hit my head on the cupboard. 😂
33 B: Uh-oh! Is the cupboard okay? 😂
34 Some emojis have grown bigger, and some even move or make laughing sounds.
35 A: So yesterday, I was in a restaurant, and I really needed to break wind.
36 B: And ...
37 A: Well, the music was really loud, so I just did it.
38 B: And ...
39 A: And then I realized I was listening to music with my earphones.

40 Laughing marks can represent our facial expressions and deliver our voice tones.
41 By using various laughing marks, we can show our friends how much we care for them or how happy we are with them.
42 Laugh, even in written forms, and your friends will laugh with you.
43 Me when it's cold out
44 This was me yesterday

시험대비 실력평가

p.36~39

01 closing → closed 02 ③ 03 ④
04 ⑤ 05 ④ 06 ③
07 laughing emoji 08 ④
09 calling → called
10 (A) an emoji (B) Is the cupboard okay
11 be typed 12 ② 13 quite quickly
14 Everyone knows what it means.
15 "ha-ha" 16 written laughter
17 break wind 18 ⑤
19 (2) 번 ⓐ loud ⓑ his earphones
20 ④ 21 ②, ⑤
22 express our happy feelings 23 ③
24 like 25 ② 26 laugh out loud

01 눈이 '감겨지는' 것이므로 closed로 고치는 것이 적절하다.
02 ⓑ와 ②, ⑤: 부사적 용법, ①, ④: 명사적 용법, ③: 형용사적 용법
03 무슨 이모티콘이 우리의 행복한 감정을 가장 효과적으로 표현할 수 있는지는 대답할 수 없다. ① It represents laughter in text. ② It shows a laughing face with a mouth open and eyes closed tightly. ③ It is a group of letters or symbols used to represent a facial expression. ⑤ XD does.
04 (A)와 ⑤: ~하는 것처럼, ~하듯이(접속사), ① ~이기 때문에(접속사), ② (as ~ as ...로 형용사·부사 앞에서) …와 같은 정도로 (as ~ as ...에서, 앞의 as는 지시부사, 뒤의 as는 접속사), ③ ~하는 동안에(접속사), ④ ~로서(전치사)
05 앞의 내용을 추가해서 설명하고 있으므로 Actually가 가장 적절하다. ① 그러므로, ③ 대신에, ⑤ 즉, 다시 말해서
06 '우리는 이메일이나 문자 메시지 같은 글 속에서조차 대화에서 하듯이 웃는다'고 했다.
07 그것은 '웃는 이모지'이고, '기쁨의 눈물을 흘리는 얼굴'이라고 불린다.
08 '이모지'는 작은 그림이라고 했으므로 ④번이 적절하다.
09 '이모지'라고 불리는 작은 그림이라고 해야 하므로, 과거분사 called로 고치는 것이 적절하다.
10 이모지를 사용한 대화 (2)가 이모지를 사용하지 않은 대화 (1)보다 더 시각적으로 웃음을 전달한다. 게다가 두 번째 대화에서 여자는 '너 괜찮니?'라는 말을 '찬장 괜찮니?'라는 말로 대체함으로써 더 재미있게 유머러스한 분위기를 표현한다.
11 주어 they가 These expressions를 가리키므로 수동태로 쓰는 것이 적절하다.
12 위 글의 첫 문장이 '또 다른 형태의 문자로 된 웃음은 LOL이다.'로 시작하므로, 이 글의 앞에는 '문자로 된 웃음의 형태'에 대한 소개가 있었다고 하는 것이 적절하다.
13 이 표현들은 사람들이 '상당히 빠르게' 타자 칠 수 있어서 인기를 얻었다.
14 동사 'know'의 목적어로, 의문문 "What does it mean?"을 간접의문문으로 바꿔 쓴 문장이다.
15 "하하"를 가리킨다.
16 우리는 글 속에서 "하하"와 같은 '문자로 된 웃음'의 형태를 사용할 수 있다.
17 break wind: 방귀를 뀌다, 장에서 가스를 내보내다
18 음악이 정말 시끄러워서 그냥 방귀를 뀌었는데, 자신이 이어폰을 끼고 음악을 듣고 있다는 걸 깨달았으므로 A의 심경으로는 '당황한'이 적절하다. ① 실망한, ② 편안한, ③ 상쾌한, ④ 기쁜, ⑤ 당황스러운, 쑥스러운
19 그럴 수 없었다. 그가 식당 안의 음악이 정말 '시끄럽다'고 생각하면서 방귀를 뀌었을 때, 실제로는 그가 '이어폰'을 끼고 음악을 듣고 있었기 때문이다.
20 XD는 얼굴 표정을 나타내기 위해 사용되는 이모티콘이므로, 하하와 LOL보다 우리의 행복한 감정을 더 '시각적으로' 표현한다고 하는 것이 적절하다. ③ 간접적으로
21 (A)와 ②, ⑤: [부대상황을 나타내는 구를 이끌어] …한 채로, …하면서, 'with+명사+형용사'가 다른 동작이나 행위를 할 때의 상황 설명으로 쓰여서 '…(명사)가 ~(형용사)한 채로'의 의미가 된다. ① …와 함께, ③ …을 가진, ④ …로, …을 써서[이용하여]
22 do는 'express our happy feelings'를 받은 대동사이다.
23 can't wait to 동사원형: …하기를 몹시 바라다, 어서 빨리 …하고 싶어 하다, look forward to ~ing: ~을 고대하다, be eager[anxious/dying] to 동사원형: ~하고 싶은 생각이 간절하다, ③ unwilling: 꺼리는, 싫어하는
24 such as = like: ~와 같은
25 이 글은 '우리가 이메일이나 문자 메시지 같은 글 속에서조차 대화에서 하듯이 웃는다.'는 내용의 글이므로, 제목으로는 '글에서 "하하"라고 웃을 수 있나요?'가 적절하다.
26 농담이나 우스운 광경 혹은 행복감은 우리를 '소리 내어 웃게' 만들 수 있다.

서술형 시험대비 p.40~41

01 (A) happy (B) do (C) since
02 laugh even in our writings
03 laughter
04 It stands for "Rolling On the Floor Laughing."
05 It shows a laughing face with a mouth open and eyes closed tightly.
06 LOL and ROFL are → An emoticon is 또는 a group of letters or symbols used to represent a facial expression → forms of written laughter
07 like 08 our friends
09 If you laugh, even in written forms, your friends will laugh with you.
10 (A) how much (B) how happy
11 They can represent our facial expressions and deliver our voice tones.
12 represents
13 Have a safe trip tomorrow. Make sure you don't miss me too much.
14 (A) (the emoticon) XD (B) ha-ha and LOL

01 (A) 감각동사 feel의 보어로 형용사를 써야 하므로 happy가 옳다. (B) laugh를 받는 대동사를 써야 하므로 do가 옳다. (C) 'long ago'는 과거의 기점을 나타내는 말이므로 since가 옳다. for+기간
02 대화에서 하듯이 '글 속에서조차 웃는다'를 가리킨다.
03 우리는 우스운 것이나 행복을 경험할 때 '웃음'을 터뜨릴 뿐만 아니라, "하하"와 같은 문자로 된 '웃음'의 형태를 사용함으로써 글 속에서도 웃음소리를 표현할 수 있다. burst into laughter: 웃음을 터뜨리다
04 ROFL은 '바닥을 구르면서 웃기'를 의미한다.
05 with를 보충하면 된다. 'with+명사+형용사'가 다른 동작이나 행위를 할 때의 상황 설명으로 쓰여서 '…(명사)가 ~(형용사) 한채로'의 의미가 된다.
06 '이모티콘'은 얼굴 표정을 나타내기 위해 사용되는 한 무리의 문자나 상징이다. 또는 LOL과 ROFL은 '문자로 된 웃음의 형태들'이다.
07 care for: 좋아하다
08 '우리의 친구들'을 가리킨다.
09 명령문, and ~ = If you로 문장을 시작한 다음, 콤마 다음의 and를 생략하고 나머지 부분을 쓰면 된다.
10 다양한 웃음표시를 사용하는 것은 우리가 친구들을 '얼마나' 좋아하는지 또는 그들과 함께 있어서 '얼마나 행복한지'를 그들에게 보여 줄 수 있게 해준다.
11 웃음 표시는 '우리의 얼굴 표정을 나타내고 우리의 목소리 어조를 전달할 수' 있다.
12 stands for = represents: …을 의미하다, 상징하다, 나타내다
13 2mrw = tomorrow, u = you
14 만약 당신이 당신의 행복한 감정을 더 시각적으로 표현하기를 원한다면, '하하와 LOL'보다 '이모티콘 XD'를 사용하는 것이 낫다. It would be better for you to ~ than to …: …하는 것보다 ~하는 것이 낫다

영역별 핵심문제 p.43~47

01 whole 02 ④ 03 ⑤ 04 ①
05 present 06 ① 07 ② 08 ⑤
09 ③
10 I'm glad to find someone who feels the same.
11 ⑤ 12 ④ 13 ①
14 which → who
15 (1) He has two cats which are black.
(2) He has two cats, which are black.
(3) I saw a child who was wearing a yellow cap.
(4) I saw a child, who was wearing a yellow cap.
16 ② 17 ③ 18 who
19 (1) Can you tell me why you want to be a teacher?
(2) Please tell me what your new science teacher is like.
20 ② 21 ①, ⑤ 22 ③
23 because[as] they can be typed quite quickly
24 that → which 25 ③ 26 ②
27 ②
28 Can you guess why Mira is smiling?
29 and, him

01 반의어 관계다. 인기 있는 : 인기 없는 = 전체의 : 일부분의
02 (a) 웃음 표시는 우리의 얼굴 표정을 나타내고 우리의 목소리 어조를 전달할 수 있다. (b) 많은 웃는 이모지가 온라인에서 사용될 수 있고, 그래서 사람들은 다양한 방식으로 자신들의 웃음을 표현할 수 있다.
03 '말하기 보다는 쓰기와 관련된'의 의미로 '쓰여진'이 적절하다.
04 '감정을 나타내기 위해 이메일 등에서 사용되는 얼굴 표정을 나타내는 일련의 짧은 키보드 기호'
05 (A) 만약 여러분이 착하게 지냈다면, 산타는 내일 멋진 선물을 줄 거예요! (B) 그룹을 이룬 학생들은 어떻게 특정 문제에 대한 그들의 결론에 이르게 되었는지를 발표할 것입니다. present는 명사로 '선물', 동사로 '발표하다, 제시하다' 등의 의미로 사용된다.
06 book은 동사로 사용될 때 '예약하다'로 사용된다.
07 엄마가 방과 후에 축구하는 것을 허락하지 않는다는 말로 기분이 언짢아 보인다가 적절하다.
08 민수의 기분을 묻는 말에 → (C) 매우 신난다고 답하고, → (D) 왜 신났는지 묻는 말에 → (B) 새로 온 학생이 그의 학교

축구팀이었고 자신의 팀에 축구 선수가 필요하다는 대답이 오고 → (A) 그 말을 들으니 기쁘다는 대답이 오는 것이 자연스럽다.

09 B가 초조하다고 말하고 있으므로 '수학 숙제 가져오는 걸 잊어버렸어.'라는 말이 가장 자연스럽다.

10 글의 흐름상 A와 B가 둘 다 초조함을 느끼고 있기 때문에 '같은 감정을 가진 사람을 찾아서 기뻐.'라는 의미가 되도록 주어진 단어를 배열한다.

11 They는 Minsu와 Yujin을 가리키고, 그들이 광선 막대기와 카메라를 가지고 온다는 말은 Nari가 이모지가 귀엽고 나는 그들의 이모지가 마음에 든다는 말 다음에 오는 것이 자연스럽다.

12 민수와 유진이는 광선 막대기와 카메라를 가지고 올 거라고 나리가 말하고 있다.

13 주절이 'Do you think'일 때 간접의문문의 의문사는 맨 앞으로 보내진다.

14 선행사 the Reds는 한국 축구팀을 응원한다는 내용으로 보아 사람을 의미한다.

16 간접의문문은 '의문사+주어+동사'의 순서로 쓰고, 반드시 의문사를 제외한 문장의 주어와 동사는 평서문의 형태로 되돌려야 한다.

17 a. 주절이 'Do you think'일 때 간접의문문의 의문사는 맨 앞으로 보내지므로 'Where do you think they will go?'로 쓴다. c. 간접의문문은 평서문의 어순이어야 하므로 'Did you ask me where he went?'로 쓴다. e. 선행사 'a watch'를 'which was broken'으로 설명해 주는 것이 자연스럽다. Minji가 선행사가 아니다.

18 첫 번째 문장은 간접의문문의 의문사 'who'가 필요하고, 두 번째 문장은 선행사 'a man'을 설명하는 계속적 용법의 관계대명사 'who'가 필요하다.

19 간접의문문의 어순인 '의문사+주어+동사'의 형태로 쓴다.

20 뒤에 such as emails or texts가 나오므로, 우리는 '글' 속에서조차 웃는다고 하는 것이 적절하다.

21 ⓑ와 ①, ⑤: 계속 용법, ②, ④: 경험 용법, ③ 완료 용법

22 이 글은 '우리가 이메일이나 문자 메시지 같은 글 속에서조차 대화에서 하듯이 웃는다.'는 내용의 글이므로, 주제로는 '우리는 글 속에서조차 웃을 수 있다.'가 적절하다. laugh: (소리 내어) 웃다

23 주어 they가 These expressions를 가리키므로, 수동태로 쓰는 것이 적절하다.

24 관계대명사 that은 계속적 용법으로 쓸 수 없기 때문에 which로 고치는 것이 적절하다.

25 XD는 알파벳 X와 D가 아니라, 입을 벌리고 눈을 질끈 감은 채 웃는 얼굴을 보여 주는 이모티콘이다.

26 이 글은 '웃음 표시의 역할'에 관한 글이다. ① pros and cons: 찬성과 반대, ③ the weak point: 약점

27 웃음 표시는 우리의 목소리 어조도 전달할 수 있다.

28 Can you guess 다음에 간접의문문 순서로 쓰는 것이 적절하다. Why can you guess Mira is smiling?(×): 동사가 guess인 경우에도 Yes/No로 대답할 수 있으면 의문사를 guess 다음에 써야 한다.

29 계속적 용법의 관계대명사는 '접속사+대명사'로 바꿀 수 있다.

단원별 예상문제

p.48~51

01 various　02 ②　03 I'm glad to hear that.

04 (1) to have video chats online

(2) to make Jihun a photo book as a goodbye gift

05 I'm glad to give him something meaningful.

06 ④　07 ③　08 ⑤　09 ②

10 ③, ⑤

11 (1) Do you know where Tom worked last year?

(2) She made chocolate cookies for me, which were very delicious.

(3) I met Sue, who gave me a free ticket.

12 (1) Do you know what the color red means?

(2) This is the uniform of the Reds, who cheer for the Korean soccer team.

13 written　14 ②　15 ⑤　16 facial

17 and it　18 ③　19 the cupboard

20 ③, ④　21 ③

22 It's a small picture which is available to use online.

23 how much we care for them or how happy we are with them

24 ④

01 유의어 관계이다. 기회 - 다양한

02 다른 무언가를 나타내기 위해 사용되는 표시, 모양 또는 물체

03 Minsu의 축구팀이 새로운 선수를 필요로 하는 상황에 새로 전학 온 친구가 이전 학교에서 축구 선수였다는 것을 알고는 Minsu가 신이 나 있다. 이 상황에서 MIso가 기쁨을 표현하는 것이 적절하다.

04 (1) Yena와 Jihun이는 온라인으로 화상 채팅을 할 것이다. (2) Yena와 Seho는 Jihun이에게 이별 선물로 사진 책을 만들어 줄 것이다.

05 '~해서 기뻐'는 'I'm glad to+동사원형'을 이용하고, something은 형용사가 뒤에서 수식하므로 meaningful이 something 뒤에 와야 한다.

06 몇몇 학생들이 학교 청소하는 것을 돕고 있다고 말하고 있기 때문에 매우 기분이 좋은 상태라는 것을 알 수 있다.

07 '~에 관해 걱정하다'는 의미로 'be worried about'을 사용한다.

08 Yunju는 Jjhun이가 이사를 가게 되어 기쁜 것이 아니라, Jihun이가 완전히 새로운 나라에 가게 되어 흥분된다는 말을 듣

고서 안심이 되어 기쁘다고 말했다.

09 (A): 내 개가 아프다는 말에 대해 유감을 나타내는 표현이 적절하다. (B) '닭튀김을 먹게 되어 기뻐!'라고 말하고 있으므로 기대감을 나타내는 표현이 적절하다.

10 두 개의 절을 하나로 연결하는 접속사 'and'와 주어 'he'가 필요하고 두 단어를 하나로 합치면 'who'로 쓸 수 있다.

11 (1) 간접의문문은 '의문사+주어+동사'의 순서로 쓰고, 반드시 의문사를 제외한 문장의 주어와 동사는 평서문의 형태로 되돌려야 한다. (2) 선행사가 복수 명사 'chocolate cookies'이므로 관계대명사 뒤에 이어지는 동사도 복수형으로 써야 한다. (3) 내용상 순서대로 일어난 상황이므로 주절과 관계사절의 시제를 일치시킨다.

12 (1) Do you know의 목적어로 간접의문문을 '의문사+주어+동사'의 어순으로 쓴다. (2) 선행사 'the Reds'를 설명하는 계속적 용법의 관계대명사를 선행사 뒤에 이어 쓴다.

13 '문자로 된' 웃음이라고 해야 하므로 'written'이 적절하다.

14 ⓑ와 ②: 작품(명사), ① (어떤 직장에서) 일하다(동사), ③ 공장, 제작소(명사), 종종 works로 단수 취급함, ④ (기계 장치 등이) 작동되다(동사), ⑤ (기계의) 움직이는 부분, 장치(명사)

15 '셰익스피어조차도 "하하"를 자신의 작품에 사용하였다'고만 되어 있다.

16 face의 형용사 facial을 쓰는 것이 적절하다.

17 계속적 용법의 관계대명사는 '접속사+대명사'로 바꿀 수 있다.

18 이 글은 문자로 된 웃음 형태인 LOL, ROFL과 문자 메시지에서 웃음을 나타내는 이모티콘인 XD를 사용하여 글 속에서 웃음을 표현하는 방법들을 설명하는 글이므로, 제목으로는 '글에서 어떻게 웃음을 표현할까'가 적절하다.

19 '너 괜찮니?'라는 말 대신 '찬장 괜찮니?'라는 말을 사용함으로써 더 유머러스한 분위기를 표현할 수 있다.

20 (A)와 ③, ④: 부사적 용법, ①, ⑤: 명사적 용법, ②: 형용사적 용법

21 a few를 various로 고치는 것이 적절하다.

22 '이모지'는 온라인에서 사용될 수 있는 작은 그림이다.

23 with를 보충하면 된다.

24 '어떤 종류의 웃음 표시를 사람들이 가장 좋아하는지'는 대답할 수 없다. ① They can represent our facial expressions. ② They can deliver our voice tones. ③ We can show our friends how much we care for them or how happy we are with them. ⑤ Yes. If we laugh even in written forms, our friends will laugh with us.

서술형 실전문제

p.52~53

01 (A) Some students are helping me clean the school.
(B) My mom won't let me play soccer after school.

02 why are you excited?

03 (1) He booked four tickets for the VTS concert.
(2) They sent messages with emojis.

04 (1) She wrote a poem about love. / who wrote a poem about love
(2) The letter cheered him up. / which cheered him up

05 (1) and he (2) and it 06 has been used

07 laugh 08 (A) writings (B) conversations

09 (A) be typed (B) open (C) used

10 quite quickly

01 (A) 'help+목적어+동사원형' 구문을 사용한다. (B) 'let+목적어+동사원형' 구문을 사용한다.

02 Minsu가 자기 반에 새 학생이 한 명 와서 정말 신난다고 말하고 있다. Miso 입장에서는 새 학생이 와서 Minsu가 신난 이유를 물어보는 것이 자연스럽다.

03 (1) 지호는 왜 행복한가? (2) 민수와 유진이는 지호에게 무엇을 보냈는가?

04 두 문장을 연결해 주는 접속사와 앞 문장의 선행사와 같은 명사를 결합하여 관계대명사로 연결한다. 선행사가 사람인 경우는 'who', 사물인 경우는 'which'를 쓴다.

05 계속적 용법으로 쓰인 관계대명사는 '접속사+대명사'로 바꾸어 쓸 수 있다.

06 현재완료 수동태로 쓰는 것이 적절하다.

07 laugh를 받는 대동사이다.

08 그것은 우리가 '글' 속에서조차 '대화'에서 하듯이 웃기 위해 사용하는 문자로 된 웃음의 한 형태이다.

09 (A) 주어 they가 These expressions를 가리키므로 수동태인 be typed가 옳다. (B) 입이 열려 있는 것이므로 open이 옳다. open: 열려 있는, with a mouth open: 입을 벌리고, (C) 얼굴 표정을 나타내기 위해 '사용되는' 한 무리의 문자나 상징이라고 해야 하므로 used가 옳다. used는 과거분사로, 뒤에서 명사를 수식하는 형용사 역할을 한다.

10 사람들은 "Laugh Out Loud"라는 전체 글자를 쓰는 대신 LOL을 사용함으로써 그들의 글에서 상당히 빠르게 웃음을 표현할 수 있다.

창의사고력 서술형 문제

p.54

|모범답안|

01 A: How are you feeling? B: I'm happy. I got a good grade. / A: How are you feeling? B: I'm angry. Someone broke my glasses. / A: How are you feeling? B: I'm sad. My brother is sick in bed.

02 (1) which is the capital city of France
(2) which is a Hawaiian dance form
(3) My role model is Messi, who is the best soccer player.
(4) This is my new English teacher, Ms. Tylor, who comes from South Africa.
03 (A) why (B) a cat (C) white

단원별 모의고사

p.55~58

01 ④	02 bottom	03 ②	04 ④
05 ⑤	06 ③	07 ④	

08 They will bring light sticks and a nice camera.
09 happier, booked, messages, bring light sticks and a nice camera
10 How are you feeling 또는 How do you feel

11 ③	12 ④	13 ①	14 ⑤

15 who is one of the most famous artists of our time

16 ②	17 ①	18 ⑤	19 ②, ⑤
20 these expressions		21 which[that] are	
22 ③	23 ②, ④	24 ③, ⑤	

25 broke wind

01 ④번의 '어떤 것을 의미하는 것으로 받아들여지다'는 'represent'에 대한 설명이다.
02 반의어 관계이다. 일부분의 : 전체의 - 맨 위의: 밑바닥의
03 보는 것 또는 시력과 연결되는 식으로
04 B의 기분이 언짢아 보이고 괜찮은지 묻는 말에 어울리는 대답을 찾는데, 다음에 나오는 G의 '그녀에게 한 번 더 말씀드려 보지 그러니?'라는 말로 미루어 보아 ④번이 적절하다.
05 빈칸 다음의 Yunju의 대답이 그 말을 들으니 기쁘다고 했기 때문에 ⑤번이 적절하다.
06 기분을 묻는 말에 가장 좋아하는 음식을 요리해서 지루하다고 답하는 것은 어색하다.
07 주어진 문장은 '그들이 정말로 기쁘다고 말했어.'라는 내용으로 그들에게서 메시지를 받았다는 말 다음에 오는 것이 적절하다.
08 민수와 유진이는 VTS 콘서트에 무엇을 가지고 올 것인가?
10 상대방의 기쁨이나 슬픔 등의 감정에 대해 물을 때 사용하는 표현으로 'How are you feeling?'이나 'How do you feel?'을 사용한다.
11 Jihun이가 아부다비로 이사 가서 기분이 어떤지 Minsu에게 물어보고 → (B) 슬프다는 감정을 표현한 다음 지훈이가 그리울 거라는 말 다음에 → (C) 본인도 또한 슬프다고 공감하고, 하지만 아부다비를 방문할 수 있다는 기쁨의 표현에 → 마지막으로 (A) 굉장하다며 새로운 나라로 여행할 기회를 얻게 되어 기쁘다는 말이 오는 것이 적절하다.
12 이별 선물로 Jihun에게 사진 책을 만들어 주자는 제안에 좋은 생각이라고 동의하고 있으므로 빈칸에는 ④가 적절하다.
13 ② I wonder what went wrong. ③ Do you know what I mean? ④ I don't know whether he can do it. ⑤ Tell me who broke the window.
14 의문사가 주어인 경우에는 의문사 뒤에 바로 동사가 이어지며, 주절이 'Do you think'일 때 간접의문문의 의문사는 맨 앞으로 보내진다.
16 ② 간접의문문에서 의문사구 'how high'를 함께 써야 한다.
17 '~인지'의 의미를 가진 의문사가 없는 간접의문문이 들어가야 하므로 'whether'가 적절하다.
18 주어진 문장의 it에 주목한다. ⑤번 앞 문장의 "Ha-ha"를 받고 있으므로 ⑤번이 적절하다.
19 actually = in fact = as a matter of fact: 실제로, 사실, ① 아마, ③ 정확히, 꼭, 틀림없이, ④ 특히
20 '이 표현들(LOL과 ROFL)'을 가리킨다.
21 used 앞에는 '주격 관계대명사+be동사'가 생략되어 있다. used는 과거분사로, 뒤에서 명사를 수식하는 형용사 역할을 하며 'a group of letters or symbols'를 수식하고 있다.
22 이 글은 문자로 된 웃음 형태인 LOL, ROFL과 문자 메시지에서 웃음을 나타내는 이모티콘인 XD를 사용하여 글 속에서 웃음을 표현하는 방법들을 설명하는 글이므로, 주제로는 ③번 '우리는 LOL, ROFL, XD를 사용함으로써 글에서도 웃음을 표현할 수 있다'가 적절하다.
23 grow[become/get]+비교급: 더 ~해지다
24 ③과 ⑤의 내용은 언급되어 있지 않다.
25 '방귀를 뀌었다'를 가리킨다.

Lesson 2

Let's Make Our Town Better

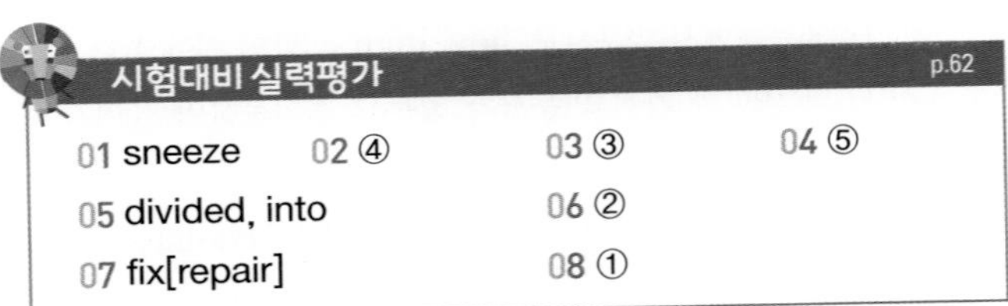

시험대비 실력평가 p.62

01 sneeze 02 ④ 03 ③ 04 ⑤
05 divided, into 06 ②
07 fix[repair] 08 ①

01 '재채기(sneeze)를 할 때, 공기와 종종 작은 액체 방울들이 갑자기 코와 입에서 여러분이 통제할 수 없는 방식으로 나온다.'
02 그 호텔은 끔찍했다! 우선, 우리 방이 너무 작았다.
03 불평하다: 무언가 잘못되었거나 만족스럽지 않다고 말하다
04 양로원: 병들고 매우 나이 든 사람들이 살고 의학 치료와 돌봄을 받는 곳
05 'A를 B로 나누다"는 'divide A into B'를 사용한다.
06 (A) 못 생긴 식품은 멋진 비주얼의 모습을 지니고 있지 않은 과일과 야채이다. (B) 중국과 미국의 친선 농구 경기가 볼썽사납게 되었다.
07 유의어 관계이다. 끈, 줄 : 수리하다
08 • 최근, Hawking이 충격적인 아이디어를 제안해서 세계를 놀라게 했습니다. • 흥미롭게도, 작은 다채로운 무지개가 하늘에 걸려 있습니다!

서술형 시험대비 p.63

01 (1) pot (2) heavy (3) hanging (4) corner
02 divide
03 leaders, set up, board, leaders, popular
04 (1) kitchen, 부엌 (2) dust, 먼지
(3) admit, 인정하다 (4) suggest, 제안하다
05 (1) (m)ess (2) (s)weaty (3) (s)neezed
(4) (n)ewspaper

01 (1) 그 여자는 화분을 창문 옆에 두었다. (2) 무거운 상자는 꿈쩍도 하지 않는다. (3) Jason은 벽에 그림을 걸고 있다. be동사 뒤에 현재분사(hanging) 형태가 적절하다. (4) 이 상자를 구석에 두자.
02 '부분 또는 그룹으로 분리하다'라는 의미로 divide가 적절하다.
03 class leader: 학급 반장, set up: 설치하다, 세우다, board: 판, popular: 인기 있는
04 (1) '음식이 보관, 준비, 조리되고, 설거지를 하는 방' (2) 건물 내부의 표면을 덮는 분말 형태의 건조한 오물 또는 매우 작은 건조한 토양, 모래 또는 기타 물질 조각 (3) 특히 내키지 않게 무언가가 사실이라는 것에 동의하다 (4) 자신이 무엇을 해야 하는지, 어디로 가야 하는지 등에 대한 당신의 생각을 누군가에게 말하다
05 (1) 내 침실이 너무 지저분해서 엄마가 나에게 방을 청소하라고 말씀하셨다. (2) 여름이 너무 덥고 땀이 많이 나기 때문에 그녀는 여름을 싫어한다. (3) 왜 재채기할 때 입을 막지 않았니? (4) 아빠는 매일 아침 신문을 읽으신다.

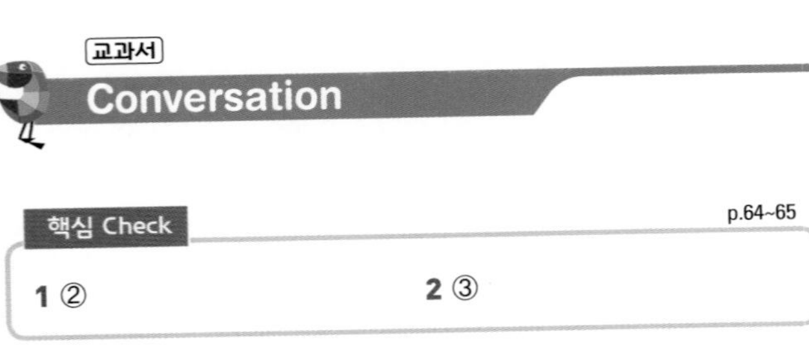

교과서

Conversation

핵심 Check p.64~65

1 ② 2 ③

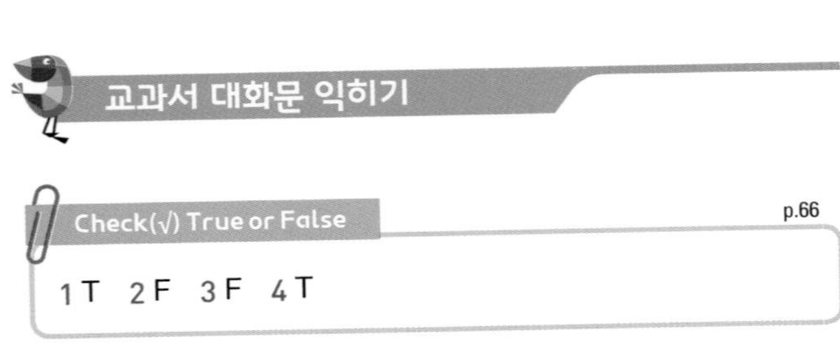

교과서 대화문 익히기

Check(√) True or False p.66

1 T 2 F 3 F 4 T

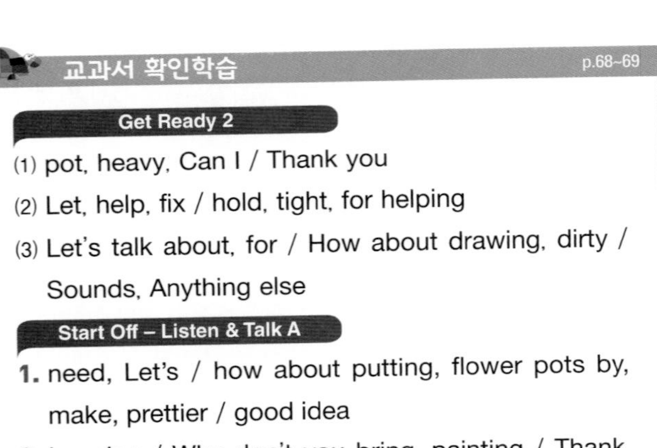

교과서 확인학습 p.68~69

Get Ready 2

(1) pot, heavy, Can I / Thank you
(2) Let, help, fix / hold, tight, for helping
(3) Let's talk about, for / How about drawing, dirty / Sounds, Anything else

Start Off – Listen & Talk A

1. need, Let's / how about putting, flower pots by, make, prettier / good idea
2. hanging / Why don't you bring, painting / Thank, for saying, bring, mine
3. about, corner, Any / How about making, corner, bring / suggesting

Start Off – Listen & Talk B

Don't / Let's talk, together / put, member, helpful for us to learn, members' / plan, school year / help, remember / suggesting

Step Up – Real-life Scene

talk about, better / Let, trash / agree, Why don't we / bench / helpful, the elderly / How about putting, make, more beautiful / suggesting, shall we

Fun Time

Let's talk / Why don't we / Thank, for

Express Yourself A

1. coming, talk about / under, most, cleaned, planted / popular, among
2. school gate, What do you think of / leaders set up, put up, a lot, events / Let's thank

시험대비 기본평가 p.70

01 Thank you for helping me.

02 ④ 03 ⑤ 04 ②

01 '~해서 고마워하다'라는 표현으로 'Thank you for 동명사/명사'를 사용한다. 동사 help를 동명사 helping으로 바꾸어야 한다.

02 '~하는 게 어때?'라는 제안의 표현으로 적절하지 않은 것은 ④번이다. 'Why didn't we draw ~?'는 '왜 우리가 지저분한 벽에 그림을 그리지 않았니?'라는 의미의 의문문이다.

03 깨끗한 학교 프로젝트에 대한 대화로 나무 아래의 모퉁이 주변을 청소하고 나무를 심었다는 말이 가장 자연스럽다.

04 '누가 샌드위치를 만들 것인가'에 대한 의견을 묻는 말에 '내가 하겠다.'고 말한 것으로 보아 자원해 줘서 고맙다는 대답이 가장 자연스럽다.

시험대비 실력평가 p.71~72

01 ④ 02 (A) making (B) suggesting

03 Let me help you fix the bench.

04 (h)elpful 05 ③ 06 ⑤ 07 ②

08 ④ 09 What do you think of it?

10 set up the board 11 Why don't you

12 my pictures 13 take → bring

01 '~에 관해 이야기하자'라는 표현으로 'Let's talk about ~'을 사용한다.

02 (A)와 (B)는 모두 전치사 뒤에 오는 말로 동명사나 명사 형태가 적절하다. 동사 make와 suggest를 모두 동명사로 바꾸어 준다.

03 '…가 ~하도록 하게 하다'라는 표현으로 'Let+목적어+동사원형'을 사용한다. 그리고 '…가 ~하는 것을 도와주다'라는 표현으로 'help+목적어+동사원형'을 이용하여 영작한다.

04 '상황을 개선하거나 쉽게 만드는 데 유용한 도움을 제공하는'의 뜻으로 'helpful(유용한, 도움이 되는)'이 적절하다.

05 벽을 어떻게 꾸밀 것인지에 대해 여러 의견을 제시해 준 것에 대해 고마워한다는 표현이 적절하다.

06 'Let's talk about ~'은 '~에 대해서 말해 보자'라는 뜻으로 함께 대화하고자 하는 주제를 소개할 때 쓰는 표현이다.

07 위 대화의 내용으로 보아 마을을 더 좋게 만드는 방법에 대해 이야기 나누고 있다는 것을 알 수 있다.

08 벤치 위에 무엇을 둘 것인지는 대화에서 언급되어 있지 않다.

09 '~에 관해 어떻게 생각하니?'는 'What do you think of ~?'를 사용한다.

10 질문: 학급 반장들은 판에 포스터를 붙이기 전에 무엇을 했는가?

11 제안하는 표현으로 'Why don't you+동사원형~?'을 쓸 수 있다.

12 밑줄 친 'mine'은 소유대명사로서 앞 문장의 'my pictures'를 가리킨다.

13 take: 가져가다, 휴대하다 bring: 가져오다, (사람을) 데려오다

서술형 시험대비 p.73

01 They will put some flower pots around the bench.

02 Why don't we clean the place together?

03 (A) Let's talk about it together.
(B) We also need our plan for this school year on the wall.
(C) Thank you for suggesting great ideas, everyone.

04 How about making a small library in the corner of the club room?

01 질문: '그들은 버스 정류장을 더 아름답게 만들기 위해 무엇을 할 예정인가?' - '그들은 벤치 주변에 몇 개의 화분을 놓을 것이다.'

02 '~하는 게 어때?'라는 표현은 'Why don't we+동사원형 ~?'을 이용한다.

03 (A) '~에 관해 말해 보자'라는 뜻으로 함께 대화하고자 하는 주제를 소개할 때 쓰는 표현이 적절하다. (B) 빈칸 다음에서 G가 '우리가 중요한 학교 행사를 기억하는 데 정말 도움이 될 거야'라고 말하는 것으로 보아 '이번 학년 계획도 필요하다'라는 말이 적절하다. (C) 대화의 마지막에 '좋은 의견을 내줘서 고맙다'라는 말이 적절하다.

04 '~하는 게 어때?'라는 의견을 제시할 때 사용하는 표현으로 'How about+-ing(동명사)?'를 사용한다. 동사 'make'를 동명사 'making'으로 바꾸어 준다.

교과서

Grammar

핵심 Check

p.74~75

1 (1) had (2) had left (3) turned

2 (1) much (2) a lot (3) very

시험대비 기본평가

p.76

01 (1) was much more difficult than I expected
(2) dogs much more than cats
(3) where you had put the box
(4) the house had been newly painted

02 (1) My teacher was looking at the pictures that her students had drawn.
(2) When I arrived at the station, the train had just left.
(3) I jumped much[far, even, a lot] higher than he did.
(4) He grew far taller than his father.

03 (1) When I entered the classroom, my friends had prepared for my birthday party.
(2) When I got up, my husband had eaten all the sandwiches.

01 (1), (2) 비교급을 강조할 때 'much+비교급+than' 순서로 쓴다. (3), (4) 과거보다 더 이전의 일은 'had+과거분사'로 나타낸다.

02 (1) 그녀의 학생들이 그림을 그린 것은 능동이므로 과거완료 능동태(had+과거분사)로 쓴다. (2) 내가 역에 도착한 것보다 기차가 떠난 것이 그 이전의 일이므로 과거완료로 쓴다. (3) 비교급을 강조할 때는 'many'를 사용하지 않는다. (4) 'far'는 비교급을 강조하는 단어이고 'than' 또한 비교급과 같이 써야 하므로 tall의 비교급 taller를 쓴다.

03 과거의 특정 시점보다 더 이전에 일어난 일이나 그 때까지 지속된 상태를 나타낼 때 과거완료시제 (had+과거분사)를 사용한다.

시험대비 실력평가

p.77~79

01 ④ 02 ⑤ 03 ③ 04 ②
05 ③ 06 ③
07 he had already fixed my bike 08 ③
09 (1) When Jiyeon came back home, she found that her mother had already set the table for her.
(2) He is much cooler than you think. I'm sure you will like him.
10 ⑤ 11 ④
12 (1) had (2) left (3) even (4) harder (5) a lot
13 ②
14 looks even younger than her daughter
15 She behaved much more kindly than I had expected.
16 (1) had cooked (2) had washed (3) had fixed
17 ③
18 He was surprised that he hadn't locked the door.
19 ③ 20 ⑤ 21 ③

01 비교급을 강조할 때는 'much/far/even/still/a lot+비교급'의 형태로 쓴다. 'really, very, many' 등은 쓸 수 없다.

02 선생님이 말씀하신 것보다 미국 남북전쟁이 더 이전의 일이지만 역사적 사실은 과거완료로 쓰지 않고 항상 과거로 쓴다. had been → was

03 ①, ⑤ 동사를 수식하는 부사구 'a lot' ②, ④ 비교급을 강조하는 'a lot' ③ 명사를 수식하는 'a lot of'

04 'I'가 알게 되기 전부터 'she'가 아팠기 때문에 두 문장을 합쳤을 때 그녀가 아픈 것은 과거완료로 쓰고 알게 된 것은 과거시제로 쓴다.

05 ③은 비교급을 강조하는 'much'이고, ①, ②, ④, ⑤는 셀 수 없는 명사를 수식하는 형용사 'much'이다.

06 눈사람을 만든 것이 눈사람을 파괴한 것보다 더 이전이고, 눈사람을 꾸며주는 관계대명사절이 수동이 되어야 하므로, 'destroyed - had been made'가 적절하다.

07 already는 had와 p.p 사이에 위치한다.

08 내가 소리를 지른 것보다 내 동생이 이어폰을 고장 낸 것이 더 이전의 일이므로 'had yelled'는 'yelled'로, 'broke'는 'had broken'으로 써야 한다.

09 (1) Jiyeon이 집에 온 것보다 어머니가 상을 차린 것이 더 이전의 일이므로 과거완료 'had already set'으로 써야 한다. (2) cool의 비교급은 'cooler'이므로 'much cooler'로 써야 한다.

10 빈칸에는 과거완료를 완성시킬 과거분사가 필요하므로 과거형 took은 적절하지 않다.

11 New York으로 이사 온 것보다 LA에 산 것이 더 이전의 일이므로 이사 온 것은 과거(moved)로, LA에 산 것은 과거완료(had lived)로 쓴다. ②는 접속사 after의 쓰임이 어색하다.

12 (1) 과거완료가 적절하므로 'had'를 사용한다. 'get up'을 수동태로 쓰는 것은 적절하지 않다. (2) 과거완료를 완성해 줄 had 뒤에 과거분사가 필요하므로 'left'가 적절하다. (3) 비교급 'younger'는 'even'과 함께 쓰는 것이 적절하다. 'so'는 비교급과 쓰지 않는다. (4) 비교급을 강조하는 much가 있으므로 'harder'를 쓰는 것이 적절하다. (5) 비교급 'nicer'는 'a lot'과 쓰는 것이 적절하다.

13 'a lot'은 비교급을 강조하는 단어로 비교급 more difficult 앞에 위치하는 것이 적절하다.

14 비교급을 강조하는 'even'을 비교급 younger 앞에 넣어 문장을 완성한다. more young으로 쓰지 않도록 주의하고, 'many'는 비교급을 강조할 때 쓰지 않는다.

15 그녀가 행동한 것보다 내가 예상한 것이 더 이전이므로 과거완

료 'I had expected'로 쓴다. 행동이 훨씬 더 친절하다고 했으므로 'more kindly' 앞에 비교급을 강조하는 'much/far/even/still/a lot'을 쓴다.

16 Mr. Han이 집에 돌아오기 전에 있었던 일들을 과거완료 시제로 쓴다.

17 첫 번째 문장은 비교급을 강조하는 'much/far/even/still/a lot' 중 하나를 써야 하며, 셀 수 없는 명사 interest와 어울리는 것은 'much'이다.

18 놀란 것보다 문을 잠그지 않은 것이 더 이전이므로 놀란 것은 과거(was surprised)로, 잠그지 않은 것은 과거완료(hadn't locked)로 쓴다.

19 early의 비교급은 earlier이다. much more early → much earlier

20 비교급을 강조할 때는 'very'를 쓰지 않고 'much/far/even/still/a lot'을 쓴다.

21 a. 비교급은 그 대상이 동일한 종류이어야 한다. me → mine[my car], c. more lovely → lovelier, d. 비교급을 강조할 때 'very'는 사용하지 않고 'much/far/even/still/a lot'을 쓴다. very more handsome → much more handsome.

서술형 시험대비 p.80~81

01 (1) Did you remember where you had put the book?
(2) When I came back home, I found somebody had broken in.
(3) Did you notice the house had been newly painted?
(4) I lost my bag (that) Mom had bought for me.
(5) When I entered the classroom, I found my teacher had already left the classroom.

02 much more beautifully

03 (1) look much more comfortable than the others
(2) much cheaper than the hand bag

04 (1) Eric played the violin much better.
(2) You should work a lot harder.

05 (1) It is raining a lot harder than yesterday.
(2) Your book is even easier to read than anything else.
(3) This book looks much more difficult than that one.

06 had never visited

07 (1) Tony threw away the gift that Jack had sent to him by mistake.
(2) Yuna showed me the notebook that she had written down a poem on.

08 (1) Jack lost the umbrella that his friend had lent to him.
(2) When I called her, she had already gone to sleep.
(3) Before I got to the theater, the movie had already finished.
(4) When I arrived at the airport, the plane had already left.
(5) Did you eat the pie that Dad had baked?

09 (1) had cleaned (2) healthier (3) called
(4) had lost (5) had gone

01 (1) 기억한 것보다 책을 놓은 것이 더 이전이므로 간접의문문으로 두 문장을 연결하면서 'did you put'을 'had put'으로 바꾼다. (2) 집에 들어온 것보다 누군가가 침입한 것이 더 이전이므로 'broke in'을 'had broken in'으로 바꾼다. (3) 집이 칠해진 것이 알아차린 것보다 더 이전이므로 'was painted'를 'had been painted'로 바꾼다. (4) 가방을 잃어버린 것보다 엄마가 사준 것이 더 이전이므로 두 문장을 관계대명사로 연결하면서 과거 'bought'를 과거완료 'had bought'로 바꾼다. (5) 교실에 들어온 것보다 선생님이 교실을 떠나신 것이 더 이전이므로 'left'를 'had left'로 바꾼다.

02 빈칸에는 부사가 필요한 자리이므로 'more beautifully'가 적절하고, 비교급을 강조하는 'much/far/even/still/a lot+비교급'의 형태로 쓴다.

03 비교급을 강조하는 문장이므로, 'much+비교급+than'의 순서로 문장을 완성한다.

04 원급을 강조할 때는 'very'를 쓸 수 있지만 비교급을 강조할 때는 'much/far/even/still/a lot+비교급'의 형태로 쓴다.

05 비교급을 강조할 때는 'much/far/even/still/a lot+비교급+than'의 형태로 쓴다.

06 그녀가 20살이 된 것(과거)보다 뉴욕에 방문한 경험이 그 이전이므로 과거완료 'had visited'를 쓴다. 'never'는 had와 과거분사 사이에 위치한다.

07 두 문장을 관계대명사를 이용하여 하나로 연결할 때 더 이전의 일은 과거완료로 쓴다.

08 (1) 우산을 잃어버린 것보다 친구가 빌려준 것이 더 이전이므로 과거완료 'had lent'로 쓴다. (2) 그녀에게 전화를 건 것보다 그녀가 잠자리에 든 것이 더 이전이므로 과거완료 'had gone'으로 쓴다, (3) 영화가 끝난 것이 과거완료이므로 극장에 도착한 것은 과거시제 'got'으로 쓴다. (4) 내가 공항에 도착한 것보다 비행기가 떠난 것이 더 이전이므로 과거완료 'had left'로 쓴다. (5) 파이를 먹은 것보다 아빠가 파이를 구운 것이 더 이전이므로 과거완료 'had baked'로 쓴다.

09 (1), (4), (5) 과거보다 더 이전의 일들은 과거완료 'had+p.p'로 쓴다. (2) 비교급을 강조하는 'much'와 비교급과 같이 쓰는 'than'이 있으므로 healthier로 쓴다. (3) 점심을 먹은 것은 과거완료 'had eaten'으로, 이후의 일은 과거시제 'called'로 쓴다.

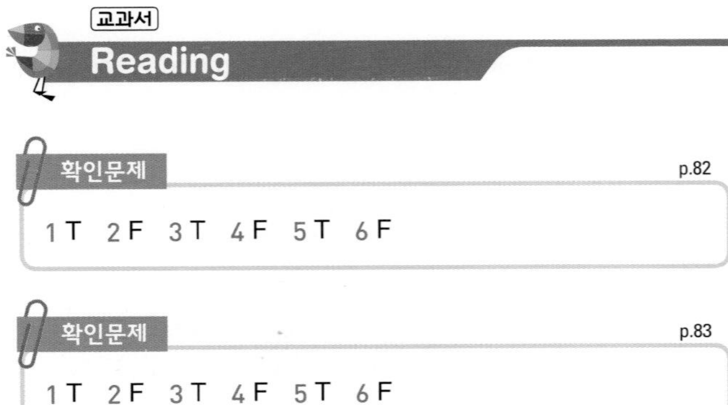

교과서

Reading

확인문제 p.82

1 T 2 F 3 T 4 F 5 T 6 F

확인문제 p.83

1 T 2 F 3 T 4 F 5 T 6 F

교과서 확인학습 A p.84~85

01 Thumbs 02 complained
03 work, far better
04 why we were working 05 across from
06 was full of, you can imagine
07 I bet 08 all ages and sizes
09 this awful mess 10 where to begin
11 just to start
12 divided, into, assigned, to 13 By lunchtime, wear
14 filled, with, were ready to 15 made us sneeze
16 At the end of 17 the toughest
18 made rows
19 stopped complaining 20 First, the lettuce
21 so fast 22 couldn't believe
23 in size in just a few days
24 what new flowers are ready
25 enjoy the sights 26 hit me
27 have been a part 28 I'm in charge of
29 will go to 30 even better, that

교과서 확인학습 B p.86~87

1 Green Thumbs
2 I complained the whole day.
3 My parents were making me work on the neighborhood project, but I had far better things to do.
4 I didn't understand why we were working on this place.
5 It was just the ugly, old, empty lot across from Johnny's Shop.
6 It was full of wild plants, fast food wraps, old newspapers, broken glass, and every other kind of dirty trash you can imagine.
7 As I looked at it that first morning, I thought, "I bet there are snakes in there, too."
8 There were twenty of us — all ages and sizes — ready to work that day.
9 I didn't think that we could clean up this awful mess and turn it into a garden.
10 We were all wondering where to begin.
11 Then Mr. Hernandez said, "The only way to do it is just to start."
12 Then, he divided the lot into four parts with string and assigned five people to each part.
13 By lunchtime, I was hot, sweaty, and glad my dad had made me wear gloves.
14 We filled fifty trash bags with waste and were ready to pull wild plants.
15 As we pulled and pulled, dust filled the air and made us sneeze.
16 At the end of the day, I had to admit the lot looked much better.
17 That first day was the toughest.
18 On the weekends that followed, we made rows, planted flower and vegetable seeds, and watered them.
19 After about two weeks, I stopped complaining when I found the plants had started popping up!
20 First, the lettuce and then the beans and the tomatoes.
21 They grew so fast.
22 I couldn't believe it!
23 The bean plants grew an inch, and the tomatoes doubled in size in just a few days.
24 Now, two months later, I like to go there every day to see what new flowers are ready to pop up.
25 Lots of people in the neighborhood meet there to enjoy the sights and to talk together.
26 Tonight, it suddenly hit me — what a good thing we did!
27 I'm proud I have been a part of it.
28 I'm in charge of picking flowers for the nursing home on Fourth Street.
29 The vegetables will go to every kitchen in our town.
30 But even better, an ugly and dirty lot that people didn't like has become a pretty garden for everyone.

시험대비 실력평가 p.88~91

01 (A) complained (B) broken (C) kind 02 ③
03 filled with 04 five 05 terrific → awful

06 ②
07 (A) wondering (B) divided (C) assigned
08 ⑤ 09 ② 10 ③
11 doubled in size in just a few days 12 ①
13 ④ 14 good → better 15 ③
16 ④ 17 ④ 18 ③, ④ 19 to pop
20 ⑤ 21 different 22 ①, ③, ④
23 ③ 24 ⑤
25 an ugly and dirty lot that people didn't like has become a pretty garden for everyone

01 (A) the whole day는 부사구로 목적어가 아니므로 about은 불필요하다. (B) '깨진' 유리라고 해야 하므로 broken이 옳다. (C) every 뒤에 단수 명사를 써야 하므로 kind가 옳다.

02 ③을 제외한 나머지는 모두 Johnny's Shop이 아니라, 글쓴이가 일해야 했던 지역을 지칭한다.

03 be full of = be filled with: ~로 가득 차다

04 그 지역을 끈으로 네 구역으로 나누었기 때문에, 총 20명을 4로 나누면 한 구역 당 '5명'이라고 하는 것이 적절하다.

05 이 '끔찍하게' 더러운 곳을 청소하여 정원으로 바꾼다고 해야 하므로 terrific을 awful이나 terrible로 고치는 것이 적절하다. terrific: 아주 좋은, 멋진, 훌륭한, awful: 끔찍한

06 '그것을 할 유일한 방법은 그냥 시작하는 것입니다.'에 가장 잘 어울리는 속담으로는 ②번 '시작이 반이다.'가 적절하다. ① 잘 생각해 보고 행동하라[돌다리도 두드려 보고 건너라]. ③ 사공이 많으면 배가 산으로 올라간다.(어떤 일에 관여하는 사람이 너무 많으면 일을 망친다는 뜻.) ④ 기회를 잘 이용하라. ⑤ 안 좋은 일은 겹쳐서 일어나기 마련이다[불운은 한꺼번에 닥친다].

07 20명의 사람들이 어디서부터 시작해야 할지 '궁금해 하고' 있을 때, Hernandez씨가 끈으로 그 지역을 네 구역으로 '나누고', 5명을 각 구역에 '배치했다.'

08 주어진 문장의 it에 주목한다. ⑤번 앞 문장의 내용을 받고 있으므로 ⑤번이 적절하다.

09 이 글은 불평하던 글쓴이가 자신이 재배한 식물들이 자라는 것을 보고 성취감을 느끼게 되는 경험을 얘기하고 있는 글이므로 제목으로는 ②번 '믿을 수 없어! 나는 원예의 재능이 있어!'가 적절하다. have a green thumb: 식물 재배를 잘하다, 원예의 재능이 있다, green thumbs: 원예의 재능(green fingers), ⑤ shortcut: 지름길, 손쉬운 방법

10 ⓐ와 ①, ②, ⑤: 관계대명사, ③, ④: 접속사

11 in just a few days: 며칠 만에

12 ⓐ와 ①: (사람, 일에 대한) 책임, 담당(명사), ② (상품·서비스에 대한) 요금(명사), ③ (요금, 값을) 청구하다[주라고 하다](동사), ④ 비난(명사), ⑤ 돌격[공격]하다(동사)

13 'The vegetables will go to every kitchen in our town.'이라고만 되어 있다.

14 문맥상 이웃 프로젝트에서 일하는 것보다 훨씬 더 나은 할 일들이 있었다고 하는 것이 적절하므로, far를 very로 고치는 것보다 good을 비교급 better로 고치는 것이 적절하다.

15 틀림없이 뱀들도 있을 것이라고 생각할 정도로 싫어하는 마음을 가지고 있는 것이므로, ③번 '꺼리는', '마지못한'이 적절하다. ① 부끄러운, ② 흥분한, ④ 기꺼이 하는, 자발적인, 열렬한, ⑤ 침착한, 차분한

16 그 장소는 볼품없고, 오래되고, 텅 빈 지역이었다. ordinary: 보통의, 평범한, ① complaint: 불평, ② have+사람+원형부정사: ~에게 …을 하도록 시키다, ③ figure out: 이해하다

17 이 글은 불평하던 글쓴이가 자신이 재배한 식물들이 자라는 것을 보고 성취감을 느끼게 되는 경험을 얘기하고 있는 글이므로, 주제로는 ④번 '고진감래'가 적절하다. ① 다다익선, ② 유비무환, ③ 급할수록 돌아가라; 급히 먹는 밥이 체한다. ⑤ 안 좋은 일은 겹쳐서 일어나기 마련이다[불운은 한꺼번에 닥친다]

18 ⓐ와 ③, ④: 열[줄](명사), ①, ②, 노[배]를 젓다(동사), ⑤: 노[배]를 저어 …를 태워[데려다] 주다(동사)

19 start는 목적어로 동명사와 to부정사를 쓸 수 있다.

20 ⓐ turn A into B: A를 B로 바꾸다, ⓑ assign A to B: A를 B에 배정하다

21 "모든 연령대와 몸집을 가진'은 연령과 몸집이 다 '다르다'는 뜻이다.

22 (B)와 ②, ⑤: 명사적 용법, ①: 형용사적 용법, ③, ④: 부사적 용법

23 ③ have a light bulb go on = A light goes on in one's head(brain): (아이디어 등이) 번득이다, 번쩍 떠오르다, ① hit on: 불현듯 ~을 생각해 내다[떠올리다], ②와 ④: occur to = strike: ~에게 생각이 떠오르다, ⑤ come up with: ~을 생각해 내다

24 ⓑ와 ⑤: (비교급을 강조하여) 훨씬(부사), ① …도[조차](부사), ② (무엇의 양·득점 등이) 균등한, 동일한(형용사), ③ 짝수[우수]의(형용사), ④ 평평한, 반반한(형용사)

25 관계대명사절인 that people didn't like가 선행사인 an ugly and dirty lot을 수식하게 쓰는 것이 적절하다.

서술형 시험대비

p.92~93

01 I had far better things to do.
02 must / sure[certain]
03 willing → unwilling 또는 reluctant
04 (A) mess (B) wondering (C) divided
05 we should 06 assigned
07 had made 08 because of
09 (A) lot (B) lot
10 ⓐ made ⓑ planted ⓒ watered

11 the lettuce, the beans and the tomatoes
12 plants
13 an ugly and dirty lot that people didn't like has become a pretty garden for everyone
14 I'm proud of having been a part of it.
15 responsible for
16 But even better, an ugly and dirty lot people didn't like has become a pretty garden for everyone.

01 'far'를 비교급 앞에 써서 강조하는 것이 적절하다.
02 I bet = I'm sure[certain] that: 틀림없이 …이다, must be: ~임에 틀림없다
03 be willing to: 기꺼이 ~하다, be unwilling to: ~하는 것이 내키지 않다, be reluctant to: 마지못해 ~하다
04 (A) '더러운 곳'이라고 해야 하므로 mess가 옳다. mass: 덩어리, mess: (지저분하고) 엉망(진창)인 상태, (B) '궁금해 하다'고 해야 하므로 wondering이 옳다. wander: (이리저리 천천히) 거닐다, 헤매다, wonder: 궁금해 하다, (C) '나눴다'고 해야 하므로 divided가 옳다. decide: 결정하다, divide: 나누다
05 '의문사 to부정사'는 '의문사+주어+should'로 바꿔 쓸 수 있다.
06 assign: (일·책임 등을) 맡기다[배정하다/부과하다]
07 아버지가 나에게 장갑을 끼도록 한 것이 점심때보다 더 먼저 일어난 일이므로 과거완료로 쓰는 것이 적절하다.
08 공기를 메운 먼지 '때문에' 우리는 재채기를 했다
09 (A) lot: 지역, (B) lot: 앞의 a와 합쳐서 비교급 강조(훨씬)
10 모두 과거시제로 써서 병렬구문을 만드는 것이 적절하다.
11 '상추,' '콩,' '토마토'를 가리킨다.
12 필자는 '식물들'이 자라나기 시작한 것을 발견했을 때 불평하는 것을 멈추었다.
13 '우리가 했던 좋은 일'은 '사람들이 좋아하지 않았던 볼품없고 더러운 지역이 모두를 위한 예쁜 정원이 되었다.'를 가리킨다.
14 be proud of ~ing로 고치는 것이 적절하다.
15 be in charge of: ~을 담당하다, ~을 책임지고 있다, be responsible for: ~을 책임지고[책임 맡고] 있다
16 목적격 관계대명사 that을 생략할 수 있다.

영역별 핵심문제

p.95~99

01 (a)wful　02 ⑤　03 ②　04 ①
05 green thumb　06 ④　07 ③
08 ④　09 ⑤　10 ③　11 ②
12 be helpful for us to learn the new members' names　13 ②, ③
14 Oksig is much cuter than real corn.　15 ⑤
16 (1) a lot more　(2) much better
(3) much more popular
17 much
18 (1) Bill Gates is much richer than me[I am].
(2) This book is even more popular than that book (is).
(3) You dance far more gracefully than me[I do].
19 to work → work　20 ④
21 ③　22 ⑤

01 반의어 관계다. 채우다 : 비우다 = 멋진 : 끔찍한
02 (a) John은 파티에 초대받지 않았는데 그가 불쑥 나타나서 우리는 놀랐다. (b) 산의 풍경이 너무 아름다워서 그녀는 울었다.
03 '할 필요가 없는 일을 하겠다고 제안하다'라는 의미로 'volunteer(자원하다)'가 적절하다.
04 '서로 옆에 있는 사물이나 사람의 줄'의 의미로 'row(열, 줄)'가 적절하다. ④번의 'raw'는 형용사로 '날 것의, 요리되지 않은'의 의미이다.
05 '식물을 재배하는 데 상당한 재능이나 능력'
06 complain은 '불평하다'라는 뜻이다. '배정하다'는 'assign'이다.
07 '~하는 게 어때?'라는 제안의 표현으로 'What do you say to+V-ing(동명사)?'를 사용한다.
08 (C) 모두 와 줘서 고맙다는 말과 이야기할 주제를 소개하는 말이 오고 → (B) '깨끗한 학교 프로젝트' 중에서 나무 아래가 가장 마음에 든다는 말과 과학 동아리가 그곳을 청소하고 나무를 심었다는 말이 오고 → 마지막으로 (A) 나도 마음에 든다는 동의의 말이 오는 것이 적절하다.
09 동아리실에 관해 이야기해 보자는 대화의 주제를 소개한 후, '의견 있니?'라고 묻는 말에 좋은 생각이라고 답하는 것은 어색하다.
10 대화의 첫 문장 'Let's talk about how we can make our town better'에서 글의 제목이 언급되어 있다.
11 'Why don't we ~' 뒤에는 동사원형이 온다. 'cleaning'을 'clean'으로 바꾸어 준다.
12 주어진 단어 It'll 뒤에 동사원형 be를 사용하고 be동사 뒤에는 형용사 helpful이 온다. to부정사 앞에 의미상 주어 for us(목적격)를 사용한다.
13 ② more easy → easier ③ worse는 bad의 비교급이므로 more worse로 쓸 수 없다. more worse → much worse
14 비교급을 강조할 때에는 'even, still, far, much, a lot'을 쓴다. 'very'는 비교급 강조 역할을 하지 않는다.
15 버스를 놓친 것이 원인(더 이전의 일): because+(과거완료), 학교에 늦은 것이 결과(나중의 일): 주절 (과거)
16 비교급을 강조할 때에는 'even, still, far, much, a lot'을 비교급 앞에 쓴다.
17 두 번째 문장에서 비교급을 강조하는 'even/still/far/much/a lot' 중 하나가 필요한데, 첫 번째 문장에서 셀 수 없는 명사

'information'을 수식할 수 있는 것은 그 중에서 'much'이다. 그러므로 공통으로 들어갈 단어는 'much'가 적절하다.

18 비교급을 강조할 때에는 비교급 앞에 'even, still, far, much, a lot'을 쓴다.

19 '사역동사(making)+목적어+원형부정사'로 쓰는 것이 적절하다.

20 ⓑ와 ④: (특정 용도용) 지역[부지], ①, ③: (수양이) 많음, 다량, 다수, ② 운명, 운, ⑤ 제비뽑기, 추첨

21 very는 원급을 강조하고, 나머지는 다 비교급을 강조한다.

22 (A)와 ⑤: 쓰레기(명사), ① 낭비, 허비(명사), ② (기회 등을) 놓치다(동사), ③ 이용[활용]되고 있지 않은(형용사), ④ 낭비하다, 허비하다(동사)

23 쓰레기 봉투 50개를 쓰레기로 채운 것이 더 먼저 일어난 일이므로 과거완료로 쓰는 것이 적절하다.

24 ⓐ change A into B: A를 B로 바꾸다, ⓑ divide A into B: A를 B로 나누다

25 위 글은 '안내문'이다. notice: (보통 공공장소에 붙이는) 공고문[안내문], ① (신문·잡지의) 글, 기사, ③ (물품·책 등의) 목록, 카탈로그, ④ (책·연극·영화 등에 대한) 논평[비평], 감상문, ⑤ 광고

26 '참가 가능 연령'은 알 수 없다. ① 4월 17일, ② Johnny's Shop 건너편에 있는 텅 빈 지역, ③ 잡초들을 뽑고 그 지역을 청소함, ④ 장갑, 쓰레기 봉투

27 '약간의 꽃들'을 가리킨다.

28 글쓴이는 모두를 위한 '예쁜 정원'을 만든 것에 대해 자랑스러워한다.

단원별 예상문제

p.100~103

01 whole 02 ②
03 Thank you for volunteering. 04 ④
05 to put the club member list, for this school year
06 ③ 07 Thank you for saying that.
08 ② 09 (D) – (B) – (A) – (C) 10 ⑤
11 have → had
12 (1) after I had taken pictures of many different kinds of corn
(2) Oksig is much cuter than real corn.
13 (1) When we visited her, she said she had studied music for 5 years in Paris.
(2) It was strange that he didn't remember the movie that we had watched the other day.
(3) Walking is much more helpful for your health than running.
(4) The building is much larger than I expected.
14 ③ 15 (A) empty (B) full 16 ②
17 ③ 18 ① 19 A lot of, Many
20 what a good thing we did!
21 (A) a pretty garden (B) a part
22 ⓐ had drawn ⓑ had cleaned
23 (A) Art Club (B) Green Club

01 반의어 관계이다. 기억하다 - 잊다 : 부분의 - 전체의

02 어떤 것을 두 배가 되게 하다

03 감사의 표현으로 'Thank you for ~'를 사용한다. 그 다음 누가 아이들과 놀아 줄것인지 묻는 말에 B가 내가 하겠다고 말하는 것으로 보아 'volunteer'를 사용한다.

04 주어진 문장은 벽에 이번 학년의 계획이 필요하다는 내용이므로 학교 행사를 기억하는 데 도움이 된다는 말 앞인 ④번에 오는 것이 적절하다.

05 벽에 동아리 회원 목록과 이번 학년의 계획을 붙일 것이다.

06 'Don't worry about it.'은 'I'm sorry.'에 대한 대답으로 적절하다.

07 '~해서 고마워'라는 의미로 Thank you for+-ing'를 사용한다.

08 (A): 마을을 위해 무엇을 할 수 있는지에 대한 답으로 '지저분한 벽에 그림을 그리는 게 어때?'라는 제안이 적절하다. (B) '벤치를 고치는 것을 도와줄게.'라는 말에 도움을 받은 M은 감사의 말을 하는 것이 자연스럽다.

09 버스 정류장에 쓰레기가 너무 많다는 말에 → (D) 동의하고 'the place(버스 정류장)를 청소하는 게 어때?'라고 제안하는 말이 오고 → (B) '좋아'라고 말한 다음 벤치를 놓자는 말을 하고 → (A) 그것이 노인들에게 도움이 될 거라는 말 다음에, → (C) 벤치 주변에 화분을 놓자고 제안하는 말이 오는 것이 자연스럽다.

10 그들은 마을을 더 나은 장소로 만들기 위한 일을 내일 시작할 것이라고 말하고 있다. right now를 tomorrow로 바꾸어야 한다.

11 형이 집에 온 것보다 내가 설거지를 한 것이 더 이전의 일이므로 현재완료 'have done'을 과거완료로 쓰는 것이 적절하다.

12 (1) 'designed'보다 사진을 찍은 것이 더 이전의 일이기 때문에 과거완료 'had taken'을 사용하여 문장을 만든다. (2) 비교급 cuter 앞에 비교급을 강조하는 'much/still/far/even/a lot'을 '훨씬'의 의미로 사용하여 문장을 만든다.

13 (1) 그녀가 말한 것보다 그녀가 음악을 공부한 것이 더 이전에 시작된 일이므로 과거완료 'had studied'를 쓰는 것이 적절하다. (2) 주절이 과거이고 관계대명사 that절은 그 이전의 경험을 나타내는 내용이므로 과거완료 'had watched'로 쓰는 것이 적절하다. (3) Walking과 running을 비교하는 문장이므로 'helpful'을 비교급으로 써야 한다. (4) 비교급을 강조하는 어휘로 'very'를 쓸 수 없으므로 'even/still/far/much/a lot' 중에 하나를 쓴다.

14 필자는 훨씬 더 나은 할 일들이 있었는데 부모님이 이웃 프로젝

트에서 일하게 시켜서 억지로 일을 하게 된 것이라서 하루 종일 '불평했다'고 하는 것이 적절하다. ① 사과하다, ② 칭찬하다, ④ 보상하다, ⑤ 제의[제안]하다, 권하다

15 그곳은 잡초, 패스트푸드 포장지, 낡은 신문들, 깨진 유리, 그리고 상상할 수 있는 모든 다른 종류의 더러운 쓰레기로 '가득 찬' 단지 '텅 빈' 지역이였다.

16 ⓐ와 ②: 대과거 용법, ①, ④: 경험 용법, ③, ⑤: 계속 용법

17 '상추'가 제일 먼저 나왔다.

18 ①은 명사적 용법이고, 나머지는 다 부사적 용법이다.

19 A (great) number of도 가능하다. lots of = a lot of: 수와 양이 많을 때 다 사용할 수 있음.

20 '우리가 얼마나 좋은 일을 했는가!'를 가리킨다.

21 처음에 사람들은 볼품없고 더러운 그 지역을 좋아하지 않았지만 그곳이 모두를 위한 '예쁜 정원'이 되었고, 글쓴이는 그런 대단한 일을 한 것의 '일부'였다는 것에 자랑스러워한다.

22 꽃을 그린 것과 연못을 청소한 것이 날개를 그린 것과 물고기를 연못에 넣은 것보다 먼저 일어난 행동이므로 과거완료로 쓰는 것이 적절하다.

23 '미술 동아리'와 '환경 동아리' 덕분에 학교의 환경이 좋아졌다. change for the better: 좋아지다

서술형 실전문제 p.104~105

01 (A) how about putting some flower pots by the windows
(B) Thank you for suggesting it

02 Let's talk about the volunteer work for our town.

03 (1) There is too much trash at the bus stop.
(2) They will put a bench there for the elderly.

04 (1) ⓐthat → which (2) ⓑhave taken → had taken
(3) ⓔthem → it

05 (1) had had (2) had told (3) had lived

06 I bet

07 why we were working on this place

08 every other kind of dirty trash that[which] you can imagine

09 to complain → complaining

10 **1인치 자라났고, 토마토는 며칠 만에 크기가 두 배가 되었다**

01 (A) 'How about+동명사(V-ing)?'를 사용한다. 의미상 창문 옆에 화분을 두다는 표현이 적절하므로, 'putting some flower pots by the windows'를 쓴다. (B) 감사의 표현은 'Thank you for+명사/동명사'를 이용한다. 동사 suggest는 동명사 suggesting 형태로 바꾸어 준다.

02 '~에 대해서 말해 보자'의 뜻으로 함께 대화하고자 하는 주제를 소개할 때 'Let's talk about ~'을 사용한다.

03 (1) 마을의 문제가 무엇인가? (2) 그들은 버스 정류장을 청소한 후에 무엇을 할 것인가?

04 (1) 관계대명사의 계속적 용법에서는 'that'을 사용하지 않고, 선행사가 사람이면 'who' 또는 'whom'을, 사물이면 'which'를 쓴다. (2) 주절의 동사 'designed'보다 after절의 동사가 더 이전의 일이므로 'had taken'으로 쓰는 것이 적절하다. (3) 'Oksig'을 지칭하므로 'it'으로 쓴다.

05 (1) 우리는 엄마가 집에 오시기 전에(과거) 즐거운 시간을 보냈다.(과거완료) have a good time: 즐거운 시간을 보내다 (2) 어제 나는 내 친구가 거짓말을 했다는 것을(과거완료) 알게 되었다.(과거) tell a lie: 거짓말을 하다 (3) Mark는 Irene과 결혼하기 전에(과거) 그의 가족과 함께 살았었다.(과거완료) live with one's family: 가족과 함께 살다

06 I bet = It is certain that = I'm sure[certain] that: 틀림없이 …이다

07 '의문사+주어+동사'인 간접의문문의 순서로 쓰는 것이 적절하다.

08 you can imagine 앞에 목적격 관계대명사 'that[which]'이 생략되어 있다.

09 불평하는 것을 멈춘 것이기 때문에, 동명사로 고치는 것이 적절하다. stop ~ing: ~하기를 그만두다, stop to부정사: ~하기 위해서 멈추다

10 본문의 마지막 부분을 쓰면 된다.

창의사고력 서술형 문제 p.106

|모범답안|

01 (1) A: Let's talk about the class field trip. Who will take pictures of our activities?
B: I will. I can do it well.
A: Thank you for volunteering.
(2) A: Let's talk about the club festival. Who will make posters?
B: I will. I can do it well.
A: Thank you for volunteering.
(3) A: Let's talk about the sports day. Who will run a 100 meter race?
B: I will. I can do it well.
A: Thank you for volunteering.

02 (1) I had stayed up late playing games last night
(2) he had worked out so hard
(3) she had lost her shoes
(4) she had already watched it before

03 (A) drew wings (B) had drawn flowers
(C) put some fish (D) had cleaned

단원별 모의고사

p.107~110

01 ①　02 (a)wful　03 ③　04 ⑤
05 ④　06 ②　07 ⑤
08 to put the club member list on the wall
09 It'll be helpful for the elderly.　10 ②
11 ②　12 ③　13 ⑤
14 (1) they had set up the board
(2) they had cleaned the pond
(3) they had drawn flowers
15 had never visited　16 ②
17 imaginable
18 I didn't think that we could clean up this awful mess and turn it into a garden.
19 ④　20 flower and vegetable seeds
21 ③　22 ④　23 worse → better

01 ①번은 '누군가에게 특정한 직업이나 일을 맡기다'라는 'assign(배정하다, 배치하다, 맡기다)'에 대한 설명이다.
02 유의어 관계이다. 불평하다 - 끔찍한
03 '다른 사람들이 고려할 아이디어, 가능한 계획 또는 행동을 언급하다'라는 의미로 suggest가 적절하다.
04 ⑤: 누가 방문객을 안내할 거니?라고 묻는 말에 '국립공원으로 가는 게 어때?'라고 답하는 것은 어색하다.
05 '그림을 좀 거는 게 어때?'라는 제안에 B의 마지막 말이 '내가 내 그림 중에서 하나를 가져올게.'라고 말하고 있으므로 빈칸에는 '그림을 가져오는 게 어때?'라는 말이 자연스럽다.
06 A의 빈칸 다음의 말이 '지저분한 벽을 누가 칠을 할 거니?'라고 묻는 것으로 보아 ②번이 가장 적절하다.
07 ⑤번은 전치사 for 뒤에 동사 suggest를 쓸 수 없다. 동명사 suggesting으로 고쳐야 한다.
08 대명사 It은 '벽에 동아리 회원들 목록을 붙이는 것'을 가리킨다.
09 인칭대명사 it(그것은)이 주어로, '도움이 될 거야'는 미래 의미로 조동사 will be helpful을 사용한다. 동사 'help'는 형용사 'helpful'로 바꾸어 준다. 마지막으로 'the+형용사'는 복수명사로 '어르신들'의 의미로 'the elderly'를 쓴다.
10 나머지는 모두 '~하자, ~하는 게 어때?'라는 의미의 제안을 할 때 사용하는 표현이다. ②번은 'let+목적어+동사원형' 구문으로 '~가 …하도록 허락하다'라는 의미이다.
11 ① much loudly → much more loudly '비교급+than'의 형태로 써야 한다. ③ much more cheap → much cheaper ④ very bigger → much bigger 비교급을 강조하는 단어로 'very' 대신 'much/still/far/even/a lot'을 써야 한다. ⑤ much wiser → much more wisely 일반 동사 'spend'를 꾸며줄 부사의 비교급이 필요하다.
12 엄마가 그의 이름을 기억한 것보다 그를 본 적이 있는 것이 더 이전이므로 과거완료 'had seen'으로 쓰는 것이 적절하다.
13 일반동사 'work' 다음에는 부사의 비교급 'more diligently'가 필요하고 그 앞에 강조의 부사 'much'를 쓴다.
14 흐름상 알맞은 내용을 과거완료시제로 변형하여 쓴다.
15 지후는 지난달에 처음으로 그 동물원에 방문했다. = 지후는 지난달 전에는 그 동물원에 가 본 적이 없었다.(과거인 지난달 보다 이전 시제인 과거완료를 쓴다.)
16 ⓐ와 ②, ③: 형용사적 용법, ①, ④: 명사적 용법, ⑤: 부사적 용법
17 imaginable: 상상할 수 있는, 생각할 수 있는(강조하기 위하여 명사의 앞이나 뒤, 형용사의 최상급, 또는 all, every, no 다음에 쓴다.)
18 turn A into B: A를 B로 바꾸다
19 Hernandez씨는 그 지역을 끈으로 '네' 구역으로 나누었다.
20 '꽃과 채소 씨앗'을 가리킨다.
21 ⓑ와 ③: 대략, 약, ① …에 대해(무엇의 '주제'나 '연관성'을 나타냄), ② [to부정사와 함께] 막 …하려고 하여, ④ 도처에, 여기저기, ⑤ …주위[둘레]에
22 자랑스러운, 앞에 what a good thing we did!라는 말이 있으므로, ④번이 적절하다. ① 부끄러운, ② 실망한, ③ 초조한, ⑤ 속상한
23 사람들이 좋아하지 않았던 볼품없고 더러운 지역이 모두를 위한 예쁜 정원이 되었으므로, '훨씬 더 좋은 것은'이라고 하는 것이 적절하다.

Lesson 3

Laugh First and Then Think

시험대비 실력평가 p.114

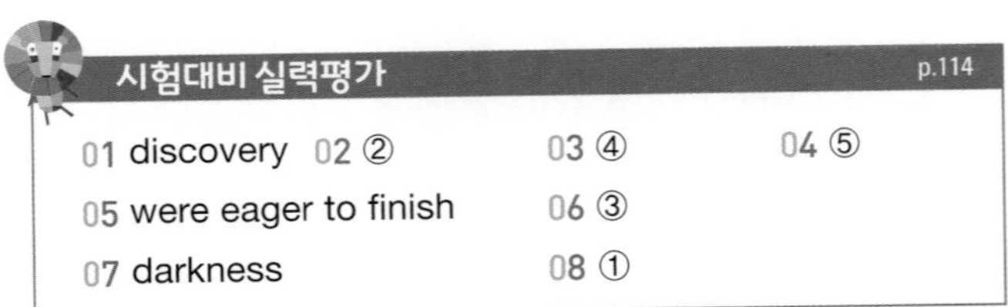
01 discovery 02 ② 03 ④ 04 ⑤
05 were eager to finish 06 ③
07 darkness 08 ①

01 '처음으로 어떤 것을 발견하는 행위'란 뜻의 '발견(discovery)'이 적절하다.

02 • 그 고양이와 그 개 사이의 우정은 매우 특이하다. • 몇몇 사람들은 돼지, 이구아나 심지어 뱀과 같은 특이한 애완동물을 키운다.

03 학위를 받기 위해서 공부하는 가장 높은 수준의 교육 기관

04 배에서 일하는 사람

05 '어서 ~하고 싶어 하다'는 'be eager to+동사원형'을 사용한다.

06 (A) 7월 16일에 한국어 말하기 대회가 미국 캘리포니아에서 열렸다. (B) 그 소년은 반 학생들 앞에서 연설을 했다.

07 '형용사 – 명사' 관계이다. 형용사에 '–ness'를 붙여 명사로 만들 수 있다.

08 (A) 그 대문은 사람들이 공원에 들어가는 것을 막는다. keep+목적어+from V-ing: …가 ~하지 못하게 하다 (B) Leonardo da Vinci의 그림들은 많은 돈의 가치가 있다.

서술형 시험대비 p.115

01 (1) bored (2) repeatedly (3) A number
(4) received
02 award
03 (1) navy, **해군** (2) magnet, **자석**
(3) invent, **발명하다** (4) ceremony, **의식, 식**
04 not only, but also, invention, useful enough
05 (1) (a)ccept (2) (h)umor (3) (e)conomics
(4) (f)illed (5) (i)maginative

01 (1) 지루하지 않게 기내에 게임을 가지고 와라. 사람이 지루하다는 의미로 'get bored'를 사용한다. (2) 동사 sang을 수식하는 부사(repeatedly)가 적절하다. (3) '많은 학생들'이란 의미로 a number of students를 사용한다. (4) 과거 시점인 '지난(last) 크리스마스'가 있으므로 과거동사 received가 적절하다.

02 '업적을 기리기 위해 주어지는 상이나 기타 인정의 표시'의 의미로 award가 적절하다.

03 (1) 배와 함선으로 이루어진 군대 (2) 다른 철을 끌어당기는 금속 조각 (3) 새로운 것을 만들거나 디자인하거나 생각해 내다 (4) 특별한 전통을 가진 공식적인 공개 행사

04 A뿐만 아니라 B도: not only A but also B, 발명: invention, 충분히 유용한: useful enough

05 (1) 이 회사의 직원들은 고객들로부터 어떠한 선물도 받지 않았다. (2) 나는 유머 감각이 좋다고 생각한다. (3) 나는 은행원이 되기 위해 대학에서 경제학을 공부할 것이다. (4) 큰 상자는 가난한 사람들을 위한 따뜻한 옷으로 가득 차 있다. (5) 그 동화 작가는 상상력이 매우 풍부하다.

교과서

Conversation

핵심 Check p.116~117

1 I'm really looking forward to it.
2 (D) → (B) → (C) → (A)

01 '기대하다'의 의미로 forward를 포함하는 것은 'look forward to'이다.

교과서 대화문 익히기

Check(√) True or False p.118~119

1 T 2 F 3 T 4 F 5 F 6 T 7 T 8 T

교과서 확인학습 p.121~123

Get Ready 2

(1) solved a lot of, I'm sure, award / think so / keep, crossed
(2) winner, award / to get, prize / I'm sure, Good luck
(3) looking forward to / make, laugh, get the prize
(4) keep my fingers crossed

Start Off – Listen & Talk A

1. can't wait for / What, going to do / practiced, for / looking forward to / Actually, a little worried, afraid, make, mistake / Don't worry, do, job, my fingers crossed
2. take part in / m going to, end / forward, seeing / sure, win / do your best, keep my fingers crossed

Start Off – Listen & Talk B

are you coming / going, for me to try / sure, do great, keep, crossed / perform, other / sounds fun, looking forward, watching, stage

Start Off – Speak Up

looking forward to, model, ready / so, nervous / do well, keep, crossed

Step Up – Real-life Scene

field trip, talent show / like, do, jokes / looking forward to it / show, sure / worry, do great, keep my fingers crossed / Let, show, Guess / sound like / show / make, laugh out loud

Fun Time

m going to / sounds great, m really looking forward to

enter, m worried about / keep my fingers crossed

Express Yourself A

1. Can you tell me, invention / a pair of special, clean, floor / win a prize, keep
2. interesting, cutting board, feeder / not only, board but also, feeder, at the same time / idea / looking forward, using

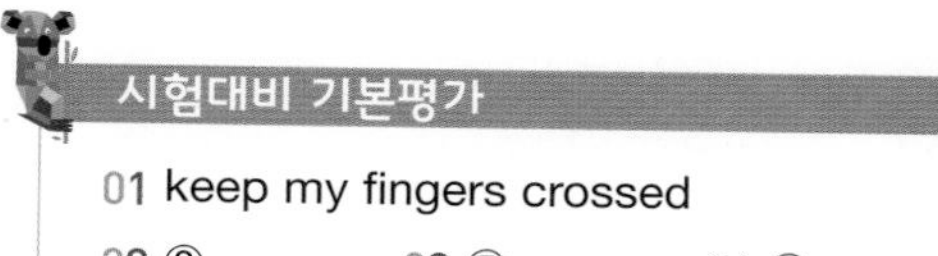

시험대비 기본평가 p.124

01 keep my fingers crossed

02 ③　03 ⑤　04 ②

01 상대가 하는 일이 잘 되기를 기원하면서 '행운을 빌어!'라고 할 때 'I'll keep my fingers crossed (for you)!'라고 한다.

02 빈칸 뒤의 말이 결과의 접속사 so로 연결되어 '그러니 네가 상을 탈 거야.'라고 말하는 것으로 보아 빈칸은 Best Joker상을 타는 이유가 나오는 것이 타당하다.

03 그 상을 받고 싶다는 G의 말에 대한 대답으로 '네가 이번에는 그 상을 탈 거라고 확신해.'라고 말하는 것이 적절하다.

04 '준비가 됐니?'라는 말에 그런 것 같다고 말한 다음 but으로 이어지는 문장으로 보아 앞 문장과 대조되는 단어가 오는 것이 적절하다.

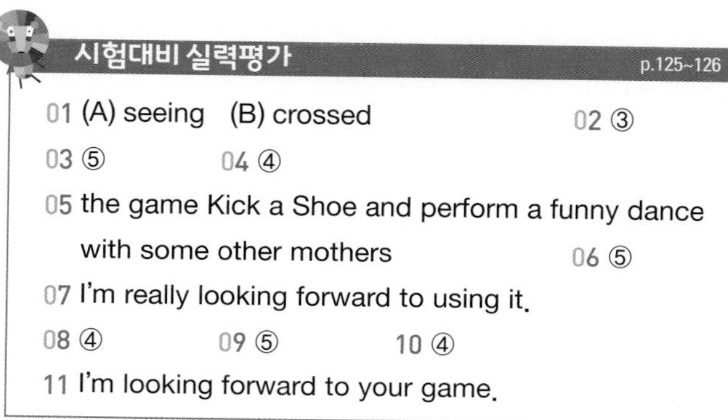

시험대비 실력평가 p.125~126

01 (A) seeing　(B) crossed　02 ③

03 ⑤　04 ④

05 the game Kick a Shoe and perform a funny dance with some other mothers　06 ⑤

07 I'm really looking forward to using it.

08 ④　09 ⑤　10 ④

11 I'm looking forward to your game.

01 (A) 전치사 to 뒤의 동사를 동명사로 바꾸어야 한다. (B) '동사(keep)+목적어(my fingers)+목적보어'의 5형식 구문으로 목적어와 수동의 관계일 때는 과거분사(crossed)가 적절하다.

02 소윤의 엄마가 경기에 뛰기를 원한다는 내용은 언급되어 있지 않다.

03 ⑤번은 'look forward to+동명사/명사' 형태를 취한다. watch를 watching으로 바꾸어야 한다.

04 (A)는 행운을 빌어주는 표현이다. ④번은 긴장한 상대에게 긴장을 풀어주는 표현이다.

05 'Kick a Shoe' 게임에 참가하고, 다른 엄마들과 코믹 댄스를 할 것이다.

06 빈칸 다음에 '너는 동시에 두 가지를 할 수 있어.'라고 말하는 것으로 보아 도마와 새 모이통 둘 다로 사용 가능하다는 것을 알 수 있다.

07 '~을 기대한다'의 의미로 'be looking forward to -ing'를 이용한다.

08 주어진 문장은 '내가 나의 연기의 한 부분을 보여 줄게.'라는 의미로 'Guess who?' 앞에 들어가는 것이 적절하다.

09 Jimin이 몇 번이나 장기 자랑에 참가했는지는 대화에서 언급되어 있지 않다.

10 빈칸 다음의 엄마가 '그날 무엇을 할 거니?'라는 말로 보아 ④가 가장 자연스럽다.

11 '~을 기대하고 있다'는 'be looking for+명사/동명사'를 사용한다.

서술형 시험대비 p.127

01 (A) I'm (really) looking forward to it.
(B) I'll keep my fingers crossed!

02 He talked like his English teacher.

03 It is not only a cutting board but also a bird feeder.

04 I'm afraid I'll make a mistake.

05 I can't wait for the sports day.

01 (A) 기대를 표현하는 말은 'be looking to+명사/동명사'를 사용한다. (B) 기원을 표현하는 말은 'keep one's fingers crossed'를 사용한다.

02 질문: 대화에서 Jimin은 누구처럼 말했는가?

03 'A뿐만 아니라 B도'의 의미로 'B as well as A'는 'not only A but also B'를 사용한다.

04 빈칸 앞에 '사실은, 전 조금 걱정이 돼요.'라고 말하는 것으로 보아 '실수할까봐 겁나요.'라는 말이 적절하다.

05 '~가 기다려진다'라는 표현은 'I can't wait for+명사'를 이용한다.

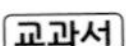

Grammar

핵심 Check
p.128~129

1 (1) strong enough (2) to win (3) for young students
2 (1) intensely (2) but (3) are they

시험대비 기본평가
p.130

01 (1) popular enough to win the award
(2) are easy enough to sing
(3) brave but also very nice
(4) is not only lovely but also smart
02 (1) Their music is great enough to make their fans excited.
(2) Their fans are excited enough to cry out.
(3) Pinocchio is not only popular but also very nice.
(4) I know not only the meaning of "eager" but also the meaning of "eagerness".
03 (1) The singer is tall enough to reach the shelf.
(2) The flower is big enough to cover the woman's face.

01 (1), (2) '~할 만큼 충분히 …한'의 문장은 '형용사/부사+enough to+동사원형'의 형태로 쓴다. (3), (4) '~뿐만 아니라 …도 역시' 의 문장은 'not only ~ but also ...'의 형태로 쓴다.
02 (1) 'enough'는 형용사/부사 뒤에 위치한다. (2) 'enough' 다음에 to부정사를 쓴다. (3) 'not only ~ but also ...'에 be동사의 보어로 둘 다 형용사를 써야 한다. (4) 'not only ~ but also ...' 사이에 두 어구의 형태를 일치시킨다.
03 '~할 만큼 충분히 …한'의 문장은 '형용사/부사+enough to+동사원형'의 형태로 쓴다.

시험대비 실력평가
p.131~133

01 ⑤ 02 ③ 03 ④ 04 ⑤
05 ⑤ 06 ③
07 The room is big enough to accommodate up to 100 people. 08 ④
09 (1) He was so diligent that he could finish the work. 또는 He is so diligent that he can finish the work.
(2) Tom as well as his parents is eating chicken. 또는 His parents as well as Tom are eating chicken.
10 The puzzle was easy enough for me to solve.
11 ①
12 (1) nice enough (2) too (3) to fight
(4) wear it (5) it can run 13 ①, ④
14 This building is strong enough to survive a heavy storm.
15 The book is interesting enough to read several times.
16 ④ 17 ⑤
18 The river is deep enough for a huge ship to sail on.
19 ③ 20 (1) lovely (2) strong

01 enough는 형용사와 부사는 뒤에서, 명사는 앞 또는 뒤에서 수식한다. 형용사 'shy'를 앞에서 수식하는 단어로 'enough'를 사용할 수 없다. ⑤에는 'too'가 적절하다.
02 의미가 올바른 것은 ②, ③, ⑤이나 어법까지 적절하게 쓰인 문장은 ③이다. ③ 나뿐만 아니라 Oliver도 독일어를 학생들에게 가르친다. ① 나와 Oliver 둘 중 한 사람이 독일어를 학생들에게 가르친다. ② 나뿐만 아니라 Oliver도 독일어를 학생들에게 가르친다.(teach → teaches) ④ 나와 Oliver 둘 다 독일어를 학생들에게 가르치지 않는다. ⑤ 나와 Oliver 둘 다 독일어를 학생들에게 가르친다.(teaches → teach)
03 형용사 'warm'을 뒤에서 수식하면서 'to부정사'와 짝을 이루는 단어로 'enough'가 적절하다.
04 'enjoy'는 동명사를 목적어로 하는 동사이므로, 'not only 동명사 but also 동명사'의 형태로 써야 한다.
05 ①~④: (원인) 날씨가 매우 추웠다. (결과) 우리는 교실에 머물렀다. ⑤는 '날씨가 너무 추워서 우리는 교실에 머물 수 없었다.'의 뜻으로 의미가 전혀 다르다.
06 첫 번째 문장에서 접속사 'that'과 함께 쓸 수 있는 것은 'so'이다. 두 번째 문장에서 형용사 'sad'를 앞에서 수식하면서 'to부정사'와 함께 쓸 수 있는 것은 'too'이다.
07 '~할 만큼 충분히 …한'의 문장은 '형용사/부사+enough to+동사원형'의 형태로 쓴다.
08 'so+형용사/부사+that+주어+(can)+동사원형'은 '형용사/부사+enough to+동사원형'의 형태로 문장을 전환한다.
09 (1) 주절과 that절의 시제를 맞춘다. (2) 'as well as' 앞에 있는 주어의 수에 동사를 맞춘다.
10 'enough to'를 사용하여 문장을 만들 때, 문장의 주어와 'to부정사'의 주어가 다를 경우, 부정사의 의미상 주어 'for+목적격'을 부정사 앞에 넣는다. 이때 문장의 주어가 'to부정사'의 목적어 자리에 중복되어 나타나지 않도록 목적어를 쓰지 않아야 한다.
11 'Not only ~ but also ...'가 주어로 쓰일 경우 동사의 수의 일치는 'but also'와 쓰인 주어에 맞춰야 하므로 ①의 동사 'are'를 'is'로 쓰는 것이 올바르다.

12 (1), (2) 부사 'enough'는 형용사나 다른 부사를 뒤에서 수식한다. (3) '형용사/부사+enough to+동사원형'의 형태로 문장을 쓴다. (4) that절에서는 목적어를 생략하지 않는다. (5) 접속사 'that' 다음에는 '주어+동사'의 형태가 오는 것이 올바르다.

13 ② John이 아니고 Mary가 ③ Mary와 John 둘 다 아닌 ⑤ John 또는 Mary 둘 중 한 명이

14 '~할 만큼 충분히 …한'의 문장은 '형용사/부사+enough to+동사원형'의 형태로 쓴다.

15 '~할 만큼 충분히 …한'의 문장은 '형용사/부사+enough to+동사원형'의 형태로 쓴다.

16 ④ '그는 너무 힘이 세서 그 모든 책을 나를 수 없다.'는 내용상 어색하므로 'too strong' 대신 'strong enough'를 쓰는 것이 자연스럽다. (그는 그 모든 책을 나를 수 있을 만큼 충분히 힘이 세다. ① 그는 너무 어려서 학교에 갈 수 없었다. ② 날씨가 너무 더워서 우리는 수영장에 갔다. ③ 그녀는 진실을 지지할 만큼 용감했다. ⑤ 그 상자는 어린이가 들어 올릴 수 있을 만큼 가볍다.

17 상관접속사 'both A and B'가 주어일 때, 그 주어는 복수이다. 그러므로 동사는 'were'가 적절하고, 형용사 'hungry'를 뒤에서 수식하면서 to부정사와 함께 쓸 수 있는 단어로 'enough'가 적절하다.

18 '~할 만큼 충분히 …한'의 문장은 '형용사/부사+enough to+동사원형'의 형태로 쓴다.

19 • 그는 매우 똑똑하다. • 그는 500 조각 퍼즐을 맞출 수 있다. → '그는 500 조각 퍼즐을 맞출 수 있을 정도로 똑똑하다.'에 적절한 문장은 ③이다.

20 두 단어가 짝을 이루어 하나의 접속사 역할을 하는 상관접속사에서는, 사용된 두 어구의 형태를 일치시킨다. 첫 번째 문장은 'heavy'와 같은 형용사인 'lovely'가 적절하고, 두 번째 문장은 be동사의 보어인 형용사 'strong'이 적절하다.

서술형 시험대비

p.134~135

01 (1) Eric is not only kind but also smart.
(2) Not only Jake but also you are a student.
(3) She was not only hardworking but also honest.
(4) Not only you but also he runs fast.
(5) Not only you but also he is going to join our club.

02 (1) This invention is useful enough to make your life much easier.
(2) Your smile is bright enough to light up the classroom.
(3) You not only make us happy but also help us (to) get along well.

03 (1) You can use it as a table for playing table tennis as well as as a door.
(2) She was kind enough to show me how to use chopsticks.

04 (1) Mark visited not only his mother but also his friends.
(2) This building is strong enough to survive a heavy storm.
(3) He is tall enough to touch the ceiling.
(4) They sell not only eggs but also milk.
(5) The box is too heavy for the girl to move.

05 The water is clean enough for us to drink.

06 (1) but also as a cup holder
(2) but also for storing things
(3) but also as lights

07 (A) He is a painter as well as a teacher.
(B) She looks not only friendly but also wise.

08 (1) He is tall enough to be a basketball player.
(2) Sumin ran fast enough to get there on time.
(3) The girl was brave enough to speak in front of many people.
(4) It is warm enough to play outside.
(5) He's cheerful enough to make us feel happy.

01 '~뿐 아니라 …도 역시'의 문장은 'not only ~ but also ...'의 형태로 쓴다. 상관접속사가 주어를 연결할 때에는 but also와 함께 쓰인 주어에 동사의 수를 맞춘다.

02 (1), (2) '~할 만큼 충분히 …한'의 문장은 '형용사/부사+enough to+동사원형'의 형태로 쓴다. (3) '~뿐 아니라 …도 역시'의 문장은 'not only ~ but also ...'의 형태로 쓴다.

03 (1) 'not only ~ but also ...'는 '... as well as ~'로 바꾸어 쓸 수 있다. (2) 'so+형용사/부사+that+주어+(can)+동사원형'은 '형용사/부사+enough to+동사원형'의 형태로 문장을 전환한다.

04 (1) 'not only ~ but also ...'의 문장에서 but은 생략하지 않는다. (2) 'enough to+동사원형'의 형태로 쓴다. (3) 'enough tall'로 형용사 'tall'을 뒤에서 수식하면서 to부정사와 같이 쓰는 것이 자연스럽다. (4) 상관접속사를 쓸 때는 두 어구의 형태가 같아야 하는데, 'They sell milk.'가 자연스러우므로, 전치사 'to'를 쓰지 않는다. (5) 'too ~ to ...'에서 문장의 주어와 to부정사의 목적어가 같을 때 그 목적어는 쓰지 않는다.

05 'enough to'를 사용해서 문장을 쓸 때 문장의 주어와 to부정사의 행위자가 다르면 to부정사 앞에 의미상 주어를 'for 목적격'의 형태로 쓴다.

06 두 단어가 짝을 이루어 하나의 접속사 역할을 하는 상관접속사는 짝을 이루는 두 어구의 형태를 일치시켜야 한다. (1) 'as an umbrella'와 'as a cup holder' (2) 'for going up and down'과 'for storing things' (3) 'as shoes'와 'as lights'

07 두 단어가 짝을 이루어 하나의 접속사 역할을 하는 상관접속사

에서는 사용된 두 어구의 형태를 일치시킨다. 첫 번째 문장은 직업을 나타내는 'a teacher - a painter'가 적절하고, 두 번째 문장은 동사 'look'의 보어인 형용사 'wise - friendly'가 적절하다.

08 (1) 형용사 'tall'을 뒤에서 수식하면서 to부정사와 같이 쓰려면 'enough'를 쓰는 것이 자연스럽다. (2) 'enough'는 형용사/부사의 뒤에 위치한다. (3) '그 소녀는 많은 사람들 앞에서 말할 수 있을 만큼 충분히 용감하다'라고 하는 것이 문맥상 자연스러우므로 'too'를 'enough'로 바꾸어 쓴다. (4), (5) 'enough to부정사'의 형태가 올바르다.

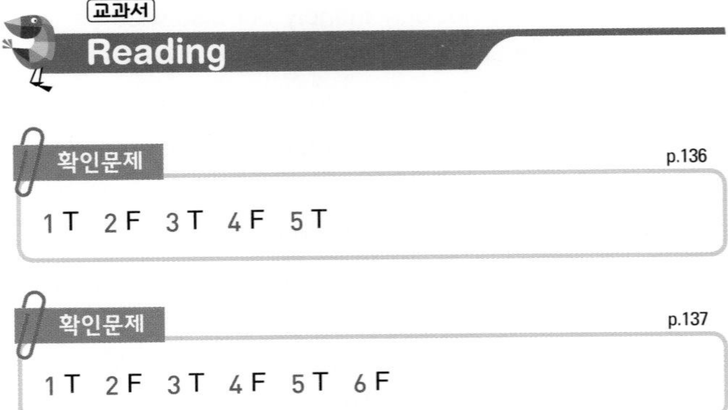

교과서

Reading

확인문제 p.136

1 T 2 F 3 T 4 F 5 T

확인문제 p.137

1 T 2 F 3 T 4 F 5 T 6 F

교과서 확인학습 A p.138~139

01 Ig Nobel
02 happens, backward
03 did research
04 enough to
05 Maybe
06 how about
07 one
08 are awarded for, laugh, think
09 by honoring the unusual, the imaginative
10 are presented by
11 is, filled with, laughable
12 for
13 To save, instead of
14 laugh out loud
15 won an award
16 succeeded in floating
17 a sense of humor
18 bring, to
19 in, for
20 keeps running away
21 Not only, but also, makes
22 a number of, keep, from getting bored
23 two words each
24 an eight-year-old girl called
25 worth less than
26 Throwing, is
27 ends with, did
28 do not receive
29 great honors like
30 a lot more fun

교과서 확인학습 B p.140~141

1 The Ig Nobel Prize
2 "What happens when you walk backward while you are carrying a cup of coffee?"
3 Han Jiwon, a Korean high school student, did research on this topic in 2015.
4 Is this research project good enough to win a Nobel Prize?
5 Maybe not.
6 But how about an Ig Nobel Prize?
7 He won one in 2017 for this fun research.
8 The Ig Nobel Prizes are awarded for discoveries that "first make one laugh and then think."
9 They were started in 1991 by AIR magazine to increase people's interest in science by honoring the unusual and the imaginative.
10 The prizes are presented by real Nobel winners in Sanders Theater at Harvard University.
11 The room is usually filled with people who are eager to cheer for the brave scientists with their "laughable" research.
12 The U.K. Navy won the Ig Nobel Prize for Peace in 2000.
13 To save money, the Navy made its sailors shout, "Bang!" instead of using real bombs.
14 Is that funny enough for you to laugh out loud?
15 Andre Geim also won an award that year.
16 He succeeded in floating a live frog in the air by using magnets.
17 "In my experience, if people don't have a sense of humor, they are usually not very good scientists," he said when he accepted his award.
18 If that still does not bring a smile to your face, how about this?
19 In 2005, Gauri Nanda won the Ig Nobel Prize in Economics for inventing an alarm clock.
20 It keeps running away until the sleeper finally gets out of bed.
21 Not only the winners' fun studies but also the ceremony for the Ig Nobel Prizes makes people laugh.
22 There are a number of interesting things that keep people from getting bored.
23 The opening and closing speeches are just two words each: "Welcome. Welcome." and "Goodbye. Goodbye."
24 If someone talks for too long, an eight-year-old girl called Miss Sweetie Poo shouts repeatedly, "Please stop! I'm bored."

25 Each winner receives ten trillion Zimbabwean dollars, which is worth less than one U.S. dollar.
26 Throwing paper planes is another fun tradition.
27 The Ig Nobel Prize ceremony ends with the words, "If you didn't win a prize — and if you did — better luck next year!"
28 The winners do not receive lots of money.
29 And the awards are not great honors like the Nobel Prizes.
30 But the Ig Nobel Prizes make science a lot more fun!

시험대비 실력평가

p.142~145

01 ⑤ 02 ③ 03 ④ 04 ⑤
05 ③ 06 shouting → shout
07 funny enough for you to laugh
08 He won it in 2000. 09 ③ 10 ③, ④
11 are → is 12 ③ 13 ②
14 won a prize 15 ④ 16 ②
17 awarded 18 ④
19 ⑤ 20 running 21 using magnets
22 (A) with (B) did (C) like
23 Unless you won a prize
24 (A) Ig Nobel (B) Nobel (C) Ig Nobel
25 ③ 26 The Ig Nobel Prizes
27 ⓐ unusual people ⓓ imaginative people

01 ⓐ on: ~에 관하여, ⓑ for: (이유·원인을 나타내어) ~으로
02 ③번 다음 문장의 But에 주목한다. 주어진 문장의 내용과 상반되는 내용을 뒤이어 소개하고 있으므로 ③번이 적절하다.
03 "first make one laugh and then think"로 고치는 것이 적절하다.
04 돈을 아끼기 위해, 해군에서는 선원들에게 진짜 폭탄을 사용하는 대신에 "쾅!"이라고 소리치게 했다고 하는 것이 적절하다. ② fake: 가짜의, blow: 강타, ④ artificial: 인공적인
05 be eager[anxious/dying] to 동사원형 = be eager[anxious/dying] for 명사[동명사] = long to 동사원형 = long for 명사[동명사]: ~하고 싶은 생각이 간절하다, be anxious about: ~에 대해 염려하다
06 사역동사(made)의 목적격보어이므로 shouting을 원형부정사 shout로 고치는 것이 적절하다.
07 so ~ that ... can = enough to
08 영국 해군이 이그노벨상을 탄 것과 같은 해에 탔다고 했으므로, 2000년에 탔다.
09 ⓑ와 ③: 살아 있는(형용사), ① 살다[생존하다](동사), ② 생방송[생중계/실황]으로(부사), ④ (공연이) 라이브의, 실황인(형용사), ⑤ (기록이나 기억에) 남다(동사)
10 ⓐ와 ①, ②, ⑤: 반복해서, ③, ④: 갑자기
11 금액을 나타내는 ten trillion Zimbabwean dollars는 단일 개념으로 생각해서 단수동사로 받는다.
12 만일 누군가가 너무 오랫동안 말을 하면 Miss Sweetie Poo가 "Please stop! I'm bored."라고 외친다고 했으므로, 수상 연설을 길게 해야만 한다는 것은 이그노벨상 시상식의 재미있는 전통에 해당하지 않는다.
13 very는 원급을 강조하는 말이고, 나머지는 다 비교급을 강조하는 말이다.
14 'did'는 'won a prize'를 대신하는 대동사이다.
15 (B)와 ④: ~와 (똑)같이[마찬가지로], …처럼(전치사), ①과 ③ (~을) 좋아하다(동사), ② 비슷한(형용사), ⑤ ~한대로[처럼](접속사)
16 돈을 아끼기 위해, 해군에서는 선원들에게 진짜 폭탄을 사용하는 대신에 "쾅!"이라고 소리치게 했다고 하는 것이 적절하다. ①과 ⑤: ~에 더하여, ~뿐 아니라, ③ ~에 덧붙여, ~와 마찬가지로, ④ ~에도 불구하고
17 present: (특히 공식적인 의식을 통해) 주다, 수여[증정]하다, award: <사람에게 상·장학금 등을> (심사하여) 수여하다, 주다
18 '시상식 시기'는 알 수 없다. ① 진짜 노벨상 수상자들, ② Sanders Theater at Harvard University, ③ '웃기는' 연구를 한 용감한 과학자들을 열렬히 격려하고자 하는 사람들, laughable: 웃기는, 터무니없는, ⑤ 영국 해군
19 '사람들이 유머 감각이 없다면, 그들은 대개 별로 훌륭한 과학자가 아니다'라는 앞 문장의 Andre Geim의 말과 어울리는 말로는 ⑤번이 적절하다. ① 안락, 편안, ② 후회, ③ 존경, ④ inner: 내면의
20 keep ~ing: 계속해서 ~하다
21 '자석을 이용해서' 그 일을 해냈다.
22 (A) '이그노벨상 시상식은 ~로 끝난다.'고 해야 하므로 with가 적절하다. end with: (…으로) 끝나다, end up: 결국 (어떤 처지에) 처하게 되다, (B) 'won a prize'를 대신하는 대동사이므로 did가 적절하다. (C) 노벨상과 '같은'이라고 해야 하므로 like가 적절하다. like: ~와 같은, alike: [형용사] (명사 앞에는 안 씀) (아주) 비슷한
23 unless = if ~ not
24 비록 '이그노벨'상의 상금이 많지 않고 수상자들이 '노벨'상 수상자들처럼 훌륭한 영광을 얻는 것도 아니지만, '이그노벨'상은 과학을 훨씬 더 재미있게 만든다.
25 ⓐ와 ③: 부사적 용법의 부사 수식 용법, 나머지도 다 부사적 용법이지만 ① 판단의 근거, ② 목적, ④ 결과, ⑤ 원인
26 '이그노벨상'을 가리킨다.
27 the+형용사 = 복수 보통명사

서술형 시험대비 p.146~147

01 (A) awarded (B) honoring
02 Is this research project good enough to win a Nobel Prize?
03 (A) Ig Nobel Prize (B) fun
04 Real Nobel winners present the prizes in Sanders Theater at Harvard University.
05 save money
06 To save money, the Navy made its sailors shout, "Bang!" instead of using real bombs.
07 unless people have a sense of humor
08 (A) floating (B) a sense of humor
09 The ceremony for the Ig Nobel Prizes as well as the winners' fun studies makes people laugh.
10 (1) **개회사와 폐회사는 단지 두 마디이다.**
(2) **만일 누군가가 너무 오랫동안 말을 하면, Miss Sweetie Poo라고 하는 여덟 살짜리 여자아이가 "제발 멈춰요! 지루해요."라고 계속 외친다.**
(3) **각 수상자는 미국의 1달러보다 가치가 낮은 10조의 짐바브웨 달러를 받는다.**
(4) **종이비행기를 날린다.**
11 Maybe this research project is not good enough to win a Nobel Prize.
12 interest in science

01 (A) 이그노벨상이 '수여된다'고 해야 하므로 awarded가 적절하다. award: ~에게 〔상벌·장학금 따위〕를 주다, 수여하다, reward: 보상[보답/사례]하다, (B) '높이 평가함으로써'라고 해야 하므로 honoring이 적절하다. honor: 존경하다, ignore: 무시하다
02 enough는 형용사를 뒤에서 수식한다.
03 그는 한국의 고등학생이었고, 2015년에 그가 했던 '재미있는' 조사 때문에 2017년에 '이그노벨상'을 받았다.
04 Real Nobel winners를 주어로 하여 고치는 것이 적절하다.
05 돈을 아끼기 위해, 해군에서는 선원들에게 진짜 폭탄을 사용하는 대신에 "쾅!"이라고 소리치게 했다.
06 '돈을 아끼기 위해, 해군에서는 선원들에게 진짜 폭탄을 사용하는 대신에 "쾅!"이라고 소리치게 한 것'을 가리킨다.
07 unless = if ~ not
08 Andre Geim은 자석을 이용해서 살아 있는 개구리를 공중에 '띄우는 데' 성공했고 이그노벨상을 받았다. 그는 수상 연설에서 '유머 감각'을 좋은 과학자의 필수적인 자질로 언급했다.
09 not only A but also B = B as well as A: A뿐만 아니라 B도
10 뒤에 이어지는 내용 네 가지를 쓰면 된다.
11 'Maybe this research project is not good enough to win a Nobel Prize.'에서 'Maybe not.'만 남긴 것이다.
12 *AIR* 잡지는 특이하고 창의적인 사람들을 높이 평가함으로써 '과학에 대한 사람들의 흥미'를 늘리기 위해 그것들을 시작했다.

영역별 핵심문제 p.149~153

01 unusual 02 ③ 03 worried 04 ⑤
05 ① 06 ④ 07 laughing → laugh
08 ⑤ 09 ③ 10 ④ 11 ③
12 ⑤
13 Not only Marie Curie but also her daughter was awarded the Nobel Prize.
14 ③ 15 ③
16 by email as well as on the phone
17 (1) Ted was kind enough to carry my bag.
(2) Vivian worked hard enough to save lots of money.
(3) The yard is so big that we can ride bikes in it.
18 ② 19 who[that] is 20 ②
21 by 22 so, that, can
23 (B) ②, ④, ⑤ (C) ①, ③ 24 ③, ④
25 ⑤ 26 ②
27 This invention is so useful that it can make your life much easier.
28 ④

01 반의어 관계이다. 유용한 – 쓸모없는 : 일반적인 – 특이한
02 (a) 우리는 비가 왔기 때문에 수영장에서 나와야 했다. (b) 그 나라의 대통령은 전쟁을 끝내고 평화를 가져오기를 희망했다.
03 '일어날지도 모르는 문제나 불쾌한 일들에 관해 생각하고 있기 때문에 불행한'의 의미를 갖고 본문의 단어 worry를 활용한 형용사 'worried'가 적절하다.
04 액체의 위에 있고 가라앉지 않다
05 하기를 자랑스러워하는 어떤 것
06 imaginative는 '상상력이 풍부한'이라는 뜻이고, '가상의'는 'imaginary'를 사용한다.
07 사역동사 make는 목적보어 자리에 동사원형을 사용한다.
08 '준비됐니?'라는 말에 B가 '음, 그런 것 같아, 하지만 자신 있어'라고 말하는 것은 어색하다. '준비되었지만 긴장이 되다 또는 불안하다'라는 의미가 오는 것이 자연스럽다.
09 사역동사 let은 목적보어 자리에 동사원형을 사용한다. to show를 show로 바꾸어야 한다.
10 대화의 첫 문장 '수학여행 장기 자랑에서 무엇을 할 거니?'라는 물음에 대한 대답에서 '장기 자랑을 기대하기'라는 것을 알 수 있다.
11 수업 시간에 선생님들이 말하는 것을 흉내 내고 농담도 할 사람은 미소가 아니라 지민이다.
12 주어진 문장의 'that'은 원인과 결과를 나타내는 'that'이다. 이와 같이 쓰인 것은 ⑤이다. ①, ② 명사절을 이끄는 접속사 ③, ④ 관계대명사
13 'Not only ~ but also ...'가 주어로 쓰일 경우 수의 일치는 'but also'와 쓰인 주어에 맞춘다.

14 ③ '방은 내가 책을 읽을 수 있을 정도로 충분히 어두웠다.'의 뜻으로 어색한 문장이다.

15 a. jump → jumps, c. such → so, e. making → to make

16 'not only ~ but also ...'는 '... as well as ~'로 바꾸어 쓸 수 있다.

17 (1), (2) '~할 만큼 충분히 …한'의 문장은 '형용사/부사+enough to+동사원형'의 형태로 쓴다. (3) 'so+형용사/부사+that+주어+동사'의 형태로 '매우 ~해서 …할 수 있다'라는 의미의 문장을 쓴다.

18 turn off the light: 불을 끄다

19 주격 관계대명사와 be동사가 생략되어 있다.

20 ⓑ와 ①, ④: 동명사, ②, ③, ⑤: 현재분사

21 ⓐ 행위자를 나타내는 by, ⓑ by ~ing: ~함으로써

22 ~ enough to = so ~ that ... can

23 (B)와 ②, ④, ⑤: 'a+보통명사'를 받은 대명사, (C)와 ①, ③: 일반인을 나타내는 대명사

24 ⓐ와 ①, ②, ⑤: 마침내, 결국, ③ 무엇보다도, ④ 적어도

25 ⑤ Gauri Nanda가 발명한 자명종은 잠자는 사람을 계속 쫓아다니는 것이 아니라, 잠자는 사람이 결국 침대 밖으로 나올 때까지 계속 도망을 다닌다.

26 ⓐ와 ② (자격·기능 등이) ~으로(전치사), ① [이유·원인] ~이므로, ~이기 때문에(접속사), ③ [보통 'as ~ as ...'로 형용사·부사 앞에서] …와 같은 정도로('as ~ as ...'에서, 앞의 as가 지시부사, 뒤의 as는 접속사), ④ [때] ~일 때(접속사), ⑤ [비례] ~함에 따라, ~할수록(접속사)

27 ~ enough to = so ~ that ... can

28 not only[just/simply/merely] A but also B = B as well as A = not only[just/simply/merely] A but B as well: A뿐만 아니라 B도, not A but B: A가 아니라 B

단원별 예상문제

p.154~157

01 float 02 ③ 03 Break a leg

04 ②

05 He's going to talk like his teachers do in class and tell some jokes.

06 ③ 07 and → or, one thing → two things

08 I'll keep my fingers crossed

09 ④ 10 ⑤

11 not only putting → not only for putting 12 ③

13 (1) Tommy is not only strong but also wise.

(2) She has not only knowledge but also courage.

(3) I'm good at not only dancing but also singing.

(4) Not only you but also he wants to see the movie.

14 What happens when you walk backward while you are carrying a cup of coffee?

15 ②, ⑤

16 *AIR* magazine started them in 1991

17 ③ 18 successful 19 ④

20 (A) laugh (B) think 21 ⑤

22 ①, ②, ③ 23 to throw 24 ④

01 반의어 관계이다. 뒤로 - 앞으로 : 가라앉다 - 뜨다

02 '폭발할 물질로 만들어진 무기'란 의미로 '폭탄'이 적절하다.

03 'Break a leg!(행운을 빌어!)'라는 표현은 주로 공연이나 행사, 경기 등을 앞두고 있는 사람에게 '행운을 빌어!'라고 격 려할 때 자주 쓰인다.

04 지민이 '수업 시간에 선생님들이 말하는 것을 흉내 내고 농담도 할 거야.'라는 말에 → (E) 그것이 기대된다는 말이 오고 → (A) 쇼에 대한 걱정을 말하고 → (D) 긴장을 풀어주며 행운을 비는 표현이 나오고 → (B) 감사의 대답이 온다. 그래서 네 번째 오는 대화는 (B)가 적절하다.

05 질문: 지민은 장기 자랑에서 무엇을 할 것인가? - 지민은 수업 시간에 선생님들이 말하는 것을 흉내 내고 농담도 할 것이다.

06 대화의 흐름상 긴장한 상대방에게 행운을 비는 말이나 긴장을 풀어주는 표현이 오는 것이 적절하다. ③번의 '포기하지 마!'라는 의미는 들어가기에 어색하다.

07 첫 문장은 '이것은 도마니, 아니면 새 모이통이니?'라는 의미로 and를 or로 바꾸어 준다. 그리고 도마일 뿐만 아니라 새 모이통이기도 하다고 했기 때문에 동시에 두 가지를 할 수 있다.

08 '행운을 빌어!'라고 할 때 'I'll keep my fingers crossed!'라고 한다.

09 민지의 엄마가 농구를 할 것을 기대하고 있는 것은 아니다.

10 ⑤번은 빨리 상을 받고 싶다는 의미고, 나머지는 상대에게 행운을 빌어주는 표현이다.

11 '~뿐 아니라 …도 역시'의 문장은 'not only ~ but also ...'의 형태로 쓰고 상관접속사에 쓰인 두 어구의 형태를 일치시켜야 한다. 이때 'but also'에서 'You can use it for controlling the TV.'가 적절한 문장이므로 'not only' 부분을 for+동명사의 형태로 바꾸어 써야 한다.

12 not only 대신 not just[simply, merely]를 쓸 수 있다.

13 (1)~(3) '~뿐 아니라 …도 역시'의 문장은 'not only ~ but also …'의 형태로 쓰고 상관접속사에 쓰인 두 단어의 모양을 일치시켜야 한다. (4) 상관접속사에 주어가 쓰인 경우 'but also' 뒤의 주어에 동사의 수를 일치시킨다.

14 '커피 한 잔을 들고 가면서 뒤로 걸을 때 무슨 일이 일어날까?'를 가리킨다.

15 ⓑ와 ②, ⑤: 관계대명사, ① 지시형용사, ③ 접속사, ④ 지시대명사

16 *AIR* magazine을 주어로 하여 고치는 것이 적절하다.

17 ⓐ in: [성질·능력·기예 등의 분야를 한정하여] ~에서, ⓑ for: [이유·원인] ~ 때문에, ~으로 (인하여)

18 succeed in ~ing = be successful in ~ing

19 위 글은 '초청장'이다. ② 요약, 개요, ③ (신문·잡지의) 글, 기사, ⑤ 광고

20 이그노벨상을 타기 위해서는 사람들을 '웃게' 만드는 것이 사람들을 '생각하게' 만드는 것보다 더 중요하다.

21 누가 상을 수여할지는 알 수 없다. ① In 1991. ② First make one laugh and then think. ③ Thursday, September 14, 2017 6:00 PM. ④ In Sanders Theater at Harvard University.

22 keep/stop/prevent/prohibit A from ~ing: A가 ~하지 못하게 하다, ④ 허락하다, ⑤ 격려[고무]하다, 용기를 북돋우다

23 to부정사를 진주어로 해서 바꿔 쓸 수 있다.

24 개회사와 폐회사는 각각 단지 두 마디이다.

서술형 실전문제

p.158~159

01 I'm looking forward to watching you on the stage.
02 talent show, talk like, tell some jokes, looking forward to
03 I'm looking forward to seeing you at the race.
04 (a) was named (c) have (e) was awarded
05 good enough
06 the unusual and the imaginative
07 (A) laugh (B) think
08 (A) makes (B) is (C) is
09 There are a number of interesting things that[which] keep people from getting bored.
10 It is "Goodbye. Goodbye."

01 '~을 기대한다'의 의미로 'be looking forward to+동명사'를 사용한다.

02 지민과 미소는 장기 자랑에 대해 이야기하고 있다. 지민은 수업 시간에 선생님들이 말하는 것을 흉내 내고 농담도 할 것이다. 미소는 그의 쇼를 기대하고 있다.

03 Soyun이 100미터 달리기를 할 것이라는 말에 네가 경주에서 달리는 모습을 보는 것이 기대된다는 표현이 적절하다.

04 (1) be named after: ~의 이름을 따서 짓다 (2) 선행사가 복수명사 people이므로 동사는 'have'로 쓰는 것이 올바르다. (3) 'Not only ~ but also ...'가 주어로 쓰일 경우 동사의 수의 일치는 'but also'와 쓰인 주어에 맞춰야 한다.

05 밑줄 친 ⓐ는 이 연구 과제가 이그노벨상을 받을 만큼 '충분히 훌륭할까'?를 의미한다.

06 the+형용사 = 복수 보통명사

07 *AIR* 잡지는 과학에 대한 사람들의 흥미를 늘리기 위해 1991년에 그것들을 시작했다. 만약 어떤 발견이 먼저 '웃기고' 나서 다음에 '생각하게' 만들 수 있다면, 그것은 그 상을 수상할 수 있다.

08 (A) not only A but also B에서는 B에 동사의 수를 일치시키고, 위 문장에서는 the ceremony가 B에 해당하므로 makes가 적절하다. (B) which의 선행사는 ten trillion Zimbabwean dollars이고, 돈은 단수 취급하므로 is가 적절하다. (C) 동명사가 주어일 때 단수 취급 하므로 is가 적절하다.

09 keep A from ~ing: A가 ~하지 못하게 하다

10 폐회사는 '안녕. 안녕'이다.

창의사고력 서술형 문제

p.160

|모범답안|

01 (A) A: I'm going to go camping with my parents.
B: Wow! That sounds great.
A: Yeah, I'm really looking forward to it.
(B) A: I'm going to have a basketball game next week, but I'm worried about it.
B: Don't worry. You'll do great. I'll keep my fingers crossed.
A: Thank you.

02 (1) He is clever enough to understand the novel.
(2) He is rich enough to buy the building.
(3) He speaks not only English but also Chinese.
(4) He is interested in not only basketball but also volleyball.

단원별 모의고사

p.161~166

01 ④ 02 eagerness 03 ③
04 ② 05 ① 06 ⑤ 07 ④
08 ④ 09 (A) crossed (B) watching
10 (1) to talk like his teachers do in class
(2) to tell some jokes 11 ③
12 Do I sound like our English teacher?
13 He is very popular as well as nice.
14 She is both beautiful and lovely.
15 She is neither smart nor creative.
16 ④ 17 ①, ④ 18 ③
19 We were brave enough to face the strong enemy.
20 Ted is so old that he can talk about the topic.
21 He has not only knowledge but also experience.
22 I must look after the children as well as feed the animals.
23 (1) cutting a pizza
(2) but also for picking up a piece of pizza

24 (1) Not only she but also you have to leave here.
(2) Not only I but also my brothers like to play with dogs.
(3) Not only I but also my best friend is from Busan.
25 ⓐ an Ig Nobel Prize
ⓑ 커피 한 잔을 들고 가면서 뒤로 걸을 때 무슨 일이 일어날까?
26 makes → make 27 ④ 28 ①
29 a sense of humor
30 (A) an alarm clock (B) gets out of bed
31 the number of → a number of / keeps → keep
32 which is worth less than one U.S. dollar

01 ④번은 '1,000,000,000,000이라는 수'란 의미로 1조를 가리킨다. 'trillion'이 적절하다. 'million'은 '백만'이다.
02 '형용사-명사' 관계이다. 행복한-행복 : 열렬한-열망
03 '당신이 계획한 것을 성취하다'라는 의미로 '성공하다'가 적절하다.
04 춤 대회에 나가게 되어 걱정이 된다는 친구에게 긴장을 풀어주는 ②번의 대답이 가장 적절하다.
05 G의 말에 우리를 항상 웃게 만든다고 했기 때문에 Best Joker 상을 받기를 기대한다는 말이 자연스럽다.
06 민호는 항상 우리를 웃게 만든다는 A의 말에 B가 '걱정하지 마. 너는 잘할 거야.'로 대답하는 것은 어색하다.
07 ④번은 대화의 흐름상 실수할까봐 겁난다고 했기 때문에 '거의 걱정이 되지 않는다.'라는 의미의 'little'을 '조금 걱정이 된다.'라는 의미의 'a little'로 바꾸는 것이 적절하다.
08 G의 마지막 말인 '무대에 선 엄마 모습을 보는 것이 기대돼요.'라는 말로 볼 때 ④에 들어가는 것이 적절하다.
09 (A)는 동사 keep의 목적보어 자리로 목적어인 my fingers의 수동 동작을 나타내는 과거분사 crossed가 적절하다. (B)는 look forward to(전치사) 뒤에 동명사 watching이 적절하다.
10 Jimin은 장기 자랑에서 수업 시간에 선생님이 말하는 것처럼 말하고, 농담을 할 것이다.
11 (A)는 대동사로 앞 문장의 동사 talk을 대신한다.
12 일반동사 의문문으로 'sound like our English teacher'와 중복되는 부분이 생략되어 있다.
13 '~뿐 아니라 …도 역시'의 문장을 'as well as'를 사용하여 쓸 때 강조하는 단어('…도 역시'에 해당하는 말)를 먼저 쓴다.
14 'both A and B'는 'A와 B 둘 다'의 뜻이다.타나다
16 'not only ~ but also ...'의 상관접속사에 쓰인 두 단어의 모양을 일치시켜야 한다. 일반동사 'sing'은 부사와 함께 써야 하므로 형용사 happy는 부사 happily로 쓰는 것이 적절하다.
17 'too ~ to ...'를 사용하여 문장을 만들 때, 문장의 주어와 'to부정사'의 주어가 다를 경우, 부정사의 의미상 주어 'for 목적격'을 to부정사 앞에 넣는다. 이때 문장의 주어가 'to부정사구'의 목적어 자리에 중복되어 나타내지 않도록 목적어를 쓰지 않아야 한다. 'so ~ that'을 사용할 때는 목적어를 생략하지 않는다.
18 a. to put → for putting, b. dance → danced, d. could → can
19 'so+형용사/부사+that+주어+(can)+동사원형'의 문장은 '형용사/부사+enough to+동사원형'의 형태로 전환할 수 있다.
20 'so+형용사/부사+that+주어+(can)+동사원형'의 문장은 '형용사/부사+enough to+동사원형'의 형태로 전환할 수 있다.
21 'not only ~ but also ...'는 '... as well as ~'로 바꾸어 쓸 수 있다.
22 'not only ~ but also ...'는 '... as well as ~'로 바꾸어 쓸 수 있다.
23 (1) 전치사 다음에는 동명사구를 쓴다. (2) 'not only for 동명사'이므로 'but also for 동명사'로 쓴다.
24 'Not only ~ but also ...'가 주어로 쓰일 경우 동사의 수의 일치는 'but also'와 쓰인 주어에 맞춘다. (1) you (2) my brothers (3) my best friend가 주어이고 이 주어에 동사의 수를 일치시킨다.
25 ⓐ '이그노벨상', ⓑ "What happens when you walk backward while you are carrying a cup of coffee?"를 가리킨다.
26 주격 관계대명사 that의 선행사가 복수형인 discoveries이기 때문에 make로 고치는 것이 적절하다.
27 ⓐ와 ①, ③, ④, ⑤: 부사적 용법, ②: 명사적 용법
28 상은 '진짜 노벨상 수상자들'에 의해 수여된다.
29 Andre Geim에 따르면, 매우 훌륭한 과학자가 되기 위해서는 대체로 '유머 감각'이 필요한 조건이다.
30 Gauri Nanda는 잠자는 사람이 결국 침대 밖으로 나와야만 끌 수 있는 '자명종'을 발명했기 때문에, 2005년에 이그노벨 경제학상을 받았다.
31 '많은' 재미있는 것들이라고 해야 하므로 a number of로 고치는 것이 적절하다. the number of: ~의 수, a number of: 많은, that의 선행사가 a number of interesting things이므로 keep으로 고쳐야 한다.
32 be worth: ~의 가치가 있다

교과서 파헤치기

Lesson 1

단어 TEST Step 1 p.02

01 건강에 좋은 02 농담 03 예매하다, 예약하다
04 전달하다 05 그리워하다
06 구할 수 있는, 이용할 수 있는 07 초조한
08 표현 09 글로 쓴, 글로 표현된
10 신사 11 실제로 12 추측하다, 짐작하다
13 선물 14 인간적인, 인간의 15 다양한
16 어조, 말투 17 방귀를 뀌다 18 시각적으로
19 인기 있는 20 완전한, 전체의, 전부의
21 기회, 가능성 22 얼굴의 23 점심시간
24 ~부터, ~ 이후 25 궁금해 하다
26 드디어, 마침내, 마지막으로 27 약속하다; 약속
28 웃음 29 나타내다, 대표하다
30 심지어, ~조차 31 문자, 편지 32 의미 있는
33 눈물 34 이사하다 35 계속해서 연락하다
36 ~와 같은 37 ~을 좋아하다
38 ~을 의미하다, 상징하다 39 큰 소리로 웃다
40 점점 ~해지다 41 ~와 같은 …
42 ~을 몹시 기다리다
43 ... (명사)가 ~(형용사) 한 채로

단어 TEST Step 2 p.03

01 joke 02 actually 03 stick
04 meaningful 05 deliver 06 expression
07 laughter 08 gentleman 09 finally
10 available 11 book 12 healthy
13 whole 14 human 15 promise
16 tone 17 miss 18 facial
19 written 20 visually 21 nervous
22 popular 23 present 24 quite
25 represent 26 move 27 guess
28 wonder 29 chance 30 tear
31 various 32 letter 33 cupboard
34 fried 35 laugh out loud 36 can't wait for
37 stand for 38 the same ~ as 39 care for
40 keep in touch 41 happier than ever
42 take a look at 43 be worried about

단어 TEST Step 3 p.04

1 various, 다양한 2 form, 형식, 방식
3 written, 글로 쓴 4 available, 구할 수 있는
5 visually, 시각적으로 6 since, ~ 이후
7 type, 타자 치다, 입력하다 8 deliver, 전달하다
9 gentleman, 신사 10 represent, 나타내다, 대표하다
11 conversation, 대화 12 symbol, 상징
13 book, 예약[예매]하다 14 emoticon, 이모티콘
15 human, 인간의, 인간적인 16 guess, 추측하다

대화문 TEST Step 1 p.05~07

Get Ready 2

(1) look happy, right / really sad, sick, at all / That's too bad

(2) be, good day, Take a look / glad to eat, can't wait for lunch break

(3) How, feeling, helping, clean / glad to hear that

(4) upset, all right / let, play, after school / Why don't you

Start Off – Listen & Talk A

1. moving, another country, How, feeling / excited to, whole / to hear, was worried about / Actually, miss, a lot / keep in touch / Let's have

2. is moving, How, feeling / going to miss / is going, invite, promised / glad to have, chance, travel

Start Off – Listen & Talk B

how are you feeling / feeling, sad, moving away / sorry, don't be, video chats / Why don't we, as, goodbye gift / something meaningful

Start Off – Speak Up – Mission

How are you / feeling / glad to hear that

Step Up – Real-life Scene

How, feeling / happier, ever / why, didn't you / booked / about / got messages / How cute, emojis, bring, light sticks / I'm glad to hear that, lots of fun

Fun Time

How, feeling / nervous, forgot to bring, How are / nervous, too, glad to find, who feels / too / How / happy, got, grade / angry, broke

Express Yourself A 1

How are / glad to get a present / present / which, sent for / wonder how high, can fly / Let me show

Express Yourself A 2

How, feeling / to cook, favorite / to know what it is / which, delicious, healthy / to try / Wait for, minutes

Check Yourself – Listen & Speak 1

how are you feeling / excited, have, in our class / why, excited / on, team, As you know, needs / I'm glad to hear, hope, joins

Get Ready 2

(1) B: You don't look happy. Are you all right?
G: No, I'm really sad. My dog is sick. He won't eat.
B: That's too bad.

(2) B: It'll be a good day today! Take a look at today's lunch menu.
G: Wow! I'm glad to eat fried chicken! I can't wait for lunch break.

(3) W: Good morning, Mr. Lee. How are you feeling?
M: I'm feeling very happy this morning. Some students are helping me clean the school.
W: I'm glad to hear that.

(4) G: You look upset. Are you all right?
B: My mom won't let me play soccer after school.
G: Why don't you ask her one more time?

Start Off – Listen & Talk A

1. G: Jihun, you're moving to another country next week. How are you feeling?
B: I'm excited to go to a whole new world, Yunju.
G: I'm glad to hear that. I was worried about you.
B: Actually, I'm sad, too. I'll miss all of you a lot.
G: Let's keep in touch online.
B: Okay. Let's have video chats often.

2. G: Minsu, Jihun is moving to Abu Dhabi in the UAE next week. How are you feeling?
B: I'm sad. I'm going to miss him a lot.
G: I'm sad, too, but I'm also happy. We can visit Abu Dhabi. He is going to invite us. He promised.
B: That's great! I'm glad to have a chance to travel to a new country.

Start Off – Listen & Talk B

B: Yena, how are you feeling?
G: I'm feeling very sad, Seho. My best friend Jihun is moving away.
B: Really? I'm sorry. But don't be so sad. You two can have video chats online.
G: You're right.
B: Why don't we make him a photo book as a goodbye gift?
G: Great idea. I'm glad to give him something meaningful.

Start Off – Speak Up – Mission

A: How are you feeling today?
B: I'm feeling happy. Today's lunch is great.
A: I'm glad to hear that.

Step Up – Real-life Scene

Nari: Hi, Jiho. How are you feeling?
Jiho: I'm happier than ever, Nari.
Nari: I know why. You did it, didn't you?
Jiho: Yes. I finally booked four tickets for the VTS concert!
Nari: Good job. Did you tell Minsu and Yujin about that?
Jiho: Sure. Oh, I just got messages from them. They said they are really happy. Look.
Nari: How cute! I like their emojis. They will bring light sticks and a nice camera.
Jiho: I'm glad to hear that. We're going to have lots of fun!

Fun Time

A: How are you feeling?
B: I'm nervous. I forgot to bring my math homework. How are you feeling?
A: I'm nervous, too. I have a math test tomorrow. I'm glad to find someone who feels the same.
B: Me, too.
A: How are you feeling?
B: I'm happy. I got a good grade. How are you feeling?
A: I'm angry. Someone broke my glasses.

Express Yourself A 1

G: How are you feeling today?
B: I'm really glad to get a present for my birthday.
G: What is the present?
B: It's this drone, which our grandpa sent for my birthday.
G: Wow! I wonder how high it can fly.
B: Let me show you.
G: Thanks.

Express Yourself A 2

G: How are you feeling?
M: I'm really glad to cook my favorite food.
G: I want to know what it is.
M: It's *japchae*, which is delicious and healthy.
G: I want to try some.
M: Okay. Wait for 30 minutes!

Check Yourself – Listen & Speak 1

G: Minsu, how are you feeling?
B: I'm really excited, Miso. We have a new student in our class. His name is Kim Kihun.
G: So why are you excited?
B: He was a soccer player on his school team. As you know, my team needs a player.
G: I'm glad to hear that. I hope he joins your team.
B: Thanks a lot.

본문 TEST Step 1 p.11~13

01 How, in, Texts
02 Laughter, human
03 laugh out loud, joke
04 even, writings, as, conversations
05 How, we, that
06 form, written laughter
07 what it means
08 has been used since
09 Even, in, works
10 gentlemen, good night
11 anything important happens, let
12 *Much*, Act, Scene
13 Another, written laughter
14 stands for, Out Loud
15 quite, Rolling on, Laughing
16 expressions, popular, be typed
17 Have, safe trip
18 Make sure, don't miss
19 try, sure, miss
20 for wishing, safe trip
21 represents laughter, text
22 with, open, closed tightly
23 not a word
24 used, represent, facial expression
25 emotion, expresses, feelings, visually
26 can't wait to
27 with tears of joy
28 small, called, emoji
29 laughing, available, laughter, various
30 hit, head, cupboard
31 Are, okay
32 hit, head, cupboard
33 Is, cupboard, okay
34 have grown, laughing sounds
35 needed to break wind
37 loud, so, just did
39 realized, listening, with, earphones
40 facial expressions, voice tones
41 By, care for, with
42 Laugh, written forms, and
43 when, cold out
44 was me yesterday

본문 TEST Step 2 p.14~15

01 How, Texts
02 Laughter, human
03 laugh out loud, somthing funny
04 laugh even in our writings, as
05 How, that
06 form, written laughter
07 what it means
08 has been used since
09 in his works
10 gentlemen, good
11 anything important
12 Act, Scene
13 Another, written laughter
14 stands for Laughing, Loud
15 Rolling on the Floor Laughing
16 expressions, because, can be typed
17 Have a safe trip
18 Make sure, miss
19 miss u
20 wishing me a safe trip
21 represents laughter
22 laughing face with, open, closed tightly
23 a word
24 which, used to represent a facial expression
25 expresses, more visually
26 can't wait to
27 These days, face with tears of joy
28 called
29 available to use, various ways
30 hit my head
31 okay
32 hit, on the cupboard
33 okay
34 have grown bigger, even move, laughing sounds
35 needed to break wind
37 loud, so, just did it
39 realized, listening to, with my earphones
40 represent, facial expressions, deliver, voice tones
41 By using, care for, with them
42 Laugh, written forms, and, laugh
43 cold out
44 This was

본문 TEST Step 3 p.16~18

1 글에서는 어떻게 "하하"라고 웃나요?
2 웃음은 인간 고유의 것이다.
3 우리는 농담을 듣거나 우스운 것을 보거나 행복감을 느끼면 소리 내어 웃는다.
4 우리는 이메일이나 문자 메시지 같은 글 속에서조차 대화에서 하듯이 웃는다.
5 어떻게 그렇게 하는가?
6 "하하"는 문자로 된 웃음의 한 형태이다.
7 모두가 그것이 무엇을 의미하는지 안다.
8 실제로 그것은 오래전부터 사용되어 왔다.
9 셰익스피어조차도 "하하"를 자신의 작품에 사용하였다.
10 DOGBERRY: 하하하! 자, 신사분들, 좋은 밤 보내시오.
11 그리고 만일 뭔가 중요한 일이 일어난다면 나를 찾아서 알려 주시오.
12 (셰익스피어, 헛소동, 3막 3장 4쪽)
13 또 다른 형태의 문자로 된 웃음은 LOL이다.
14 그것은 '크게 소리 내어 웃기'를 상징한다.
15 사람들은 또한 ROFL도 꽤 자주 사용하는데, 그것은 '바닥을 구르면서 웃기'를 의미한다.
16 이 표현들은 상당히 빠르게 타자를 칠 수 있어서 인기를 얻었다.
17 A: 내일 안전한 여행을 해.
18 나를 너무 많이 그리워하지 않도록 해. LOL
19 B: 좋아. 너를 그리워하지 않도록 할게. LOL.
20 안전한 여행을 기원해 줘서 고마워.

21 XD 또한 문자 메시지에서 웃음을 나타낸다.
22 그것은 입을 벌리고 눈을 질끈 감은 채 웃는 얼굴을 보여 준다.
23 XD는 단어가 아니다.
24 그것은 이모티콘이고, 얼굴 표정을 나타내기 위해 사용되는 한 무리의 문자나 상징이다.
25 이모티콘 XD는 우리의 행복한 감정을 하하와 LOL보다 더 시각적으로 표현한다.
26 나는 디즈니랜드에 가는 게 몹시 기다려져. XD
27 요즘 사람들은 '기쁨의 눈물을 흘리는 얼굴'인 를 사용한다.
28 이것은 '이모지'라고 불리는 작은 그림이다.
29 많은 웃는 이모지가 온라인에서 사용될 수 있고, 그래서 사람들은 다양한 방식으로 자신들의 웃음을 표현할 수 있다.
30 A: 찬장에 머리를 부딪쳤어.
31 B: 오, 이런! 너 괜찮니?
32 A: 찬장에 머리를 부딪쳤어.
33 B: 어 어! 천장 괜찮니?
34 어떤 이모지들은 크기가 커졌고, 또 어떤 것들은 심지어 움직이거나 웃음소리를 내기까지 한다.
35 A: 그래서 어제 나는 식당에 있었는데 정말 방귀를 뀌어야 했어..
36 B: 그리고 …
37 A: 음, 음악이 정말 시끄럽길래 나는 그냥 뀌어 버렸어.
38 B: 그리고 …
39 A: 그리고 그때 나는 내가 이어폰을 끼고 음악을 듣고 있다는 걸 깨달았지.
40 웃음 표시는 우리의 얼굴 표정을 나타내고 우리의 목소리 어조를 전달할 수 있다.
41 다양한 웃음 표시를 사용함으로써, 우리는 친구들을 얼마나 좋아하는지 또는 그들과 함께 있어서 얼마나 행복한지를 그들에게 보여 줄 수 있다.
42 웃어라, 문자로 된 형태로라도. 그러면 친구들도 여러분과 함께 웃을 것이다.
43 추울 때 내 모습이네.
44 이건 어제의 나야.

본문 TEST Step 4-Step 5

p.19~23

1 How Do You "Ha-Ha" in Your Texts?
2 Laughter is human.
3 We laugh out loud when we hear a joke, see something funny, or feel happy.
4 We laugh even in our writings, such as emails or texts, as we do in our conversations.
5 How do we do that?
6 "Ha-ha" is a form of written laughter.
7 Everyone knows what it means.
8 Actually, it has been used since long ago.
9 Even Shakespeare used "ha–ha" in his works.
10 DOGBERRY: Ha, ha, ha! Well, gentlemen, good night.
11 And if anything important happens, find me and let me know.
12 (Shakespeare, Much Ado About Nothing Act 3, Scene 3, Page 4)
13 Another form of written laughter is LOL.
14 It stands for "Laughing Out Loud."
15 People also use ROFL quite often, which means "Rolling on the Floor Laughing."
16 These expressions have become popular because they can be typed quite quickly.
17 A: Have a safe trip 2mrw.
18 Make sure u don't miss me too much. LOL
19 B: OK. I'll try to make sure I don't miss u. LOL
20 Thanks for wishing me a safe trip.
21 XD also represents laughter in text.
22 It shows a laughing face with a mouth open and eyes closed tightly.
23 XD is not a word.
24 It's an emoticon, which is a group of letters or symbols used to represent a facial expression.
25 The emoticon XD expresses our happy feelings more visually than ha–ha and LOL do.
26 I can't wait to go to Disneyland. XD
27 These days, people use — a "face with tears of joy."
28 This is a small picture called an "emoji."
29 Lots of laughing emojis are available to use online, so people can express their laughter in various ways.
30 A: I hit my head on the cupboard.
31 B: Oh, my! Are you okay?
32 A: I hit my head on the cupboard.
33 B: Uh-oh! Is the cupboard okay?
34 Some emojis have grown bigger, and some even move or make laughing sounds.
35 A: So yesterday, I was in a restaurant, and I really needed to break wind.
36 B: And ...
37 A: Well, the music was really loud, so I just did it.
38 B: And ...
39 A: And then I realized I was listening to music with my earphones.
40 Laughing marks can represent our facial expressions and deliver our voice tones.
41 By using various laughing marks, we can show our friends how much we care for them or how happy we are with them.

42 Laugh, even in written forms, and your friends will laugh with you.
43 Me when it's cold out
44 This was me yesterday

구석구석지문 TEST Step 1

p.24

Self-study Guide

1. when you live
2. live in
3. Could you, when the next bus will come
4. in ten minutes

Link to the World

1. what the color red means
2. who cheer for, means
3. traffic light
4. Of all the meanings, never fails

Express Yourself C

1. guess what my brother got
2. got, from, who lives in

구석구석지문 TEST Step 2

p.25

Self-study Guide

1. A: Can you tell me where you live?
2. B: Sure. I live in Mokpo.
3. A: Could you tell me when the next bus will come?
4. B: Sure. It will come in ten minutes.

Link to the World

1. Do you know what the color red means.
2. • This is the uniform of the Reds, who cheer for the Korean soccer team. Red means "power" on this uniform.
3. • Red on a traffic light means "stop."
4. • Of all the meanings of red, "love" is my favorite. "Love never fails."

Express Yourself C

1. Yeji: Can you guess what my brother got for his birthday?
2. He got a drone from our grandpa, who lives in Busan.

Lesson 2

단어 TEST Step 1

p.26

01 끔찍한, 지독한 02 땀투성이의, 땀에 젖은
03 반장 04 더러운 05 두 배가 되다
06 활동 07 다른, 그 밖의 08 텅 빈, 비어 있는
09 제안하다 10 재채기하다 11 기쁨
12 쓰레기 봉투 13 걸다, 매달다 14 끈, 줄
15 힘든 16 채우다
17 불평하다, 투덜거리다 18 수리하다
19 인정하다, 시인하다 20 먼지
21 상추 22 이웃, 인근 주민 23 ~ 중에, ~ 사이에
24 쓰레기 25 포장지 26 상상하다
27 콩 28 도움이 되는, 유용한
29 궁금해 하다, ~할까 생각하다
30 쓰레기 더미, 지저분함, 엉망진창
31 배정하다, 배치하다, 맡기다 32 광경
33 단단히, 꽉 34 인기 있는
35 ~에 공들이다[애쓰다]
36 ~을 맡아, ~을 담당하여
37 설치하다, 마련하다 38 ~을 돌보다
39 A를 B로 채우다 40 A를 B로 나누다 41 A를 B로 바꾸다
42 ~할 준비가 되다 43 갑자기 나오다, 불쑥 나타나다

단어 TEST Step 2

p.27

01 awful 02 dirty 03 suggest
04 double 05 fill 06 complain
07 fix 08 trash bag 09 dust
10 helpful 11 hit 12 string
13 assign 14 imagine 15 tight
16 empty 17 pleasure 18 admit
19 among 20 wrap 21 sweaty
22 bean 23 sneeze 24 hang
25 tough 26 popular 27 row
28 sight 29 trash 30 lettuce
31 mess 32 neighborhood 33 nursing home
34 heavy 35 be full of 36 take care of
37 set up 38 turn A into B 39 work on
40 be ready to-V 41 divide A into B 42 across from
43 in charge of

단어 TEST Step 3 p.28

1 lot, 부지, 구획 2 fix, 고치다 3 fill, 채우다
4 awful, 끔찍한 5 tough, 힘든 6 sweaty, 땀에 젖은
7 empty, 텅 빈, 비어 있는 8 volunteer, 자원하다
9 complain, 불평하다 10 double, 두 배가 되다
11 admit, 인정[시인]하다 12 assign, 배치하다, 맡기다
13 suggest, 제안하다 14 dust, 먼지
15 nursing home, 양로원 16 hang, 매달다

대화문 TEST Step 1 p.29~30

Get Ready 2

(1) flower pot, heavy, Can I / kind, Thank you
(2) Let me help, fix / hold, tight, for helping
(3) Let's talk about, for / How about drawing, dirty / Sounds, Anything else

Start Off – Listen & Talk A

1. need, Let's / how about putting, flower pots by, make, prettier / good idea
2. How about hanging / Why don't you bring, good at painting / Thank, for saying, bring, mine
3. about, corner, Any / How about making, corner, bring / for suggesting

Start Off – Listen & Talk B

Don't / right, Let's talk, together / need to put, member, helpful for us to learn, members' / also need, plan, school year / help, remember / suggesting

Step Up – Real-life Scene

talk about, better / Let me tell, trash, bus stop / agree, Why don't we / cam put, bench, too / helpful, the elderly / How about putting, around, make, more beautiful / for suggesting, shall we / problem

Fun Time

Let's talk, town party / Why don't we cook / Thank, for

Express Yourself A

1. for coming, talk about / under, most, cleaned around, planted / popular place among
2. Let's talk, school gate, What do you think of / leaders set up, put up, a lot more, events / Let's thank, class leaders

대화문 TEST Step 2 p.31~32

Get Ready 2

(1) B: The flower pot looks heavy. Can I help you, Ms. Min?
W: You're so kind. Thank you very much.
(2) G: Let me help you fix the bench.
M: Please hold this tight. Thank you for helping me.
(3) B: Let's talk about what we can do for our town.
G: How about drawing pictures on the dirty walls?
B: Sounds good. Anything else?

Start Off – Listen & Talk A

1. B: What do we need in our club room? Let's talk about it.
G: Sure. Well, how about putting some flower pots by the windows? They'll make our room prettier.
B: That's a good idea. Thank you, Jiu.
2. B: How about hanging some pictures?
G: Good. Why don't you bring one of your pictures? You're good at painting, Seho.
B: Thank you for saying that. I'll bring one of mine.
3. B: Let's talk about the corner this time. Any ideas?
G: How about making a small library in the corner of the club room? I will bring some books tomorrow.
B: Great idea! Thank you for suggesting it, Minju.

Start Off – Listen & Talk B

G: Seho, we need something on the wall, too. Don't you think so?
B1: You're right. Let's talk about it together.
G: I think we need to put the club member list there. It'll be helpful for us to learn the new members' names.
B2: That's a good idea. We also need our plan for this school year on the wall.
G: Right! That'll really help us remember important school events.
B1: Thank you for suggesting great ideas, everyone. We are a good team.

Step Up – Real-life Scene

G1: Let's talk about how we can make our town better.
B: Let me tell you first. There's too much trash at the bus stop.
G2: I agree. Why don't we clean the place together?
B: Good. We can put a bench there, too.
G1: Great idea. It'll be helpful for the elderly.
G2: How about putting some flower pots around the

bench? They'll make thebus stop more beautiful.

G1: Thank you for suggesting great ideas, everyone. Then, shall we start tomorrow?

G2, B: No problem.

Fun Time

A: Let's talk about the town party.

B: Okay. Why don't we cook *bibimbap*?

A: Wonderful. Thank you for your idea.

Express Yourself A

1. M1: Thank you for coming, everyone. Let's talk about the Clean School Project.

W: I like the corner under the tree most. The Science Club cleaned around the corner and planted the tree.

M2: I like it, too. It is a very popular place among the students.

2. M1: Let's talk about the school gate this time. What do you think of it?

W: The class leaders set up the board and put up some posters. We can know a lot more about school events.

M2: Right! They did a good job. Let's thank the class leaders.

본문 TEST Step 1

p.33~34

01 Green Thumbs
02 complained, whole day
03 work, neighborhood, far better
04 why we were working
05 ugly, empty, across from
06 full, wraps, other, imagine 07 at, bet, there, too
08 ages, sizes, ready, work
09 up, awful mess, into 10 where to begin
11 only way, just, start
12 divided, into, assigned, to
13 By lunchtime, sweaty, wear
14 filled, with, ready, pull
15 filled, made us sneeze
16 end, admit, much better 17 first, the toughest
18 followed, rows, seeds, watered
19 about, stopped complaining, up
20 First, lettuce, then, beans 21 grew so fast
22 couldn't believe 23 doubled, size, few
24 later, every, what, ready
25 Lots, there, enjoy, sights
26 suddenly hit, what, thing
27 proud, have been, part
28 charge, picking, nursing home
29 will go to, in
30 even better, that, become

본문 TEST Step 2

p.35~36

01 Thumbs
02 complained, whole day
03 making, work, far better, to do
04 why we were working
05 ugly, empty, across from
06 was full of, wraps, broken, every other kind, you can imagine
07 I bet, bet there are, too
08 all ages and sizes, ready to work
09 clean up this awful mess, turn, into
10 where to begin
11 only way to do, just to start
12 divided, into, with string, assigned, to
13 By lunchtime, sweaty, wear gloves
14 filled, with waste, were ready to pull
15 As, dust filled, made us sneeze
16 At the end of, had to admit, much better
17 the toughest
18 made rows, watered
19 stopped complaining, popping up
20 First, the lettuce 21 grew so fast
22 couldn't believe
23 in size in just a few days
24 later, what new flowers are ready
25 Lots of, to enjoy the sights 26 suddenly hit me
27 proud, have been a part
28 I'm in charge of picking, nursing home
29 will go to
30 even better, that, has become

본문 TEST Step 3

p.37~38

1 식물을 잘 키우는 사람들
2 나는 온종일 불평했다.
3 우리 부모님은 나를 이웃 프로젝트에서 일하게 하셨지만, 나에게는 훨씬 더 나은 할 일들이 있었다.
4 나는 우리가 왜 이곳에서 일하고 있어야 하는지 이해하지 못했다.
5 그곳은 그저 Johnny's Shop 건너편에 있는 볼품없고, 오래되고, 텅 빈 지역이었다.
6 그곳은 잡초와 패스트푸드 포장지와 낡은 신문, 깨진 유리,

그리고 상상할 수 있는 모든 다른 종류의 더러운 쓰레기로 가득 차 있었다.

7 그 첫날 아침에 그곳을 보았을 때, 나는 "틀림없이 저 안에는 뱀들도 있을 거야."라고 생각했다.

8 그날 일할 준비가 된 — 모든 연령대와 몸집을 가진 — 우리 20명이 있었다.

9 나는 이 끔찍하게 더러운 곳을 청소하여 정원으로 바꿀 수 있다고 생각하지 않았다.

10 우리는 모두 어디서부터 시작해야 할지 궁금해 하고 있었다

11 그때 Hernandez 씨가 "그것을 할 유일한 방법은 그냥 시작하는 것입니다."라고 말했다.

12 그러고 나서, 그는 그 지역을 끈으로 네 구역으로 나누고, 5명을 각 구역에 배치했다.

13 점심 무렵, 나는 덥고, 땀이 났으며, 아버지가 나에게 장갑을 끼도록 한 것이 기뻤다.

14 우리는 쓰레기 봉투 50개를 쓰레기로 채웠고, 잡초를 뽑을 준비가 되어 있었다.

15 우리가 뽑으면 뽑을수록, 먼지가 공기를 가득 메워서 재채기가 나왔다.

16 그날이 끝날 무렵, 나는 그 지역이 훨씬 더 나아 보인다는 것을 인정해야 했다.

17 그 첫날이 가장 힘들었다.

18 그다음 주말에 우리는 열을 만들고, 꽃과 채소 씨앗을 심고, 물을 주었다.

19 약 2주 뒤, 나는 식물들이 자라나기 시작한 것을 발견했을 때 불평하는 것을 멈추었다!

20 처음에는 상추, 그러고 나서, 콩과 토마토.

21 그것들은 아주 빨리 자랐다.

22 나는 믿을 수가 없었다!

23 콩 식물은 1인치 자라났고, 토마토는 며칠 만에 크기가 두 배가 되었다.

24 두 달이 지난 지금, 나는 매일 어떤 새로운 꽃들이 피어날 준비가 되었는지 보러 그곳에 가는 것을 좋아한다.

25 이웃의 많은 사람이 그곳에서 만나 풍경을 즐기고 함께 이야기를 나눈다.

26 오늘 밤, 갑자기 생각났다 — 우리가 얼마나 좋은 일을 했는가!

27 나는 내가 그 일의 일부였다는 것이 자랑스럽다.

28 나는 'Fourth Street'에 있는 양로원을 위해 꽃을 따는 일을 맡았다.

29 채소들은 우리 마을의 모든 부엌으로 갈 것이다.

30 하지만 훨씬 더 좋은 것은, 사람들이 좋아하지 않았던 볼품없고 더러운 지역이 모두를 위한 예쁜 정원이 되었다는 것이다.

본문 TEST Step 4-Step 5

p.39~42

1 Green Thumbs

2 I complained the whole day.

3 My parents were making me work on the neighborhood project, but I had far better things to do.

4 I didn't understand why we were working on this place.

5 It was just the ugly, old, empty lot across from Johnny's Shop.

6 It was full of wild plants, fast food wraps, old newspapers, broken glass, and every other kind of dirty trash you can imagine.

7 As I looked at it that first morning, I thought, "I bet there are snakes in there, too."

8 There were twenty of us — all ages and sizes — ready to work that day.

9 I didn't think that we could clean up this awful mess and turn it into a garden.

10 We were all wondering where to begin.

11 Then Mr. Hernandez said, "The only way to do it is just to start."

12 Then, he divided the lot into four parts with string and assigned five people to each part.

13 By lunchtime, I was hot, sweaty, and glad my dad had made me wear gloves.

14 We filled fifty trash bags with waste and were ready to pull wild plants.

15 As we pulled and pulled, dust filled the air and made us sneeze.

16 At the end of the day, I had to admit the lot looked much better.

17 That first day was the toughest.

18 On the weekends that followed, we made rows, planted flower and vegetable seeds, and watered them.

19 After about two weeks, I stopped complaining when I found the plants had started popping up!

20 First, the lettuce and then the beans and the tomatoes.

21 They grew so fast.

22 I couldn't believe it!

23 The bean plants grew an inch, and the tomatoes doubled in size in just a few days.

24 Now, two months later, I like to go there every day to see what new flowers are ready to pop up.

25 Lots of people in the neighborhood meet there to enjoy the sights and to talk together.

26 Tonight, it suddenly hit me — what a good thing we did!

27 I'm proud I have been a part of it.

28 I'm in charge of picking flowers for the nursing home on Fourth Street.

29 The vegetables will go to every kitchen in our town.

30 But even better, an ugly and dirty lot that people didn't like has become a pretty garden for everyone.

구석구석지문 TEST Step 1

p.43

After You Read A

1. visited, after school
2. while, were looking
3. picked, flowers, took, to, nursing home
4. proud that, mad, for everyone

Do It Yourself

1. Our, Symbol
2. which, drew as, my town
3. designed, had taken, many different kinds of corn
4. much cuter than
5. everybody likes it

Link to the World

1. the largest, in the world
2. is made up of
3. are built over
4. There are, police stations, post offices
5. much more, than
6. is called

구석구석지문 TEST Step 2

p.44

After You Read A

1. I visited the town garden after school.
2. Some people were talking while they were looking at the beautiful garden.
3. I picked some flowers and took them to the nursing home.
4. I'm proud that we made a pretty garden for everyone.

Do It Yourself

1. Our Town Symbol
2. This is Oksig, which I drew as a symbol of my town.
3. I designed this after I had taken pictures of many different kinds of corn.
4. Oksig is much cuter than real corn.
5. I hope everybody likes it.

Link to the World

1. • Kampong Ayer is the largest "water village" in the world.
2. It is made up of about 40 small villages.
3. • All the houses are built over the water.
4. • There are schools, police stations, gas stations, and post offices.
5. It is much more beautiful than you think.
6. It is called the Venice of Asia.

Lesson 3

단어 TEST Step 1

p.45

01 용감한	02 발견	03 대학, 대학교
04 뒤로	05 폭탄	06 뜨다
07 실수	08 존중하다; 명예	
09 창의적인, 상상력이 풍부한		10 아마도
11 수여하다; 상	12 개막	13 발명, 발명품
14 웃기는	15 의식, 식	16 저장하다
17 가치; ~의 가치가 있는		18 받아들이다
19 자석	20 열렬한, 간절히 바라는	
21 반복적으로	22 응원하다	23 전통
24 공연하다	25 실제로, 사실은	26 경제학
27 해군	28 수여하다	29 관심
30 연구, 조사; 조사하다		31 선원
32 유용한	33 1조	34 드문, 특이한
35 ~ 대신에	36 계속 ~하다	37 ~에 성공하다
38 큰 소리로 웃다	39 ~에 참여하다	
40 A가 ~하지 못하게 하다		
41 ~을 (열렬히) 하고 싶어 하다		
42 ~에서 떠나다, 나가다		43 행운을 빌다

단어 TEST Step 2

p.46

01 accept	02 opening	03 backward
04 discovery	05 eager	06 repeatedly
07 perform	08 economics	09 float
10 peace	11 honor	12 bomb
13 brave	14 award	15 ceremony
16 invention	17 while	18 laughable
19 actually	20 unusual	21 navy
22 magnet	23 maybe	24 mistake
25 sailor	26 tradition	27 research
28 trillion	29 useful	30 worth
31 imaginative	32 interest	33 university
34 receive	35 less than	36 instead of
37 succeed in	38 take part in	39 laugh out loud
40 keep -ing	41 get out of	42 be eager to
43 keep A from -ing		

단어 TEST Step 3

p.47

1 live, 살아 있는 2 award, 수여하다 3 sailor, 선원
4 trillion, 1조 5 accept, 받아들이다 6 magnet, 자석
7 navy, 해군 8 backward, 뒤의 9 discovery, 발견
10 float, 뜨다, 띄우다 11 research, 연구, 조사
12 invent, 발명하다 13 eager, 열렬한, 간절히 바라는
14 honor, • 명예 • 존경하다
15 imaginative, 창의적인, 상상력이 풍부한
16 university, 대학

대화문 TEST Step 1

p.48~50

Get Ready 2

(1) solved a lot of, I'm sure, win, award / think so / keep, crossed
(2) winner, award / to get, prize / I'm sure, get, prize, Good luck
(3) looking forward to / make, laugh out loud, get the prize
(4) get, award, keep my fingers crossed

Start Off – Listen & Talk A

1. can't wait for / What, going to do / practiced, for a few weeks / looking forward to / Actually, a little worried, afraid, make, mistake / Don't worry, do, job, my fingers crossed
2. take part in / m going to run, end / looking forward, seeing / sure, win / do your best, keep my fingers crossed

Start Off – Listen & Talk B

are you coming / going to play, for me to try / sure, do great, keep, fingers crossed / going to perform, other mothers / sounds fun, looking forward, watching, stage

Start Off – Speak Up

looking forward to, model, ready / so, nervous / do well, keep my fingers crossed

Step Up – Real-life Scene

field trip, talent show / going to, like, do in class, jokes / looking forward to it / show, sure / worry, do great, keep my fingers crossed / Let me show, act, Guess / sound like / going to show / make, laugh out loud

Fun Time

m going to travel / sounds great, m really looking forward to

going to enter, m worried about / Don't worry, keep my fingers crossed

Express Yourself A

1. Can you tell me, invention / a pair of special, clean, floor / win a prize, keep, crossed
2. looks interesting, cutting board, feeder / not only, board but also, feeder, at the same time / idea / really think so / looking forward, using

Get Ready 2

(1) G: You solved a lot of problems in class. I'm sure you'll win the Class Brain award.
B: Do you really think so?
G: Of course. I'll keep my fingers crossed for you, Sangjun!

(2) B: The winner of the Oh So Sweet award will get some candies.
G: Oh, I want to get the prize.
B: I'm sure you'll get the prize this time. Good luck, Jiu!

(3) B: I'm looking forward to the Best Joker award this time.
G: Ha-ha. You always make us laugh out loud. So you'll get the prize, Yunki. Good luck.
B: Thank you.

(4) B: Minji, you're a happy girl. I think you'll get the Ms. Cheerful award. I'll keep my fingers crossed!
G: Oh, thank you, Jiho.

Start Off – Listen & Talk A

1. G: Mom, I can't wait for the sports day.
W: What are you going to do on that day, Minji?
G: I'm going to play basketball for my class. We've practiced hard for a few weeks.
W: Oh, I'm looking forward to your game.
G: Actually, I'm a little worried. I'm afraid I'll make a mistake.
W: Don't worry. You'll do a good job. I'll keep my fingers crossed!

2. W: Soyun, are you going to take part in any races on the sports day?
G: Sure. I'm going to run a 100 meter race at the end of the day.
W: Wow, I'm looking forward to seeing you at the race.
G: But, Mom, I'm not sure I'll win the race.
W: Just do your best. I'll keep my fingers crossed!

Start Off – Listen & Talk B

G: Mom, are you coming to the sports day?
W: Sure. I'm going to play the game Kick a Shoe. This will be the first time for me to try it.
G: Don't worry. I'm sure you'll do great. I'll keep my fingers crossed for you!
W: Thank you. I'm also going to perform a funny dance with some other mothers.
G: That sounds fun. I'm looking forward to watching you on the stage.

Start Off – Speak Up

A: I'm looking forward to the model airplane contest tomorrow. Are you ready?
B: Well, I think so, but I'm nervous.
A: You will do well. I'll keep my fingers crossed!

Step Up – Real-life Scene

Miso: We're going on a field trip next Tuesday. What are you going to do in the talent show, Jimin?
Jimin: I'm going to talk like our teachers do in class and tell some jokes.
Miso: Wow! I'm really looking forward to it.
Jimin: Will everyone like my show? I'm not sure.
Miso: Don't worry. I'm sure you'll do great. I'll keep my fingers crossed!
Jimin: Thank you, Miso. Let me show you one part of my act. Guess who? "Goood Jooob!"
Miso: Ha-ha, you sound like our English teacher.
Jimin: Do I? I'm going to show you more at the show.
Miso: Great! You always make us laugh out loud.

Fun Time

A: I'm going to travel to Jejudo next week.
B: Wow! That sounds great.
A: Yeah, I'm really looking forward to it.

A: I'm going to enter the dance contest next week, but I'm worried about it.
B: Don't worry. You'll do great. I'll keep my fingers crossed.
A: Thank you.

Express Yourself A

1. G: Can you tell me something about your invention?
B: They are a pair of special shoes. You can also clean the floor with them.
G: Great! I'm sure you'll win a prize. I'll keep my fingers crossed!

2. B: This looks interesting. Is this a cutting board or a bird feeder?
G: It is not only a cutting board but also a bird feeder. You can do two things at the same time.
B: That's a great idea!
G: Do you really think so?
B: Yes. I'm really looking forward to using it.

본문 TEST Step 1

p.54~56

01 Ig Nobel Prize
02 happens, backward while, carrying
03 did research on, topic
04 research, enough to win
05 Maybe not
06 how about
07 won, fun research
08 awarded for, laugh, think
09 interest, honoring, unusual, imaginative
10 are presented by, winners
11 filled with, cheer, laughable
12 won, for, in
13 To save, instead of
14 enough, laugh out loud
15 also won, award
16 succeeded in floating, using
17 sense, humor, accepted, award
18 bring, to, face, how
19 in, for inventing, alarm
20 keeps running away, out
21 Not only, but, makes
22 number, keep, from, bored
23 opening, closing, words each
24 called, shouts repeatedly, bored
25 trillion, which, worth less
26 Throwing, is another, tradition
27 ends with, win, did
28 winners, receive lots of
29 awards, great honors like
30 a lot more fun

본문 TEST Step 2

p.57~59

01 Ig Nobel Prize
02 happens, backward while, carrying
03 did research, topic
04 good enough to win
05 Maybe
06 how about
07 won one, fun reserch
08 are awarded for discoveries, laugh, think
09 to increase, interest, by honoring the unusual, the imaginative
10 are presented by real Nobel winners
11 is, filled with, eager to cheer, laughable
12 won, for
13 To save, made, shout, instead of using
14 funny enough, laugh out loud
15 won an award
16 succeeded in floating, by using magnets
17 a sense of humor, when, accepted, award
18 bring, to, how about
19 in, for inventing
20 keeps running away, gets out of
21 Not only, but also, makes, laugh
22 a number of, keep, from getting bored
23 opening, closing speeches, two words each
24 an eight-year-old girl called, repeatedly
25 ten trillion, which, worth less than
26 Throwing, is, tradition
27 ends with, win, prize, did
28 do not receive
29 great honors like
30 a lot more fun

본문 TEST Step 3

p.60~61

1 이그노벨상
2 “당신이 커피 한 잔을 들고 가면서 뒤로 걸을 때 무슨 일이 일어날까?”
3 한국의 한 고등학생인 한지원은 2015년에 이 주제에 관해 연구했다.
4 이 연구 과제는 노벨상을 받을 정도로 훌륭할까?
5 아마도 아닐 것이다.
6 하지만 이그노벨상은 어떤가?
7 그는 이 재미있는 연구로 2017년에 상을 탔다.
8 이그노벨상은 ‘먼저 웃기고 나서 다음에 생각하게 하는’ 발견에 수여된다.
9 그것은 특이하고 창의적인 사람들을 높이 평가함으로써 과학에 대한 사람들의 흥미를 늘리기 위해 AIR 잡지에 의해 1991년에 시작되었다.
10 그 상들은 하버드 대학의 Sanders 극장에서 진짜 노벨상 수상자들에 의해 수여된다.
11 그 방은 대개 ‘웃기는’ 연구를 한 용감한 과학자들을 열렬히 격려하고자 하는 사람들로 가득 찬다.
12 영국 해군은 2000년에 이그노벨 평화상을 탔다.
13 돈을 아끼기 위해, 해군에서는 선원들에게 진짜 폭탄을 사용하는 대신에 “쾅!”이라고 소리치게 했다.
14 그것이 당신이 큰 소리로 웃을 정도로 우스운가?
15 Andre Geim도 그해에 상을 탔다.
16 그는 자석을 이용해서 살아 있는 개구리를 공중에 띄우는 데 성공했다.
17 그는 상을 받을 때, “내 경험상, 사람들이 유머 감각이 없다면, 그들은 대개 별로 훌륭한 과학자가 아니다.”라고 말했다.
18 그것이 아직도 당신의 얼굴에 미소를 띠게 하지 않는다면, 이것은 어떤가?
19 2005년에 Gauri Nanda는 자명종을 발명해서 이그노벨 경제학상을 받았다.
20 그것은 잠자는 사람이 결국 침대 밖으로 나올 때까지 계속 도망을 다닌다.
21 수상자들의 재미있는 연구뿐만 아니라 이그노벨상 시상식도 또한 사람들을 웃게 만든다.

22 사람들이 지루해하지 않도록 하는 재미있는 것들이 많이 있다.
23 개회사와 폐회사는 단지 두 마디이다: "환영합니다. 환영합니다."와 "안녕. 안녕."
24 만일 누군가가 너무 오랫동안 말을 하면, Miss Sweetie Poo라고 하는 여덟 살짜리 여자아이가 "제발 멈춰요! 지루해요."라고 계속 외친다.
25 각 수상자는 10조의 짐바브웨 달러를 받는데, 그것은 미국의 1달러보다 가치가 낮다.
26 종이비행기를 날리는 것은 또 다른 재미있는 전통이다.
27 이그노벨상 시상식은 "만일 당신이 상을 타지 못했다면 – 그리고 만일 탔다면 – 내년에는 좀 더 많은 행운이 있기를!"이라는 말로 끝이 난다.
28 수상자들은 많은 상금을 받지 않는다.
29 그리고 그 상은 노벨상같이 훌륭한 영광은 아니다.
30 하지만 이그노벨상은 과학을 훨씬 더 재미있게 만든다!

본문 TEST Step 4-Step 5 p.62~66

1 The Ig Nobel Prize
2 "What happens when you walk backward while you are carrying a cup of coffee?"
3 Han Jiwon, a Korean high school student, did research on this topic in 2015.
4 Is this research project good enough to win a Nobel Prize?
5 Maybe not.
6 But how about an Ig Nobel Prize?
7 He won one in 2017 for this fun research.
8 The Ig Nobel Prizes are awarded for discoveries that "first make one laugh and then think."
9 They were started in 1991 by *AIR* magazine to increase people's interest in science by honoring the unusual and the imaginative.
10 The prizes are presented by real Nobel winners in Sanders Theater at Harvard University.
11 The room is usually filled with people who are eager to cheer for the brave scientists with their "laughable" research.
12 The U.K. Navy won the Ig Nobel Prize for Peace in 2000.
13 To save money, the Navy made its sailors shout, "Bang!" instead of using real bombs.
14 Is that funny enough for you to laugh out loud?
15 Andre Geim also won an award that year.
16 He succeeded in floating a live frog in the air by using magnets.
17 "In my experience, if people don't have a sense of humor, they are usually not very good scientists," he said when he accepted his award.
18 If that still does not bring a smile to your face, how about this?
19 In 2005, Gauri Nanda won the Ig Nobel Prize in Economics for inventing an alarm clock.
20 It keeps running away until the sleeper finally gets out of bed.
21 Not only the winners' fun studies but also the ceremony for the Ig Nobel Prizes makes people laugh.
22 There are a number of interesting things that keep people from getting bored.
23 The opening and closing speeches are just two words each: "Welcome. Welcome." and "Goodbye. Goodbye."
24 If someone talks for too long, an eight-year-old girl called Miss Sweetie Poo shouts repeatedly, "Please stop! I'm bored."
25 Each winner receives ten trillion Zimbabwean dollars, which is worth less than one U.S. dollar.
26 Throwing paper planes is another fun tradition.
27 The Ig Nobel Prize ceremony ends with the words, "If you didn't win a prize — and if you did — better luck next year!"
28 The winners do not receive lots of money.
29 And the awards are not great honors like the Nobel Prizes.
30 But the Ig Nobel Prizes make science a lot more fun!

구석구석지문 TEST Step 1 p.67

Self-study Guide

1. words
2. showed, eagerness to learn
3. get, meaning
4. not only, but also

Express Yourself C

1. Stairs
2. These, Magic
3. not only, going, but also, storing
4. useful enough to make, much easier

Link to the World

1. Nobel Prize
2. named after, Swedish scientist
3. is awarded to, who, great work
4. all the winners, the youngest
5. at the age of, had fought, children's rights

6. received, three times
7. Not only, but also, was awarded

구석구석지문 TEST Step 2

p.68

Self-study Guide

1. New words again!
2. He showed great eagerness to learn new things.
3. Oh, I get the meaning of "-ness."
4. Now I know not only the meaning of "eager" but also the meaning of "eagerness."

Express Yourself C

1. Magic Stairs
2. These are Magic Stairs.
3. You can use them not only for going up and down but also for storing things.
4. This invention is useful enough to make your life much easier.

Link to the World

1. The Nobel Prize
2. The Nobel Prize was named after Alfred Nobel, a Swedish scientist.
3. It is awarded to people who have done great work for the world.
4. Of all the winners, Malala Yousafzai is the youngest.
5. She won the Nobel Prize at the age of 17 because she had fought for women's and children's rights.
6. The Curie family received the Nobel Prize three times.
7. Not only Marie Curie but also her daughter was awarded the Nobel Prize.

MEMO

MEMO

MEMO

적중 100

영어 기출 문제집

정답 및 해설

천재 | 정사열